SOUTH ASIA IN 2008
A REVIEW

South Asia in 2008
A Review

Edited by

HERNAIKH SINGH
TRIDIVESH SINGH MAINI

First published 2009

ISBN 978-81-7304-830-2

Published by
Ajay Kumar Jain *for*
Manohar Publishers & Distributors
4753/23 Ansari Road, Daryaganj
New Delhi 110 002

Typeset by
Kohli Print
Delhi 110 051

Printed at
Salasar Imaging Systems
Delhi 110 035

Contents

C. Terrorism and Security

II. ECONOMIC DEVELOPMENT

A. Economic Reforms

III. REGIONAL AND INTERNATIONAL RELATIONS

A. South Asian Regionalism

B. South Asia–China Relations

C. South Asia–South-East Asia Relations

D. South Asia–United States Relations

Foreword

THE INSTITUTE of South Asian Studies is pleased to present *South Asia in 2008: A Review*, a compilation of its policy briefs and insights written in the course of last year.

2008 was an eventful year for South Asia. There was a return of democracy in Bangladesh, Bhutan, Pakistan and Nepal; the removal of President Pervez Musharraf and the assassination of Benazir Bhutto in Pakistan; the conclusion of the India–United States nuclear deal; the terrorist attacks on the Indian High Commission in Kabul and in Mumbai; and the onset of the global downturn and the economic challenges to the South Asian region.

Throughout 2008, the Institute has kept a close watch on these events and has produced a steady stream of analyses of these key developments. These analyses not only provide incisive insights, they also examine the impact and implications of things happening in South Asia on South-East Asia and Singapore.

This publication is categorised into three broad sections: Politics and Governance; Economic Development; and Regional and International Relations.

The section on Politics and Governance covers issues related to the domestic politics of the South Asian countries. These include the elections in Pakistan, Bangladesh and Nepal, and the transition towards democracy in Bhutan. The results of the recently-held assembly elections in India and a comprehensive analysis of the state elections of 2008 are also included in this section. Terrorism is a major threat to peace and security in South Asia. There are analyses of the Mumbai attacks, the attack on the Indian embassy in Kabul and the conflict in Sri Lanka under this section.

Included in the section on Economic Development are papers on the Indian and Pakistan budgets; the impact of inflation on the South Asian economies; and the possible impact of the United Progressive Alliance's victory in the trust vote on economic reforms.

The fiscal and monetary policies followed by the South Asian governments, which are extremely important in view of the current state of economies the world over, are also discussed.

Infrastructure development is also an important issue for many, if not all, the countries in the region. For this reason, this section looks at issues of education, urban transport, agriculture and the industrial corridor from Delhi to Mumbai. There is also an analysis of development and governance in several key states in India.

There is an appreciation of the increasing interconnectedness between South Asia and the rest of the world and this section includes several papers dealing with the impact of the sub-prime crisis on the Indian economy, and the responses of the South Asian economies to the global recession and the oil shock.

The last section on Regional and International Relations touches on regionalism in South Asia and its relations with South-East Asia, China, the United States and Russia. The papers cover economic cooperation, foreign policy, strategic and security issues. Apart from the India–United States civilian nuclear deal, India–Pakistan talks, visit of the Russian prime minister to India and possibility of greater cooperation between South Asia and South-East Asia, there is also an analysis on the possible impact of the Barack Obama presidency on the India–Pakistan relationship.

The Institute intends to publish an annual 'Year in Review', and we hope you will find our analyses informative and useful.

TAN TAI YONG
Director
Institute of South Asian Studies

SECTION I

POLITICS AND GOVERNANCE

A. Centre–State Relations

1

Prime Minister Manmohan Singh in Arunachal Pradesh: Buttressing the Claims

S.D. MUNI

(*13 February 2008*)

In territorial disputes, it is said that possession is three-fourth of the claim. Dr Manmohan Singh's visit to Arunachal Pradesh—where India's claims are disputed by China—within two weeks of his state visit to China was obviously a move to reinforce and reassert that the area belongs to India.

This assertion had a three-pronged manifestation. First, Dr Singh loudly and clearly proclaimed that Arunachal Pradesh is an integral part of India. He said, 'Arunachal Pradesh is our land of (the) rising sun. . . . I sincerely hope that, like the sun, Arunachal Pradesh will rise from the east as a new star and become one of the best regions of our country.' Secondly, he visited the men in uniform posted on the border with China in the area at Lohitpur to boost their morale by praising them as guardians of 'long-term peace in the region'. He announced an allocation of nearly Rs 1 crore to improve facilities at the army transit camp and provide for satellite phones there. The implied message perhaps was that the area would be held, if need be, by the use of force.

Thirdly, he announced several projects worth Rs 4,000 crore to boost connectivity of the region with the rest of India, stimulate its developmental activity and integrate it more closely with the fast growing economy of the country. These projects, the prime minister said, 'will contribute to the economic development of the state and create new employment opportunities for the youth of Arunachal Pradesh'. He further added that, 'it is only through these measures and through the all round development of Arunachal Pradesh that we can ensure that the nation moves ahead in step towards a glorious future'. The thrust of these projects is on building infrastructure in the areas of power, and rail, road and air links. An interesting component of these infrastructure projects is the proposed daily helicopter link between Guwahati and Tawang. The Buddhist monastery in Tawang, built in 1681 by the Tibetan Lama Lodre Gyatso on the command of the fifth Dalai Lama Nagwang Lobsang Gyatso, claims its cultural lineage from Tibet. The Chinese claims on Tawang are based on this lineage.

A number of considerations could have been behind Dr Singh's move to undertake this visit to Arunachal Pradesh. There has been a lack of progress in Sino–Indian border negotiations. During his visit to China, his hosts refused to exchange their version of maps of the boundary and the draft note prepared by them on the disputed areas and proposed accommodations, and reiterated their own claims on Arunachal Pradesh, particularly Tawang. There have been several instances of the Chinese troops encroaching on the Arunachal Pradesh region besides elsewhere along the border. The Indian army has been raising the question of such encroachments and there have been allegations that the Indian prime minister, in view of the burgeoning bilateral trade and economic relations, was soft on China in this regard. This visit was to send a message that the Indian establishment was not soft on sensitive aspects of the border issue. This was also evident in the strong statements of External Affairs Minister Pranab Mukherjee on 16 June 2007 and the Defence Minister A.K. Anthony on 18 June 2007. Allegations of softness towards China were also levelled by the opposition Bharatiya Janata Party (BJP) that the prime minister was under pressure from the Left in his approach to China. The BJP member of parliament from Arunachal Pradesh, Khiren Rijiiu, voiced these charges even during Prime Minister Singh's visit to Arunachal Pradesh. He said that the Chinese were pursuing an aggressive stance in this region and through repeated encroachments, have taken some of its territory from the Taksin area. Prime Minister

Singh's visit was in response to these pressures from both within and outside the government.

While sending strong messages to the Chinese as well as internal distractors, the visit can also be seen as a much needed step towards stimulating the developmental process in not only Arunachal Pradesh but the whole of the northeastern region. The inclusion of Mani Shankar Aiyar, the minister for north-eastern affairs, in the prime minister's delegation was important. Developing the north-eastern region and linking it to India's 'Look East' policy has been vigorously argued by Mr Aiyar. There is huge hydropower potential, based on the run of the river projects in this region which has remained neglected for decades. Prime Minister Singh promised to his audiences in Arunachal Pradesh that by developing micro-hydro-power projects, along with the use of solar power and grid based power, all the villages of the region can be electrified within a period of two years. He also pointed out that, 'Our government has given the highest priority to the development of the north-eastern region, including Arunachal Pradesh.' He has been acutely aware of the fact that territorial claims cannot be sustained if there is even the slightest degree of disaffection among the people living in the border/disputed areas.

During the past couple of years, the Chinese have been asserting their claims on Arunachal Pradesh in a rather aggressive manner. On the eve of the Chinese President Hu Jintao's visit to India in November 2006, the Chinese ambassador in New Delhi, Sun Yuxi, had publicly announced that the whole of the Arunachal Pradesh state belonged to China, and not just the Tawang. In April–May 2007, the Chinese authorities had refused to grant a visa to an Indian Administrative Service officer from Arunachal Pradesh for his China visit under the pretext that since the area belonged to China, no visa was required by the people living there as they were going to their own country. In view of this position, it was rather surprising the Dr Manmohan Singh's visit to Arunachal Pradesh did not evoke any reaction from China, not at least for the first week of the visit. The onset of the Chinese New Year festivities is not an adequate reason to explain this lack of reaction from the

Chinese side. The academics working in China's government-funded think-tanks such as the China Institute for Contemporary International Relations and the Chinese Academy of Social Sciences did take an exception to this visit and indicated that this would harm the smooth development in Sino–Indian bilateral relations. However, after more than a week, the Chinese officials protested against the prime minister's visit to Arunachal Pradesh. Taking exception to Dr Singh's description of Arunachal Pradesh as 'our land of (the) rising sun', the Chinese said that it was 'not proper' to make such statements at a time when the two countries were engaged in talks over the boundary question. The Chinese objection was strongly rebutted by Foreign Minister Mukherjee on 8 February 2008 when he stated that 'Arunachal Pradesh is an integral part of our country . . . we have elected members in our parliament from Arunachal Pradesh . . . and therefore . . . it is quite obvious that prime minister will visit any part of the country.' The foreign minister's reaction to a lowly Chinese official and his mild 'performa' reaction, as it could be called was advisedly tailored to administer a strong rebuff.

The contrast in the latest Chinese objections to their earlier position on Arunachal Pradesh is a clear indication that the Chinese have softened unless (there is) a stronger reaction in the offing still. The Chinese have relented even on the question of issuing visas to people from Arunachal Pradesh. Is this an indication that China is gradually shifting towards 'accommodating' India's claims, as it had done earlier on the question of Sikkim? One may recall here that during Mao's times, Sikkim and Arunachal Pradesh (then called North East Frontier Agency), along with Nepal and Bhutan, were considered the fingers of the Chinese palm, Tibet. This is no longer the Chinese position on Nepal, Bhutan and Sikkim. Perhaps, their position on Arunachal Pradesh is also falling in this line. May be, the earlier stronger position of China was to test the strength of India's commitment to Arunachal Pradesh. This shift in the Chinese position, if true, may be in conformity with the 11 April 2005 agreement on the 'Political Parameters and Guiding Principals for the Settlement of the India–China Boundary

Question' which in its Article VII says that, 'In reaching a boundary settlement, the two sides shall safeguard due interests of their settled population in border areas.' Even Article V underlines 'national sentiments, practical difficulties and reasonable concerns and sensitivities of both sides and the actual state of border areas', while referring to 'historical evidence'.

2

Karnataka State Assembly Elections: Implications for the UPA Government

E. SRIDHARAN

(10 June 2008)

THE KARNATAKA state assembly elections were held in May 2008. The principal opposition party, the Bharatiya Janata Party (BJP), which led the National Democratic Alliance (NDA) (the national coalition government) from 1999 to 2004, won to form its first government in a southern state. The result is important because it has broad implications for the political prospects of the ruling Congress-led United Progressive Alliance (UPA) coalition government in the general elections due by May 2009. In this brief, the Karnataka elections will be analysed at two levels: first, the elections themselves at the state level and, second, their possible implications for the UPA at the national elections.

Karnataka, an economically booming state in south India, with India's information technology capital, Bangalore, as its capital, has had three principal parties since the 1980s. These were the Congress, which ruled the state since Independence except for a term each in the 1980s and 1990s; the Janata Dal (Secular) [JD(S)], a regional offshoot of the original Janata Dal, itself a descendant of the Janata Party that ruled the state for a term in the 1980s, led by former Prime Minister H.D. Deve Gowda (1996–7); and the BJP, which rose to a vote share of 28 per cent in the state in the 1991 general elections. It has, since then, steadily expanded and consolidated its base to become one of the two leading parties in the state by vote share for both parliamentary and state assembly elections since the late 1990s.

In 2004, the BJP won the majority of parliamentary seats in the state in the general elections, as well as the single largest number of seats (79) of the state assembly's 224 seats, ahead of the Congress (65 seats) and the JD(S) (58 seat).[1] However, the Congress and the JD(S) came together and formed a post-elections coalition government, which collapsed in 2006. Thereafter, the JD(S) formed an alternative coalition with the BJP in which the JD(S) agreed to share the chief ministership with the BJP for 20 months each, out of the 40 months left of the assembly's five-year term, and took its turn first. However, when it came to handing over the chief ministership to the BJP, the JD(S) chief minister, H.D. Kumaraswamy, reneged and early elections were precipitated in May 2008.

The BJP won the elections, acquiring a near-majority of 110 out of 224 seats, and joined with five independent candidates to form a government. There are several salient points about the elections results. Compared to 2004, the BJP experienced a substantial 5.4 per cent swing of votes in its favour, rising to 33.9 per cent from 28.5 per cent in 2004. This gave it a 31 seat jump from 79 to 110. The Congress also saw an increase of seats from 65 to 80 and received 34.6 per cent of votes, compared to 35.3 per cent in 2004, a loss of only 0.7 per cent. In fact, it remained the largest single party in vote share, being 0.7 per cent ahead despite the small loss of vote share and the more than 5 per cent swing in favour of the BJP. The JD(S)'s vote share declined by only 1.5 per cent from 20.6 per cent in 2004 to 19.1 per cent in 2008. However, it only won 28 seats, compared to 58 in the last elections. The BJP's 5.4 per cent increase in vote share came largely at the expense of the 'Independents' and 'Others'.

The BJP's winning of 30 more seats is due to the vagaries of the first-past-the-post system, due to the relative concentration of its votes in some parts of the state, while the Congress party's votes were more evenly spread. Viewed in terms of Karnataka's five regions, the BJP and the Congress were neck-to-neck in vote share in the northern region, the BJP's traditional stronghold, and the BJP was a distant third behind the Congress and the JD(S) in the southern (old Mysore) region, the JD(S)'s only stronghold, excluding the Bangalore urban region. It was in the Bangalore urban, coastal and central regions that the BJP notched a 5 per cent lead over the Congress.

While losing to the BJP in these three regions, the Congress also faced stiff competition from the JD(S) in the southern region. Inflation and the 'sympathy factor' for the BJP, as it was perceived to have been cheated out of its share of power by a duplicitous JD(S), were probably also factors that contributed to the BJP's victory. It should be noted that the JD(S), with 19 per cent of the vote, cannot be counted out of the equation altogether. A possible Congress–JD(S) pre-elections coalition in 2009 remains a formidable combination, arithmetically speaking. After all, they were general elections allies in 2004.

In the larger national context, it needs to be added that the Scheduled Caste (SC)-based Bahujan Samaj Party (BSP), despite running candidates in the state, did not make a dent, failing to win any seats and managing runner-up status in only two constituencies. However, there were 15 constituencies in which the Congress was the runner-up, 14 constituencies in which the BJP was the runner-up and eight constituencies in which the JD(S) was the runner-up. In these instances, the BSP's votes exceeded the victory margin, thereby making it a potential spoiler not only for the Congress, but also for the JD(S) and the BJP, since it cannot be assumed that all SC votes went only to the Congress, despite the latter being the traditionally preferred party of the SCs.

What do the elections mean for the prospects of the Congress-led UPA government and for the BJP-led NDA coalition in the national elections due by May 2009 at the latest?

First, it is a psychological blow for the Congress and the UPA and a morale booster for the BJP and the NDA. This will be the first BJP government in the south, a breakthrough for the BJP, and equivalent to its forming state governments on its own for the first time in 1990, if we ignore the Jana Sangh (later renamed BJP)-dominated Janata Party governments in some Hindi-belt states in 1977–80.

Second, the Karnataka elections' blow to the Congress followed several others in a row in 2007 and 2008. The Congress' performance in the state assembly elections since the 2004 general elections has been rather poor.

In 2004, in the four states that had assembly elections simultaneously with parliamentary elections, the Congress lost Orissa to the Biju Janata Dal (BJD)–BJP coalition, lost Sikkim to the regional Sikkim Democratic Front, won Andhra Pradesh decisively from the Telugu Desam and formed a post-elections coalition government with the JD(S) in Karnataka. Later in 2004, it won Maharashtra and formed a coalition government with its Nationalist Congress Party (NCP) ally, and won Arunachal Pradesh. The Congress and the UPA seemed to be consolidating their parliamentary victory by bagging major states such as Andhra Pradesh, Maharashtra and Karnataka.

In 2005, it won Haryana but lost Bihar and Jharkhand, the latter essentially because it failed to maintain its winning coalition of 2004.

In 2006, it won Assam and Pondicherry (a union territory), lost Kerala to its ally at the centre, the Left Front, while the latter retained power in West Bengal. A Congress ally, the Dravida Munnetra Kazhagam, along with its minor local allies, won Tamil Nadu.

In 2007, the tide seemed to turn against the Congress and the UPA. It won only tiny Manipur and Goa, losing Punjab to the Akali Dal–BJP alliance, and losing Uttarakhand, Gujarat and Himachal Pradesh to the BJP, all decisively, while making no gains in Uttar Pradesh, which was won decisively by the BSP, a potential threat to the Congress party's SC vote base nationally.

In 2008, the Left retained power in Tripura while the Congress lost in Meghalaya and Nagaland, all small northeastern states. The Congress also lost in Karnataka to the BJP.

Thus, in the eleven state assembly elections in 2007 and 2008 to-date, the Congress lost nine, winning only tiny Manipur and Goa. Apart from losing Uttar Pradesh to the BSP, the Congress lost all the major states to the BJP or its NDA allies. Four major Hindi-belt states, namely, Rajasthan, Madhya Pradesh, Chhattisgarh, all ruled by the BJP, and Delhi (technically a union territory), ruled by the Congress, are scheduled to have state assembly elections by November 2008, as are Jammu & Kashmir, and Mizoram, with the possibility of early elections being called in Orissa by a confident BJD–BJP alliance. This will be the critical round of state assembly elections before the general elections.

How does the Congress stand in these elections and in the general elections in 2009 following the Karnataka elections? The BJP cannot win in Jammu & Kashmir, and Mizoram but the Congress and its allies may also lose to local parties, and these are small states. In Rajasthan, Madhya Pradesh and Chhattisgarh, the anti-incumbency factor should, in theory, help the Congress but a lot depends on whom the electorate blames for rising inflation, the ruling party at the centre or the state? Inflation, crucially, food prices, and, more generally, the economic situation, in the immediate run-up to the elections, will be critical. In this context, the decision to raise petrol and diesel prices in early June 2008 rather than closer to the elections is an electorally-shrewd move. Also critical is whether the BSP runs candidates in all these states and how much they do or do not cut into the SC votes of the Congress. Wild card events like terrorist strikes that are plausibly attributable to Islamist groups might also help the BJP attack the Congress on security and, in a coded way, appeal to latent Hindu communal/anti-Muslim sentiment in sections of the electorate.

Third, a critical issue for 2009 would be the forging of pre-elections alliances. It needs to be remembered that, in November 2003, the Congress lost Rajasthan, Madhya Pradesh and Chhattisgarh, but became 'coalitionable' in a swathe of states such as Andhra Pradesh, Karnataka, Jharkhand, Tamil Nadu, Maharashtra, Jammu & Kashmir, and Himachal Pradesh, and, hence, nationally, and won the 2004 elections.[2]

In a national political context, in which even the most optimistic scenarios for each of the two major parties gives them no chance of achieving a majority on their own, the key to forming a national government is the pre-election coalitions they manage to tie up. For each, it means both retaining major allies and adding more without giving up too many seats in their stronghold states. Viewed this way, what is the scenario at the present moment? The Congress alliance has been fraying, with the Telangana Rashtra Samithi

(TRS) in Andhra Pradesh exiting the UPA (though in recent by-elections to the both assembly and parliamentary seats, it performed very poorly), the Peoples Democratic Party in Jammu & Kashmir, and the NCP in Maharashtra having somewhat strained relations with the Congress. However, the Congress has reabsorbed the defecting splinter group in Kerala. Although Mamata Banerjee's Trinamool Congress left the NDA, it has not rejoined or allied with the Congress. Crucially, there appears to be an incipient coalition of the Samajwadi Party and the Congress in Uttar Pradesh. Even in Karnataka, the Congress will be formidable if it coalesces with the JD(S), arithmetically speaking. And it has to put together the 2004 coalition in Bihar and Jharkhand (UPA minister Ram Vilas Paswan's party contested independently in the 2005 Bihar assembly elections and helped the NDA win). If it can keep/add the coalition allies mentioned, especially in Maharashtra, Tamil Nadu, Jharkhand and Uttar Pradesh, and exploit anti-incumbency in at least one or two major BJP-ruled Hindi-belt states, the UPA will remain a serious contender in 2009.

Conversely, for the BJP and the NDA, the need to keep/add allies includes forming an alliance in Tamil Nadu with the principal opposition party there, Jayalalitha's All India Anna Dravida Munnetra Kazhagam, with the Telugu Desam (which has left the NDA) and/or the TRS in Andhra Pradesh, preventing a Congress–JD(S) alliance in Karnataka, sabotaging the continuation of the Congress–NCP alliance in Maharashtra while preserving the alliance with the Shiv Sena, preserving alliances with the Janata Dal (United) in Bihar, Jharkhand and Karnataka, and with the BJD in Orissa, with the Akali Dal in Punjab, and bringing the Trinamool Congress back into the NDA in West Bengal. Whether a BJP–BSP alliance is forged in Uttar Pradesh, and on what terms, in response to a possible Samajwadi Party–Congress alliance, is crucial.

All in all, the field remains wide open and it is far too early to write the political obituary of the Congress and the UPA after Karnataka.

NOTES

1. Indian election statistics are available at the Election Commission of India's website: www.eci.gov.in.
2. For how the Congress became 'coalitionable' in 2004 and won, see E. Sridharan, 'Electoral Coalitions in the 2004 General Elections: Theory and Evidence', *Economic and Political Weekly*, vol. XXXIX, no. 51, 18–24 December 2004, 5418–25. For the BJP's expansion using coalitions as a strategy, see E. Sridharan, 'Coalition Strategies and the BJP's Expansion, 1989–2004', *Commonwealth and Comparative Politics*, vol. 43, no. 2, July 2005, pp. 194–221. For regional party strategies, see E. Sridharan, 'Coalitions and Party Strategies in India's Parliamentary Federation', *Publius*, vol. 33, no. 4, Fall 2003, 135–52.

SECTION I

POLITICS AND GOVERNANCE

B. Political Parties and Processes

3

Benazir Bhutto (1953–2007) Assassinated: Pakistan in Turmoil

ISHTIAQ AHMED

(4 January 2008)

THE GENERAL elections in Pakistan, scheduled for 8 January 2008, have been postponed till 18 February 2008. This decision was taken by the Pakistan Election Commission in the wake of the assassination of former prime minister of Pakistan and leader of the Pakistan People's Party (PPP), Benazir Bhutto. Riots broke out in many parts of Pakistan but they were more severe in the province of Sindh to which Bhutto and her family belong. The destruction of government buildings and infrastructure has been staggering. The offices of the Election Commission, polling booths, the voters' list, police stations, petrol pumps, railway stations and railway carriages, trucks and private cars have been torched by angry mobs. Sindh has been practically burning. The government deployed the military in Sindh with orders to shoot at sight. Pakistan could be on the brink of a civil war.

The dastardly crime took place after she had addressed a mammoth public meeting in Rawalpindi on 27 December 2007 to solicit votes for the general elections announced for 8 January 2008. Rawalpindi is less than 10 km from Pakistan's capital, Islamabad. The headquarters of the Pakistan Army are located in Rawalpindi as are the head offices of its intelligence services. Rawalpindi has aptly been described as a garrison town. Yet, the writ of the state has been flouted many times in recent months in Pakistan. Only on 30 November 2007, the present author was in Islamabad to attend a conference when a suicide bomber blew himself up and a number of policemen and ordinary citizens. Apparently, the culprit wanted to enter the area where the top generals of the army have their residences. When he was intercepted, he decided to kill himself and the police.

Ms Bhutto was fully aware of the dangers and even claimed to have received information that attempts on her life would be made, but she was a daring individual. Just some months before her return to Pakistan in October 2007, after living eight years in self-exile, she said in an interview, 'No real Muslim will kill a woman, because Islam forbids it. Such a person will burn in hell forever.' But the terrorists struck her immediately upon her arrival to Pakistan. The convoy, comprising cars, trucks, police jeeps, motorbikes and thousands of people on foot to take her from Karachi Airport to the mausoleum of the founder of Pakistan, Mohammed Ali Jinnah, was attacked viciously with two bomb blasts by a suicide bomber. The utter savagery and mayhem it caused left at least 149 people dead and more than 500 injured. She survived unhurt on that occasion.

So, one can only wonder what convinced her to go out in the public and address gatherings. At the time of the first attack, she said in a press conference that she had received intelligence from a friendly country that three men in the government—two holding ministerial positions, and the third, a powerful civil servant—were planning her murder and that she had informed President Musharraf about it. Now, an American journalist has revealed that he had received an e-mail from Ms Bhutto in which she complained that proper security and protection were not being provided to her and, if she became a victim of a terrorist attack, Musharraf would bear the responsibility.

President Musharraf and his ministers have rejected all such allegations. Musharraf actually advised her not to return to Pakistan yet because he claimed to have intelligence suggesting that she would be attacked if she did. We should also remember that Islamist terrorists had already made three attempts on Musharraf's life. Among those who took part in those attacks were some lower ranking air force personnel. Therefore, Musharraf's complicity in her murder does not make any sense, especially because both were reportedly moving towards some power-sharing deal brokered by the United States.

Al Qaeda declared in a message put up on an Islamist website that her death brings to an end 'America's most precious asset in Pakistan' but denied having a hand in her killing. Ms Bhutto had made several statements that from the Al Qaeda point of view are anathema. She said that she would actively take part in the war on terror and help root it out of Pakistan. Even more provoking was her statement that her government would allow the Americans access to the mastermind behind Pakistan's nuclear weapons programme, Dr Abdul Qader Khan, who was kept in house detention under pressure from the United States. Even Musharraf, who has worked closely with the Americans, had turned down the request to let them interrogate him. In ideological and political terms, therefore, Ms Bhutto was a greater challenge to the Islamist extremists.

Such pronouncements by Ms Bhutto undoubtedly earned her the wrath of not only Islamists but ultra-nationalist and jingoistic elements in the Pakistan military and intelligence establishment. Musharraf has not been in full control of these apparatuses for quite some time, although the military, as a whole, remains loyal to him. The Pakistan government has accused Baitullah Mahsud for ordering the assassination of Ms Bhutto, which a spokesperson for Mahsud has denied. There are some reports that rogue elements of the Special Services Group, an elite commando formation in the Pakistan army, may have been involved in shooting her down. The government has claimed that Ms Bhutto died of a deep wound she received when she fell in her car and not from gunshots.

Among the disgruntled sections of Pakistani society, especially the Sindhis, who form the second largest ethnic nationality in the Pakistani federation, the Musharraf government is being perceived as responsible for creating conditions that led to the assassination of Ms Bhutto. The Sindhis have a long catalogue of grievances against the federal government of Pakistan, which they allege is dominated by the military recruited mainly from the dominant Punjab province. Ms Bhutto's father, Zulfikar Ali Bhutto, was overthrown by General Zia-ul-Haq in 1977. Later, he was hanged on allegations of having ordered the murder of a political opponent by the Supreme Court in which four judges, all Punjabis, found him guilty, while the other three non-Punjabis did not. In Sindhi perception, it was a case of judicial murder.

Ms Bhutto's brother, Murtaza, was gunned down some years ago. Punjabi police officers were blamed for that murder though his wife and children alleged that Ms Bhutto's husband, Asif Ali Zardari, was involved in the crime. Mr Zardari has also been blamed for massive corruption during Ms Bhutto's two stints as prime minister. Both she and her husband are alleged to have robbed the Pakisan exchequer of a staggering amount of US $1.5 billion. Anyhow, the assassination of Ms Bhutto has created a family of Sindhi martyrs. Popular perceptions are always swayed when someone is cruelly killed. If the government is not able to bring the situation under control quickly, other parts of Pakistan may go up in flames. Almost all the political parties opposed to General Musharraf decided to boycott the election when the news of Ms Bhutto's assassination became known. Now, they have agreed to take part in the election scheduled for 18 February 2008. There can be no doubt that several months of agitation in Pakistan during 2007 against the authoritarian policies of General Musharraf have greatly weakened him and the parties which support him.

The United States and its allies are greatly worried that if the current wave of instability does not ebb soon, the Islamists may stage a takeover. In that case, control over Pakistan's nuclear arsenal could pass into the hands of extremists who could threaten regional and world security. This doomsday scenario is not very likely to materialise at present because the top military generals are not Islamists and their hold over the military apparatus remains firm. There are also reports from the United States' media that the Americans have succeeded in gaining control over Pakistan's nuclear arsenal—something which the Pakistan government has strongly denied.

The forthcoming elections would probably be the most divisive since 1971 when East Pakistan broke away from Pakistan. The PPP is expected to benefit from the huge sympathy wave currently sweeping Pakistan.

4

One Year in Office: An Assessment of Bangladesh's Caretaker Government

M. SHAHIDUL ISLAM

(*15 January 2008*)

IN THE FACE of a political crisis, a caretaker government took over control in Bangladesh on 12 January 2007, giving the people the hope of a new dawn. After one year, however, instead of celebrations, the Dr Fakhruddin Ahmed-led interim cabinet has found itself in the midst of a series of problems, if not crises. Just before the first anniversary of the government, half of its advisers had to leave office due to poor performance and public dissatisfaction. The sky-rocketing prices of essentials has also affected the popularity of the government. The common people in Bangladesh now think that the country's economic outlook and political prospects are no better, if not worse, than those during the so-called democratic governments. This paper evaluates the performance of the current army-backed caretaker government during the last one year.

According to the Bangladesh Constitution, the caretaker government's prime objective is to arrange parliamentary elections within 90 days of its taking over office. The current interim government, however, had other ideas. Instead of holding free and fair elections, the government announced a long list of reform agenda immediately after assuming power. To carry forward the reforms, it needed to extend its control beyond the 90 days. The Bangladeshi people, Bangladesh's development partners and donor agencies concurred with the authorities as the country badly needed reforms in some crucial areas. These would not be possible under the so-called democratic regimes, due to political considerations.

The apolitical caretaker government inherited a legacy which can be characterised by, *inter alia*, an inefficient bureaucracy, weak and highly politicised institutions, a corrupt political system, and distorted market mechanisms. To clean up the country's corrupt-political culture, the army-backed government arrested more than 200 top-level politicians, including two ex-prime ministers, Sheikh Hasina and Khaleda Zia, on allegations of corruption. Some political bigwigs have already been punished through trials in so-called 'kangaroo' courts. The authorities have banned all kinds of political activities and gatherings, both indoor and outdoor. They have insisted on internal reforms of political parties so as to create a transparent and accountable party system. To break the political monopoly of the Bangladesh Nationalist Party and the Awami League, attempts have been made to initiate a third wave in politics.

The interim government reconstituted the Election Commission and the Anti-Corruption Commission, framed new laws to tackle corruption and ratified the United Nations Convention against corruption. The judiciary has been separated from the executive body of the government. The authorities have taken some stern actions against unscrupulous businessmen who are believed to be controlling the markets through syndication (oligopolistic market).

However, these highly ambitious reforms have not delivered the desired outcomes, at least in the short run. The anti-corruption campaign has slowed down economic activities. The growth in the industrial and agriculture sectors is either negative or very low. The government's borrowing from the state-owned banks has been increasing at an alarming rate. The rate of inflation has crossed the double-digit mark and the level of unemployment has soared, resulting in a state of stagflation in the Bangladesh economy. More importantly, business confidence in the economy has decreased and this is a big worry for the country.

According to the Bangladesh Bureau of Statistics, the overall inflation in Bangladesh was 8.25 per cent on a twelve-month annual average and 10.06 per cent on a point-to-point basis in October 2007 whereas the food-inflation hit 11.73 per cent in the same period. The value of local and foreign investment proposals submitted to the Bangladesh Board of Investment reportedly plunged by 68 per cent and 98 per cent respectively in the first quarter of the present fiscal year. As a result, the growth rate in Bangladesh is predicted to be lower than the fiscal years of 2005–6 and 2006–7. The World Bank projected a 5.5 per cent growth rate for the fiscal year of 2007–8, though the Bangladesh Bank believes that the economy will enjoy a 6 per cent plus gross domestic product growth in the same period.

The present government's reform measures in the last one year were supposed to improve the sociopolitical and economic systems of the country. It offered so much promise. So what went wrong? There are several reasons for the failure of the government to deliver.

First, the authorities, in many cases, dealt with corruption too heavy-handedly. It was a huge mistake tackling political and business corruption simultaneously. The arrest of alleged corrupt political leaders did not directly harm the economy. However, the actions against dishonest businessmen and their business practices created panic in the business community. Consequently, local traders and entrepreneurs limited their business operations and foreign investors were not confident in investing in new projects. Moreover, the government shut down some state-owned production units which had been incurring losses. As a result, hundreds of workers lost their jobs and there was limited employment generation. In short, the economy could not absorb the sudden shocks that resulted from the reforms.

Second, the interim government, which consists of 10 advisers, has been overseeing 42 ministries. This is humanly impossible, given the magnitude of the challenges facing the country. Moreover, the government initiated reforms beyond the number of areas that it could possibly manage. As such, the government has been stretched and distracted from the key tasks at hand.

Third, the interim government's assumption of power coincided with mounting fears of a food price spiral on global markets and high energy prices. Moreover, in the last six months, Bangladesh faced two major natural disasters (summer floods and Cyclone Sidr) which damaged standing crops, among others, and escalated food prices. Though the government was not at fault, these rises and events have placed additional burden on the government, with the Bangladeshi people looking to it for assistance and directions.

It is perhaps too soon to expect results from the government. The reforms put in place may not necessarily bring about immediate benefits. There is a trade-off between short-term losses *versus* long-run gains in any reform, regardless of the extent of the political and economic shake-up. Quite simply put, there is no gain without pain.

Nevertheless, in the short-run, the reforms have reaped dividends in some areas. For instance, the Chittagong port, known for its administrative bottlenecks, has raised port efficiency by 30 per cent and the cost of doing business in the port is now 40 per cent less, according to a World Bank assessment. Many tax evaders have been brought back into the tax net. More importantly, the ongoing reforms have created a social awareness which could help reduce corrupt activities in the long run.

Despite the caretaker government delivering mixed results in the past 12 months, Bangladesh cannot afford to let it fail. There is no real alternative until a new democratic government is installed through parliamentary elections. On its part, the interim government should learn from its mistakes in the first year and should prioritise the tasks at hand. With the state of some macroeconomic variables being very shaky, economic management should be the immediate priority. At the same time, the caretaker government should take necessary measures to increase food supply in the market.

The caretaker government cannot also afford to be distracted from its main objective of holding general election before the end of this year. To do so, it should expedite the electoral reforms, including lifting the ban on political activities as soon as possible, if not, immediately. There is also an urgent need to start constructive dialogue with the major political parties. The general election and, consequently, the installment of a democratically-elected government is the only way to bring the country back on track.

5

The Pakistan Elections: A Political Analysis

ISHTIAQ AHMED
(22 February 2008)

After nine years of military and quasi-military rule, which included a contrived and rigged election in 2002, Pakistanis finally went to the polls on 18 February 2008. Notwithstanding fear of terrorist attacks at election booths, over 46 per cent of eligible voters cast their vote. The environment was most explosive: manifest rigging would have set in motion mass protests. The large number of foreign observers and Pakistani volunteers who monitored the election agreed that the elections were, by and large, free and fair. Clearly the people voted for change.

Since early 2007 March when President Musharraf blundered by declaring Chief Justice Iftikhar Muhammad Chaudhry of the Pakistan Supreme Court non-functional—a novel euphemism for dismissal—on charges of abuse of public office, his worries only multiplied. His secular-liberal support base began to diminish rapidly. The lawyers came out protesting and continued their campaign despite repression. They were joined by civil society actors concerned with human rights and civil liberties and also political cadres from opposition parties.

The Islamists were already up in arms against him for allegedly waging the United States' war on terror on Muslims, many of them being fellow Pakistanis, ironically once trained by both Pakistan and the United States to wage jihad in Afghanistan. In early July 2007 Musharraf ordered a crackdown on the heavily-armed Islamists barricading in the Lal Masjid in Islamabad. Hundreds of people were killed. Revenge terrorist attacks by the Islamists followed immediately. They mainly targeted government functionaries but completely innocent people were also not spared.

By early October 2007, it was clear that the government was desperately trying to bring the situation under control. Musharraf's controversial re-election as president on 6 October 2007 by legislators whose term was ending in a few weeks; the imposition of a state of emergency on 3 November 2007 and arrest of thousands of political and civil society activists, followed by withdrawal of emergency on 16 December 2007 under intense pressure from the United States, the British Commonwealth, European Union and the people already in the streets—all these were sure signs of a government deeply in trouble. Musharraf deposed some other judges of the Supreme Court and replaced them with handpicked men. More voices within Pakistan and from outside now began to demand that Musharraf should leave and free and fair elections be held. He agreed on 27 November 2007 to give up his job as chief of army staff, but insisted that he was an elected civilian president.

The Americans had been trying hard to arrange some power-sharing arrangement between him and Benazir Bhutto but her assassination on 27 December 2007 plunged Pakistan into deep chaos, especially Sindh from where the Bhuttos hailed. The situation was brought under control by the army being deployed in the disturbed areas with order to 'kill on sight'. The election date was moved from 8 January 2008 to 18 February 2008. Under the circumstances, when the people voted on 18 February 2008 they were expressing an opinion on either keeping or changing the government. There can be no doubt that they voted overwhelmingly for change.

The National Assembly of Pakistan comprises 342 elected members—272 general seats and 70 reserved seats for non-Muslims (10) and women (60). The two main parties in opposition to President Musharraf—the Pakistan People's Party (PPP) now led by Asif Ali Zardari, the husband of the assassinated Benazir Bhutto, won 87 seats and the Pakistan Muslim League-Nawaz [PML(N)], led by Mian Muhammad Nawaz Sharif, secured 66 seats. They will also get on a proportional basis the major share of the 70 reserved seats for non-Muslim minorities and women.

Elections were held for 268 general seats while for the remaining four general seats they have been postponed. The results of 258 general seats have been released thus far. There was certainly a sympathy vote in favour of the PPP in the wake of Ms Bhutto's assassination. However, even the PML(N) did impressively well. It undoubtedly won admiration in its home base of Punjab because Sharif remained consistently opposed to any compromise with Musharraf. Both parties were already agreed on the Charter of Democracy of 2006, which calls for a common front to restore democracy in Pakistan. Zardari and Sharif have expressed an interest in forming a coalition government. A majority of 172 is needed to form the government. Both parties will probably need to include a minor party or some independents to form a coalition government.

The situation in the provinces is also indicative of the opposition performing much better but, in the Punjab, the Pakistan Muslim League-Quaid-e-Azam [PML(Q)] has done comparatively better than what it gained for the National Assembly from the Punjab. In the crucial North-West Frontier Province, where the Taliban and pro-Al Qaeda elements have their stronghold, the people voted for the secular Awami National Party. In Baluchistan, the Baluch nationalist parties and groups boycotted the election. In sharp variance with the rest of Pakistan, the PML(Q) emerged as the main winner. There will probably be coalition governments in the provinces too.

The coming weeks will be a test of nerves as well as foresight for the three key players: Musharraf, Sharif and Zardari. With regard to nerves, the contest is going to be between Sharif and Musharraf. The former refuses pointblank to accept the latter as president and has given a call for him to quit. Musharraf remains adamant that he is the elected president of Pakistan. Zardari has avoided an open confrontation with Musharraf saying that the parliament will decide if Musharraf should remain president or not. He has taken the same position on the re-instatement of Justice Chaudhry and other judges who have been removed from the Supreme Court.

On the other hand, Lahore's *Daily Times* of 21 February 2008 has reported that the government has re-activated a number of cases in a Swiss court against Zardari involving the illegal stashing of 60 million Swiss francs in a bank in that country. This tactic might make Zardari fall in line in case he starts cooperating too closely with Sharif.

With regard to foresight, the issue at stake is providing Pakistan a stable government. Historically, the PPP and PML(N) have been bitter rivals, though the rivalry has little to do with ideology: it was a zero-sum game for gaining power. The only thing which has brought them together now is their common grudge against Musharraf. It may be recalled that Sharif was banned from returning to Pakistan by the Musharraf regime while Benazir had gone into self-exile to evade being put on trial for alleged corruption by her and Zardari to the tune of US $1.5 billion. Benazir and Sharif were able to return to Pakistan some time ago only when the United States and Saudi Arabia respectively exerted intense pressure on Musharraf.

Musharraf has spoken about a government of reconciliation and his willingness to work with any government. Will this be acceptable to Sharif? Not easily at all. His party remains firmly behind him. The best thing for Musharraf to do will be to quit. But in case he is not willing to budge, a lot will depend on how Zardari plays his cards.

Whatever government finally comes into power, it will have to address the egregious problems of poverty, illiteracy, rising inflation and unemployment and the scourge of terrorism in Pakistan. Will it be able to do this in the overall framework of democracy and pluralism? This will depend on the ability of the elected representatives of the people and the government to keep the Islamists at bay. Whereas a role for Islam in the polity will always be accommodated in Pakistan, the question always is how much? In a free and fair election, Pakistanis have always voted for middle parties and Islamists have never won more than 5 per cent of the total vote. The rise of radical Islam in Pakistan has been the product of elite power games and not of some mass support from the general public.

The provinces of Baluchistan and Sindh have a long catalogue of grievances against the Punjabi-dominated central government. A federal system which enhances the economic and financial powers of the provinces will have to be considered to render secessionist threats unattractive. Under all circumstances, a return to military rule or quasi-military rule will be profoundly demoralising for the people of Pakistan.

As far as Pakistan's international and regional commitments are concerned, the new government will have to convince the rest of the world that rooting out terrorism remains its priority and that Pakistan's nuclear arsenal will not fall into the hands of the Islamists. With the new chief of army staff, General Kayani, in power, co-operation between the elected representatives of the people and the military should be the normal and natural way to tackle these issues.

Pakistan's economy has been doing quite well in the last few years, recording an annual growth rate of around 7 per cent. The basic fiscal and financial policies needed to latch on to the growing Asian prosperity east of Pakistan are already in place. If somehow Nawaz Sharif can be brought back into parliament, he will undoubtedly have a pivotal role to play in managing the economy because he is essentially a very successful entrepreneur.

Pakistan's greatest curse has been that its leaders are prone to corruption and that too on a massive scale. Perhaps this time around, with the internet and global networking in place, the media and civil society will be better prepared to expose such wrongdoing.

6

Yousaf Raza Gilani: Pakistan's New Prime Minister

ISHTIAQ AHMED
(*25 March 2008*)

YOUSAF RAZA GILANI (Makdoom Syed Yousaf Raza Gilani), was elected to the Pakistan National Assembly on 18 February 2008 on a ticket of the Pakistan People's Party (PPP) of Benazir Bhutto. After several weeks of suspense and speculation, during which intense consultations and negotiations within the PPP and between the PPP and its coalition partners, the Pakistan Muslim League-Nawaz [PML(N)], the Awami National Party (ANP), the Jamiat Ulema-e-Islam-F and the Muttahida Qaumi Movement (MQM) took place, Gilani was nominated on 22 March 2008 as the PPP candidate for the pivotal post of prime minister. On 24 March 2008, he was elected prime minister of Pakistan. He secured 264 votes of the newly elected legislators while his rival and leader of the opposition, Chaudhri Pervaiz Elahi, of the Pakistan Muslim League-Quaid-e-Azam [PML(Q)], received only 42 votes. He is to be sworn in as prime minister on 25 March 2008 by President Pervez Musharraf.

Gilani hails from a prominent landowning family of Multan in the Seraiki-speaking areas of southern Punjab. Multan is an ancient city and is known for the very large number of Sufi shrines located in it. Gilani's family are custodians of one of the prominent Sufi shrines, that of their ancestor, Musa Pak. They belong to the Qadri Order which is one of the largest in the Muslim world and subscribes to Sunni doctrines. It was founded in Baghdad by Shaikh Abdul Qadir Jilani (died 1166), from whom Gilani's family trace their descent.

Gilani's forefathers held important positions during the Mughal and British periods. His father, Alamdar Hussain Gilani, was a member of the Pakistan National Assembly and served as a minister in the early years after Pakistan became independent. Yousaf Raza Gilani received his early education in Multan and then did his BA from the Forman Christian College, Lahore and an MA in Journalism from the Punjab University, Lahore (1976). He is married and has four sons and a daughter.

Gilani's induction into politics began in 1978 from the platform of the Pakistan Muslim League during the rule of General Zia-ul-Haq (1977–88). He was a cabinet member during the government of Prime Minister Muhammad Khan Junejo (1985–8). He served as minister of housing and works from April 1985 to January 1986 and railways minister from January 1986 to December 1986.

In 1988, Gilani joined the PPP. He became a close aide of the late Benazir Bhutto. In Benazir Bhutto's first government (1988–90), he served as minister of tourism from March 1989 to January 1990 and again as minister of housing and works from January 1990 to August 1990. In her second stint as prime minister (1993–6), Gilani was elected speaker of the National Assembly in which position he stayed till February 1997. He has been elected several times as member of National Assembly from Multan. In the recent 2008 elections, he defeated the PML(Q) candidate, Sikandar Hayat Bosan.

Gilani was arrested on 11 February 2001 by the Musharraf government on charges of misuse of office while he was the speaker. Allegedly, he hired 600 people of dubious qualifications from his constituency on government payroll, inflicting a loss of Rs. 30 million annually. He was convicted by an anti-corruption court and spent nearly six years in prison. He was finally released on 7 October 2006. He has always maintained his innocence and has blamed the Musharraf regime for victimising him for his steadfast loyalty to the PPP and the late Benazir Bhutto.

There is wide speculation that Asif Ali Zardari, chairperson of the PPP, appointed through a written will of his wife, Bhutto, will soon get himself elected to the National Assembly through a by-election and will then replace Gilani but other reports suggest that the PPP wants to retain him as prime minister for the full term until 2013, provided he presents himself as a competent and effective prime minister. His continuation in office will naturally depend also on the stability of the coalition government. His close associates do not see him as a weak person and he is reportedly capable of making bold independent decisions.

Among the first orders he has issued after being elected as prime minister is the removal of all hindrances on the movement of the deposed chief justice of Pakistan, Iftikhar Muhammad Chaudhry, and other such judges of the Pakistan Supreme Court. For several months now, these honourable judges of Pakistan's Supreme Court have virtually been kept in detention.

It will be quite difficult for him to work smoothly with President Musharraf. Not only does he head a coalition government in which the two biggest parties, the PPP and the PML(N), have a long list of grievances against the president, Gilani himself was incarcerated by President Musharraf for nearly six years.

One can expect his government to act determinedly to curtail the extraordinary powers acquired by the president through different constitutional and legal subterfuges to dismiss an elected government and other such related subjects. He will most certainly proceed with a resolution being passed by the National Assembly, quashing the removal of the chief justice and his colleagues since this has already been agreed upon by the PPP and PML(N).

7

Post-Election Pakistan: Is there Hope or Despair for the People?

IFTIKHAR A. LODHI

(*27 March 2008*)

THE BRIEF EUPHORIA that followed the 18 February 2008 polls in Pakistan seems to have died down and the harsh realities of an immature polity are beginning to surface. Despite the decision of the Pakistan Muslim League-Nawaz PML(N) and the Pakistan People's Party (PPP) to form the government, as well as President Pervez Musharraf's promise to work with the new government, the prophecies of an Islamist takeover and/or Pakistan's disintegration have become a recurrent theme.

The turmoil in Pakistan today is far less intense than that in Iraq and Afghanistan. However, Pakistan is under greater international scrutiny and, therefore, cause for greater concern, due to its nuclear weapons, its strategic geography, and it being a front line ally in the United States-led 'war on terror'. If Pakistan fails in any way, it will be a failure of the United States, which is already mired in Iraq and Afghanistan and its 'war on terror'.

However, the very actions that Washington believes will bring stability to Pakistan are a readymade recipe for greater instability and turmoil in the country. The narrowly defined and misplaced United States strategic interests have been and are in direct conflict with the democratic aspirations of the Pakistani people. The recent poll clearly showed that the people want change and/or, at least, want to get rid of President Musharraf and his coterie, the Pakistan Muslim League-Quaid-e-Azam PML(Q). Yet, the Bush administration has been staunchly supporting Musharraf. Whilst the country was deciding on the new government, the United States tried to broker a deal between Musharraf's supporting party, the PML(Q), and the largest winning party, the centre-left secular PPP, by sidelining the second largest winning party, the centre-right PML(N).

The current coalition between PPP and PML(N), which has defied the United States pressure, faces many challenges such as addressing sociopolitical and economic issues and the issue of nation building. However, even before the two parties can start to work on the larger national agenda, they will need to resolve their own differences. There are wide differences, ideological and tactical, between the two parties.

Firstly, the two parties do not agree on how the 'war on terror' should be fought. While the slain leader of PPP, Benazir Bhutto, asserted that the scourge of terrorism would be dealt with an iron hand, she never elaborated a strategy. She vaguely argued that the Pakistan military was not doing enough and needed direction. One is not too sure how the PPP would be able to muzzle the Pakistan army which is not known to take orders from its elected leaders. Nawaz Sharif, head of the PML(N), on the other hand, is known to be sympathetic to the Islamists, if not the extremists. After winning elections, he has asked Washington to 'define the war on terror'. He made a similar call to the Americans on 25 March 2008.

The Pushtun nationalist secular-centre-left Awami National Party that swept away the elections in north-western region has suggested initiating talks with the militants, differentiating between Al Qaeda and Pakistani Taliban.

Secondly, the two parties have differing views on the role of President Musharraf in any future government setup. He has vowed to stay on and has stated that he would support the new government. However, the civil society and the PML(N) have called for his resignation. Though the PPP is willing to work with him, apparently on Washington's demand, it wants to curtail his powers. On the other hand, the Pakistan army has not given any categorical assurance of backing him, though the army chief, General Kayani, has mentioned that the army is not distancing itself from Musharraf.

Thirdly, the two parties had originally differed on the issue of the restoration of the supreme court judges. The lawyers' movement to reinstate the deposed judges has been able to sustain itself effectively over one year despite pressure from various groups. President Musharraf could not have imagined such a reaction when he sacked Chief Justice Iftikhar Chaudhry on 9 March 2007. The movement, though primarily initiated and controlled by the legal fraternity, soon gained support from the civil society. The newly established television channels also played a critical role in this episode. While the PML-N fully supported the movement, the PPP initially remained silent. Nevertheless, both parties have lately agreed to restore the judges. In fact, one of the first orders issued by Yousaf Raza Gilani after being elected as prime minister, backed by the PPP and PML(N), is the removal of all hindrances on the movement of the deposed chief justice and other such judges.

It now seems that Washington is starting to realise that it is Pakistan, and not Musharraf, which is its indispensable ally in the 'war on terror'. The recent statements from the United States Department suggest that it may willy-nilly succumb to the demands of the Pakistanis. If the Bush administration chooses to keep its support for Musharraf at the expense of state institutions and political stability in any conflicting situation, it would cost Pakistan dearly. The problem of American support for President Musharraf lies with two widely-held misperceptions in Washington. First, he is the only guarantee for Pakistan's cooperation in fighting extremists and if he is not present on the political scene, the Islamists would take over the country. Secondly, he, or generally the army, alone can hold the country together which would otherwise fall apart.

The Islamist takeover threat has, honestly, been blown out of proportions. There is no way that the Islamic parties can come to power, either by democratic means or through staging a mass uprising. A cursory look at the history of Pakistan reveals that the Islamic parties, even the moderate ones, have never enjoyed popular support. Though Pakistan came into existence in the name of religion, its founding father Mohammed Ali Jinnah clearly had a vision of a secular state. The Westernised elite in Pakistan have followed his footsteps since then. The largest ever number of popular vote for all religious parties put together was 10 per cent in 2002. They secured 68 seats in the National Assembly. This was really an aberration as the Pakistani people had voted for the religious parties in widespread anger over the United States' attack on Afghanistan. In the recent polls, generally believed to be fair and free, these religious parties were able to secure only six seats in the National Assembly.

There are also fears of an Islamist rebellion within the Pakistan army. Such propositions overlook the history and structure of the institution and that of civil–military relations. There have been more than a dozen such attempts in the past from middle and high rank officers with different ideologies, communist as well as Islamist. All such attempts were easily and quickly put down. The Pakistan army is highly professional and, since the times of the British, it has been engaged in combats in Islamist rebellions in and outside the country. It was the army who nurtured the Islamists with the help of the United States for its strategic purposes in Afghanistan. There are reportedly some lower and middle rank officers who are sympathetic to the Islamists but these are unlikely to influence the overall control and command structure of the army.

Similarly, the disintegration theory does not stand scrutiny either. The only active nationalist movement that has a secessionist agenda today in Pakistan is the Baluch movement. The movement turned into armed insurgency in 2005. However, it lacks the widespread support of the masses. Comparisons have been drawn between today's Pakistan and Pakistan in 1970 when the then East Pakistan became Bangladesh. The fact that Bangladesh and Pakistan are separated by a thousand miles of hostile Indian territory leaves any comparison inappropriate. Moreover, the Bengalis are a homogeneous population and much larger than West Pakistan's population. The Awami League of Sheikh Mujeeb then enjoyed popular support, including a strong bureaucracy. And yet the final victory was secured with the intervention of the Indian army. None of these situations are present today or are likely to take place in Pakistan.

There are allegations by Islamabad that 'foreign powers' are fanning the flames in Baluchistan. Many of these Baluch groups have been operating from Afghanistan and their financial and political centres are established in the Middle East, the United Kingdom and the United States. Whilst the grievances on the backwardness of the province are legitimate, the Baluch rebels are largely private militias of tribal chieftains. They are reportedly motivated by the prospects of Baluchistan's potential wealth and the role it will play in 'the new great game' in which they want their share. Nevertheless, the approach taken by President Musharraf to tackle these problems was flawed. There must be a political solution to the grievances of the Baluch people. Similarly, a whole-hearted multipronged strategy is required to fight Islamic extremism in the long run.

At the moment, there remains a lack of trust between the progressive elements of the civil society, including the elected democratic parties, and the Washington-backed Musharraf regime. At a time when the two centrist parties will form a coalition government, Washington will need to back them whole-heartedly even if it means Musharraf losing some, if not all, of his power as a result.

8

Bhutan: Marching Towards Democracy

S.D. MUNI

(3 April 2008)

THE YEAR 2008 may go down in the history of South Asia as the year of democratic institutionalisation and electoral processes. After Pakistan's elections on 18 February, Bhutan followed on 24 March and Nepal is all set to hold its first ever Constituent Assembly polls on 10 April. All these elections are a manifestation of the strong upsurge for democracy against the erstwhile autocratic governance in these countries. The case of Bhutan has, however, been different as the Bhutanese elections were cast in a unique political context. Unlike the situation in Nepal and Pakistan, the elections were not precipitated by any grassroots upsurge for political change and representative governance. The Bhutanese people were happy to be governed by their traditional monarchy whose criteria for development was defined by the unique concept of 'Gross National Happiness', to contrast it with 'Gross National Product', felt and enjoyed, not only materially but also 'spiritually', by its people. Bhutan's call for democracy was a top-down gift to his people by the king, Jigme Singhye Wangchuk, much against the unwillingness and initial resistance by his ministers and associates as well as his subjects. Compare this with the Nepal king in Bhutan's close proximity, who was hellbent on going to any length in retaining his hold over power. He even resorted to direct rule under the pretext of dealing with the 10-year old Maoist insurgency. Also contrast the Bhutan king's initiative with the military regimes in Pakistan and Myanmar. While the military regime in Pakistan, succumbed to the idea of democratic elections under severe domestic and international pressures, the regime in Myanmar has defied the international community, by and large, and suppressed the protests led by the monks on the question of accommodating democratic aspirations of the people.

Much before the culmination of democratic upsurge in its neighbourhood, the king of Bhutan decided in 2005 to open up his traditional monarchy to political liberalisation. He took the initiative to institute democracy by handing over executive power to elected representatives. Towards that goal, he launched the process of drafting a new constitution that made the king a constitutional head and transferred effective executive powers to an elected parliament. He went around his country discussing the draft constitution and pleading with his people to learn to rule themselves through their elected representatives. To the skeptics and indifferent masses, who seemed happy with the ways they were being traditionally governed, he argued the advantages of a representative system. The new Constitution makes it mandatory for the future Bhutanese kings to retire at the age of 65. The king can also be removed by a two-thirds vote in the parliament. King Jigme Singhye Wangchuk himself abdicated in favour of his 26 years old eldest son, Jigme Khesar Namgyal Wangchuk in 2006. Political parties were reintroduced in April 2007 by lifting a 50-year old ban on them. Elections to constitute the lower house of parliament were announced for March 2008.

There has, of course, been political pressure from the people for democracy in Bhutan decades before the king's initiative. The Bhutan State Congress launched a futile popular movement for democracy during the early 1950s. Again during the early 1990s, Bhutan witnessed a democratic struggle which was effectively put down. Both these earlier movements had been dominated by the Nepalis living in southern Bhutan and, accordingly, there was a clear ethnic dimension to them, directed against the Drukpa people and their traditional monarchy. The possibility of these movements being in the background of King Jigme Singhye's initiative cannot be ruled out. But the trigger for his move must have been provided by the events in his neighbourhood where centuries of autocratic monarchical rule had turned people violent, giving rise to the Maoist insurgency. There have also been growing concern about the possibility of Maoist influence and infiltration among the ranks of the Bhutanese refugees settled in United Nations camps in Nepal since the early 1990s. The king could also sense the unfolding aspects of globalisation where democracy and human rights had come to occupy centre-stage in political discourse. One would not know the succession tensions within the royal family in Bhutan where court intrigues and jealousies had not been unheard phenomena. In all, it was prudent and far-sighted on the part of the king to decide in favour of broadening the base of authority and legitimacy before forces of history overtook the tiny kingdom. The events in Tibet have borne out the wisdom of the king's moves.

The Bhutan elections are unique not only because they were ordered by the king, but also unlike in other South Asian countries, they are based on educational qualifications. Under the newly framed election laws, no one can contest parliamentary elections without having a graduate degree. Bhutan has a very small graduate community of just 3,000 persons. This is also indicative of the fact that, in a country where literacy is still only 42 per cent, the graduate community may mostly come from the upper and elite sections of the society. The degree of management of the elections was also evident in the screening of the contesting parties. One of the parties, the Druk Peoples' Unity Party, was disqualified due to what was described as a lack of 'credible leadership'. It was alleged that more than 75 per cent of the party members were school dropouts. The elimination of the third party also reduced the two-stage electoral process into a direct one stage process. According to election laws, the first stage of the elections was to filter out all but the two highest ranking (in terms of votes secured in the first stage) parties for the second and the final stage process. The Election Commission had also disqualified a candidate of the Peoples' Democratic Party (PDP) who tried to play up the problem of Bhutanese of Nepal origin. This was done to send a firm message that there was no room in Bhutan for communal and sectarian politics. There was a clear decision to keep the Nepali issue out of the political process. No person could contest the elections if any of his/her parents were a migrant Bhutanese. Both the parents had to be Bhutan born. The electoral process was also kept free of religious issues as the monks were not eligible to vote. No wonder, there were no sensitive or contentious issues. In fact, there was not much to distinguish between the two major contenders, the PDP and the Druk Phuensum Tshogpa (DPT) or Bhutan Peace Party. While the DPT promised a compact government, equal and just treatment to all the citizens and high standard for political conduct, the PDP tried to lure the voters by offering them salary raise and infrastructure development, including an airport in eastern Bhutan.

It was a keenly contested election. Of more than 318,000 registered voters, 79.4 per cent cast their votes. Even the king appealed for the exercise of franchise right by all the Bhutanese. Senior administrators actively participated in the campaign. People walked long distances from their homes to cast their votes. Some expatriate Bhutanese also came from the United States and Europe to participate in the elections. The Election Commission gave 100,000 Bhutanese rupees to each of the candidates along with essential election material. In addition to this, a candidate could spend 100,000 Bhutanese rupees of his/her own to boost his/her electoral prospects. The Election Commission also organised a television debate between the leaders of the contending parties. There were corruption charges by the DPT against PDP, saying that the latter was bribing the voters but such charges were stoutly countered.

Election results stunned all calculations. Analysts in Bhutan and India had expected a close fight, with the difference of not more than five to ten seats between the winner and the loser. Even the DPT, which emerged as the overwhelming winner, had not expected more than 30 seats in the 47 contested ones. It finally won 45 seats and the PDP which was routed, won only two seats. The PDP has asked for re-poll or, at least, a serious investigation into the factors that caused such a landslide in favour of the DPT. This heavily-lopsided outcome has been attributed to various factors. Some have blamed automatic voting machines for their faulty mechanism or improper use. Others have given credit to the campaigning style of the DPT and the impressive articulation by its leader, Jigme Y. Thinley, in the debate as well as during the campaign. The DPT also had five senior ministers in its ranks, and there was the impression that this party had the real blessings of the king, though the PDP had a leadership related to the royal family. The active canvassing by senior civil servants for the DPT further confirmed this impression. Since the election was seen as a gift from the king, the voters chose the party that was seen as the king's real party.

Bhutan's top-down experiment in democracy, therefore, starts with a parliament having an extremely weak opposition. Even the two elected PDP members have threatened to resign if the causes of their party's rout are not sincerely investigated. To compensate for the weak opposition, the DPT leader and prime minister-elect has promised accountable, corruption-free and transparent governance down to the constituency level. He has assured that he will do everything to 'establish firm foundations for a great democracy' under constitutional monarchy. He stated that, 'We are all subjects of one king. And in this small country, we are all family'.

While the international community has welcomed the democratic initiative of Bhutan, some criticism has been levelled at the neglect of Nepali refugees who have been languishing for years in Nepal and India. More than a 100,000 of the refugees were not included in the voters list and were not allowed to participate in the elections. Even according to the Bhutanese government's official position, while most of these refugees were illegal migrants into Bhutan, some of them could be Bhutanese citizens. What about their voting rights? These refugees have been infiltrated by extremist elements, including members of Bhutan Communist Party, closely affiliated to the Nepal Maoists. They tried to disrupt the elections by exploding bombs in various parts of Bhutan since January 2008 and on the eve of elections. These extremists have been opposing third party solution to the refugee problem wherein these refugees would be repatriated to the United States (about 60,000) and about 20,000 in some of the European countries. The process of repatriating these refugees to the West has already begun.

Though the ethnic issue was kept carefully out of the electoral process, it will need to be addressed seriously by the new democratic establishment. There are nine Nepali members of the DPT elected to the parliament but this is far less than the number warranted by the population size of the Nepalis in Bhutan, even after excluding the Nepal-based refugees. The dispersal of refugees will not resolve Bhutan's ethnic issue if the Nepalis living in Bhutan and accepted as Bhutanese citizens are not given a sense of belonging and equal participation in its political and economic life. Though Bhutan is the second richest South Asian country in terms of per capita income (of approximately US $1,200), there are wide income gaps in the society. Judicious policy initiatives will be needed to bridge these gaps if social harmony and 'national happiness' are to be ensured.

The new government will also confront a foreign policy challenge in the form of an assertive and sensitive China. Bhutan's boundary issue with China remains to be resolved. There have been discussions between Bhutan and China on the issue and much of the tension areas have been sorted out but its final resolution is linked to the resolution of Sino–Indian boundary question due to tri-junctions and historical imperatives. The revival of the Tibet issue has the potential of vitiating the Sino–Indian boundary question. China has also built up an impressive spread of infrastructure in the Himalayas, with roads reaching up to the Bhutanese borders. There have been Bhutanese objections to some of the road links creeping into the areas claimed by Bhutan. Intrusion by Chinese shepherds into Bhutan's pasture lands had also raised tensions between them on a number of occasions earlier.

As for India, a stable, democratising, friendly and confident Bhutan is the best security asset in the turbulent Himalayas. India recently revised its treaty relations with Bhutan to the satisfaction of the kingdom. While India has been supporting Bhutan's gradual transition to democracy, the prime minister-elect of Bhutan, Jigmye Thinlay, has promised to further strengthen the 'unique friendship and understanding' prevailing between the two countries.

9

The Pakistan Federal Cabinet: More of the Same or Something New?

ISHTIAQ AHMED

(*11 April 2008*)

THE ISLAMIC REPUBLIC of Pakistan is a federal, parliamentary democracy which exercises its authority within the limits imposed by Islamic injunctions. The Pakistan Constitution vests executive powers for the federation as a whole in the prime minister and his cabinet, but through a number of ordinances and amendments enacted during the dictatorships of General Zia-ul-Haq and General Pervez Musharraf, the president has been given extraordinary powers to dismiss the prime minister and to dissolve parliament in case he is convinced that the government is not functioning properly. It will be interesting to see if the newly-elected government will seek to change this situation in favour of a strong prime minister and make the presidency a titular office. The Pakistan parliament is bicameral. It consists of an upper house, the Senate, elected by the provincial assemblies and the Federally Administered Tribal Areas (FATA), and a lower house, the National Assembly, elected directly by the citizens on the basis of universal adult franchise.

After the recent elections in Pakistan on 18 February 2008, a coalition government comprising the two main winners the Pakistan People's Party (PPP), and the Pakistan Muslim League-Nawaz [PML (N)], along with the Awami Nationalist Party (ANP), Jamiyat Ulema-e-Islam-Fazlullah [JUI-(F)] and an independent member from FATA was formed.

Prime Minister Yousaf Raza Gilani was sworn in by President Pervez Musharraf on 24 March 2008 in a solemn and tense ceremony as the leaders of the PPP, PML(N) and ANP boycotted it.

Slogans were shouted by some of the PPP leaders in favour of the assassinated Benazir Bhutto. The swearing-in of the federal cabinet on 31 March 2008 was even more charged with tension and anxiety as the ministers from the PML(N) initially were reluctant to be sworn in by President Musharraf but later took the oath of office wearing black armbands to express their objection to him continuing in office. In any case, the formalities were completed. There are 11 PPP, nine PML(N), two ANP, one JUI(F) ministers and one minister from the independents. The distribution, according to political party and portfolios, is as follows:

(i) The ministers from the PPP are Chaudhry Ahmed Mukhtar (Defence); Makhdoom Shah Mehmood Qureshi (Foreign Affairs); Sherry Rehman (Information and Broadcasting); Qamar Zaman Kaira (Kashmir Affairs and Northern Areas); Syed Khursheed Ahmed Shah (Labour, Manpower and Overseas Pakistanis); Senator Farooq H. Naik (Law and Justice); Nazar Muhammad Gondal (Narcotics Control); Humayun Aziz Kurd (Population Welfare); Syed Naveed Qamar (Ports and Shipping, with additional charge of Privatisation and Investment); Najamuddin Khan (States and Frontier Regions); and Raja Pervaiz Ashraf (Water and Power).

(ii) The ministers from PML(N) are Chaudhry Nisar Ali Khan (Senior Minister, Communications with additional charge of Food, Agriculture and Livestock); Shahid Khaqan Abbasi (Commerce); Tehmina Daultana (Culture); Ahsan Iqbal (Education, with additional charge of Minorities); Muhammad Ishaq Dar (Finance, Revenue, Economic Affairs and Statistics); Khawaja Muhammad Asif (Petroleum and Natural Resources, with additional charge of Sports); Sardar Mehtab Abbasi (Railways); Rana Tanveer Hussain (Defence Production); and Khawaja Saad Rafique (Youth Affairs, Science and Technology).

(iii) The other ministers include JUI(F)'s Senator Rehmatullah Kakar (Housing and Works); ANP's Haji Ghulam Ahmad Bilour (Local Governments and Rural Development); and Nawabzada Khawaja Muhammad Khan Hoti (Social Welfare, Special Education); and FATA MNA Hameedullah Jan Afridi (Environment).

The post of foreign minister has been given to PPP's Shah Mahmood Qureshi. He was one of the persons in contention for the post of prime minister. He has almost the same background as Prime Minister Gilani in that he comes from an influential, perhaps the most influential, landowning family of Multan who are custodians of the most revered Sufi masters—Shaikh Bahauddin Zakariya and Shah Rukhne Alam—in that ancient town of southern Punjab. Qureshi is a PPP heavyweight and may have been given the foreign ministry by PPP President Asif Ali Zardari with a view to maintaining a balance between these two influential families. He does not have any previous experience of foreign affairs but has been elected a member of the National Assembly in the past also. He will probably maintain the policy already established by the foreign office of normalising relations with India and Afghanistan and maintaining good relations with China, the Arab world and the Muslim nations in general. Zardari and Sharif have, in recent times, given statements favouring increasing economic interaction with India and more people-to-people contacts through the liberalisation of visa and related matters. Also, on Kashmir, the ideas expressed by them suggest that it will not be allowed to obstruct the normalisation of ties with India. Qureshi will probably tow this line as it seems now to be anchored in the Pakistan foreign office as well.

The defence ministry has gone to PPP's Chaudhry Mukhtar Ahmed. He belongs to a wealthy industrial family of Lahore which made its fortune by pioneering factory-level manufacturing of shoes. They own Services Industries with headquarters in Gujrat, north of Lahore. Ahmed has also been a steadfast member of the PPP since long. He too was tipped as the prime minister, but in the subsequent horse-trading that followed behind closed doors, he was given the defence portfolio. Upon becoming minister, he reportedly described Musharraf as a great asset for Pakistan but has subsequently denied that he said so. He is generally considered to have good relations with Musharraf and the military establishment. He is also a friend of Zardari—both met in jail when they were charged with various financial irregularities. The defence ministry enjoys a high status as it is the link between the civilian government and the military establishment.

The finance ministry has been allotted to PML(N)'s Ishaq Dar from Lahore. It was expected that, since Nawaz Sharif and his brother, Shahbaz Sharif, belong to an industrial family and have a keen interest in the promotion of commerce and production, this key ministry will go to their party. Since neither of them are, at present, a member of parliament because of some legal hurdles, Dar has been given this portfolio. He is of Kashmiri descent and a relative of Nawaz Sharif. He served as finance minister in Nawaz Sharif's government which was toppled by General Musharraf in 1999. During that period, he distinguished himself by making export-oriented growth the cornerstone of his economic strategy. After sanctions were imposed on Pakistan when it tested nuclear devices at the end of May 1998, Dar successfully negotiated an International Monetary Fund (IMF) rescue package to avert an economic crisis. Though that package was not able to prevent the crisis hitting Pakistan severely, it is generally recognised that those measures mitigated the impact of the sanctions. He enjoys the reputation of being business friendly and in favour of globalisation and Pakistan's greater integration into the world economy. He will certainly favour greater trade with India and can even be induced to evolve a Pakistan 'Look East' policy, if he has not been thinking of one already.

Some other important political figures in the federal cabinet are PPP's Sherry Rahman, a prominent female journalist of Urdu-speaking origin from Karachi, a human rights activist and a close friend and aide of Benazir Bhutto. She has been assigned the ministry of information and broadcasting. In the last few days, some ministers from the last government, the chief minister of Sindh, Arbab Ghulam Rahim, and federal minister, Dr Sher Afghan Niazi, have been physically assaulted by angry mobs. The attack on Rahim was shown on private television channels but was later taken off the air and questions have been asked if Rahman had issued the orders to that effect.

Another heavyweight in the federal cabinet is PML(N)'s Chaudhry Nisar Ali Khan (senior minister, communications with additional charge of food, agriculture and livestock). He hails from northern Punjab and has been an elected member of parliament many times from Rawalpindi district. He served as federal minister for petroleum and natural resources, and provincial coordinator during 1990–3 in the government of Nawaz Sharif. Again from 1997–9, he was federal minister for petroleum and natural resources and special assistant to the prime minister.

The PPP has its strongest hold in Sindh from where both Benazir Bhutto and Asif Zardari hail. Makhdoom Amin Rahim, custodian of a famous Sufi shrine and landlord was initially tipped as the frontrunner for the post of prime minister but Zardari overruled him probably because he enjoyed a strong position in the PPP rank and file besides being a leading member of Sindhi feudal society and could, therefore, be difficult for Zardari to control once he became prime minister. Zardari has chosen to balance the Sindhi presence in the federal cabinet by including PPP's Syed Khursheed Ahmed Shah (labour, manpower and overseas Pakistanis) and Syed Naveed Qamar (ports and shipping, with additional charge of privatisation and investment). Both are important members of the PPP and enjoy significant influence in the Sindhi feudal society.

Qamar Zaman Kaira of the PPP has been given the ministry of Kashmir affairs. He hails from Punjab. He is known as a hard working party worker who has helped greatly in organising the PPP in the Punjab. Although the Kashmir ministry is primarily responsible for the affairs of the Pakistani-administered Azad Kashmir, it also monitors the overall situation in the Indian-administered Kashmir. It remains to be seen what specific ideas of his own he will bring in order to solve that outstanding issue with India. Prime Minister Gilani and Indian Prime Minister Manmohan Singh have exchanged conventional greetings and spoken to each other. The media has reported that the Indian premier is likely to visit Pakistan soon. It is very unlikely that the new cabinet will spoil its relations with India by assuming some intransigent position on Kashmir.

Given the recent history of violence and terrorism as well as the arrest of peaceful agitators against the authoritarian policies of President Musharraf from March 2007 onwards when he declared Chief Justice Iftikhar Muhammad Chaudhry non-functional, the new government will face an uphill task of establishing law and order in the country. This crucial task has been assigned to PPP's Senator Farooq H. Naik who is the new minister for law and justice. He is a Punjabi. He is a lawyer and has very close relations with PPP's chief Zardari. He has represented Benazir Bhutto and her husband in several legal cases. He will have to bring under control the escalating violence that had taken place recently when two former close members of the pro-Musharraf's administration, Ghulam Rahim and Sher Afghan Niazi, were badly assaulted by angry mobs. There were ugly scenes of violence in Karachi as well where nine people, six of them lawyers, were killed in clashes between different political factions. Naik has condemned, in very strong words, the stoning to death of a man and women in the tribal areas after a self-styled Islamic court found them guilty of adultery. He has also ordered an inquiry into the death of a Hindu worker at the hands of his Muslim co-workers at a garment factory in Karachi after a heated discussion on religion. He was accused of blasphemy and killed in a gruesome manner by fanatical Muslims.

On the whole, the post of prime minister and other key ministries (foreign affairs, finance, defence and law and order) have been allotted to Punjabis, whose province, Punjab, is Pakistan's largest in terms of population as well as the dominant one in terms of the origins of the military and bureaucratic apparatuses. While the federal cabinet and federal governments and cabinets are now taking shape, there are rumours that Zardari may be planning to secure the prime minister post for himself but that remains to be seen. There can be no denying that serious differences exist between the two leaders, Zardari and Sharif, on the acceptance of Musharraf as president and on the restoration of the chief justice and other judges of the Supreme Court deposed by Musharraf. It is widely believed that Zardari and before him, his wife Benazir Bhutto, had already worked out a deal brokered by the United States with Musharraf on power-sharing. Zardari continues to be working on such an agenda while Sharif is adamant that Musharraf should be removed as president through legal and constitutional means, and the chief justice and other judges be put back on the benches. But both Zardari and Sharif are not at present members of parliament.

Therefore, it will be interesting to see whether the federal cabinet develops internal cohesion and works as one team led by an independent prime minister or whether it will take its cue from the party bosses.

Although suicide bombing has noticeably declined in Pakistan after the new government announced that it would seek to end terrorism though not only through military means. It will seek political solutions too and bolster such efforts with economic support to the poverty-ridden tribal areas of Pakistan from where most of the suicide bombers are recruited. The fact that the PML(N) is part of the coalition government and its leader, Nawaz Sharif, has had a soft spot for conservative Islamic ideas, can mean that channels of communication with the militants can be established with greater ease and trust. Such a liaison can also mean that the extremists gain concessions on greater adherence to dogmatic Islamic law by the government. On the whole, the federal cabinet consists of urbane, modern educated individuals who would probably eschew close identification with either the left or the right.

It is, however, far from certain that the new government will survive and consolidate itself. The coming days and weeks will severely test its ability to govern Pakistan successfully, and if it survives, then the transition to a civilian, democratic and peace-oriented government will be smoothened.

10

Nepal Constituent Assembly Elections: The Dawn of a New Era?

NISHCHAL NATH PANDEY

(18 April 2008)

THE HISTORIC elections for a Constituent Assembly in Nepal are finally over, not only with 60 per cent voter turnout but also with a fair amount of violence. The Nepalese voted for the first time in nine years on 10 April 2008 to choose a 601-member special assembly. There were 74 political parties, including one with all women candidates and another formed by a former Japanese national. There were 17.5 million voters and over 80,000 observers, alongside high-profile individuals such as former United States president, Jimmy Carter, and the son of former Japanese prime minister, Ryutaro Hashimoto. The new assembly is expected to draft a new Constitution for the country and abolish the Hindu monarchy. The monarchy has ruled the complex Nepali State, comprising 22 different principalities of various ethnic groups, for 239 years.

The elections were the culmination of a 2006 peace deal with Maoist guerrillas to end a decade-long civil war. However, violence marred the run-up to the polls with a series of bomb blasts, abductions and disturbances. The Election Commission confirmed that several people were killed, including two candidates, and polls were postponed in more than 100 booths. The killing of seven Maoists cadres in the Dang district just one day prior to polls nearly sparked off a massive protest by the Maoists but was assuaged by the chairman of the Maoist Party, Comrade Prachanda.

Based on available information on the polls, the Maoists are heading towards an absolute majority, leaving the other parties far behind. The other two mainstream parties, the Nepali Congress

(NC) and the United Marxist Leninist (UML) are expected to suffer massive losses at the elections, having had their vote banks considerably eroded over the years. Of the 601 assembly members, 240 will be elected directly and 335 through a proportional electoral system, a complicated procedure for Nepal's nascent democratic system. The remaining 26 members will be nominated by the prime minister.

The Maoists are well ahead not only in the direct elections but also in proportional voting where they have secured 32.41 per cent of the total votes counted thus far. As of 16 April 2008, they have already secured 119 seats in the direct elections, whereas the NC has only 33 seats and the UML only 30.

The biggest loser in the elections is the NC which has never been so weak in its entire history. The results have been a big blow personally to Prime Minister Koirala whose entire family fared badly at the polls. His daughter Sujata, nephew Shekhar, cousin Sushil and close confidante Mahesh Acharya were well beaten at the polls. His home minister, Krishna Prasad Sitaula, also lost in his home constituency in Jhapa district.

Similarly, for the UML, the election results came as a huge surprise and shock. Its powerful general secretary, Madhav Kumar Nepal, lost in both his constituencies while party stalwarts such as education minister, Pradip Nepal, and former foreign minister, K.P. Oli, were also routed.

Another major significant outcome of the polls was the poor show of the parties based in the Terai (southern plains), mainly the Madheshi Janadhikar Forum (MJF) and Tarai-Madhes Democratic Party, which did not bag as many seats as expected. Initially, analysts had hoped that these parties would emerge as king-makers in case of a hung parliament. Most certainly, Nepal will officially become a republic once the first sitting of the Constituent Assembly votes against the institution of monarchy.

These have been landmark elections, not only because they addressed a 57-year old promise made by the King Tribhuvan after the successful revolution of 1950 of letting the people draft their own Constitution, but also because there were more women representatives from the Terai region, who had hitherto been excluded from the upper echelons of government, as well as former Maoist guerrillas. The real challenge for Nepal will be the post-elections period and how the new leaders, the United Nations and the international community will handle the intricate constitution making process with such a large number of members coming from a diverse range of socially-disadvantaged communities.

All parties, including the armed groups in the Terai, will need to work closely with the interim government and with one another to ensure a smooth transition to the new legislature and government. The MJF will be watching events unfold from the sidelines. The MJF spearheaded a bloody uprising of the Terai people last year that led to the killing of more than 70 people. It had, earlier, described the elections as a historic opportunity for the Nepali people to consolidate the peace process and to create a more democratic and inclusive future for their country. The leader of the MJF, Upendra Yadav, contested and won against the prime minister's daughter.

These elections will expose the tensions amongst Nepal's ethnic communities vying for partial to complete autonomy, most notably in the Terai where the Madhesi community is clamouring for power. Although the Terai parties were not able to muster seats even in the Terai districts, the interim legislature has agreed on a federal system of governance. However, Nepal's interim Constitution has not elaborated on the type of federal structure the country will have. This is likely to be a very sensitive issue for the Constituent Assembly to handle.

The new government will also need to look at security sector reforms, the key issues being the integration of the former Maoist guerrillas into the Nepal army. It is likely that the Maoists would want to be included into the Nepal army, a proposition the chief of the army staff, General Rukmangud Katuwal, had vehemently and publicly opposed in the past. However, with the Maoists emerging to be the duly elected and legitimate government, General Katuwal will have to obey the orders of his political masters.

Another challenge, albeit not a major one, is the issue of a 'secular state' declared by the interim parliament. This has been questioned by Hindu groups in Nepal and in north India. Eighty per cent of the population of the country is Hindu and there has been some tension between the majority Hindus and the minority Muslims recently, including one episode of a bomb blast at a mosque in Biratnagar town in southern Nepal.

Furthermore, during the last one month, Kathmandu witnessed protests almost on a daily basis by Tibetan refugees who have been living in Nepal from the 1950s. An incident of vandalism at the consular section of the Chinese embassy led to the Chinese ambassador in Nepal meeting Prime Minister Koirala and demanding security for his embassy along with a more effective curb on anti-China protests. At the same time, the Nepal government has come under condemnation from across the globe for being too harsh on Tibetan protesters. One international media group has called the Nepal police a proxy of its Chinese counterpart. Nepal has inadvertently become a front line state on the Tibetan issue.

Nepal's economy is also in dire straits. Besides being in depression, the country suffers from a shattered infrastructure. Besides the country has a high rate of unemployment, with about one-third of the Nepalese living on less than US $1 a day. The Constituent Assembly elections have provided the opportunity for change and development in Nepal. However, the new government has the unenviable task of managing a highly sensitive and volatile political system, as well as a rebuilding the economy. It will need the support of the key political players to turn the country around. Only then can the people of Nepal truly witness the dawn of a new era in their country.

11

The Unravelling of Coalition Politics in Pakistan

RAJSHREE JETLY

(16 May 2008)

THE RECENT breakdown of talks between the Pakistan Muslim League-Nawaz [PML(N)] and the Pakistan People's Party (PPP) on the reinstatement of the judiciary and the withdrawal of federal ministers by the PML(N) from the ruling coalition have threatened to derail coalition politics in Pakistan and deal another body blow to the process of democratisation in the country. At the heart of this matter is the reinstatement of judges of the supreme court who were deposed by President Musharraf under emergency rule and the Provisional Constitutional Order of 3 November 2007. Both the PML(N) and the PPP agreed in the Bhurban declaration of 9 March 2008 that the judges would be reinstated through a resolution within 30 days of the formation of the government.

With the expiry of the first 30 April 2008 deadline, further talks were held in Dubai and London to resolve the matter. However, the expiry of the second deadline on 12 May 2008 precipitated the extreme reaction by Nawaz Sharif to pull out his party's nine ministers from the 24-minister federal cabinet, while the coalition has not completely disintegrated—the resignations of the PML(N) have yet to be accepted by Prime Minister Yousaf Raza Gilani—it has clearly been pushed to the brink. This brief examines the contentious issue of the restoration of the judiciary and the consequences an impasse on this matter may have on Pakistan's political struggle for democracy.

Background to Coalition Politics and the Judicial Crisis

Pakistan has been in a state of extreme turmoil, especially over the last 18 months. The holding of elections on 18 February 2008, however, infused new hopes for the revival of the democratic process and the end of the military rule of Musharraf. The election results gave an overwhelming mandate to the democratic parties, the PPP and the PML(N), which together accounted for 154 out of 267 directly contested, seats and they formed a coalition government. The coalition, however, was built on very shaky grounds, and largely united by a common cause, namely, the ouster of Musharraf. Historically, the two parties have been bitter rivals with competing ideologies and agendas.

The independence of the judiciary became an issue of national significance with the dismissal of the chief justice, Iftikhar Chaudhry, on 9 March 2007. The restoration of the judiciary has become the single most important political issue in Pakistan, symbolising the country's struggle for democracy and ouster of military rule. While it is a source of popular support and legitimisation, it is also a potential time bomb, as there is nothing to prevent a fully restored judiciary from revisiting the constitutional cases involving the legitimacy of Musharraf's presidency, which could open another Pandora's Box of uncertainty and additional turmoil in Pakistan.

Disintegration of The Coalition Over The Restoration of The Judiciary

While both the PPP and the PML(N) are in broad agreement on the need to restore the judiciary, the deadlock lies in the modalities rather than on the final objective. The PML(N) wants the judges reinstated unconditionally through a resolution to be passed in the national assembly with a simple majority. Its position is that this is in line with the Bhurban Declaration and reflective of the will of the people.

The PPP, on the other hand, is insisting on a comprehensive constitutional political solution of the problem. It wants a comprehensive constitutional package to strengthen the judiciary as a whole, going beyond the reinstatement of the judges and linking the restoration of the judiciary to constitutional reforms, including limiting the powers of top judges and reducing their tenure. The PPP, while willing to reinstate the sacked judges, does not want to remove the current judges who were appointed to replace the judges dismissed by Musharraf. Although negotiations between the two parties are still continuing to break the impasse, the prospects of a breakthrough remain uncertain.

On closer analysis it appears that both parties have their own agendas and are acting in their own self-interest rather than for the larger good of the country. In some ways, both parties are victims of the personal agendas of their leaders, Sharif and Asif Ali Zardari. Sharif has his personal scores to settle with Musharraf who ousted him from power in the 1999 coup. Some believe that the real reason PML(N) wants former Chief Justice Chaudhry and his colleagues restored is to see that there is a chance of Musharraf being ousted from the presidency on the grounds of his ineligibility to stand as a presidential candidate. At the same time, PML(N) does not want to be out of power and understands that it cannot push too far on this issue. Thus, it has maintained that it will not dissolve the coalition and will continue to support it on an issue-by-issue basis. Severing ties from the coalition runs the risk of the PPP seeking support from pro-Musharraf elements to form the government. This would completely isolate the PML(N) and leave Sharif at the mercy of his nemesis. His tightrope act has allowed Sharif, at least in theory, to live up to publicly-stated principles and, thus, retain the moral high ground.

The PPP, on the other hand, is driven largely by the personal fears and compulsions of its leader, Zardari who, like Musharraf, does not want to see the return of some of the sacked judges, particularly former Chief Justice Chaudhry, who might take a view that the legal challenges to the National Reconciliation Ordinance, an amnesty Musharraf granted to Zardari, former Premier Benazir Bhutto and others against graft cases could be upheld. Zardari is also reported to be comfortable with the present Chief Justice, Abdul Hameed Dogar, who, in a petition against the condition of graduation to contest parliamentary elections, ruled that a person need not have a bachelor's degree to become a parliamentarian, paving the way for Zardari to contest the forthcoming by-election slated in June 2008.

Possible Consequences of The Disintegration of the Coalition

A disintegration of the coalition will have negative repercussions on Pakistan's politics and economy. There is widespread concern that the political parties are not able to hold the country together. This has led to uncertainty in terms of policies and disruption of government services and functions, particularly law and order, and security. Related to this is the fear that continuing political instability could fuel popular disenchantment and lead to a resurgence of civil unrest. Pakistanis have already been provoked into taking to the streets and it will not take much to push the country into renewed civil strife.

More significantly, the split in the coalition could change the political fortunes of Musharraf whose power has been largely curtailed since the February polls. If the PML(N) decides to sit in the opposition, then there is a chance that Musharraf's party, the PML(Q), could join the coalition despite the PPP's denials of this possibility. Even if the coalition does not dissolve, weakening it will have the inevitable consequence of strengthening Musharraf. Cynics—and even the not so cynical—will argue that this scenario would be perfectly acceptable to the United States. There is speculation in some quarters that the United States' pressure on Zardari is responsible for the PPP's delaying tactics, as the United States is keen to have Musharraf in place for continuity of its policies on the war on terror.

Invariably, the decision of the PML(N) to quit the federal cabinet has cast a shadow on the investment climate and has shaken the already low investor confidence in the national economy. The formation of a democratic government had raised the hopes of the business community which yearned for political stability for economic growth and recovery. But the recent events have shattered these hopes, and Pakistan will suffer the consequences not just of the loss of investor confidence but a deeper malaise in business confidence and economic fundamentals.

Conclusion

It will be a real pity if the gains as a result of the 18 February 2008 elections are frittered away. The PPP and the PML(N) owe it to the people of Pakistan to get beyond their political differences and personal interests and act in the genuine interest of the nation to restore democracy in a country beleaguered for too long by military rule and dictators. The restoration of the judiciary is critical because it reflects the people's will and because it is a bulwark institution in a democracy.

In addition, this is the first time, or at least the first in a long time, that Pakistan has a judiciary that is willing to stand up to the military and defend democracy. The judiciary's previous history in civil–military conflicts has not been exemplary and if the political parties are genuine about restoring democracy, they must restore the judiciary. If the political elite fail to resolve their differences, Pakistan will be condemned to repeat its familiar past of political mismanagement, giving the army yet another opportunity to stage a comeback. The least that the people of Pakistan deserve is for the political parties to put their act together and save their country. Otherwise, one may well be forced to ask if Pakistan is really ready for democracy or perhaps, more pertinently, whether its political leaders are ready for it.

12

The Walkout in India: No Longer 'Left' in the Lurch

BIBEK DEBROY

(9 July 2008)

WITH THE LEFT [the Communist Party of India-Marxist (CPI-M), the Communist Party of India, the Forward Bloc and Revolutionary Socialist Party] planning to meet President Pratibha Devisingh Patil on 9 July 2008 and submit a letter withdrawing support from the United Progressive Alliance (UPA) government, the overall numbers game seems simple. There are two vacancies and the Lok Sabha now has 543 members. A simple majority requires 272 members. The UPA (the Congress, Rashtriya Janata Dal, Dravida Munnetra Kazhagam, the Nationalist Congress Party, Pattali Makkal Katchi, Jharkhand Mukti Morcha, Lok Janshakti Party, Kerala Congress, the Muslim League, Republican Party of India, All India Majlis-e-Ittehadul Muslimeen, Peoples Democratic Party, Sikkim Democratic Front and three Independents) has 231 seats (the Congress has 153 seats).

With the Left's 59 members of parliament having quit, the UPA has lost its majority. However, to all intents and purposes, the Samajwadi Party (SP) has provided support to the UPA through its 39 members, leaving UPA with only two members short of a majority. But it isn't that simple. There is dissidence within the SP too, and at least seven (if not 10) of its members of parliament may not end up supporting the government. Indeed, there are question marks about support from some of the UPA constituents too. Though these are political parties with single-digit members of parliament (one or two), even one member of parliament matters. Therefore, the Congress cannot be sure about the numbers yet and will try to get support from other political parties like Rashtriya Lok Dal (Ajit Singh), Janata Dal Secular (Deve Gowda), Telangana Rashtra Samithi, Trinamool Congress, National Conference, Shiromani Akali Dal and Independents.

Horse-trading is best conducted in private, not in public. The first question, therefore, is, will the president ask the government to face a trust vote in parliament? A petulant Left has asked for this. However, it is unlikely to relish the prospect of being seen voting with the Bharatiya Janata Party (BJP). Nor would the SP like to see some of its members of parliament defy a whip. The president, who is understandably kindly disposed towards the Congress and would hate to confront a hard decision, has a soft option. The Constitution does not clearly require a test on the floor of the house, particularly for a functioning government, and a precedence of going by letters of support was set by the then president in 1998.

In all probability, nothing is going to happen within the parliament. Outside the parliament, the SP's turnaround almost certainly ends the Third Front or the United National Progressive Alliance as a pre-poll alliance and perhaps increases the probability of a pre-poll alliance between the BJP and All India Anna Dravida Munnetra Kazhagam, Telugu Desam Party, Jharkhand Vikas Morcha, Indian National Lok Dal, Asom Gana Parishad and even Marumalarchi Dravida Munnetra Kazhagam. The Bahujan Samaj Party should also feel threatened because the Congress–SP tie-up is not only for Delhi, but also for states like Maharashtra and Uttar Pradesh. However, all such alliances are likely to be post-poll alliances.

It is certain that the general elections will be postponed. In any event, early elections had been ruled out after inflation increased, and the Karnataka elections did not go the way the Congress had expected them to. An earlier argument doing the rounds that anti-incumbency against the BJP in Madhya Pradesh and Rajasthan would work in favour of the Congress if the general elections coincided with state-level elections, no longer seems to be doing the rounds. While one can quibble about the indicator used to measure inflation, it is reasonably certain that inflation should ease off after December 2008. Hence, the government is likely to last its full term, with a vote on account (rather than a full-fledged budget) in February 2009. Other than the inflation issue, there is not much support within the UPA, and even within the Congress, for triggering off a general election on the nuclear deal, which not too many people understand. In any event, something that is seen to side with the Americans does not normally win votes in India.

The impasse over the nuclear deal fundamentally boiled down to a clash of egos between two individuals—Prime Minister Manmohan Singh and the leader of the Left, Prakash Karat. One of the perennial mysteries is the prime minister's decision to grant an interview to *The Telegraph* newspaper in August 2007, read primarily in the east, calling the Left's bluff and triggering off the crisis.

Having failed to achieve much on economic reforms (the Right to Information Act has been diluted, the step towards value-added tax is a legacy of the National Democratic Alliance, as is the road construction programme), Prime Minister Singh seems to be driven by the motive that his legacy for posterity will be what he leaves in the area of external relations, including the nuclear deal. There is an interesting titbit of information resulting from an application under the Right to Information Act, filed in Mumbai. In the last 10 years, Rs 3.71 billion has been spent by Indian prime ministers on travelling abroad. Of this, almost one-third (Rs 1.2 billion) was spent by the present prime minister in 2005 and 2006. The simple point is that there is not much empathy within the Congress (this includes Mrs Sonia Gandhi) for Dr Singh's obsession with the nuclear deal and within the CPI(M) for Karat's rigidity. In the latter case, to take one example, the West Bengal government is concerned that several projects [airport modernisation, East-West metro in Kolkata, the Special Economic Zone (SEZ) at Nayachar in Haldia] might get held up because a friendly government no longer exists in Delhi.

Not all existing members of parliament get nominations for re-election. For those who get such nominations, the success rate is around 50 per cent. Why would one, therefore, want to lose the privileges for anything up to 10 months? The argument is much stronger if one is a minister. Logically, Somnath Chatterjee can no longer continue as a speaker. However, less clear is the fallout for Karat and Dr Singh within their respective political parties. Nonetheless, the latter has Mrs Gandhi's trust, a position that not many within the Congress enjoy.

Under the assumption that the Congress heads a government that comes back to power in 2009, since it would be too early for Rahul Gandhi to become prime minister, Dr Singh's return as prime minister is quite possible. By present calculations, the outcome of the 2009 elections is anyone's guess, barring the demise of the Third Front. The BJP faces a leadership and infighting crisis, but has been rejuvenated by the state election results. The Congress will suffer from anti-incumbency (inflation is only one part of this) and the delimitation exercise, which has made many more constituencies urban, perceived to be a gain for the BJP and a relative loss for the Congress.

The nuclear deal is still uncertain. India has to first get nuclear proliferation safeguards approved by the International Atomic Energy Agency and then obtain a waiver from the Nuclear Suppliers Group. It is only after this that it can be presented to the United States Congress, which already has a packed legislative agenda for 2008. And in the likely event of a Democrat presidency, the United States' support may also be lacking. The Left has been perceived as an element that blocked economic reforms—telecommunications; insurance; civil aviation; agriculture; foreign direct investments in retail; pensions; intellectual property rights; privatisation; and SEZs. One might tend to think that, with the Left out of the way, reforms will now proceed. The hypothesis about the Left alone being responsible for blocking reforms is incorrect. There is not much support for reforms even within the Congress, not to speak of its new-found allies, who could have easily become allies in 2004, avoiding the present mess. Certainly, in the run-up to general elections, one should not expect reforms. The pound of flesh that these allies want is not clear yet. The Reserve Bank of India governorship and lucrative ministerial berths like finance, defence and petroleum have been mentioned as a possible price, but there could be more. Nothing comes free.

13

Musharraf's Resignation: A Cause for Celebration and Concern for Pakistan

RAJSHREE JETLY

(*25 August 2008*)

ON 18 AUGUST 2008, President Pervez Musharraf bowed to the inevitable and resigned from his post, two months short of the 10th anniversary of his coup d'état when he ousted Prime Minister Nawaz Sharif. In his resignation speech, Musharraf insisted that he was not guilty of any of the charges being made against him and that he was acting in the best interest of Pakistan by stepping down to avoid a protracted power struggle and political uncertainty. Despite his protestations, the writing was on the wall following the 18 February elections when the people spoke loudly and clearly through the ballot box, shifting the power base away from Musharraf to the civilian parties led by Sharif and Asif Ali Zardari. The nail in the coffin was provided by Musharraf's two indispensable backers—Pakistan's military and the United States, both of which were clearly reassessing whether continued support of Musharraf might prove to be an unacceptable liability. Without their full support, Musharraf had no choice but to step down. Already, the provincial assemblies in Punjab, Sindh, the North-West Frontier Province and Baluchistan had tabled motions with overwhelming support demanding Musharraf seek a vote of confidence, and it was obvious that he would have failed.

One might wonder why Musharraf's two institutional backers may have had a change of heart. Arguably, the military, under General Kayani, was genuinely trying to extricate itself from the political mess and give civilian rule a chance. Equally importantly, it was not going to risk having a former chief of army staff being impeached, as this would tarnish the military's reputation of which it was fiercely protective. The United States, guided by its own security interests in the region, was also beginning to accept that not only was Musharraf fast becoming the wrong horse to bet but that other alternatives were viable. It is rumoured that Prime Minister Yousaf Raza Gilani's visit to Washington last month was to convince President George W Bush to stop supporting Musharraf. It would be reasonable to speculate that Prime Minister Gilani would have reassured Washington that its primary interests in Pakistan would not be compromised, and that the new democratic government would continue to support the United States' fight against Al Qaeda and Taliban militants.

The one theoretical, but wholly unrealistic, option left would be for Musharraf to exercise his power under Article 58(2)(b) of the Constitution to dissolve the assemblies and impose presidential rule. Musharraf, in fact, referred to this possibility in his resignation speech but dismissed it. Clearly, any such attempt would have failed as he would not have the political support of his party or allies and he would not have had the necessary logistical support of the military.

On the face of it, Musharraf's resignation was the best news for Pakistan. By all accounts, the resignation was widely celebrated as a victory for democracy and vindication of the recent popular uprisings and civil society struggles. To that extent, Musharraf's removal was significant because it removed the final obstacle to the return of democratic, civilian rule. As we saw, even though the 1998 elections delivered an overwhelming mandate to the political parties and were seen as a vote against Musharraf, he continued to remain president. His continuation in office became an impediment in the smooth functioning of the government and rankled political parties who wanted to pursue democratic reform. The fact that President Musharraf, even at his weakest, could, in theory, use Article 58(2)(b) to dismiss the elected assemblies and re-establish his position was akin to the sword of Damocles hanging over Pakistani democracy.

There is, however, another side to the story. The focus on

Musharraf has diverted attention from the more acute problems of soaring inflation and spiralling food and oil prices, as well as the sliding foreign exchange reserves and drop in foreign investment. In addition, terrorism remains the biggest threat to Pakistan's stability and a concerted effort is vital to tackling this problem. The last thing that Pakistan wants at this stage is political uncertainty and lack of direction in the fight against terrorism. The Indian national security adviser, M.K. Narayanan, has drawn attention to this danger, saying, 'We abhor the political vacuum that exists in Pakistan. It greatly concerns us.'

Clearly, Musharraf's resignation is cause for both celebration and concern. The key question is what implications this will have on the political stability and security of the nation. This turns on three dynamics: the relationship between the domestic political parties, principally the Pakistan People's Party (PPP) and the Pakistan Muslim League-Nawaz [PML(N)]; the relationship between the military and civilian rule; and the relationship between the United States and the civil/military leadership in Pakistan. There is no running away from the fact that there is a huge shadow of uncertainty over the future of Pakistan in terms of the presidency, the political parties and the military.

In terms of the domestic political parties, both the PPP and the PML(N) did come together to form the government, but they are political rivals with their own agendas. The glue holding the two parties together has been the common goal of ousting Musharraf. Now that he has stepped down, there is a real danger that innate differences and, more significantly, the intractable divergence on the critical issue of the restoration of the judiciary could tear the coalition apart. The PML(N) has insisted that all the judges, including former chief justice, Iftikhar Chaudhry, who had been dismissed by Musharraf during the Emergency, should be reinstated through a simple majority resolution passed by the parliament. The PPP, on the other hand, wants to link the restoration of the judiciary to broader constitutional reform, including changes in the terms and powers of judges. The speculation is that the leader of the PPP, Asif Ali Zardari, does not want the return of some of the judges, especially the former chief justice, for fear that old corruption cases against him shall be reopened. The PML(N) is holding steadfast to the need for restoration of the judges, failing which it would pull out of the coalition, throwing Pakistani politics into further chaos.

The military has been undoubtedly the centre of power in Pakistan; sometimes ruling directly through coups, but always lurking in the background as king-maker or power broker. It is likely to continue playing that role in the foreseeable future also. But for now, the military has chosen to adopt a low profile and has allowed the civilian political process to continue. This is a win-win situation for the military; a successful democratic transition will help repair the military's image as a supporter of democratisation, but if the political parties continue to put self-interest over national interest and implode the coalition, it will create a perfect excuse for the military to move in once again on the pretext of rescuing a dysfunctional state. The military, in any case, has its plate full with increased militant activities along the border areas, including a recent direct attack against a key military installation, resulting in almost 80 deaths and over 100 injured. How this civil–military relationship plays out over the coming period will be crucial to Pakistan's return to full democracy.

Finally, the role of the United States and its relationship with the civil and military leadership is an important factor. The United States' number one foreign policy concern with respect to Pakistan is the war on terrorism. Musharraf had been a favoured leader, as he had been accommodative of United States' interests. As a military dictator, Musharraf was not constrained in adopting policies that may not have been popular domestically. This is not a luxury that the political parties have, and it is not clear to what extent the PPP and the PML(N) have a consensus on the strategies to be adopted in the struggle against militancy and terrorism. If the parties have divergent policies on this, then whichever party is more United States-friendly will secure the United States' support. The issue will then inevitably become politicised, thereby undermining a concerted national effort. For example, Sharif has already indicated to the United States that Pakistan would adopt strategies that were apposite to Pakistan's interest, which would include greater negotiation and mediation with militant groups. The United States is not comfortable with too much emphasis placed on negotiation, for fear that this could allow the militants to regroup and strengthen themselves. Whether this means that the United States may, if it deems necessary, support the military instead of the democratic parties is something that cannot be ruled out.

Finally, while all this political uncertainty hangs over Pakistan, the immediate question of who is going to be president is an equally important one. The Election Commission has announced 6 September 2008 as the date for presidential elections. Several names have surfaced as potential contenders, including Zardari. It will be very interesting indeed if Zardari does snare the top post.

14

Elections in Pakistan: New President, Same Old Story

RAJSHREE JETLY

(*11 September 2008*)

UNTIL EIGHT months ago, no one would have predicted that Asif Ali Zardari would become a pivotal figure in Pakistani politics, much less the president of Pakistan. Better known as the controversial spouse of former prime minister, Benazir Bhutto, Zardari's name was tainted with allegations of corruption and linked to extortion and murder. He spent eleven years in jail though none of the charges were proven in court before being bailed out by then-President Pervez Musharraf through the National Reconciliation Ordinance. But he has overcome all odds to be elected Pakistan's president.

Zardari's election victory was impressive, winning 481 out of 702 Electoral College votes. The other two candidates were Pakistan Muslim League-Nawaz's [PML(N)] Saeeduzzaman Siddiqui, who secured 153 votes and Pakistan Muslim League-Quaid-e-Azam's [PML(Q)] Senator Mushahid Hussain Sayed who garnered 44 votes. A breakdown of the total electoral votes shows that Zardari won convincingly at both the national and provincial levels. He secured 281 out of 436 votes at the national level in both houses of the parliament (of which 10 were declared invalid). In comparison, Siddiqui and Senator Hussain managed only 111 and 34 votes respectively.

The Pakistan People's Party's (PPP) strength was further reinforced at the provincial assemblies where its nominee, Zardari, swept all votes in the Sindh assembly, and scored convincing victories in Baluchistan and the North-Western Frontier Province

(NWFP) over his two rivals. Only in Punjab, did he come in second (22 electoral votes) as compared with 35 votes won by Siddiqui. The PPP had clearly overtaken PML(N) in securing allies in the run-up to the presidential polls. With the support of such parties the Awami National Party, the Muttahida Qaumi Movement, and Jamiat Ulema-e-Islam, the PPP knows that it can survive at the centre and provincial assemblies even after the exit of PML(N) from the government. Since the presidential nominees were fielded along party lines, the results can be seen as a reflection of the present strength of these three parties in Pakistan. The PPP is now in a commanding position, with its members occupying the key positions of president, prime minister, speaker and deputy speaker, as well as being in government in all four of Pakistan's provinces.

From one view, the presidential election results may be seen as the culmination of an anti-Musharraf wave, leading to the full restoration of democracy with a civilian government and a civilian head of state. However, according to a Gallup poll of 2,000 people, almost half were not in favour of any of the three candidates and only 26 per cent approved of Zardari.

A more cynical view is that Zardari's ascension to the presidency is a stab in the back for the democratic movement in Pakistan, which was based largely on the demand for the restoration of the judiciary and the curtailment of presidential powers enshrined in Article 58(2)(b). In fact, it was Zardari's failure to live up to expectation on these two issues that led Nawaz Sharif to pull out of the coalition. Article 58(2)(b) allows the president to dissolve the National Assembly and sack the elected prime minister, and both the PPP and the PML(N) had agreed in the 2006 Charter of Democracy to repeal these anti-democratic presidential powers. Zardari has said that he would redress the balance of power between the presidency and the parliament, and this is something that he would need to act on urgently. His record, however, is not that encouraging, given that he has prevaricated on the issue of the full restoration of the judiciary, choosing instead to reinstate a few judges.

Pakistan's new president may have been elected by a comfortable margin, but he has tremendous challenges ahead of him. One of the major problems that Zardari will have to deal with, first and foremost, is the rising militancy in Pakistan. Suicide attacks are increasing, and even on the day of the election, a suicide bomber blew up a police post in the NWFP, killing 31 people.

Second, Pakistan's economy is in dire straits, with unemployment and under-employment rising, inflation soaring at 25 per cent and foreign investment, which had been steadily increasing since 2001, showing almost no increase in the last year. The Pakistani rupee has depreciated by 20 per cent this year and the Karachi Stock Exchange has lost a third of its value over the same period.

Apart from the economic crisis, Zardari has to keep a watchful eye on Sharif, who despite having declared that he would not attempt to bring down the government, is already working quietly behind the scenes to revive the alliance between his party and the PML(Q) and to consolidate his support base. Zardari has to decide whether to continue trying to work with Sharif or whether to take him on. Recently, rumours surfaced that the PPP was targeting Sharif and the PML(N) when it was reported that the National Accountability Bureau, which operates under the ministry of law, was reopening corruption cases against Sharif and members of his family. The PPP leadership has been quick to quash these rumours, stating that it does not believe in political victimisation. The PML(N) remains very strong in Punjab, which is the largest province in terms of population and the PPP has to be politically sensitive to this in its electoral calculations.

However, to be at all effective, Zardari's first priority must be to establish his credibility. This will require the repeal of Article 58(2)(b), the restoration of the judiciary, giving up the co-chairmanship of the PPP to respect the non-partisan nature of the presidential post, and quelling the rising militancy. Failure to do any of these will lead to further destabilisation of democratic politics in Pakistan and could result either in another popular uprising and potential civil unrest or pave the way for the return of the military. So far, the military, under General Kayani, has remained passive and has allowed the civilian parties to continue their struggles. However, Pakistan's history has shown that the military will not hesitate to act if it deems necessary.

The trouble is that carrying out each of the above tasks could have a detrimental consequence on Zardari. Repealing Article 58(2)(b) would mean stripping himself of considerable power as president. Fully restoring the judiciary risks the danger of the NRO being opened up for scrutiny. Quelling militancy requires firm action against a segment of his own people and working closely with the United States, which could lead to speculations of Zardari being too close to the United States. Pakistan's military is unlikely to tolerate a president who gives any appearance of condoning foreign military offensives within Pakistan's borders, as happened just three days before the presidential election when United States forces launched an attack against an Al Qaeda target in South Waziristan. Zardari is, thus, between the proverbial rock and the hard place, as he has to balance various competing interests, including his own domestic political constituency, the provincial interests, the military and the United States.

Pakistan may have a new president but its underlying problems remain. It will be interesting to see if and how Zardari will inject a fresh approach in addressing these problems and propelling Pakistan towards full democracy and economic recovery.

15

Return of the Two *Begums*: A 'Hobson's Choice' for Bangladesh?

M. SHAHIDUL ISLAM

(17 September 2008)

AFTER AN 18-MONTH roller coaster ride, Sheikh Hasina and Khaleda Zia, the two former prime ministers and heads of the two major political parties in Bangladesh, the Bangladesh Awami League (BAL) and the Bangladesh Nationalist Party (BNP) respectively, have returned to the country's political scene. The caretaker government that took over on 11 January 2007, with a strong military backing and an overwhelming support from the masses, has finally given up its 'minus-two formula' and other political reform packages, realising the ineluctable reality that it is ultimately these two *begums* who hold the key to lead (or mislead) the nation.

The comeback of these two matriarchs is no less dramatic than the return of the king in the famous movie *The Lord of the Rings*. This popular movie shows how even the least of us can change the world through courage, commitment and determination. But the reality for the common people in Bangladesh is far from fiction. For the country's 150 million people, it is rather a 'Hobson's choice'.[1]

The interim government is apparently looking for a safe exit strategy, leaving the country in the hand in either of the two *begums*. Apprehensions over the parliament pools and a potential army takeover are fast fading, and it is highly likely that a new democratically-elected government will be at the helm of affairs in the country by early 2009, if not earlier.

A Tale of Three Regimes: Have all of them Failed?

The fundamental question is whether the return of the so-called 'illiberal democracies',[2] led by Sheikh Hasina and Khaleda Zia, will be able to solve the country's prolonged political malaise? If not, then what are the alternative forms of governance available for the country? Did either the cantonment or the caretaker governments deliver any better results than the illiberal democracies? To comprehend these questions, it is worth looking at the brief history of the different forms of regimes that the nation has witnessed to date.

Since its inception in 1971, Bangladesh has been ruled mainly by military and democratically-elected governments. But neither the military nor the illiberal democracies have been able to fulfil the Bangladeshi people's expectations. A few caretaker governments, *inter alia*, have also governed the nation, albeit their tenure, excepting the current caretaker government, has been short due to constitutional obligations.[3]

The poor performance of the military rulers and less than impressive developments during the Khaleda Zia and Sheikh Hasina's regimes led the Bangladeshi people to believe that they would perhaps be better off under a non-partisan plain-clothed government. After all, the three successive apolitical caretaker governments in 1991, 1996 and 2001 with their 90-day tenure, had captured the Bangladeshi people's hearts and minds. But the fourth caretaker government (2006–7) lost its credibility and collapsed eventually, as it was highly politicised by the then-BNP government.

When the new, army-backed non-partisan caretaker government took over in January 2007, it received widespread support, both at home and abroad. This is because the three successive governments since the fall of the military government in 1990 had failed to deliver any roadmap to the nation. The political leaders' involvement in widespread corruption and politicisation of almost all the institutions had caused much frustration among masses. Moreover, the two major political parties' bitter rivalries had kept the country in permanent turmoil.

As a result, the current interim government's reform agenda received overwhelming support from the people. There was also no hue and cry when it decided to extend its tenure beyond 90 days. It has been 18 months since the apolitical caretaker government took over the country. However, it has achieved mixed results. It implemented some important institutional reforms that were not possible under the so-called democratic governments, due to political considerations. But it suffered on the economic front. In a sense, this was rather unfortunate as the caretaker government's assumption of power coincided with mounting fears of a food price spiral in global markets and high energy prices. Another important reason for its economic failure was its inability to gain the confidence of businesses and investors, and this can be traced to the uncertainty over its tenure. Further, the interim government, which consists of 10 advisers, has been overseeing 42 ministries. This is humanly impossible, given the magnitude of the challenges facing the country.

On the whole, the 18-month long tenure of the current interim government has not totally proven that a non-partisan plain-clothed government can do a better job for the country, as compared to the other forms of governments in Bangladesh.

Sheikh Hasina and Khaleda Zia: A 'Hobson's Choice'?

The sad truth for Bangladesh is that, regardless of how bad the leadership of the BAL and the BNP may be, it is highly likely that the two parties will continue to remain on Bangladesh's political scene in the near future. If the long due parliament elections are held by the end of this year, it is expected that either the BAL or the BNP will return to power. This means that one of the two *begums* could come back to power soon. What does it mean for the Bangladesh people? For them, it is really a Hobson's choice—they either accept an illiberal democracy (led by Khaleda Zia or Sheikh Hasina) or have nothing at all.

The acute dilemma for the masses is that there is no 'third power' in Bangladesh politics that they could support and vote into power. There have been several attempts to initiate a third front in Bangladesh politics to break the political monopoly of the BNP and the BAL. There has also been an attempt to reform the major political parties. However, nothing has worked for the interim authority.

Routine fair and free elections have failed to institutionalise democracy in Bangladesh. The business people who dominate in Bangladesh politics are mainly responsible for the malfunctioning of the parliament. After being elected into power, they use the mandate given to them by the people for their own personal gains rather than to look after the needs of the people. The country's major institutions have also been routinely politicised. The 'winners take all' policy often creates conflicts of interest between the BNP and the BAL. All these issues have been responsible for the current sad state of affairs in Bangladesh, a country which held so much promise for its people but which has failed to deliver on all fronts—social, political and economic.

Two Silver Linings

The key question now is whether the BAL and BNP will learn some lessons from history. If the past is any guide, there is very little hope, really.

However, there are two silver linings. First, the current interim government's sweep against political corruption may help the Bangladeshi people judge the candidates during elections according to their corruption records[4] *inter alia* and this may keep the politicians in some sort of check. The second silver lining is the presence of a strong anti-incumbency factor that exists in Bangladesh's politics. Indeed, it was this main consideration that prompted the then-BNP government to politicise the fourth caretaker administration. As the gap between performance and promises remains wide, people normally oust the immediate past government in parliamentary elections. As such, one can hope that the major political parties will learn from their past mistakes and help to refine the country's political system.

In the best interests of Bangladesh's 150 million people, the speed of change needs to be much faster than the current pace, if change is going to take place at all, and it needs to happen in the short run. After all, as famously observed by great economist John Maynard Keynes, 'we are all dead in the long run'.

NOTES

1. The phrase is believed to have originated from Thomas Hobson (1544–1630), a livery stable owner in Cambridge, England, who, in order to rotate the use of his horses, offered customers the choice of either taking the horse in the stall nearest to the door or taking none at all.
2. The term is owed to Fareed Zakaria, a noted political and foreign policy analyst. For details, see 'The Rise of Illiberal Democracy', *Foreign Affairs*, November/December 1997.
3. In the parlance of institutional government, a caretaker government is one which normally takes care of the state administration for an interim period until a regular new government is formed (Banglapedia, available at www.banglapedia.net/). Article 58B [under chapter IIA] of the Bangladesh Constitution legitimises the caretaker government. The tenure of a caretaker government is generally three months. The current army-backed interim government which took over in January 2007 has extended its tenure to beyond the length set by the Bangladesh Constitution and there are some controversies about the nature of the government.
4. The Anti-Corruption Commission of Bangladesh has disclosed the corruption records of the top political leaders of BNP and BAL, among others.

16

Maldives: Towards Open Polity

S.D. MUNI

(*31 October 2008*)

DEMOCRACY IS definitely on the move in South Asia. After Bhutan, Nepal and Pakistan, it has turned corner in Maldives, a republic of 1,192 islands in the splendid Indian Ocean. Asia's longest ruling autocrat, Maumoon Abdul Gayoom, lost his presidency in the elections held in October 2008 to Mohamed Nasheed 'Anni', who suffered six years of prison for waging a democratic struggle against the Gayoom regime. Mohamed Nasheed 'Anni' had been declared a 'Prisoner of Conscience' by Amnesty International, a human rights organisation.

The spark of democracy was lit in Maldives in 2003 when protests against the death-in-custody of a young man, detained under charges of drug abuse, snowballed into demands for greater political freedom and democracy. This emerged as the first major challenge to President Gayoom since his assumption of power in 1978. In between, there have been a couple of coup attempts, including a serious and determined one in 1988, which was put down with military help from India. Street protests and international pressures forced President Gayoom to introduce political reforms under which political parties were allowed in 2004, and a new Constitution was adopted in 2007, providing for an open election for the presidency. The 2005 elections of the *Majlis* (Maldivian national parliament) took place on party basis for the first time. Until then, President Gayoom had been elected six times, each time for a five-year term, on a simple 'yes' or 'no' vote without anyone contesting his candidacy.

The October 2008 elections were held under the newly-introduced political reforms. A seven-point criterion was introduced for a prospective presidential candidate. This included having Maldivian parentage (both mother and father), being at least 35 years of age, not being a foreign national, not being a Sunni Muslim, etc. The first round of elections held on 8 October 2008 was contested by six candidates belonging to five parties, with one independent candidate. There are 10 parties registered with the Maldives Election Commission, but some of the smaller ones formed coalitions to put up strong candidates. President Gayoom of Dhivehi Raiyyithunge Party and Mohamed Nasheed 'Anni' of Maldives Democratic Party (MDP) emerged as the principal contenders after the first round of the polls, obtaining 40.63 per cent and 25.09 per cent of the votes respectively. Since a winning candidate had to cross the 50 per cent vote limit, they had to have a second round. The votes secured by the remaining candidates in the first round were as follows: Hasan Saeed (Independent)—16.54 per cent; Gasim Ibrahim (Republican Party)—15.4 per cent; Umer Naseer (Islamic Democratic Party)—1.44 per cent; and Ibrahim Ismail (Social Liberal Party)—0.18 per cent. The first round was conducted peacefully but it was marred by a number of irregularities. Some of the voters' lists reached wrong polling booths located in various atolls, causing confusion, and the identity cards of a number of voters could not be distributed to them in time, causing difficulties in their casting of ballots. Finally, all those who were in the queue at polling booths were allowed to vote.

These difficulties were taken care of during the second and decisive round of polling which was held on 28 October 2008. Earlier, the run-off poll date was fixed for 29 October 2008, but due to school examinations, it had to be pre-poned, as the schools were converted into polling booths. Voters who could not find their names in the voters' list for the first round were also accommodated for the second round by the Election Commission. Of the 209,000 eligible voters, more than 86 per cent, that is, 179,343 voters cast their ballots in the second round. Polling was also organised for voters staying outside Maldives. President Gayoom was confident that it would be easy for him to take his tally to 50 per cent from 40 per cent, by exploiting divisions among the political parties. This, however, did not happen, as all the opposition parties decided to unite behind Mohamed Nasheed 'Anni' as the opposition candidate to defeat President Gayoom, giving him a comfortable lead of 54.21 per cent. President Gayoom could muster only 45.79 per cent, barely 3 per cent more than his first round tally. He gracefully accepted defeat saying, 'I accept the results . . . and I respectfully congratulate Mr Mohamed Nasheed and his party . . . I am declaring my full support to him. . . . In this change we are approaching, I assure you, we will make this a peaceful process.' The new president is expected to take office on 11 November 2008, exactly 30 years after President Gayoom assumed power.

The core issue in the election was democracy—liberalising the political system. Most of the opposition leaders had worked with President Gayoom at one time or another and were eventually alienated as a result of the authoritarian style of functioning and the heavy reliance on nepotism, cronyism and corruption in the administration. Once they fell from favour of the president, they were treated harshly, even jailed and tortured. There was, therefore, a considerable degree of personal anger between Gayoom and his opponents, which made the campaign highly personalised. President Gayoom was portrayed as a dictator and equated with Robert Mugabe of Zimbabwe. He, in turn, labelled his opponents as inexperienced and personally motivated. In the last leg of his campaign, President Gayoom also accused Mohamed Nasheed 'Anni' of deviating from Islam and gravitating towards Christianity. President Gayoom claimed credit for improving Maldives' economy and making it a paradise of tourism in Asia. It was indeed under his regime that the per capita income of Maldives grew to nearly US $1,500, making it the richest South Asian country. President Gayoom also projected himself as the originator of democracy in Maldives, as it was he who started the political and constitutional reforms in the island republic.

President Gayoom's claims were strongly discounted by the opposition. They brought out numerous instances of torture and political repression under the Gayoom regime. In one of the interviews with Al Jazeera television network, President Gayoom was found fumbling in explaining the offences of the opposition leader Mohamed Nasheed 'Anni' that necessitated his long periods of detention. The opposition explained that the fruits of progress made by Maldives have been distributed unequally, benefiting a chosen few families around the president. There are also accusations of rampant corruption in the Gayoom administration and, despite the high per capita income, 21 per cent of the population live below the poverty line, with very poor facilities for health, education and employment for the ordinary people. With regard to corruption, the independent Attorney-General of Maldives, otherwise appointed by President Gayoom, released a damning report, highlighting instances of misappropriation of millions of dollars. The release of this report days before the run-off poll for the presidency exposed the credibility of President Gayoom's campaign. In the capital, Atoll of Male, more than 100,000 people are cramped in a small area of 2.5 sq. km. The opposition candidate Mohamed Nasheed 'Anni' promised to address the problems of poverty, health and housing. He assured the voters that he would develop tourism and fisheries sectors and harness vast marine resources to create job opportunities. He also laid emphasis on education and proclaimed that after winning the elections, he would convert the Presidential Palace into a university campus. On the whole, he promised a 'New Maldives' of political freedom and economic progress.

The new Maldivian president faces a number of challenges. The problem is not with his lack of experience because there are a number of people in the newly-energised political space of the island republic with experience in the administration. There is also a clear agenda of building transparent, efficient and liberal political institutions to deliver good governance to the people of Maldives.

The difficulties of the new president may arise on two political counts. President Gayoom has lost but he still has a substantial support of nearly 45 per cent in the island. President-elect Mohamed Nasheed 'Anni' has assured that he will steer clear of the politics of vendetta and revenge and even the outgoing President Gayoom has promised to cooperate with the new leader. However, there are inherent incompatibilities between the approaches of these two leaders in addressing the problems of Maldives. Mohamed Nasheed 'Anni's' challenge is to blunt these incompatibilities and forge creative cooperation to take advantage of the experience and understanding of the outgoing leadership without endorsing his regime's distortions.

Secondly, the other political parties and groups have lent support to the MDP leader just on the one-point agenda of ousting President Gayoom. There are otherwise ideological, political and personality-oriented differences among the opposition coalition. The tensions arising out of these differences would start impinging on the dynamics of creating a 'New Maldives' sooner than later. The Nepal example is there for anyone to draw lessons from. In particular, there are extremist streaks among the president-elect's support groups. It would be a challenge to keep Maldives on a liberal, moderate and progressive social track while drawing on the support of the diverse political groups.

Lastly, the global economic meltdown will adversely affect the Maldivian economy as well, particularly its tourism sector which contributes 28 per cent to its gross domestic product. The new leader and his administration have to ensure development and equitable distribution of the fruits of development to aspiring Maldivians. One hopes that the dedication of the president-elect and his team to their pronounced goals, and their youthful enthusiasm will help them meet these political and developmental challenges and the 'New Maldives' of their dreams will start taking shape soon.

17

State Assembly Election Results in India: Dispelling the Many Commonly-held Notions of Indian Elections

TRIDIVESH SINGH MAINI

(*12 December 2008*)

THE RECENT assembly elections, dubbed by many as the 'semi-finals' of the 2009 Lok Sabha polls, in five states—Chhattisgarh, Delhi, Madhya Pradesh, Mizoram and Rajasthan—sprung many surprises. The Congress won three states and the Bharatiya Janata Party (BJP) two. To many observers, the results came as a surprise, perhaps including for the Congress, considering that the elections in Rajasthan and Delhi were held in the aftermath of the Mumbai terrorist attack.

The state assembly election results challenged many commonly-held assumptions. Firstly, the re-election of BJP governments in Chhattisgarh and Madhya Pradesh and the Congress in New Delhi once again falsified the notion of anti-incumbency. For the BJP governments in Chhattisgarh and Madhya Pradesh, their victory takes them into a second term while for the Congress, its victory in Delhi ensures a third term. The chief ministers of all these states—Sheila Dikshit (Delhi), Raman Singh (Chhattisgarh) and Shivraj Singh Chauhan (Madhya Pradesh)—fought mainly on the plank of development. In fact, Dikshit had to contend with the burden of the Congress government's failure at the central level, which included the issues of inflation and terrorism. To make things worse for Sheila Dikshit, voting in Delhi took place three days after the rampage in Mumbai. Many expected this to dent Dikshit's otherwise bright chances, especially after the aggressive ad campaign by the BJP and Congress-bashing for being too soft on terror. Yet she managed to win convincingly.

Secondly, high polling in Madhya Pradesh, Chhattisgarh and Delhi did not go against the incumbents as had been expected. The three states had approximately 60 per cent polling, and in all these states, the sitting governments did well. It was only Rajasthan where high polling actually resulted in the incumbent government being voted out of power. Vandita Mishra, writing for *The Indian Express*, remarked, 'Anti-incumbency is not an iron law of nature. Incumbency can be a good thing and people will turn out in large numbers to vote for a party in government again if it is seen to have delivered.'

Thirdly, none of the so-called 'star campaigners' from Delhi or other states can really take the credit for their party's victory. Ultimately, the issue of development played a key role in the electoral outcomes of Delhi, Chhattisgarh, Madhya Pradesh and Rajasthan. Pankaj Vohra, a columnist for *The Hindustan Times*, aptly remarked, 'The results prove that wherever the chief ministers could project positive achievements and development activities of their governments, their parties won.'

Fourthly, while these assembly elections, in no way, indicate the fact that the Congress party's handling of security issues is *par excellence*, the three–two elections result definitely shows that people are equally disgruntled with the BJP and do not really feel that the latter has a magic wand to solve issues such as terrorism. Mishra stated that:

> Terror—or how safe we are—is certainly an issue, and given the attacks in Delhi, Jaipur and then Mumbai, the Congress-led United Progressive Alliance (UPA) was on the defensive. But the BJP's formulation of the issue failed to strike a credible chord. Its campaign that the UPA was 'soft on terror' didn't translate into 'we know how to keep you safe'. Its 'blood-stain' ad asking for votes even as the siege was on in Mumbai put off many voters.

In fact, interestingly according to Vohra, many believe that in spite of it being soft on terror, Congress is still looked at as being a more nationalistic party. According to him, 'For the common man, the Congress had won the 1965 and 1971 wars against Pakistan and its governance generates a greater sense of assurance than the jingoistic stance of the BJP.' Apart from this, terrorism in many ways is looked at as a war on the nation and the people generally back the government of the day. A *Times of India* editorial stated that:

> Significantly, Rajasthan and Delhi voted after the Mumbai carnage and both opted for the Congress. In these states, the BJP ran an aggressive campaign on terrorism and even took out advertisements against the Congress style of governance. That strategy may have backfired. Sure, terrorism is a major concern but people seem to have refused to read party politics into it. They recognise terrorism, especially the kind witnessed in Mumbai, as a war waged on the nation.

If one were to look at the lessons for the BJP and the Congress, rather than bringing cheer to either camp, the elections brought to the fore the lack of leadership at the national level, more so in the case of the BJP. The Congress too faces the same problem to a degree. These elections, to some degree, obliterated that problem because, in spite of facing incumbency of 10 years in Delhi, the terrorist attacks and the rise of the Bahujan Samaj Party, the Congress managed to triumph. Similarly, in Rajasthan, in spite of not having a leader to take on Vasundhara Raje Scindia, the Congress managed to win. The BJP, with L.K. Advani as its prime ministerial candidate, on the other hand, tried hard to play up the issue of terrorism and inflation and projected Gujarat's chief minister, Narendra Modi, as its 'star campaigner'. Modi, thought to be prime minister material, failed in the national capital, which provides a good measure of the nation's mood. In politics, a week is a long time and anything can happen. The state elections proved just that—the BJP needs a re-think on not only its handling of sensitive issues such as terrorism but also the choice of 'star campaigners'.

As far as the Congress is concerned, Dikshit's re-election, losses in Madhya Pradesh and Chhattisgarh, and a not very convincing victory in Rajasthan should teach the party something about projecting a leader. While in Delhi, the party did more or less project Dikshit as the leader, it did not do so in Madhya Pradesh,

Chhattisgarh and Rajasthan. The BJP played up this issue, with Advani remarking during the election campaign that, 'Have you seen a cricket team saying it will decide the name of its captain after the match is over? The same is the case with the Congress.' It is time the party projected a leader for 2009 so that the country knows who is captaining the Congress.

It would be incorrect to dub the current assembly results as an indicator of what will happen in the general elections in 2009. In December 2003, the BJP emerged victorious in three assembly elections and yet lost the Lok Sabha polls. Only one thing can be said clearly though—in spite of failures on many fronts, the Congress has been able to win three states. This means that the BJP has more to worry about than the Congress has to celebrate. While the Congress is reticent to project a leader, the BJP miscalculates. The general election of 2009 will show us which will prove to be less harmful.

18

An Overview of the November–December 2008 Provincial Elections in India

PARANJOY GUHA THAKURTA

(17 December 2008)

Introduction

THE OUTCOME of the elections to the legislative assemblies of five Indian provinces or states, namely, Chhattisgarh, Delhi, Madhya Pradesh, Mizoram and Rajasthan, that became known on 8 December 2008, indicates that voters in the world's largest democracy are becoming increasingly mature. Even as votes are cast in favour of candidates and political parties that provide (and not merely promise) good governance, anti-incumbency sentiments remain pronounced in many parts of the country. In addition, India's voters—poor and uneducated though many of them may be—appear less likely to be influenced by emotive issues related to terrorism, religion, caste and community and seem to be more concerned with what could be considered substantive issues pertaining to economic and social development. The results of the recently-concluded assembly elections have made the country's two largest political parties, the Indian National Congress (INC) and the Bharatiya Janata Party (BJP), introspect about their future while drawing up strategies in the run-up to the forthcoming fifteenth general elections that, it now seems, will be conducted on schedule in April–May 2009.

The Backdrop

In December 2003, the right-wing, Hindu nationalist BJP, leading the National Democratic Alliance (NDA) coalition, which was then in power in New Delhi, was exuding confidence. That month, the party had, without the support of its allies, comfortably won the elections to the assemblies of Chhattisgarh, Madhya Pradesh (in central India) and Rajasthan (in the west). What was small consolation for the INC, then in the opposition, was that the country's centrist 'grand old party' managed to retain its hold over the government of the National Capital Territory of Delhi. At that time, a section within the BJP was rather keen on bringing forward the fourteenth general elections in India that could have been held as late as September–October 2004. This section argued that the party's 'India Shining' advertising campaign would persuade a substantial section of the electorate to return the BJP-led NDA coalition to power. It was even contended by some in the party that the BJP would have more members of parliament (MP) in the Lok Sabha (the Lower House of India's parliament) and would be less dependent on its coalition partners.

Elections were conducted ahead of schedule in April–May and on 13 May 2004, after the poll outcome was clear, leaders of the BJP were shocked to realise that their party had shrunk in size and that the NDA coalition would not be in a position to form India's federal government. A Centre–Left coalition led by the Congress, called the United Progressive Alliance (UPA), went on to form the government with crucial 'outside' support from a group of 60-odd MPs belonging to four Left parties led by the Communist Party of India (Marxist) [CPI(M)].

Four years down the line, the Congress went on to lose a series of state elections in different parts of the country. On 22 July 2008, the UPA won a vote of confidence in the Lok Sabha after parting ways with the Left—following a bitter dispute over the nuclear agreement between India and the United States—and after obtaining the support of the regional Samajwadi Party that currently has a notable presence in the country's most populous state, Uttar Pradesh.

Given past experience, most political observers are of the view that the November–December 2008 elections to five state legislative assemblies of Chhattisgarh, Delhi, Madhya Pradesh, Mizoram and Rajasthan should not be seen as a 'curtain raiser' or a 'semi-final' of sorts before the fifteenth general elections that are scheduled to take place in April–May 2009. (The results of the elections to the Jammu & Kashmir assembly would be known on 24 December 2008.) At the same time, the outcome of the five assembly elections was closely watched for possible pointers to the political mood that would prevail in the country before the general elections.

The 26–8 November 2008 terrorist attacks in Mumbai took place when the elections were on in particular states. The upsurge in belligerent nationalism that followed the terrorist attacks, especially among sections of the urban middle and upper classes (that had avidly viewed the live television coverage of the incidents in Mumbai) was expected to lead to more votes being cast in favour of the BJP that has accused the Congress of being 'soft' on terror. The high—in some cases, record—voter turnout in the national capital of Delhi and other states was interpreted to mean that sections of the electorate would exercise their franchise against incumbent governments. But that was not to be—not in Delhi, Chhattisgarh and Madhya Pradesh.

Anti-incumbency sentiments have strengthened across India in recent years. Roughly 40 per cent of the MPs and half the members of legislative assemblies (MLAs) have not been re-elected in national and state elections that have taken place over the last decade and a half. While some MPs and MLAs have been rejected by their parties as candidates, most have been voted out. Each of the last four Lok Sabhas constituted in 1996, 1998, 1999 and 2004 saw around 250 new faces in a Lower House comprising 543 members. States where anti-incumbency sentiments have not been evident in recent years have been few and far between and include West Bengal, Bihar, Gujarat and Madhya Pradesh.

The November–December 2008 assembly elections witnessed anti-incumbency sentiments prevailing in all the states that went to the polls barring one, that is, Chhattisgarh. These sentiments were, however, not strong enough to dislodge the ruling party in three out of the five states, Delhi, Madhya Pradesh and Chhattisgarh, while in Rajasthan and Mizoram, the incumbent regimes were replaced by the Congress. The number of MLAs belonging to the ruling parties came down in each of the five states with the notable exception of Chhattisgarh. One way anti-incumbency sentiments were countered was by refusing tickets to sitting MLAs considered less than capable or responsive to their constituents. In both Chhattisgarh and Madhya Pradesh, the BJP chief ministers, Raman Singh and Shivraj Singh Chauhan respectively, denied tickets to over a third of the legislators who had been elected in 2003—this strategy considerably helped the governments in these two states retain power. In the past a similar strategy has assisted the ruling Left Front led by the CPI(M) in West Bengal and the BJP government in Gujarat headed by Narendra Modi.

Delhi

The biggest surprise of the recently-concluded assembly elections was the victory of the incumbent Congress government in Delhi led by Sheila Dikshit. No chief minister of Delhi has served two full terms like Dikshit, leave alone three terms. Few within the Congress—not to mention the BJP—could have imagined that she would lead her party to a third straight victory and join the ranks of venerable chief ministers of the country with long terms—these include individuals such as Jyoti Basu (West Bengal), Gegong Apang (Arunachal Pradesh), Mohan Lal Sukhadia (Rajasthan), M.G. Ramachandran (Tamil Nadu) and Manik Sarkar (Tripura). Clearly, many voters in the national capital believed that her administrative capabilities would be superior to those of her political rival from the BJP, Vijay Kumar Malhotra, who had earned a reputation of being a 'giant killer' after he defeated (current prime minister) Manmohan Singh from the South Delhi Lok Sabha constituency in the 1999 general elections.

Dikshit's victory also reinforced the point that a tall leader can make voters repose faith in a political party that may not exactly be becoming more popular. Delhi's voters were also able to distinguish between local issues, regional issues and even larger national issues. If the BJP could have replicated its performance in the April 2007 elections to the Municipal Corporation of Delhi—when it won 168 out of 272 wards with the Congress winning in only 64 wards—the party should have won the 2008 assembly elections with a comfortable majority. But this did not happen, surprising many political observers. An important factor that helped Dikshit was divisions in the BJP; the party's general secretary Arun Jaitley was first selected as the BJP's chief ministerial candidate for Delhi but Malhotra was selected after Jaitley decided he was not interested.

In 1993, the BJP won 49 out of the 70 seats in the assembly while the Congress won 14 seats; in 1998, the Congress won 52 seats and the BJP 15, while in 2003, the Congress won 47 seats and the BJP 20. The number of Congress MLAs in the Delhi assembly has come down to 42; the party's vote share declined from 48.1 per cent in 2003 to 40.3 per cent in 2008. The number of seats won by the BJP went up by three to 23; the party's vote share rose from 35.2 per cent to 36.4 per cent. The Bahujan Samaj Party (BSP), led by Mayawati (currently chief minister of Uttar Pradesh), opened its account in the Delhi assembly with two seats, the party's vote share more than doubling from 5.8 per cent in 2003 to 14 per cent in 2008. The BSP played 'spoiler' to both the Congress and the BJP in over a dozen seats.

Chhattisgarh

In November 2000, when Chhattisgarh became a separate state, the Congress held 62 seats in the Vidhan Sabha or state assembly, the BJP had 22 MLAs while five seats were held by other parties. In December 2003, after assembly elections were held in the new state for the first time, the BJP swept the polls with 50 seats while the Congress obtained only 37 seats. The BJP was able to repeat this performance, thanks to Chief Minister Raman Singh's relatively non-controversial image. More importantly, what clinched the election for the incumbents was the state government's decision to provide poor families rice at Rs 3 per kg—the public distribution scheme was strengthened considerably and corruption reduced.

The number of BJP MLAs in the Chhattisgarh assembly remained constant between 2003 and 2008 at 50, with the party's share of the total votes cast going up marginally by 1 per cent, from 39.3 per cent to 40.3 per cent. The number of Congress MLAs in Chhattisgarh went up by one, from 37 in 2003 to 38 after the

2008 election although the party's vote share rose by nearly 2 per cent from 36.7 per cent to 38.6 per cent.

What hurt the Congress was factionalism—former Chief Minister Ajit Jogi did not see eye-to-eye with former leader of the opposition in the assembly Mahendra Karma on the issue of supporting the 'Salwa Judum' force in the southern part of the state dominated by Left-wing extremists (Maoists or Naxalites). Supporters of the 'Salwa Judum' grouping of 'special police officers' describe it as a spontaneous response of local villagers against violence by underground Maoists while its critics describe it as a government-sponsored vigilante group. Unlike Karma, a former Communist who spearheaded the formation of the group, Jogi concurs with the view of civil rights activists who claim that the 'Salwa Judum' represents a failure of the state administration to enforce law and order, and curb Left-wing extremism in the tribal-dominated Bastar division of the state. Eventually, the BJP ended up gaining by winning key assembly constituencies in the division.

Madhya Pradesh

The Congress won 174 seats and 172 seats in the undivided 320-member Madhya Pradesh assembly in 1993 and 1998 respectively, while the BJP won 117 seats and 119 seats in the elections held in these two years. In November 2000, the state was bifurcated. Chhattisgarh became a separate state and the number of members in the Madhya Pradesh assembly shrunk to 230. Digvijay Singh of the Congress had served as chief minister for two terms from December 1993 to December 2003. In the December 2003 elections, the BJP won as many as 173 seats in the 230-member assembly while the number of seats with Congress drastically shrunk to 38 seats.

After the December 2008 elections, the number of BJP MLAs in the Madhya Pradesh assembly fell from 173 to 143; the party's vote share came down from 42.5 per cent to 37.6 per cent or a fall of almost 5 per cent. The number of seats won by the Congress rose from 38 to 71, although the party's vote share increased by less than 1 per cent from 31.6 per cent to 32.4 per cent. The BSP increased its tally from two to seven, its share of the vote rising from 7.3 per cent to 9 per cent; the party had 11 MLAs in the undivided Madhya Pradesh assembly in 1993 and 1998.

The Ladli Lakshmi scheme to provide education grants to young women made Shivraj Singh Chauhan popular as chief minister in Madhya Pradesh. Similar schemes had been initiated in different states, including in Uttar Pradesh during the Mulayam Singh Yadav government. However, the difference was that the scheme was implemented efficiently in Madhya Pradesh. Chauhan took a leaf out of the book scripted in 2004 by Andhra Pradesh Chief Minister Y.S. Rajshekhar Reddy by making direct contact with people in rural areas. In the process, many voters chose to ignore a scandal involving purchases of road rollers and dumpers by a firm close to the chief minister's family.

Chauhan became chief minister of Madhya Pradesh three years ago in November 2005 after the BJP leadership made Babulal Gaur step down from the post. In August 2004, Gaur had replaced Uma Bharti after she was sworn in as chief minister of Madhya Pradesh after the December 2003 elections. Bharti later rebelled against her party's leadership and formed her own party, the Bharatiya Janshakti Party. It won five seats in the latest round of polling in 2008, though she herself lost the elections.

The BJP in Madhya Pradesh under Chauhan could not have performed as well as it did had it not been helped greatly by deep divisions in the Congress that had various factions led by former Chief Minister Digvijay Singh, Union Commerce Minister Kamal Nath, MP Jyotiraditya Scindia (son of prominent Congress leader, the late Madhavrao Scindia) and Ajay Singh, son of Union Human Resources Development Minister Arjun Singh (who was chief minister of the state between June 1980 and March 1985 and again between February 1988 and January 1989). As if these factions were not enough, Congress President Sonia Gandhi and her confidantes 'parachuted' Suresh Pachauri to Bhopal (capital of Madhya Pradesh) from New Delhi to head the party in the state. Pachauri, a former minister in the union government in New Delhi and member of the Rajya Sabha (the Upper House of India's parliament) for four six-year terms, could not rejuvenate the

Congress in the state and acknowledged responsibility for the party's poor performance.

Rajasthan

The electoral contest in Rajasthan in 2008 was quite close. The Congress did not obtain a majority in the 200-member state assembly—it won 96 seats—and depends on the support of a number of independent MLAs. The party's vote share went up a bit over 1 per cent, from 35.7 per cent in 2003 to 36.8 per cent. The number of BJP MLAs in the Rajasthan assembly declined from 120 to 78; the party's vote share came down significantly by nearly 5 per cent from 39.2 per cent to 34.3. The BSP's vote share rose from 4 per cent to 4.6 per cent while the number of its MLAs went up from two to six.

After Mohan Lal Sukhadia, who was chief minister of Rajasthan continuously from November 1954 till July 1971, the only individual to have served two consecutive terms as chief minister was Bhairon Singh Shekhawat between March 1990 and November 1998—he had earlier served as chief minister of Rajasthan between June 1977 and February 1980. Shekhawat went on to become the vice-president of India. Ashok Gehlot, the current chief minister, had served as chief minister of the state between December 1998 and December 2003. In the Rajasthan assembly, the Congress won 76 seats in 1993, 153 seats in 1998 and 56 seats in 2003 while the number of BJP MLAs was 95, 33 and 120 respectively in these three elections.

Former BJP Chief Minister Vasundhara Raje was perceived as 'feudal', 'haughty' and 'imperious' in her style of functioning. She apparently sought the support of BJP veterans in the state, Jaswant Singh (former union minister who held the external affairs and finance portfolios) and Shekhawat, rather late in the day. Besides the fact that factionalism was rampant in the state, what made Raje's government unpopular was the fact that police fired on members of the Gurjar community and farmers in the state on more than 20 occasions during her tenure as chief minister. Large sections of Gurjars had disrupted normal life in Rajasthan during 2007, agitating for Scheduled Tribe status for the community.

The pattern of voting during the current round of elections in Rajasthan seems to have cut across what is often described by political analysts as 'vote banks'. Whereas political parties put up candidates belonging to particular castes and communities in specific constituencies, social formations like the Brahmins, Rajputs, Jats, Yadavs, Gurjars and Meenas did not vote along party lines in Rajasthan. This is a clear indication of voters becoming politically mature.

Mizoram

After the June 1986 agreement between the then Prime Minister Rajiv Gandhi and the one-time underground Mizo leader Laldenga, Mizoram has been relatively free from the influence of violent insurgency that has prevailed in most other states in north-eastern India. Mizoram is also among India's most literate states. The Congress had dominated the polity of Mizoram from the mid-1980s till the late-1990s. In December 1998, Zoramthanga of the Mizo National Front became the state's chief minister after his party won 21 out of the 44 seats in the state assembly. He was re-elected five years later. The 2008 assembly elections in Mizoram saw the Congress return to power with an impressive majority obtaining 32 out of 40 seats with the party's vote share going up from just over 30 per cent to nearly 39 per cent. The decline in the vote share of the MNF was relatively small, from 31.7 per cent to 30.6 per cent, but the number of MLAs belonging to the party fell drastically from 21 to 3 with former chief minister Zoramthanga himself losing the elections. The current chief minister of the state, Lalthanhawla, had earlier held the same position on two occasions between May 1984 and August 1986 and again between January 1989 and December 1998.

Conclusion

The message emanating from the outcome of the five assembly elections is that politicians and political parties are supported when they deliver on their promises—when they not merely announce programmes and schemes for economic and social development but ensure that these are actualised and executed efficiently.

In the four states in north India where assembly elections took place, the battle was between the two largest political parties in India, the Congress and the BJP. A similar situation exists in only four other states (Gujarat, Himachal Pradesh, Uttarakhand and to a lesser extent, Karnataka). In each one of the 20 other states in India, there is at least one other important political party of consequence. The aggregation of outcomes of elections in these 28 states put together has brought about a fragmentation of the country's polity. It would, therefore, be simplistic to look at the 2008 assembly elections for indicators to the likely outcome of the forthcoming general elections that are scheduled for April–May 2009.

SECTION I

POLITICS AND GOVERNANCE

C. Terrorism and Security

19

Recent Bomb Blasts in South Asia: Are the Terrorists on a Killing Spree Again?

ISHTIAQ AHMED

(*11 July 2008*)

ON 6 JULY 2008, a suicide bomber blew himself up near the Lal Masjid (Red Mosque) in the Pakistani capital, Islamabad. He succeeded in taking at least 21 lives, including those of 15 policemen. The mayhem the blasts caused was a shocking reminder of the fact that terrorist networks which had been dormant for some time are again back in the killing business.

It is intriguing to note that the government allowed the administration of the Lal Masjid to hold a conference to mark the first anniversary of a gory showdown with pitched battles being fought between Pakistani paramilitary forces and heavily-armed militants barricading inside the mosque from 3 to 10 July 2007. The loss of lives then was counted from a conservative 150 to as high as 1,500. Among the dead were some military personnel.

The Lal Masjid, an elaborate Islamic seminary, comprising several building complexes, included schools for male and female pupils. The founder of the seminary, Maulana Muhammad Abdullah, was deeply involved, with the blessings of the Pakistan army, in the Afghanistan jihad of the 1980s. He was subsequently assassinated in 1998. His two sons, Ghazi Abdul Aziz and Ghazi Abdul Rashid, took over the mantle of militant Sunni Islam. They were openly supportive of the Taliban and were bitter opponents of the United States' policies in Afghanistan and Pakistan. They began to denounce the government of General Pervez Musharraf for allegedly surrendering Pakistan's sovereignty and national security to the Americans by joining their so-called 'war on terror' against fellow Muslims, which included military action against the Taliban and Al Qaeda in the tribal belt on the Pakistan–Afghanistan border.

From early March 2007, the two brothers and their disciples embarked upon a concerted agitation to assert their power. The whole world was awestruck when global television networks flashed images of men and women clad in black robes, carrying long sticks and other weapons, raiding an alleged brothel run by a Pakistani woman and a Chinese massage parlour. The militants took the Chinese workers hostage and declared that they were going to impose the Islamic Shariah in Pakistan. The hostages were later released. However, the Islamists declared that they were going to establish Islamic courts, which would try all violators of the Shariah and punish them severely in accordance to Quranic laws.

The Ghazi brothers also issued a *fatwa* urging Muslims to overthrow General Musharraf. In practical terms, they were preaching open rebellion. The government initially tried to negotiate with the militants for a peaceful resolution of their grievances, but all efforts failed to bear fruit; hence the heavy loss of life resulting from hand-to-hand fighting as the military and paramilitary forces forced their way inside the Lal Masjid.

Fully aware of the violent not-too-distant Lal Masjid episode, it was thus surprising that the current Pakistani government allowed a conference to be held in Islamabad to commemorate last year's bloody episode. Was such a decision taken out of some genuine respect for the freedom of speech and assembly or was it a populist gesture to appease the militants? Whatever the rationale, it was indeed a terribly wrong decision.

Could it be that the new Pakistan People's Party (PPP)-led government simply does not have the perspective and competence to deal with the terrorist threat that looms large over Pakistan? After all, Prime Minister Yousaf Raza Gilani came to power only at the end of February 2008 after a long period of quasi-military rule under General Musharraf and his main political ally, the docile Pakistan Muslim League-Quaid-i-Azam.

It is perhaps also possible that the decision to allow the conference to go ahead was aimed at appeasing Nawaz Sharif, the leader of the second biggest party in the Pakistan parliament, the Pakistan Muslim

League-Nawaz [PML(N)]. Sharif has close connections with the Saudis and is known to have a soft corner for Islamism.

The PPP and PML(N) formed a coalition government after the February 2008 elections. However, the PML(N) withdrew after a few weeks because the two parties failed to develop a joint position on the restoration of the deposed judges and on President Musharraf's future. It is, therefore, also possible that the conference on the Lal Masjid episode was a gesture to keep Sharif in good humour.

The government claimed to have made proper security arrangements to prevent terrorist attacks. Several thousand policemen were reportedly stationed in Islamabad during the commemorative conference. Whatever the preparations and calculations, it has now been proven that it was a myopic and foolish decision.

The Pakistani media has reported that several speakers at the conference whipped up passions by describing the dead leaders and cadres of the Lal Masjid as martyrs in the cause of Islam. Not surprisingly, such a suggestion put the Pakistan military in the role of killers and aggressors.

In any case, following the installation of the civilian government, the militants had suspended their intense wave of suicide bombings and other types of terrorism, possibly in the hope that General Musharraf would be forced to step down as president, and Pakistan would withdraw from the war on terror and stop helping the Americans.

This did not happen. Instead, Prime Minister Gilani reiterated that Pakistan's commitment to root out terrorism remained uncompromised, albeit backed with a broad-based strategy that included economic and political reforms to neutralise the moderate sections of the tribal society. It is naïve, however, to believe that the Islamists would abandon terrorism without making all efforts to convert Pakistan and Afghanistan into theocratic tyrannies.

In the last few weeks, increasing Taliban activism has been reported in Peshawar. Also, just a day after the suicide bombing in Islamabad, six bomb blasts took place in Karachi. At least 25 people suffered grievous injuries. The same day, a suicide bomber struck the Indian embassy in the Afghanistan capital, Kabul. Forty-one people, including four Indian diplomatic staff, were killed. Under these circumstances, there is reason to fear that terrorism may increase in Pakistan.

Are the recent terrorist outrages carried out by the same group or by disparate groups? Analysts are pondering this question. It may take some time before we know the truth, if we ever know anything at all. Whatever the case, one thing is quite certain—the terrorists are on a killing spree again.

20

Attack on the Indian Embassy in Kabul: Time to Sober Up

IFTIKHAR A. LODHI

(15 July 2008)

THE 7 JULY 2008 suicide attack on the Indian Embassy in Kabul left 41 people dead and some 140 injured, including an Indian military attaché and three other Indians. Immediately after the attack, Kabul started pointing fingers at Islamabad and its Inter-Services Intelligence (ISI) agency. Though New Delhi has officially refrained from blaming Pakistan, many senior officials joined Kabul in accusing the ISI. Islamabad has categorically rejected the allegations. Although conventional wisdom suggests a strong possibility of ISI's complicity, if not Islamabad's, the ground realities may be somewhat different.

Kabul has frequently blamed Islamabad for almost all anti-occupation and anti-Karzai government attacks. The rhetoric has gone up in the recent past, less due to a formidable insurgency, and more due to President Hamid Karzai's frustrations with the mired North Atlantic Treaty Organization (NATO) forces. Relations between the two capitals are at all-time low so much so that President Karzai threatened to attack Pakistan last month.

Washington, despite condemning attacks in the strongest terms, refused to endorse allegations of Islamabad's complicity. United States defence secretary, Robert Gates, said, 'I haven't seen any evidence or proof that foreign agents were involved.' The State Department said that it believed the attack was carried out by the extremists.

There are many reasons to believe that the Taliban are behind the attack. The militants have been targeting Indian interests with increasing frequency in recent times. The current attack was the fourth in a row this year. Since 2002, the Taliban, while at large, have repeatedly demanded the departure of all Indian personnel from Afghanistan; similar demands have been made of the occupation forces.

There could be many propositions on the objective, timing and the high profile nature of the target. First, the stronger the United States–India strategic partnership grows, the more India would be on the militants' radar screen. Second, India has reportedly stepped up its military-to-military cooperation with Afghanistan in recent months, short of sending combat troops. In April 2008, Afghanistan's defence minister, A.R. Wardak, took a delegation of the Afghanistan army and air force to India and to army establishments in Kashmir, 'seeking Indian cooperation against threats of terrorism and extremism'. The militants are wary of the greater Indian role, which was instrumental in keeping President Karzai (who faces an election next year) in power, with its deep links with the Northern Alliance and efficient intelligence apparatus. Finally, a stable and peaceful cooperative relationship between Pakistan and India would be a nightmare for the militants. The militants stand to gain the most from bad blood between India and Pakistan. There is a precedent for such attacks in the recent history of the relations between the two countries. Whenever some progress is made on peace-building between the two countries, certain elements in Pakistan have attempted to sabotage it, leaving both countries pointing fingers at each other. These elements have links with the Islamic militants, Islamic political parties, and the ISI.

Pakistan's prime minister, Yousaf Raza Gilani, while condemning the attacks and rejecting allegations, said that Pakistan itself is a victim of terrorism, it wants stability in the region, and it wants to push forward with an ongoing four-year (2004–8) effort to reach peace with India. Ironically, hours before the attack, an article by a former Indian career diplomat, M.K. Bhadrakumar, appeared in the *Asia Times*, which read, 'A lot of back-channel activity has been going on between Delhi, Islamabad and Washington . . . there is a broad consensus among Pakistani politicians for normalisation of relations with India . . . so that they can devote themselves with full energy to the nation's existential crisis.'

If sabotaging rapprochement between India and Pakistan was the purpose, then the miscreants seemed to have been successful in their objective. The attack has caused a hiccup in thawing relations between the two nuclear rivals. Both countries were expected to make positive progress in the coming months on major contentious issues, as well as on cooperation in trade and the Iran–Pakistan–India gas pipeline. Coincidently, a day after the attack, Indian troops at the Line of Control exchanged fire with Pakistani troops, a rare incident since the ceasefire in 2003. India also lashed out at Islamabad during the United Nations Security Council's session on Afghanistan's future on 9 July 2008 for making peace deals with the militants.

While the Indian government, on the whole, exercised restraint, the Indian media and the strategic community, as usual, pointed fingers at Islamabad. Many demanded that India should flex its muscles in the region, while sidelining American and Pakistani sensitivities. A case in point was an editorial in the influential English daily, *Indian Express*, which stated:

> After the Kabul bombing, India must come to terms with an important question that it has avoided debating so far. New Delhi cannot continue to expand its economic and diplomatic activity in Afghanistan, while avoiding a commensurate increase in its military presence there. For too long, New Delhi has deferred to Pakistani and American sensitivities about raising India's strategic profile in Afghanistan.

However, these actions can prove a pet recipe for regional destabilisation. Pakistan has, time and again, expressed its concerns over growing Indian presence in Afghanistan. In fact, many NATO and United States officials are of the opinion that Kabul and Delhi can play a bigger role on the issue of stabilisation in the region by addressing Pakistan's concerns. For example, a former top United States diplomat, Karl Inderfurth, said at a hearing on 24 January 2009, 'Kabul should address Pakistan's concerns on India, and its allies should urge Kabul to officially accept [the] Durand Line as the border between the two South Asian neighbours.' Bhadrakumar, contends that, 'It is plain unrealistic to overlook Pakistan's legitimate interests in Afghanistan.'

Some analysts, on the other hand, contend that it is India's legitimate right to be present in Afghanistan. They believe that the attack is part of a calibrated Pakistani strategy directed at coercing India into scaling down its growing presence in Afghanistan. These analysts suspect that Islamabad may not be involved in the attack; rather the ISI, which runs its own agenda, being a 'state within a state', is responsible for the carnage. For example, India's national security adviser, M.K. Narayanan, commented on a news channel, 'We have no doubt that the ISI is behind this . . . the ISI needs to be destroyed. We made this point, whenever we have had a chance, to interlocutors across the world . . . there might have been some tactical restraint for some time, obviously that restraint is no longer present.' Pakistan has rejected these accusations.

However, the issue may not be the ISI *per se* but rather civil–military relations. The ISI works on orders of the Pakistan army with a well defined command and control structure. To suggest that the ISI is involved in the attack is to suggest that the Pakistan army is involved. However, several reasons seem to indicate that the army may not be the culprit in this regard. Today, the global and regional strategic scene is completely different from that in the 1990s. Pakistan has managed successfully to woo the United States and China. Backing the Taliban would strain its relations with the United States and alienate China, Iran and the neighbouring Central Asian countries, all of whom are wary of Islamic militancy. Islamabad appears to have abandoned the Taliban, notwithstanding the fact that there are elements supportive of them within and outside the government machinery.

Furthermore, the Pakistan army itself has been under attacks from the militants. The militants, once confined to the mountains, have created havoc in Pakistan-settled areas in the recent past, including attacks on Pakistan army cantonments; army headquarters; the Navy War College; the Intelligence Service headquarters; the Danish Embassy; the United States Consulate; and the political parties and their leaders. Pakistan has deployed more than 80,000 troops in the border regions, more than the total strength of NATO's coalition force and the Afghanistan army deployed on the border. More Pakistani troops have died in battle with the militants than Afghanistan and coalition casualities put together in the last seven years.

Despite the sacrifices it has made, the Pakistan army lacks credibility, due to its past misadventures, making it suspect in the eyes of many analysts who continue to doubt its intentions. The Pakistan army will have to go the extra mile to win its lost trust at home and abroad. On the other hand, the Karzai government and New Delhi can play a bigger role to address Pakistan's concerns. If the three capitals do not come to terms with the issues at hand and continue the blame game, the militants would be the final winners.

21

The Pakistan Inter-Services Intelligence: A Profile

ISHTIAQ AHMED
(*15 August 2008*)

IN THE PAST few weeks, Pakistan has come under intense pressure from the United States, Afghanistan and India to curb the alleged involvement of its Inter-Services Intelligence (ISI) in terrorist activities. Such pressure has been built rapidly in the aftermath of bomb blasts, some carried out by suicide bombers, in July 2008 in many parts of South Asia. Those outrages caused well over a hundred deaths. Much before the recent attacks, the ISI's power and influence in politics had gained it the reputation of 'a state within a state', suggesting that Pakistani governments, especially those formed by civilians, have little or no control over its activities. The ISI rejects such accusations, claiming that it is a professional organisation dedicated solely to gathering intelligence that would strengthen Pakistan's national survival and security.

Existing literature on spy agencies is replete with data suggesting that acting irregularly and even in illegal ways is not unusual for such organisations. Even in stable and strong democracies, governments are not always fully in control of them and they can set up their agenda rather freely. Charges that the Central Intelligence Agency (CIA) and the Federal Bureau of Investigation (FBI) sometimes act in defiance of United States governments have been made several times, but since such organisations work in great secrecy, it is not easy to find solid corroborative evidence against them that can show that they do act against the will of the government. However, the general assumption underlying the functioning of such entities is that they act under a coherent chain of command,

and, in principle, their activities are purported to enhance national security.

Pakistan's President, Pervez Musharraf, has described the ISI as 'Pakistan's first line of defence'.[1] On 5 August 2008, the Pakistan government criticised the Americans for blaming Pakistan for the recent terrorist activities. It was claimed that, on 24 May 2008, Pakistan provided the Americans with the exact location and movement of the Taliban leader, Baitullah Mehsud, who had driven to a remote South Waziristan mountain post in his Toyota Land Cruiser to address the press [among the journalists present was the BBC Pakistan correspondent]. He returned safely to his abode. The statement went on to say that the United States military has the capacity to direct a missile to a precise location at very short notice as it has done close to 20 times in the last few years to hit Al Qaeda targets inside Pakistan. However, no action was taken against Mehsud. This attitude was described by Pakistan as intriguing and confusing. Pakistan also alleged an Indian hand in the trouble in Baluchistan and also accused the Afghanistan government of protecting Baluch secessionists.

Making allegations and counter-allegations is typical of spy agencies and the exact truth may never be known to the public at large. On the other hand, it is possible that, for the resurgence of terrorism, the factors that have created the present situation are far more complex and include many other players.

In any event, it is worth recapitulating the chronology of the July terrorist attacks. On 6 July 2008, in a suicide bombing in Islamabad, 21 people lost their lives, including 15 policemen. The next day in Karachi, six crude bombs exploded in different parts of the city, causing grievous injury to 25 people. Pakistan blamed Mehsud for the attacks—he was also blamed for the assassination of Benazir Bhutto on 27 December 2007.

However, it was after the attack on the Indian embassy in the Afghanistan capital, Kabul, on 7 July 2008 that killed more than 60 people, including four members of the Indian diplomatic staff, that protests began to be aired directly against the ISI. The Afghans immediately started claiming that the attack had been masterminded by an intelligence agency of a neighbouring country. Given the strained relations between Afghanistan and Pakistan, it was not difficult to assume that the Afghans were pointing the finger at Pakistan. A few days later, India made similar accusations. President Hamid Karzai of Afghanistan went on to claim that his government had convincing evidence that suggested that the attack had been masterminded by Pakistani intelligence. Initially the CIA chief, Robert Gates, said that he had not seen any evidence of a Pakistani involvement, but soon afterwards, the United States' position changed when the Afghan and Indian points of view were presented to the Bush administration.

In the meantime, terrorist outbursts continued and bomb blasts took place in the Indian city of Bangalore on 25 July 2008 and in Ahmedabad on 26 July 2008. Some 60 people lost their lives and many more were injured. The Indian police claimed to have found dozens of unexploded bombs in Surat and other Indian towns and cities. There was no doubt that some forces were trying to instigate communal clashes between Hindus and Muslims in India, and were indeed aiming at undermining the efforts that had gone on for quite some time to develop better understanding and relations between India and Pakistan. India did not directly name the ISI for those attacks, but alleged that a Pakistani involvement in them was present even when the actual blasts might have been carried out by Indian Muslims recruited by extremist organisations.

Under the circumstances, the recent visits of Pakistan's newly elected prime minister, Yousaf Raza Gilani, to the United States and Sri Lanka were marred by constant barrage of questions and comments about Pakistan's alleged inability to control the terrorists, who were receiving support from the ISI. Thus, what was supposed to be an excellent occasion to showcase his vision of Pakistan and what he hoped to achieve as prime minster became instead an embarrassing exercise in finding arguments to exonerate Pakistan from charges of inability to control rogue elements in Pakistani society.

In the United States, President George Bush, as well as presidential candidates, John McCain and Barack Obama, and other leaders whom Gilani met, urged him to do much more to root out extremism and terrorism. The same concerns were raised by the

American media. The only positive gain was that the Congress voted in favour of a US $15 billion aid package to Pakistan, of which the major portion would be spent on economic development.

The South Asian Association for Regional Cooperation Summit which he attended immediately afterwards was dominated by Gilani assuring his South Asian counterparts that his government was determined to fight terrorism. In an interview with a Sri Lankan newspaper, he rubbished all accusations that the ISI was involved in the Kabul bombing, asserting that it took orders from him and reported to him in accordance with requirements laid down in the Pakistan constitution. In any case, in a 45-minute long meeting with Indian prime minister, Manmohan Singh, Gilani pointed out that Pakistan too was a victim of terrorism and that both Pakistan and India should work together to fight that evil. In a separate meeting with President Karzai, he promised to carry out an investigation to find out if there was any involvement of the ISI in the Kabul bombing. The question, of course, is: Does Gilani enjoy real powers as the chief executive of the Pakistan government? Gilani was indeed making a technically correct statement when he said that, constitutionally speaking, the ISI was under his jurisdiction and reported to him, but for all practical purposes, it is the chief of army staff to whom the ISI reports and takes orders from. In the past, whenever a civilian government had tried to establish its control over the ISI by appointing a general it trusted, but who was unacceptable to the military establishment, the latter trumped over it by appointing its own men to strategic positions dealing with intelligence on internal politics. In this way, the ISI continued to maintain a watch on the activities of the civilian government itself.

In order to make sense of why the ISI enjoys, in actual reality, such wide discretionary powers and is allegedly involved in terrorism, we need to look at it in a historical perspective.

The ISI was founded in 1948 to facilitate intelligence gathering and sharing between the three main sections of the armed forces: the army, navy and air force. There are other military and civilian intelligence agencies too, but the ISI is undoubtedly the most powerful and the most politicised among them. The exact number of people who work for it is not known but estimates suggest it has at least 25,000 employees. Another 30,000 serve as informants and in other related roles. Although its official brief is about enhancing national security and, it is therefore, concerned primarily with intelligence gathering and other related activities pertaining to external threats to Pakistan, it was given a political task already in the late 1950s when General (later Field Marshal) Mohammad Ayub Khan (1958–69) ordered it to monitor opposition politicians from East Pakistan because he did not trust that Bengali police officers of the Criminal Investigation Department (CID) would do that sincerely. Similarly, Prime Minister Zulfikar Ali Bhutto (1971–7) ordered the ISI to collect intelligence in Baluchistan after an arms cache allegedly dispatched by Iraq to help Baluch separatists was uncovered in 1973. Bhutto too did not trust the Baluchis working in the CID.

General Muhammad Zia-ul-Haq (1977–88) asked the ISI to bolster the Mohajir Qaumi Movement in the Sindh province as a counterweight to the Pakistan People's Party, led by Benazir Bhutto, but the real big boost to the ISI's status and importance came during the Afghan jiḥad of the 1980s. He assigned the ISI the crucial task of setting up bases in Pakistan where Mujahideen (Islamic warriors) could be indoctrinated and trained to fight the holy war against the Soviet Red Army that had marched into Afghanistan in 1979, with a view to bolstering the fledgling communist regime that had come to power the previous year though a military coup. During this period, thousands of Islamic schools called madrasas were set up by the Islamists, where hundreds of thousands of pupils (Taliban), mainly from the Pushto-speaking tribes on both sides of the Pakistan–Afghanistan tribal belt, were indoctrinated in a severely militant type of Islamic ideology. This massive undertaking was given full help by the United States and Saudi Arabia. The ISI did not have any direct involvement in the setting up of the madrasas, but naturally the pupils indoctrinated in them were drafted into jihad operations in Afghanistan and, later, in the Indian-administered Kashmir.

After the Soviets withdrew in 1989 and the Americans hurriedly left without ensuring a smooth and stable transfer of power to

Afghan politicians, a fierce and bloody power struggle erupted among rival political and ethnic factions constituting Afghan society. While Pakistan backed the predominantly Pashtun Taliban, arch rival India threw its weight behind the Northern Alliance, comprising the Uzbek, Tajik, Hazara and other ethnic groups. The Taliban emerged victorious in that gory encounter and Pakistan's influence in Afghanistan increased dramatically.

It should not be surprising therefore that, in that process, some officers in the ISI became hardcore Islamists although the ISI, as a body, may have remained a professional organisation focusing primarily on national security. Moreover, some top military and ISI officers began to nurture the dream of establishing an Islamic superstate that would initially comprise Pakistan and Afghanistan, but would then expand into the Indian-administered Kashmir through successful jihad, and later to the Central Asian republics. Even Iran could possibly be integrated into it. From the Pakistan military's point of view, such expansion westwards would provide Pakistan 'strategic depth' *vis-à-vis* arch rival India.

The Kashmir jihad which took off soon after the withdrawal of the Soviet Union from Afghanistan was spearheaded by militant Pakistani organisations such as Laskhar-e-Taiba (LeT) and Jaish-e-Muhammad (JM). These outfits actively supported a popular uprising of Kashmiri Muslims that had emerged against Indian rule and, as a result, were involved in violent conflict with Indian troops. Later, these organisations began to expand their activities into India and the result was several terrorist outrages in both Indian-administered Kashmir as well as in other parts of India. It was widely suspected that the ISI maintained close connections with the LeT and JM.

Given these major assignments and concomitant involvement in militant operations, it should not be surprising that the ISI appropriated far more power and acquired much greater influence than is normally the case with intelligence agencies of middle level powers such as Pakistan. Also, the fact that democracy and civilian institutions never took firm roots in Pakistan and the military dominated the political scene meant that the ISI, the primary military intelligence agency, began to be dreaded as a state within a state.

However, the 9/11 terrorist attacks on the United States set in motion a worldwide campaign against terrorism. While Pakistan joined the 'war on terror' and the Musharraf regime began to arrest Al Qaeda operatives, militants active in the Indian-administered Kashmir continued to be described by it as freedom fighters. However, after the 13 December 2001 terrorist attack on the Indian parliament, pressure on President Musharraf to dissociate the state with such militancy increased enormously. In an important address to the Pakistani nation on 12 January 2002, President Musharraf declared that Pakistan remained committed to the just struggle of the Kashmiri people against Indian dominance, but that, in future, militant organisations such as the LeT and JM would not be allowed to organise jihad on Pakistani territory for engagement in the Indian Kashmir.

Such utterances did not go down well with sections of Pakistani society that sympathised with the militants. Among them were serving and retired military officers, including senior officers in the ISI hierarchy. Several unsuccessful assassination attempts were made on President Musharraf and his loyal generals. It was found that some insiders were involved in those attacks. Consequently, a reshuffling of key positions in the military and the ISI took place as President Musharraf placed his trusted men in those positions. It is, however, possible that such actions were not thorough and, therefore, some dissident ISI functionaries who harboured sympathies for the Taliban and militant organisations remained undetected.

In any case, former ISI Director, Lieutenant-General Hameed Gul, and other retired military officers as well as rightwing Islamist leaders began openly to blame the government for making Pakistan national interests subservient to those of the United States. Voices were also raised in favour of the Kashmir jihad. During 2007, the terrorists directed their wrath at the Pakistan military personnel and installations. Bomb blasts and suicide attacks took place almost every other day. As a result, hundreds of fatalities and injuries were suffered by the military. President Musharraf blamed the Taliban, but it is possible that dissident elements from the military and especially the ISI aided the Taliban in carrying out the attacks.

It is widely believed by the Pakistani military establishment that the Karzai government is closely allied to India and, therefore, Indian influence has increased significantly in Afghanistan. Such developments are seen as being inimical to Pakistani interests. It is, therefore, possible that, in the attack on the Indian embassy in Kabul, such considerations may have played some role. The Americans claim to have intercepted messages exchanged between the ISI officers and the Taliban in which the former provided information to the latter on the movement of North Atlantic Treaty Organization troops.

On the other hand, within the Pakistani tribal areas, bloody clashes between the Taliban and the Pakistani military continue. In the last few months, hundreds of Pakistani military personnel have lost their lives in such encounters. The military and the ISI have also continued to render help to the Americans in tracking down Al Qaeda operatives. Thus, the military establishment, which includes the ISI, apparently plays contradictory roles in the current situation.

It is, however, very unlikely that the mainstream ISI, headed currently by General Nadeem Taj, and previously by General Pervez Kayani (currently chief of army staff), had been acting in defiance of the policies of President Musharraf, when he was firmly in power before the 18 February 2008 general elections. However, after the civilian government took over in the end of February 2008, that chain of command may have become less effective. There is nothing to suggest that the linkages and networking between the ISI officials and the Taliban and militant organisations such as LeT and JM have been severed altogether.

In any event, the pressure on Pakistan to deal effectively with terrorist networks within its territory will remain. Given the thriving market for conspiracy theories in Pakistan, some people believe that the United States, Afghanistan and India are developing a joint strategy against Pakistan. If that be true, then instead of the Taliban, Al Qaeda, LeT, JM and the ISI being blamed for terrorism, the Pakistani state itself may be viewed as a rogue entity that needs to be dealt with severely. In one sense, that would be a self-fulfilling prophecy of those who believe that Pakistan is a victim of some international plot against it.

It is, therefore, in Pakistan's interest that it strives hard to crush all networks and organisations that may be involved in terrorism. The ISI should indeed play its legitimate role in gathering intelligence imperative to strengthen Pakistan's security, but such activities should conform to the overall norms and standards that international law approves for the conduct of nations.

Equally, it is important that regional and world powers should assist Pakistan in strengthening its democratic institutions and in establishing the supremacy of civilian rule. Also, efforts should be made to persuade the Pakistani and Indian military establishments and their spy agencies not to engage in a perpetual zero-sum combat to gain influence in South Asia and Afghanistan. There is the need to radically re-orient the politics of South Asia in a positive direction so that this region may benefit from the economic opportunities that are at hand. A destabilised Pakistan will inevitably carry adverse repercussions for its neighbours Afghanistan and India. Given the fact that Pakistan is a nuclear weapon state, such an outcome can spell disaster for the South Asian region as well as the rest of the world.

22

India's Tamil Politics and the Sri Lankan Ethnic Conflict

S.D. MUNI

(6 November 2008)

THE LIBERATION TIGERS of Tamil Eelam (LTTE) is, no doubt, one of the world's most powerful terrorist organisations. However, the myth of its military invincibility has been built and nurtured for a long time by a variety of vested interests, ranging from Tamil chauvinists all over the world; to even Sri Lankan politicians who saw their political fortunes in the perpetuation of the ethnic conflict. This myth was broken on at least four occasions: (i) in 1987, when the then Sri Lankan president, J.R. Jayawardane, drove the Tamil militants, including the LTTE, to the verge in his so-called 'fight to the finish'; (ii) in 1987–9, when the Indian Peace Keeping Force (IPKF) bottled up the LTTE in Vanni jungles and successfully carried out elections in the northeastern province; (iii) in 1995–6, when the then Sri Lankan president, Chandrika Kumaratunga, again cleared them from Jaffna and the eastern province, pushing them into the jungles; and (iv) now, when the Sri Lankan security forces have trapped them in their last two districts of Killinochi and Mallaithivu.

Whenever the LTTE has been militarily cornered, the Tamil politicians of India, prompted by the LTTE, have raised the issue of 'the security of Tamil people' and have pressured India into prevailing over Colombo, if necessary, through diplomatic and even military intervention, to stop the war. These politicians succeeded in 1987 when India sent its MIG fighters to drop food packets to the conflict-marooned Tamils in Jaffna. This intervention paved the way for the July 1987 Indo–Sri Lankan agreement for the resolution of the ethnic conflict. The IPKF went to Sri Lanka under the provisions of this agreement. The factors that added weight to the Tamil politicians' pressures on New Delhi then were many and varied; the most significant being the deep strategic discord between Colombo and New Delhi during Indira Gandhi's prime ministership in India. Her successor, Rajiv Gandhi, tried to persuade Jayawardane to address the issue peacefully and to seek its negotiated political resolution. However, he found Colombo deceptive and insincere. Much water has flown down the Indian and Sri Lankan rivers since then.

The political mood even in Tamil Nadu started changing with the IPKF fighting the LTTE in Sri Lanka. However, with the assassination of Rajiv Gandhi by the LTTE in May 1991, the LTTE lost much of its sympathy and support among the Tamils of India. The major Tamil parties of India broadly distanced themselves from the LTTE, though the latter's links have continued with fringe Tamil nationalist streak and the vested interests that thrive on the LTTE's smuggling and procurement network in Tamil Nadu. Marumalarchi Dravida Munnetra Kazhagam (MDMK), led by V. Gopalswamy (Vaiko), and Pattali Makkal Katchi (PMK), led by S. Ramadoss, are the two most vocal proponents of this Tamil nationalist streak and, hence, proponents of the LTTE's interests in India. Among the major parties, Dravida Munnetra Kazhagam (DMK), led by M. Karunanidhi, and All India Anna Dravida Munnetra Kazhagam (AIDMK), led by M.G. Ramachandran, had been patronising the Sri Lankan Tamil militant groups since the outbreak of the ethnic conflict across the Palk Strait in the early 1980s, or even earlier. Both these parties used these Sri Lankan militant leaders as their musclemen in Tamil Nadu politics. After the death of Ramachandran and the post-1987 conflict between the LTTE and the non-LTTE Sri Lankan Tamil militant groups, Karunanidhi continued to keep links with them. Ramachandran's successor, J. Jayalalitha, distanced herself from the LTTE. The DMK and Karunanidhi also came under scrutiny in the Rajiv Gandhi assassination probe conducted by Justice M.L. Jain. Using this as a pretext, the Congress withdrew support from the Gujral government at the centre in 1997 because the DMK was an ally of that government. Even before the present resurgence of the Sri Lankan government's war against the LTTE, the MDMK and the PMK did not relent in their advocacy of the LTTE. In 2005, their pressure, with the implicit backing of the DMK [now being an ally of the United Progressive Alliance (UPA) government at the centre], succeeded in scuttling a near-finalised defence cooperation agreement between India and Sri Lanka.

The Sri Lankan government's present campaign against the LTTE started in June 2006. Despite claims to the contrary by the Sri Lankan government, this campaign has not been without massive suffering for the ordinary Tamil people of Sri Lanka. Estimates of the number of internally-displaced people from this war have gone up to half a million. The life of Tamils living even outside the war zone, for example, in Colombo and other provinces, has been badly affected under security regulations. A number of them have disappeared while others have been displaced. More than 300 Tamils were pushed out of Colombo in want of adequate 'documentation'. The Sri Lankan government has also gagged the media and other independent sources of information on war-related issues. The international community, including the United Nations, has levelled serious charges of human rights violations on the Sri Lankan government. With the onslaught of military campaign in the north closing in on the LTTE strongholds, the excessive use of helicopter gunships and air bombardment, and the LTTE's penchant for using human shields (of innocent civilians under their control) to protect themselves, the miseries of Tamil people have increased manifold.

The deteriorating human rights situation in Sri Lanka has given spurt to Tamil Nadu's emotive politics. While the MDMK and the PMK have always been restive on the Sri Lankan Tamil issue, other radical outfits such as Viduthalai Chiruthaikal Katchi of Thirumavalavan, the Tamil Nationalist Party of Nedumaran and Periyar Dravida Kazhagam have now joined them to flaunt their support for the LTTE which is a banned terrorist organisation in India. All of them have asked India to intervene in the current Sri Lankan crisis to secure a ceasefire. The Communist Party of India added to the political momentum to this issue by calling for a strike on 2 October 2008, in solidarity with the Tamils of Sri Lanka. The Left, in its disenchantment with the UPA government on the question of Indo–US agreement, did not hesitate from using the Sri Lankan issue to mobilise support in the south and put pressure on the central UPA government and its local DMK ally. It announced that AIDMK would also join the 2 October 2008 strike. Though the Left and AIDMK have made it clear that their concern is only with the innocent Tamil civilians of Sri Lanka and not with the plight of the LTTE, their attacks have been sharp and have focused on Tamil Nadu's chief minister, Karunanidhi, and Prime Minister Manmohan Singh.

The DMK could not afford to be left out on the Sri Lankan issue while its rivals were cashing on it politically. In order to outdo his political rivals, Karunanidhi issued a strong statement on 5 October 2008, asking thousands of people to send telegrams to Prime Minister Singh, urging the central government to 'intervene immediately and stop the genocide of Tamils in Sri Lanka'. A day later, he even went to the extent of threatening the central government by saying that if it 'fails to find a solution to the problems of Tamil people, we may be forced to consider whether this government is necessary'. On 14 October 2008, he called an All-Party meeting on the Sri Lankan issue and adopted a resolution stating that 'the centre should stop the thirty-year old civil war that has resulted in thousands of Tamils' deaths in Eelam. Since Indian military aid is resulting in genocide of Tamils, this meeting urges its immediate stoppage. . . . This meeting informs the centre that if India does not fulfil the demands [the inaction] may result in the resignation of all Members of Parliament from Tamil Nadu.' Though the LTTE was not mentioned anywhere in the resolution, the reference to 'Eelam' was a clear recognition of the LTTE's separatist agenda. Kanimozhi, Karunanidhi's daughter, was the first to submit her resignation from the membership of Rajya Sabha, in response to the All-Party resolution. The submission of the resignation, not to the chairman of Rajya Sabha but to her own father, clearly underlined its tactical thrust. A number of other DMK members of parliament did likewise subsequently. Karunanidhi was clearly bashing the centre to blunt the attacks of his local rivals for his being an ally of the UPA's Sri Lanka policy. Other DMK allies such as Dr Ramadoss even asked for a separate Tamil Nadu if the centre was to ignore the demands of the Tamils. Vaiko, who had fallen out from the DMK-led alliance, threatened to take armed Tamils from Tamil Nadu to fight with the LTTE against the Sri Lankan government.

Karunanidhi succeeded in his political objective of taking the wind out of the sails of his rivals on the Sri Lankan issue. His political thunders forced the central government to launch a number of political and diplomatic manoeuvres to diffuse the issue. Prime Minister Singh called Karunanidhi on 6 October 2008 and then rushed his National Security Adviser (NSA), M.K. Narayanan, to assure the Tamil leader that everything needed to be done in relation to Sri Lanka would be done. The Sri Lankan High Commissioner was summoned by the NSA to express 'India's grave concern and unhappiness'. Minister of external affairs, Pranab Mukherjee, made a statement in Rajya Sabha saying, 'what is required in Sri Lanka is a peaceful and negotiated political settlement which allows each community to realise its own potential within the framework of a united Sri Lanka' and he promised that the 'Government of India will do all in its power to achieve this goal, to ameliorate the humanitarian conditions in Sri Lanka and has been making representations to the Government of Sri Lanka at several levels'. A week later, in another statement in the parliament, he reiterated India's concerns with regard to the 'deteriorating humanitarian situation in the northern part of Sri Lanka' and emphasised India's 'conviction that there is no military solution to the ethnic conflict'. He informed the parliament about the forthcoming visit of Basil Rajapakse, brother and senior adviser to the president of Sri Lanka, Mahinda Rajapakse, to India. This visit was the result of a telephone conversation between Prime Minister Singh and President Rajapakse.

This visit took place on 26 October 2008. Basil Rajapakse met Foreign Minister Mukherjee, Narayanan and Foreign Secretary Shiv Shankar Menon. In the statement issued after his visit, it was disclosed that the 'positive and constructive' discussions centered 'on a range of issues'. India conveyed its concerns and received the assurance that the 'safety and well-being of the Tamil community in Sri Lanka is being taken care of'. India also decided to send 'around 800 tonnes' of supplies for the 'affected civilians in the North', the delivery of which would be facilitated by the Sri Lankan government. The contrast with the 1987 situation was stark. The 'Indian side called for the implementation of the 13th Amendment' and the Sri Lankan special envoy emphasised that his government and the president were 'committed to a political process that would lead to a sustainable solution'. It is important to note that there was no reference to the 13th Amendment in the Sri Lankan response as this is a contentious issue in Sri Lankan politics. It was significant that 'both sides agreed that terrorism should be countered with resolve', meaning that the Sri Lankan government's military operations against the LTTE would continue unhindered.

After the meeting, Foreign Minister Mukherjee went to Chennai to brief Karunanidhi who, in response to Sri Lanka's assurances, called off his demand of resignations. The UPA president, Sonia Gandhi, also called Karunanidhi to calm him down. The political turmoil in Tamil Nadu on the Sri Lankan issue was pacified. It was clearly understood that neither the Sri Lankan government's war against the LTTE would be stopped, nor would India's military support to Sri Lanka be withdrawn. New Delhi appeared neither willing nor constrained to review its Sri Lanka policy and Chennai was not determined to pull down the UPA government at the centre on the Sri Lankan issue.

While New Delhi felt compelled to diffuse the coalition pressures from Tamil Nadu, it was constrained not to do anything to force Colombo to act on the question of the war or on the issue of devolution of power and political solution. Unlike in 1987, India has huge investments in Sri Lanka which cannot be exposed to the anger of the Sinhalese chauvinists by echoing the dubious emotions of Tamil chauvinists in Tamil Nadu. Sri Lanka has also been craftily playing the Pakistan and China cards to force India into following the Colombo line. Even Indian public disapproval by Narayanan of Sri Lanka's arms procurements from China and Pakistan did not make any difference in this respect. In fact, China is gradually consolidating its strategic presence in Sri Lanka and there are Sri Lankan strategic analysts who would even prescribe encouraging

China to set up monitoring posts in Sri Lanka to watch India's nuclear and missile activities on the southern peninsula if India detracts from the present policy to Colombo's disadvantage. India is also helpless in pressuring Colombo on the devolution of power to the Tamil areas because, while the LTTE is obstinate in not wanting to come to the negotiating table, the non-LTTE groups, who would be the beneficiaries of the devolution, are unable to present themselves as a united force. There seems to be a broad strategic consensus in India that de-fanging a terrorist group such as the LTTE may not be undesirable in the long run. After all, India is also battling its terrorists hard at home.

23

The Mumbai Mayhem: The Global War on Terror Comes to India

S.D. MUNI

(*1 December 2008*)

INDIA FACED ITS worst ever terror attack on 26 November 2008 in Mumbai. With unprecedented sweep and speed, the terrorists attacked 10 different locations and then settled down in three iconic buildings—the Taj Mahal Palace Hotel, Hotel Trident-Oberoi and the Nariman House (a Jewish community house)—for wanton killings and pitched battles. The grit and doggedness with which the terrorists fought, and the range of arms, ammunition and explosives with which they were equipped, underlined months of careful preparation. Interrogations of the captured terrorist have revealed details of the terrorists' entry into Mumbai through the sea route from Karachi. They had plans to blow up the Taj Hotel before possible escape. There is still confusion about the actual number of terrorists that came from outside as they came in batches. More than 10 have been shot dead and one arrested. Some of them checked into the Taj Hotel on 22 November 2008 and occupied room no. 630, where not only additional explosives and arms were stored with the help of local associates (sleeping cells and underworld contacts) but a control room was also set up for the operations. They had complete and precise reconnaissance of the three major sites. India's National Security Guard (NSG) commandos who launched the counter-operations admitted that the terrorists appeared to be fully familiar with the hotel's layout and they were as well trained and determined as the commandos.

It took India's elite NSG commandos nearly 48 hours of intense encounters to clear the sites of the terrorists. Besides the NSG, almost all other components of India's security forces, the police, army (Rapid Action Force), navy (naval commandos) and the air force (helicopter units), battled the terrorists for 60 long hours in all. The terrorists had instructions to kill up to 5,000 people and to 'kill till your last breath'. At the end of these operations, there were high casualty figures, with nearly 200 people dead and over 300 injured. Nearly 600 people were rescued from the terrorists' captivity. The dead included more than 20 foreigners (five Israelis, five Americans, three Germans, two Greeks, a Japanese, a Canadian, an Australian, a Malaysian and a Singaporean), 14 police officers, including four senior Anti-Terrorist Squad (ATS) officers and at least two NSG commandos. The dead also included the families of the general manager of the Taj Hotel (his wife and two sons) and the manager of the Nariman House (the Rabbi and his wife). These figures may be revised after the final mopping up of all the sites.

The terrorists called themselves 'Deccan Mujahedeen', largely to camouflage their real identity. The interception of their conversations revealed that they spoke a mix of Punjabi, Urdu and Hindi. According to the Mumbai police, the arrested terrorist has admitted that he was trained by Laskhar-e-Taiba (LeT), an extremist jihadi outfit in Pakistan, established during the 1980s by Osama bin Laden. Though banned in Pakistan after 2001, LeT continues to operate under the name of Jamat-ul-Dawa. It is believed to be operating not only in Pakistan and occupied Kashmir, but also in Afghanistan, Iraq, Central Asia and Africa.

The terrorists in the Mumbai attack carried fake identity cards of British, Mauritius and other nationalities to cover their real identities, though the possibility of LeT having separatist Kashmiris, alienated Indian Muslims and British rationals of Pakistani origin as recruits cannot be ruled out. There is also a strong possibility that their operations were supported by local groups and Mumbai's underworld. There is no dearth of Mumbai's underworld don Dawood Ibrahim's associates (the D-Company) offering possible help, though Dawood himself lives in Karachi and Dubai with protection from the respective establishments. He was the mastermind of Mumbai's 1993 riots. The Indian government has, for long, been requesting Pakistan to hand over Dawood but without any success. The terrorists' Mumbai operations were patterned on previous LeT-blessed Fidayeen attacks in Kashmir and the attacks in 2001 (the Indian parliament), in 2002 (the Akshardham Temple in Gujarat), in 2005 (Ayodhya) and in 2006 (Rashtriya Swayamsevak Sangh headquarters in Nagpur). As in the case in Mumbai, the terrorists carried dry fruits for their sustenance and had shown the propensity for fighting a coordinated pitched battle with the security forces. This is unlike usual terrorist acts of killing through suicide and other explosions. The imprint of Al Qaeda training and motivation were also clearly evident in the Mumbai attack.

The Mumbai attack was different from other acts of terrorism in India so far in that it focussed on foreigners. In Mumbai, the attackers primarily targetted Americans, British and Israelis. The two hotels were chosen as they are frequented by foreigners. The siege on Nariman House, and the killing of Jews and Israelis there, as in the case of Trident-Oberoi, clearly point towards Al Qaeda links to the attack. The e-mail (the origin of which has now been traced to Pakistan) sent on behalf of the terrorists in the name of 'Deccan Mujahedeen' underlined two objectives: (a) 'India should stop its atrocities on Muslims. . .'; and (b) 'the proof of atrocities on Muslims is evident in Iraq, Afghanistan and . . . Kashmir. . . .' One of the escapee hostages from Nariman House quoted the terrorists as saying that, the 'Indian army should withdraw from Kashmir and let Shariah law prevail in Muslim-dominated regions. . . .' These are the leads to suggest the role of LeT–Al Qaeda combined.

Behind the rhetoric of Kashmir, Shariah, Iraq and Afghanistan, the Mumbai attack seems to have been driven by two broader sets of objectives, namely, of hurting India and harming India–Pakistan political understanding. India's rising profile as a power of economic and political consequence in world affairs has not been palatable to some extremist sections in Pakistan. LeT's supreme leader Hafiz Mohammad Saeed's statements on 6 and 19 October 2008 before senior Lashkar leaders may be recalled where he poured venom against India and signalled that 'the only language India understands is that of force, and that is the language it must be talked to in'. India's vulnerability to terrorism and its incapacity to ensure internal security and stability can seriously erode investor confidence and subdue its growth dynamism. India's travel and tourism sectors have already started feeling the pinch of the Mumbai attack, with some Western countries issuing travel advisories to their citizens. However, if India is seen to be able to deal with the aftermath of this terrorist attack firmly, it may be able to overcome the long-term damage to its economic strength and prospects, as suggested by the owner of the Taj Mahal Palace Hotel and India's top industrialist, Ratan Tata.

The attack could also have been aimed at weakening India's political stability by vitiating its sensitive communal situation and exploiting the creeping alienation of the Muslim minority. There are disturbing reports of alienated Indian Muslims joining Al Qaeda ranks to fight against the North Atlantic Treaty Organization forces in Afghanistan. Some Indian analysts trace the beginning of Indian Muslims' alienation to the demolition of Babri Mosque (1992, Ayodhya) and claim that a Muslim activist from Hyderabad, Abu Abdel Aziz 'Barbaros', had then established links with organisations such as Al Qaeda and LeT. Incidents of communal violence in Gujarat and elsewhere have subsequently reinforced such links. It is also pointed out that security searches and indiscriminate harassment of the Muslim community following terrorist incidents on the one hand, and growing violence of 'Hindu terrorists' against Muslims in India on the other, have also alienated a number of young Muslims, particularly in Muslim-dominated cities such as Hyderabad. This, if at all, could be the rationale behind the rise of groups such as 'Indian Mujahideen'. The use of 'Deccan Mujahideen' as a cover by the Mumbai attackers was perhaps to lure alienated Indian Muslims towards building and/or further re-inforcing Indian chapters of Al Qaeda, LeT and other such extremist outfits. The challenge before India lies in insulating its society and polity from the spillover of the 'global war on terror' raging in Afghanistan.

If the objective of the attack on Mumbai was to widen the communal divide in India, its effect has been just the opposite. The sacrifice of the ATS chief of Mumbai, Hemant Karkare, in chasing the terrorists on 26 November 2008 has brought praise for him from his Hindu fundamentalist detractors who have been criticising him for his probe against the 'Hindu terrorists' involved in the Malegaon attacks. The entire police operations against the terrorists in Mumbai have been led by a Muslim officer, Hasan Gafoor. Anti-Muslim organisations such as the Shiv Sena remained quiet during the terror attack and there were no communal incidents in Mumbai triggered by this attack. The attack may have made some impact on the in-progress elections for a number of state assemblies to the disadvantage of the Congress which is in power both at the centre and in Maharashtra (with Mumbai as its capital). However, the general popular reaction has been against the politicians' attempts to 'politicise terror' for electoral purposes. If the Congress party's prospects in the forthcoming national elections are adversely affected and result in the unseating of Prime Minister Manmohan Singh, the organisers of the Mumbai attack could derive the satisfaction of having punished him for his policy of taking India strategically closer to the United States.

The second set of the terrorists' goals may be to reverse the positive trend in India–Pakistan relations, particularly in the context of a democratic government in Islamabad. A Pakistani scholar, Dr Moonis Ahmer, has boldly said that the attack '. . . is a well thought-out conspiracy to destabilise relations between the two countries'. Another London-based Pakistani analyst, Farzana Shaikh, reinforces this assumption by saying, 'If we find that indeed there was some section of the Pakistani society involved in either planning or orchestrating this attack in Mumbai, it would be a very very serious matter and certainly one which could possibly bring the two countries back to the brink of war.' The question of the Mumbai attack having Pakistani roots has been raised by the Indian government. While Prime Minister Singh described the terrorists as 'foreign based', Foreign Minister Pranab Mukherjee has blamed the involvement of 'elements from Pakistan' in the Mumbai attack. Indian leaders have been cautious in avoiding any direct reference to the involvement of the Pakistan government yet. However, India has asked Pakistan to send the chief of its military intelligence agency, the Inter-Services Intelligence (ISI), to India to share information on terrorism-related issues. The Indian assumption is that there are elements in Pakistan which are beyond the control of its new democratic government and these have a vested interest in creating mischief. The responses of the Pakistani government have also been cautious and positive so far. President Asif Ali Zardari, Prime Minister Yousaf Raza Gilani and Foreign Minister Shah Mehmood Qureshi have shown their willingness to help India in the investigations and have assured India that 'any Pakistani group if found involved in the Mumbai attack will be dealt with seriously'. It may however, be noted that, on the advice of the Pakistan army chief, General Ashfaq Parvez Kayani, President Zardari has decided to send a junior ISI officer to India, as opposed to his initial decision of sending the ISI chief. This resistance from sections of the Pakistani establishment is aimed at ensuring that Pakistan is not seen as yielding to pressure from India. They may also not be fully in favour of reigning in extremist elements as instruments to keep India contained.

While both the Indian and Pakistani sides are carefully trying to avoid precipitate actions, the situation is sensitive and New Delhi is under increasing pressure to take firm action against the perpetrators of terrorism. If New Delhi is provoked and pushed by the consequences of the terrorists' act to create heat on Pakistan's eastern border, it would yield a rationale for Pakistan's security forces to divert attention and deployment, at least partly, from the Afghanistan border. Such heat can be created in many ways. One may recall the deployment of Indian forces on the Pakistan border under 'Operation Parakram' during the previous National Democratic Alliance regime following the terrorist attack on the Indian parliament in 2001. Alternately India may decide to hit at terrorist establishments across the Line of Control. This would jeopardise the United States' 'war on global terror' in Afghanistan and delight Al Qaeda and Taliban forces as well as the extremist jihadi organisations of Pakistan. Voices have started rising from Pakistan Taliban-dominated tribal lords that they are prepared to fight on the eastern front against India if military action in their areas is put on hold. Such a diversion, or even the cooling down of India–Pakistan peace process, will also be cheered by sections of the Pakistan army and the defunct political wing of the ISI, which have never endorsed either Pakistan fighting 'the American War' in Afghanistan or improving its relations with India at the cost of the 'Kashmir issue'. These sections may be looking forward to the prospects of activating the 'Kashmir issue' in India–Pakistan relations in the context of a new United States administration which may not be averse to getting re-involved in the Kashmir dispute between the two South Asian neighbours to ensure the viability of its reinforced strategy in Afghanistan. The deep interest shown by United States president-elect, Barack Obama, in the Mumbai terror attack is reflective of these concerns. Extremist elements in Pakistan would be happy if increased United States involvement became a new source of tension between India and the United States.

India has a habit of learning through shocks and humiliations. The reflection of this shock is the resignations of home minister, Shivraj Patil, and national security adviser, M.K. Narayanan. Some more heads in the ministry of home affairs, intelligence establishments and the Maharashtra state government may roll. The Mumbai attack has exposed intelligence and security vulnerabilities of the Indian state. It has triggered a blame game between political and administrative decision makers on the one hand, and the role of the intelligence agencies on the other. The poor equipment and agility of the initial security response to such serious contingencies have also been exposed. It is hoped that the Mumbai attack would prove to be a watershed in revamping and tightening anti-terror mechanisms of the Indian state. In the wake of the Mumbai attack, the Indian people have also strongly and angrily reacted to the pathology of the political class in exploiting anything and everything that comes their way—from caste and religion to terror—for their immediate electoral gains. This may seem to be inevitable in a competitive democracy but the politicians would do better to identify some issues of national priority, such as fighting against terrorism, and ensuring the security of ordinary people, where they would shun playing politics. That would be the best tribute India's political class could pay to the dead in the Mumbai mayhem.

SECTION II

ECONOMIC DEVELOPMENT

A. Economic Reforms

24

Nepal: Political Uncertainties and Economic Challenges

MALMINDERJIT SINGH

(29 February 2008)

NEPAL, THE LAST surviving South Asian monarchy, is hoping for a fresh start as it attempts to establish a republic. This change in the Constitution by the interim legislature in December 2007, however, has to be endorsed during the Constituent Assembly elections proposed for April 2008. Nevertheless, there is a shadow of doubt over the probability of these elections as they have been postponed twice before in 2007.

The fresh waves of protests in the south of Nepal by activists of the United Democratic Madhesi Front (UDMF) since 12 February 2008 have resulted in a curfew and deployment of armed police in several districts of the Terai region which borders India. The UDMF failed to register any candidates by the 24 February 2008 deadline set for nominations. The Madhesis threaten to boycott the April 2008 general elections unless the government meets their demand for autonomy in the southern Terai region. Ironically, these elections were to be the first since the government signed a peace accord with the Maoist rebels in November 2006. The UDMF has now been joined by the Rastriya Janashakti Party (RJP) in boycotting the elections. Led by former Prime Minister Surya Bahadur Thapa, the RJP also did not submit any candidates for the April elections as it wants the Madhesi crisis to be settled first.

The implication of these latest protests in the Terai, an agricultural land, is damaging the economy as well. The protests blocked major roadways and highways, thus causing food and fuel shortages in other parts of the country, especially in Kathmandu.

As 62 per cent of Nepal's imports come from India, the Terai–Kathmandu network is central to the country. As such, the government-imposed curfew helped to unblock the main east-west road. Fuel tankers and gas trucks that arrived from India last week, were finally escorted by police to Kathmandu to ease the shortage there. This block in supply has already created a system of fuel rationing in the capital, with the government creating a fuel quota system under where vehicles are only allowed to be filled every second day based on the odd or even numbered registration plates. Even though Prime Minister Girija Prasad Koirala has confirmed that his government is willing to meet the Madhesi demands for greater rights, provided they take part in the April elections, he has rejected the Madhesi demand for autonomy. With both sides not willing to give in, there is little hope of the political protests ending anytime soon.

The constraints in the supply of fuel and key food products may result in inflationary pressures on the prices of goods in the country. Crude oil prices have more than tripled over the last five years from around US $30 to more than US $100 per barrel. Due to global increase in crude oil prices, the Nepal government hiked up the prices of petroleum products last month, only to be confronted by angry protests. Not wanting to arouse such hostilities in the wake of the Constituent Assembly elections, the government retracted its price hike decision. In doing so, though, the government has added to the financial woes of the Nepal Oil Corporation (NOC). As the debts on petrol imports from India worsen, the government needs to ask itself if it is willing to continue to pursue the costly policy of shielding consumers from the increasing global fuel prices. Undoubtedly, its decision against fuel price increases in January 2008 managed to prevent the prospects of the Constituent Assembly elections from being completely wiped out. However, the misalignment of domestic market fuel energy prices with global energy prices could be detrimental to the petroleum sector of the economy as well as worsening a deteriorating balance of trade with India.

Further, if the government continues to subsidise petroleum consumption in Nepal, its burgeoning national debt would probably lead to higher future taxes and, therefore, further add to poverty among the Nepalese people. As subsidies lead to increasing macroeconomic problems for the country, a scenario with decreasing supply and increasing demand would only lead to higher prices. In that case, larger subsidies would be needed from the government which would, inevitably, worsen the country's macroeconomic problems.

Critics have said that the Nepalese government should cut fuel taxes instead of introducing further subsidies. They argue that fuel tax, and not fuel price, is too high. The current Nepalese tax schedule on fuel, paid by the NOC as revenue to the government, consists of custom duties, charged at a flat rate on the volume of imports—value added tax (except on kerosene), local development tax and road maintenance charges. In 2006, the NOC ended up paying Nepali Rs 8 billion as tax revenue to the government. It is unlikely that the government will compromise on such a lucrative revenue, especially since it claims that this income is being re-employed in social sectors such as health care and education for the benefit of the poor. The government argues that, if it does not provide subsidies, then in the current scenario where inflation pressures have been building up, higher fuel prices could possibly lead to hyperinflation. Given the recent starving of fuel supplies, the government's argument may have some weight. However, it needs to realise that these subsidies, designed to protect the poor from escalating fuel costs, are in fact subsidising the relatively better off people who stock up fuel. Moreover, the fact that fuel prices may still increase due to current political instability, shows that inflation is inevitable. Hence, the Nepal government has to focus more on curbing the seemingly inevitable inflation as opposed to attempting to drive down the cost of fuel.

A major issue associated with inflation in Nepal lies in the policy adopted to combat it. The Nepal Rashtra Bank (NRB), the central bank of Nepal, has contained inflation within the country at 5.5 per cent over the last five years through its pegged exchange rate regime with the Indian currency. Although pegging the exchange rate provides a nominal anchor for Nepal to control inflation, the anchor used in this case may not be appropriate. With inflation lurking within the Indian economy itself, Nepal may be exposing itself to inflationary pressures from its neighbours. Thus, maintaining an exchange rate peg is not the ideal solution to Nepal's inflation problems. In addition to exposing itself to transmission shocks from India, it is also increasing the likelihood of external speculative attacks. Furthermore, an exchange rate peg entails a loss of independent monetary policy which possibly undermines the accountability of policy makers to pursue anti-inflationary policies. To make matters worse, such a strategy also exacerbates the financial fragility of the country and increases the probability of a financial crisis in Nepal. The Nepal government has to recognise the importance of monetary policy sovereignty and accord independent status to the NRB. The NRB, on the other hand, will have to complement this strategy by adopting an inflation-targeting regime that will effectively control price increases in the economy. This double-edged monetary policy strategy has worked in several countries such as the United Kingdom and Canada in controlling inflation.

Other economic challenges include the sluggish performance of the economy which has grown at only between 2 and 3 per cent since 2005, owing to the decline in the tourism and agricultural sectors. Forming almost 40 per cent of Nepal's gross domestic product, agriculture has declined in its annual growth since 2005 at levels below 2 per cent. Nevertheless, a bumper harvest this year in the vicinity of Kathmandu has kept the prices of agricultural products relatively low. Tourism, which had declined significantly in previous years due to the Maoist insurgency, picked up last year with improvements in the political climate. Particularly, tourism flows from India and South Asia increased to help provide a much needed stimulus in the economy. However, with the escalation of political tensions in the country again, the tourism sector can be expected to push the economy into further decline. Furthermore, as the Terai region is an industrial hub, instability there will be costly for the economy. As protestors attacked primarily the Indian-owned mills and factories and even shot an industrialist, Shashi Kant Agrawal, businesses remained closed under the curfew climate. This has caused a shortage of essential commodities such as rice in the capital city. With current supplies estimated to last barely more than a week, prices of such food items have soared by at least 10 per cent over the last fortnight. These indicators do not paint a healthy picture for the economy in Nepal.

The political uncertainties do not seem likely to end in the near future. Given the differences between the government and several of the political parties, elections are quite unlikely to take place in April 2008. At the same time, increases in prices of basic necessities have placed the Nepalese economy in a highly precarious situation. Indeed, an economic dilemma such as escalating inflation may jeopardise any hopes of political reforms, for the latter must be accompanied by economic liberalisation. With such mammoth challenges, only time will tell if Nepal will move on the path to becoming a republic or continue to remain in its current state of political and economic uncertainties.

25

The First Budget by the New Coalition Government in Pakistan: Economic Situation and Policy Directions

IFTIKHAR A. LODHI

(9 July 2008)

THE TROUBLED coalition government had its first federal budget (Fiscal Year 2008–9) passed[1] on 22 June 2008, after being in office for a hundred days, amid growing economic woes, political instability, and a deteriorating law and order situation. This paper analyses the budget in a broader macroeconomic framework and examines the policy initiatives that could put the economy back on track and provide the much needed relief to the common man.

This is the first budget presented jointly by two major rival parties, the right-centre, the Pakistan Muslim League-Nawaz [PML(N)] and the left-centre, the Pakistan People's Party (PPP). Despite the fact that the PPP, the leading coalition partner, is perceived as a populist party and the PML(N) as pro-business, there are no major differences, if at all, between the two on the economic front. Moreover, their economic policies do not differ from those of the previous government. Consequently, the budget is, by and large, a continuation of the policies set forth by the previous government. However, the budget has been overshadowed by the overall macroeconomic challenge of slowing growth, soaring inflation and widening fiscal and current account deficits.

> The PPP has come a long way to believe in 'private sector as engine of growth', 'open markets', and 'deregulated, decentralised and privatised economy', since sweeping away its first elections in 1970 with an agenda of establishing a 'socialist order' (by 'nationalising all major industires', while 'accepting the possibility of existence of a private sector').

Following the 18 February 2008 polls, the new government was faced with a political and economic crisis, along with a deteriorating law and order situation. The year 2007 saw Pakistan suffering from chaos and economic abyss, starting with the judicial crisis in March 2007, growing terrorist acts in urban areas, emergency rule, and the assassination of the PPP's leader, Benazir Bhutto. Besides domestic issues, global developments such as the slowdown in the United States' economy, the liquidity crisis, and soaring oil and primary commodity prices, also added to Pakistan's economic woes, given the historical vulnerability of the country's economy to external shocks.

BUDGET HIGHLIGHTS

Against all odds, Pakistan's economy has once again shown extraordinary resilience. The FY 2007–8 registered a respectable 5.8 per cent gross domestic product (GDP) growth, though far below the target of 7.2 per cent, and the actual growth rate of 6.8 per cent in FY 2006–7, pulling down the 7 per cent average GDP growth of the last four years.[2] Other macroeconomic indi-cators also showed a reverse trend.

THE TARGETS

The budget FY 2008–9 presents a 'long term perspective' in the backdrop of the following 'key assumptions about the macroeconomic conditions' in the year ahead:

- The GDP will grow by 5.5 per cent in the year 2008–9.
- Inflation will be contained at 12 per cent.
- Gross investment to GDP ratio will be maintained at 25 per cent.
- The fiscal deficit will be contained to 4 per cent.
- The current account deficit will be reduced to 6 per cent of the GDP.
- Foreign exchange reserves will be increased to US $12 billion.

Explaining the troubled economic situation, Syed Naveed Qamar, the finance minister, charged the previous government with 'policy inaction' in the face of economic crisis, shifting the 'brunt of all ills that were associated with these crises' to the current government. Nevertheless, he acknowledged the economic achievements of the outgoing administration, attributing to the 'windfalls of the aftermath of 9/11', an apparent hint to the increased formal remittances and a sizeable support, both in kind and in cash, from the partners in the 'war on terror'.[3]

The total outlay is estimated at Rs 2,010 billion (US $29.55 billion),[4] a 7.4 per cent increase from Rs 1,871 billion last year. The budget includes development spending of Rs 550 billion (US $8.08 billion), as compared to a revised spending of Rs 458 billion last year. This reflects a 20 per cent increase. Keeping in view the worsening domestic and international economic situation, it would have taken extraordinary structural initiatives to make the current budget 'poor-friendly'. Nevertheless, the budget announced some meagre populist measures, such as the Rs 34 billion (US $500 million) 'Benazir Income Support Program'; and the Rs 28 billion (US $411 million) 'People's Works Program', along with a 20 per cent increase in basic pay of all federal and defence personnel with a similar increase in pensions.

However, these measures are undermined by two most important policy changes; one, the phasing out of several subsidies, including petroleum, electricity, textile and food, which currently amount to Rs 407 billion (US $6 billion); and second, a blanket increase in the General Sales Tax from 15 to 16 per cent. Both these measures are bound to add to the existing double-digit inflation in the short run, irrespective of the distortive character of subsidies and long-run benefits of doing away with them.

Another major policy shift in the current budget was the discussion over defence spending in the National Assembly for the first time since the defence budget was classified in 1965. Despite Prime Minister Gilani's veiled promise to 'freeze the defence budget at current levels', the actual defence budget jumped 7 per cent to Rs 296 billion (US $4.35 billion) from last year's Rs 277 billion. Nonetheless, as compared to last year's 11 per cent increase, this is a welcome move.

The budget seeks to restore economic stability, growth momentum and investor's confidence by fiscal austerity; increasing agriculture and manufacturing productivity and competitiveness; spurring infrastructure development; reducing current account deficit; increasing revenue generation; and building up foreign exchange reserves while focusing on higher exports, employment generation, and increased social spending for a 'meaningful change' in the social indicators.

However, the targets (assumptions) actually reveal the limited space for manoeuvrability for the government in the face of evolving structural changes and external shocks. The targets, to begin with, are very modest, which, even if met successfully, would only slightly decelerate the economic downturn. More significantly, many of the rhetorical measures adopted could simply fail in the face of the waning state capacity to execute these policies.

The Twin Deficits: Impact of International Energy and Food Crisis

The fiscal deficit grew to 7 per cent of GDP, with an equally large current account deficit, against the target of 4.7 per cent in FY 2007–8.[5] Both the deficits are largely due to international oil and commodity price hikes apart from less than targeted revenue collections and export growth.[6]

A lack of appropriate demand estimation and price foresight on the part of the previous government contributed to the wheat crisis earlier this year. The government allowed wheat exports when prices were still low in June last year, only to be imported again at much higher prices earlier this year. Food and petroleum contributed to two-thirds of the increase in the import bill.[7]

However, much of this increase in the import bill was borne by the government in the form of subsidies, resulting in a large fiscal deficit. The outgoing administration funded deficit through borrowings from the central bank—the State Bank of Pakistan (SBP).[8] The result was compounded inflation, making monetary management difficult.[9] Inflation was precisely the reason, in the first place, for not passing the burden to the consumer.

The experts are convinced that energy and food prices will stay higher than their current levels in the foreseeable future. Therefore,

THE WAY FORWARD

- Phasing out subsidies on petroleum and electricity.
- Further shift towards natural gas for transportation and electricity generation.
- Exemption from tax and custom duty for energy saving equipment/ CNG buses.
- Accelerated efforts to import natural gas and build dams, in addition to increasing domestic exploration and production.
- Inviting foreign investments in the farm sector.
- Large tracts of land will be made available to foreign investors to induce capital and technology.
- Exemption from sales tax and other duties on imported and local supply of fertilizers pesticides and machinery.
- Exemption from the 10 per cent custom duty on import of rice seeds.
- Availability of farm credit on easy terms.
- Increased subsidy on fertilizer from Rs. 2.

it is imperative for the governments, as well as international institutions, to formulate policies for long-term solutions.[10]

The current government, upon assuming office, has adopted a multi-pronged strategy to tackle the challenges. In the long run, subsidies on petroleum and food will be phased out and resources will be enhanced through increased productivity, infrastructure development and a shift towards other alternatives of oil. In the short run, a tight monetary policy, foreign assistance and borrowings are the only options. As a first move, the government has sought Saudi Arabia's support for deferred payments on oil, a one-time US $300 million waiver, and future help in building strategic oil reserves.

Monetary Stance

The SBP, in a knee-jerk reaction to the mounting pressures, tightened its monetary policy in the last week of May 2008, the second time within four months.[11] In addition, to manage the exchange rate effectively and to stabilise the volatile stock exchange, the SBP introduced new regulations.[12] Despite the fact that the current inflationary pressures are largely due to higher government borrowings, a monetary response alone is not enough, given the lag between monetary adjustments and the real economy's response. Moreover, a tight monetary policy is likely to affect only non-energy, non-food inflation at the cost of growth. Therefore, the government's decision to phase out subsidies and other announced initiatives point in the right direction.

FISCAL DEVELOPMENTS

The tax revenue collection fell substantially short of its targets last year. The budget aims to raise tax revenues by 25 per cent in the year ahead.[13]

Pakistan's tax-to-GDP ratio has stagnated at about 10 per cent in the last decade, as compared to 17 per cent average for developing countries. The previous government embarked on a large-scale reform agenda but remained unsuccessful in raising the tax-to-GDP ratio to any significant level. Despite a 20 per cent annual increase in the number of taxpayers in the last three years, less than 2 per cent of the population pays tax, among the minimum in the region. There is a dire need to broaden the tax base. However, how the government tackles this problem has not been described in any specific terms.

On the contrary, the current budget plans to raise direct taxes ostensibly to balance the 'mismatch' between direct and indirect taxes, since the latter make up 62 per cent of total taxes. As a first step, the government has withdrawn 35 different income tax exemptions, in addition to introducing a progressive property tax. On the other hand, import duty on luxury items has also been raised along with 1 per cent increase in sales tax. As a result, any proportional change is unlikely to take place. The measures essentially mean an increased tax burden rather than an emphasis on broadening the tax base.

In addition to increasing revenue, the government targets to reduce expenditure substantially by phasing out subsidies and drastic cuts on non-development, non-salary expenditure, along with freezing the defence budget.[14] However, reining in expenditure

DIRECT TAXES

- Withdrawal of 35 income tax exemptions.
- A liberal 'Investment Tax Scheme' whereby taxpayers can voluntarily declare assets and pay 2 per cent on their market value.
- The lower bracket for tax exemption raised by 20 and 30 per cent for salaried men and women taxpayers respectively.
- A progressive 5 to 15 per cent tax on property income rather than the existing fixed 5 per cent.
- A Rs 100 per sq. ft tax on real estate developers.

INDIRECT TAXES

- Increase from 15–25 per cent import duty on luxury items to 30–35 per cent.
- Increase from 90 to 100 per cent custom duty on luxury vehicles.
- Increase in the sales tax from 15 to 16 per cent.
- Increase in the Federal Excise Duty on telecommunication services from 15 to 21 per cent and on banking, insurance and franchise services from 5 to 10 per cent.

could prove difficult as the need for large infrastructure investments and the on-going large-scale administrative reforms would require extra resources.[15] Moreover, besides political costs, the plans for a phased end to subsidies will not be trouble free. For example, the big business lobby in the textile sector has already made inroads to avail itself of Rs 30 billion discriminatory subsidies, without any such provision in the current budget.[16]

On the other hand, public debt, which was brought down to 55 per cent of GDP at the end of FY 2006–7 from 85 per cent in 2000, has started to grow due to a sharp depreciation of the rupee *vis-à-vis* the United States dollar, besides the twin deficits. This trend is likely to continue as the current government would have to bear the brunt of increased interest payments, payments on maturity of the sovereign bonds, and Paris Club payments.[17] The privatisation proceeds are also likely to decline. Although the budget announces 10 per cent shares for the workers of privatised enterprises, the government still runs into the danger of a political backlash during the process.[18]

To finance the debt and deficit, following the footsteps of the outgoing administration, the current government plans to introduce different short-term sovereign bonds and to encourage global depository receipts (GDR) by public (and private) entities. It also plans to increase interest rates on national saving certificates.[19] These steps intend to curtail borrowings from the SBP, which had reached 'alarming levels'.[20] However, the recent degrading of Pakistan's credit ratings by Moody's and Standard & Poor (S&P), and the looming political and economic uncertainties have already eroded investor confidence, making it difficult for the coalition government to pursue such policies with greater success.[21]

Growth and Investment

A dismal performance of the agriculture sector significantly contributed to a lower GDP growth: it grew by only 1.5 per cent against 3.7 per cent last year. While the services sector grew by 8.2 per cent, the manufacturing sector registered a modest growth of 5.2 per cent, with the major share coming from construction. The agriculture sector, despite its decline in overall GDP to 19 per cent, still employs half of the labour force and contributes directly or indirectly to 60 per cent of the total exports. It is therefore imperative to enhance its productivity.

The government has prioritised agriculture and allocated Rs 75 billion for improved water access, along with doubling subsidies on fertilizers and raising wheat support price, in addition to tax incentives and inviting foreign investment. The acute power shortages and a poor infrastructure significantly reduced productivity of the manufacturing and agricultural sectors. Besides measures to deal with infrastructure deficiencies, custom duty on many raw materials and equipments such as port dredgers and power plants has been reduced to zero. In addition, investments of more than US $50 million have been made free from any domestic partnership. Capital gain tax exemptions on foreign capital and tax holidays are expected to attract more foreign investment.

Investment has been the main driver of recent economic growth, followed by consumption, standing at above 20 per cent of GDP.

However, this level of investment is unsustainable, due to political uncertainties and the international situation. Economic hardship has visibly affected national and domestic savings, which declined to 14 and 11.7 per cent of GDP from 18 and 16 per cent respectively. Moreover, there has been an increase in share of private *vis-à-vis* public investment from 64 to 74 per cent in the last five years, making the economy more sensitive to investor confidence. Foreign investments have declined to US $3.6 billion (July–April) against US $5.3 billion in the same period last year, largely due to the decline in portfolio investments. If the political uncertainties continue, direct investments are likely to decline.

Social Sector

Pakistan, being a classic example of 'growth without development', attracts special attention. Despite maintaining an average 5 per cent GDP growth over the last 50 years, it ranks relatively very low (136) on the human development index. For decades, successive governments have neglected the social sector due to huge interest payments and defense budget. There have been some achievements in terms of increased per capita income and reduced poverty incidence in recent years.[22] However, spending on education and health remains low. The demographic dividend poses major challenges in terms of employment generation, given the 7 per cent unemployment, and a large underemployment incidence.[23]

The government has decided to double the development budget for education. However, there is no substantial change in the health budget, which stands at 0.6 per cent of gross national product. The 'Benazir Income Support Program' is introduced to protect the poorest of the poor through distributing Rs 1,000 per month cash grants to each qualifying household. The 'People's Works Program' will provide employment while engaging in local infrastructure development. However, both of these programmes run the danger of bureaucratic red tapes and corruption. It is highly unlikely that the benefits will reach the target groups.[24] Nevertheless, only the doubling of the development budget for education seems to be the step forward.

Conclusion

Pakistan's economy has shown resilience, and despite all odds, has continued to grow. However, international oil and commodity prices, along with a slow growth in agriculture and exports have posed serious challenges. Continued political instability, violence, and wrangling over power between the PPP and the PML(N) have put economic management on the back burner. The economic challenges are compounded by the fact that neither of the parties has a commendable record on economic management. Increased policy uncertainty is likely to impede both domestic and foreign investment.

Moreover, the lack of political direction can further weaken the government's capacity to implement the policies spelt out in the budget. However, the previously-initiated structural changes in the economy are unlikely to be reversed. The budget FY 2008–9 has set modest targets but remains largely rhetorical. The coalition partners have repeatedly made similar promises in their earlier tenures. What would make the results different this time around remains anybody's guess.

NOTES

1. The fiscal year in Pakistan starts from 1 July and ends on 30 June.
2. The data in this paper, unless otherwise stated, is from the 'Economic Survey of Pakistan, FY 2007–8', 'Finance Minister Budget FY 2008–9 Speech', and 'Budget FY 2008–9 in Brief'. These three documents are published by the Ministry of Finance, Government of Pakistan. They are available online at http://finance.gov.pk/admin/images/budget/budget[1].pdf.
3. (a) Pakistan received US $10 billion from the United States since 9/11, though two-thirds of this amount is reimbursement payments for the expenses of 100,000 troops deployed on the Pakistan–Afghanistan border.
   (b) The international financial institutions rescheduled Pakistan's debt after it joined 'the war on terror' in the aftermath of 9/11. Similarly, the military assistance given to Pakistan for being a major non-North Atlantic Treaty Organization (NATO) ally reduced pressures on domestic resources. Pakistan's Paris Club debt of US $12.5 billion was rescheduled

in 2002. In April 2003, US $1 billion American bilateral debt was written off. This is a clear signal for the capital markets that Pakistan is 'too important to default' for geo-strategic reasons.

(c) In another development, increased economic activity was witnessed, particularly in transport, construction and commodity sectors, due to supplies to NATO's International Security Assistance Force in Afghanistan.

4. By current interbank rates, Rs 68 = US $1. The June 2008 average was Rs 67.50.

5. The current account deficit is expected to be well above 7.3 per cent of GDP far above the targeted 5 per cent, a 40 per cent increase from the previous year. This was a direct result of 28 per cent increase in imports, fuelled by strong demand and high oil prices, and only 7.6 per cent increase in exports, far below the target of 12.9 per cent but still impressive as compared to last year's 3 per cent. Nonetheless, the adverse effect on the overall balance of payments was cushioned by an impressive growth in remittances. Remittances grew by 19 per cent, totalling US $5.9 billion (July 2007–May 2008).

   The impact of the rising current account deficit on the balance of payments was further compounded by capital outflows and delays in the planned floatation of a sovereign bond. Subsequently, the exchange reserve build-up began to shrink from US $16.5 billion in October 2007 to less than US $11.2 billion at the end of May 2008. The rupee depreciated against the United States dollar by 6.4 per cent between July 2007 and April 2008, despite the United States dollar's own depreciation against major currencies.

6. Oil prices surged from US $55 per barrel in January 2007 to US $140 per barrel in May 2008, a jump of more than 155 per cent. Similarly international food price index increased by roughly 40 per cent in 2007 and, in the first three months of 2008, prices rose by about 50 per cent. The prices of rice, wheat and palm oil have also increased by 78 per cent, 120 per cent and 102 per cent respectively between April 2007 and April 2008. (Islam 2008, 'Of Agflation and Agriculture').

7. Pakistan imported 80 per cent of its 127.75 million barrels of oil in FY 2006–7, constituting 27 per cent of its import bill. Petroleum imports grew by 41 per cent between July 2007 and May 2008 to reach US $9.39 billion, as compared to US $6.63 billion over the same period last year. Food and dairy imports grew by 45 per cent to US $3.28 billion from July 2007 to May 2008, as compared to US $2.26 billion over the same period last year, mainly due to wheat and palm oil.

8. 'Interim Monetary Policy Measures', State Bank of Pakistan, May 2008, p. 10. http://www.sbp.org.pk/m_policy/MPS-MAY-FY08-EN.pdf.

The subsidies increased from a provision of Rs 114 billion (US $1.67 billion—1.1 per cent of GDP) in last year's budget to Rs 407 billion (US $6 billion—3.9 per cent of GDP). As much as Rs 551 billion (US $8.10 billion—up to May 2008) has been borrowed from the Central Bank against the full year budgeted estimate of Rs 399 billion (US $5.86 billion), which is unprecedented in the country's history.

The shortfall in external financing receipts due to tight liquidity and strong credit demand made it difficult for the government to mobilise substantial amounts through treasury bills, which could have eased up inflationary pressures.

9. Consumer Price Index (CPI) inflation soared to 10.8 per cent in May 2008, as compared to 7.8 per cent last year on a 12-month moving average. The highest rise was registered in May 2008 when CPI inflation jumped to 19.3 per cent on year-on-year basis, while food inflation touched 28.5 per cent during the same month—the highest in three decades.
10. M. Shahid Islam, 'Of Agflation and Agriculture: Time to Fix the Structural Problems', ISAS Insight No. 30, 5 May 2008—Quoted International Monetary Fund. http://www.isasnus.org/events/insights/31.pdf.
11. The SBP has raised its lending rate by 1.5 per cent points to 12 per cent and the cash reserve ratio requirement by one percentage point to 9 per cent for all deposits with a maturity of more than 12 months.
12. For details of regulations see 'Interim Monetary Policy Measures', State Bank of Pakistan, May 2008. http://www.sbp.org.pk/m_policy/MPS-MAY-FY08-EN.pdf
13. To Rs 1,250 billion (US $18.38 billion) from Rs 1,000 billion (US $14.70 billion) in FY 2007–8.
14. Some of the proposed measures include ban on purchase of assets, and budgetary cuts for the Prime Minister Secretariat, National Assembly and Senate.
15. The revised total expenditure for FY 2007–8 stands at Rs 2,228.9 billion (US $32.77 billion), actually budgeted at Rs 1,875 billion (US $27.5 billion).
16. 'ECC set to grant Rs 30bn subsidy to textile sector', *Pak Tribune*, 1 July 2008, http://www.paktribune. com/news/index.shtml?202627
17. The oversubscribed US $500 million Eurobond will mature in 2009 and Sukuk will mature in 2010. Moreover, the Paris Club payments that were rescheduled in 2002 will be due in 2009.
18. The privatisation proceeds stand at Rs 1.65 billion in FY 2007–8 against the actual target of Rs 75 billion. All the public entities, which were privatised, witnessed workers' strikes in which the PPP trade unions played

an active role. Pakistan Telecommunication Corporation Limited incurred huge costs in laying off workers after Dubai-based Etislat purchased 26 per cent shares. The privatisation of Pakistan Steel Mills was stopped by the Supreme Court on charges of a non-transparent process.

19. The previous government launched controversial sovereign bonds (Euro 2004, Sukuk 2005) and a number of GDRs by public and private entities, to raise capital from international markets.
20. The SBP also advised the government to amend the Fiscal Responsibility and Debt Limitation Act 2005 to disallow borrowings from the SBP. The law introduced greater fiscal discipline and transparency along with guidelines on social sector spending.
21. Both Moody's and S&P cut Pakistan's credit ratings to five levels below investment-grade from B1 to B2. Though Moody's maintained a stable outlook, S&P opted for a negative outlook. Moody's Report read: 'weak governance, political tensions and flaws in the legal system will undermine institutions . . . sharply widening [twin] deficits . . . are reversing a multi-year trend of fiscal consolidation and debt reduction . . . renewed political discord is unlikely to provide the stable and orthodox policy framework necessary for quickly limiting these macroeconomic imbalances'. 'Pakistan Risks Losing Investor Confidence', *Business Recorder*, 14 June 2008. http://www.brecorder.com/latestindex.php?latest_id=8152&cindex=23¤t_page=1
22. The per capita income has grown at an average rate of 13.5 per cent per annum during the last six years rising from US $586 in 2002–3 to US $1,085 in 2007–8, thanks to a fourfold increase in remittances. Poverty (headcount ratio on Rs 994 per month poverty line) incidence has fallen from 28 per cent to 23 per cent during the same period.
23. Since 60 per cent of the population is under 25 years of age.
24. There are empirical studies showing the number of such programmes, which failed to do what they intended to.

26

Pakistan's Economic Crisis and the IMF Bailout Package

IFTIKHAR A. LODHI

(9 December 2008)

THE INTERNATIONAL Monetary Fund (IMF) has approved a US $7.6 billion bailout package to prevent Pakistan from defaulting on its external debt. The 23-month Stand-By Arrangement under the Fund's fast-track Emergency Financing Mechanism has provided an immediate US $3.1 billion funding to strengthen the country's fast deteriorating foreign exchange reserves. The programme seeks to preserve social stability and restore investor confidence in Pakistan by addressing its current macroeconomic imbalances. At the same time, it sends a strong signal to the international donor community about the country's improved macroeconomic prospects.

Pakistan approached the IMF for assistance in November 2008 to avert a default on its foreign payments. The country requires roughly US $15–20 billion over the next two years to avoid a Balance of Payment (BoP) crisis. The Pakistani authorities were initially reluctant to turn to the IMF because of the expected stringent conditions, terming it Plan C—the last option. Plans A and B included frontload disbursements from multilateral institutions, borrowing from the international market and making an approach to friendly countries for help. Despite receiving some support from multilateral lenders and some friendly countries, Pakistan's primary request for immediate cash infusions were turned down, given weakened investor confidence in the economy. The government then turned to the IMF.

This paper seeks to examine three key issues. First, how did an economy with robust macroeconomic indicators until last year reach this critical stage? Second, why did Pakistan's closest allies, including the United States and China, let it down? Last, what will be the likely economic and political implications of the IMF arrangement?

Anatomy of the Crisis

There is no doubt that an adverse external economic environment in the shape of unprecedented high levels of oil and commodity prices earlier this year and the current global financial crisis have largely contributed to the crisis in Pakistan today. Nevertheless, the genesis of the current crisis is internal. The key reasons for the current meltdown of the economy are continued political turmoil, deteriorating security, structural issues and the unsustainable growth policies in recent years.

Pakistan's economy has dramatically gone from high growth rates and burgeoning foreign exchange reserves to a state of crisis in less than a year. Real gross domestic product (GDP) growth has declined, foreign exchange reserves are depleted, the current account and fiscal deficits have blown up, net capital inflows have reversed significantly, inflation hovers around 25 per cent and the rupee has depreciated sharply by around 25 per cent. The Karachi Stock Exchange has been in a free-fall, nosediving from the year high of 15,000 points to 9,200 in three months, forcing the government to intervene by placing a floor and proposing a bailout plan.[1]

An imminent BoP crisis loomed large when the current government assumed office in March 2008. The current account deficit (CAD) more than doubled in the fiscal year 2008 (ending at 30 June 2008). The CAD soared to US $14.04 billion (8.4 per cent of GDP) from US $6.87 billion last year (see Figure 1), the highest in the history of the country. The fundamental source of such a steep increase in the CAD was a 57 per cent expansion in the trade deficit over the year, in addition to an increase in net outflows from income account.

Since 2001, the fast-paced liberalisation of the economy, leading to sharp reductions in tariffs and robust demand growth, caused a steady increase in imports. On the other hand, the growth in exports

Figure 1: Pakistan's Trade and Current Account Balance (FY 2003–FY 2008)

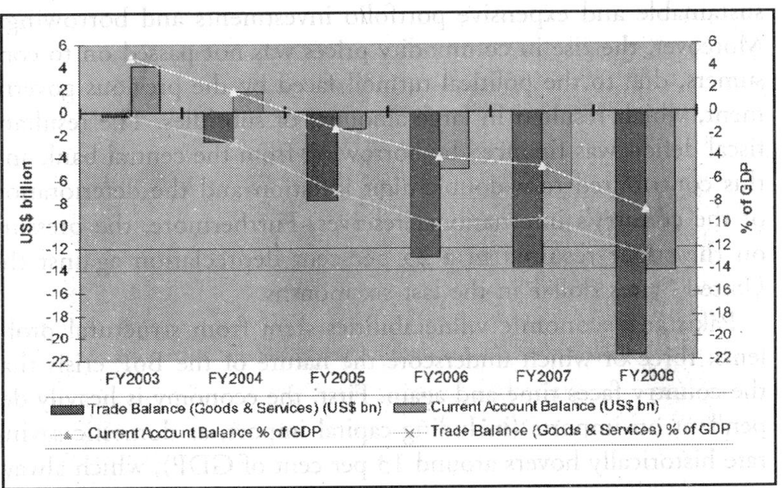

Source: State Bank of Pakistan and the IMF.

could not keep pace with imports, resulting in huge trade deficits (goods and services) over the years. The trade deficit rose to US $21.6 billion in FY 2008 from US $13.9 billion in FY 2007 and a mere US $361 million in FY 2003 (see Figure 1). Consequently, the current account balance deteriorated steadily from a surplus of US $4 billion in FY 2003 to a deficit of US $14 billion in FY 2008, despite a robust growth in remittances.

Almost half of the additional merchandise import bill in FY 2008 came from the food and oil sectors, which registered 46 per cent and 43 per cent growth respectively.[2] Nevertheless, non-oil and non-food imports grew by 21 per cent, as compared to a 12 per cent growth in exports.

In the first four months of the FY 2009 (July–October 2008), a similar trend continues. The trade deficit reached US $7.55 billion against US $5.47 billion in the same period last year, a 37 per cent increase. Furthermore, net inflows have reduced substantially, resulting in almost a doubling of the CAD to US $5.95 billion from US $2.99 billion over the same period last year.

A sustainable moderate CAD may not pose a problem as such. However, the previous government financed the deficit by unsustainable and expensive portfolio investments and borrowings. Moreover, the rise in commodity prices was not passed on to consumers, due to the political turmoil faced by the previous government, which resulted in large amounts of subsidies. The resultant fiscal deficit was financed by borrowing from the central bank and this contributed to a double-digit inflation and the deterioration of the country's international reserves. Furthermore, the pressure on the rupee resulted in a 25 per cent depreciation against the United States dollar in the last six months.

Pakistan's economic vulnerabilities stem from structural problems, three of which underscore the nature of the BoP crisis that the country faces time and again. First, the economy is heavily dependant on imports (including capital import, as domestic saving rate historically hovers around 13 per cent of GDP), which always surpasses exports. Exports, on the other hand, are limited in commodity types and destination countries, leaving the country in the current account deficit and vulnerable to external shocks. Second, the tax-to-GDP ratio (10 per cent) is far below the average 17 per cent for developing countries, and less than 2 per cent of the population is covered by the tax net. The huge government expenditure on debt payments, and defence and current spending resulted in huge fiscal deficits that reached 7.4 per cent of GDP in FY 2008. Last but not least, public debt remains as high as 55 per cent of GDP, albeit a significant improvement from 90 per cent of GDP in FY 2000. External debt makes up 27 per cent of GDP (FY 2008), down from 43 per cent in FY 1999.

However, much of the improvement in the country's debt position was the result of a favourable external environment. Pakistan's cooperation with the United States in the 'war on terror' resulted in relief in public debt amounting to about US $3.7 billion, coupled with a rescheduling of a US $12.5 billion Paris Club debt. These resulted in a substantially reduced debt service burden which was 12.8 per cent in FY 2008, as compared to 28 per cent in FY 1999. The military and economic assistance provided by the United States helped, to some extent, to ease the burden on fiscal resources.

Moreover, the liberalisation of the capital account and international controls over informal money transfers after the September 11 attacks resulted in increased investments and remittances. Since the start of FY 2008, the external and internal environments have become less favourable for borrowing. There has also been a significant decline in capital inflows. Consequently, the government failed to float planned sovereign bond and global depository receipts, due to the political turmoil at home and as a result of the global financial crisis. For all the above reasons, the foreign exchange reserves began to shrink from US $15.6 billion in October 2007 to less than US $3.5 billion in October 2008, merely enough to support four weeks of imports, in the face of maturing liabilities. As a result, external debt and liabilities, as a proportion of foreign exchange reserves, reached a staggering 900 per cent at the end of September 2008, against 300 per cent a year ago, making it impossible to fulfil international obligations.

Friends of Pakistan: Economics and the 'War on Terror'

After failing to mobilise capital from the international market, Pakistan turned to several friendly countries. Saudi Arabia, a long-time friend of Pakistan, which had helped the country out of a similar crisis in 1999 after the nuclear tests, was less than enthusiastic about Pakistan's requests for deferred payments on oil imports. Nevertheless, Pakistani government sources claim that it received a 'positive response' from the kingdom.

China, another all-weather friend of Pakistan with huge excess foreign reserves, declined any major cash infusion and President Asif Ali Zardari's visit to China in October 2008 only yielded US $500 million, with promises of investments and trade opportunities to help Pakistan. It is likely that Beijing wants to keep a low profile. Its growing investments and cooperation with Pakistan have already raised eyebrows in Washington and New Delhi. There have been suspicions that, after the India–United States nuclear deal, China and Pakistan may attempt a similar nuclear cooperation. Furthermore, it is only wise for China to let the Americans take care of their 'front line ally' in the 'war on terror'.

The United States, wary of Islamabad's commitment (and capacity) to fight militants' mounting insurgency in Afghanistan against United States-led forces, has been moving towards a multilateral approach in tackling Pakistan's crisis. The Bush administration, bogged down by the worst financial crisis since the Great Depression, has also dragged its feet on a bill promising US $1.5 billion annual economic aid over a period of 10 years for Pakistan. The aid is conditional upon Islamabad's 'performance' in the fight against militants. Washington reportedly wants Pakistan to refocus its military strategy to fighting the militants and normalising relations with India, said a Pakistani diplomat privy to the negotiations while talking to the daily *Dawn*.[3] Therefore, by involving major stakeholders in regional stability, Washington wants to share its burden on the 'war on terror'. Washington threw its weight behind the formation of the Friends of Pakistan (FoP)[4] group to help Pakistan overcome its political and economic challenges by developing a comprehensive and coordinated approach to security, development and institutional issues facing the country. The group reportedly wanted Pakistan to get an IMF loan approval which would assure careful management of the economy and instil greater investor confidence.

The IMF Arrangement and its Implications

In fact, 'by providing large financial support to Pakistan, the IMF is sending a strong signal to the donor community about the country's improved macroeconomic prospects', said IMF Deputy Managing Director, Takatoshi Kato. The Managing Director of the Fund, Dominique Strauss-Kahn, urged the donor community to 'work together and act quickly to support Pakistan's programme in order to mitigate the impact of the current economic difficulties'.

The IMF arrangement is part of a broader package which involves other multilateral institutions and donor countries. It aims to restore macroeconomic stability and investor confidence through a tightening of fiscal and monetary policies, while simultaneously preserving social stability and adequate support for the poor, stated the press release issued by the IMF. The loan tranches are subject to quarterly reviews by the IMF which has set forth certain conditions. Nevertheless, most of the 'conditions' are already part of the government's economic agenda announced during the FY 2009 budget in June this year.

The Fund stipulates bringing Pakistan's fiscal deficit down from 7.4 per cent of GDP in FY 2008 to 4.5 per cent in FY 2009 and 3.3 per cent in 2009/10 by phasing out energy and electricity subsidies and strengthening revenue mobilisation through tax policy and administration measures.

These measures, if implemented successfully, will help to meet the target to some extent, particularly the phasing out of subsidies.[5] In the short run, reforms in tax administration and, particularly the 1 per cent increase in the general sales tax (from 15 to 16 per cent implemented in the FY 2009 budget) will help raise tax-to-GDP ratio. In the medium term, the government will have to take a number of measures such as eliminating exemptions in the general sales tax and the income tax, and introducing a commercial agriculture tax.[6] There will also be cuts on development projects through 'reprioritisation', depending on loans from elsewhere. To provide support to the poor and vulnerable, spending on the social safety net will be increased from 0.6 to 0.9 per cent of GDP in FY 2009 with the help of the World Bank.

The IMF arrangement also stipulates tightening the country's monetary policy, bringing down inflation to six per cent in FY 2010 and ensuring zero government borrowing from the central bank. These measures too are in congruence with the State Bank of Pakistan's (SBP) announced monetary policy goals. In fact, the SBP has raised interest rates three times since January 2008, reaching 15 per cent in November 2008.

Nevertheless, inflation remains uncontrollable. While food and energy inflation is expected to come down with the easing of supply shortages and a fall in international oil prices, the persistent acceleration in core inflation remains a matter of concern. By October 2008, the year-on-year non-food, non-energy core inflation rose to 18.3 per cent from 13 per cent in June 2008.[7] If this trend continues, the FY 2009 inflation could reach 21 per cent, far above the target of 11 per cent set for the current year, according to the IMF and the SBP estimates.

THE DEBATE

Pakistan is in a 'Catch-22' situation. As a matter of fact, the current inflationary pressures are largely due to higher government borrowings, besides exogenous price shocks. However, the measures taken (revoking subsidies, increasing sales tax, etc.) to arrest growing fiscal deficit are fueling inflation. The large external account deficit and slowdown of capital inflows, due to domestic turmoil and international crisis, are also exerting pressure on the rupee, which has depreciated 25 per cent in six months. The net effect of depreciation in the value of the rupee, in the presence of huge inflation, has exacerbated inflation by raising input costs. Moreover, the recession in Pakistan's top export markets is also likely to hurt export growth. The IMF has already reduced Pakistan's GDP growth projections to 3.5 per cent in FY 2009. This vicious cycle is likely to cause a less than expected revenue generation and a more than targetted fiscal and current account deficit.

In view of such a scenario, a contractionary monetary policy and austere fiscal measures are not enough. Many analysts in Pakistan and abroad have criticised the IMF and the Pakistan government. A case in point is an editorial in the *Wall Street Journal* (*WSJ*) saying, 'Pakistan needs market-oriented reforms along the Chilean and Irish models, not the IMF's austerity prescriptions.'[8] Though many in Pakistan may not agree with the alternative suggested by the *WSJ*, there is an increasing concern over high interest rates, cuts on development expenditure and increase in taxes.

The IMF and the Pakistani authorities, on the other hand, are of the view that the economic crisis in Pakistan is different from global developments where many developed and developing countries have gone for fiscal stimulus and monetary easing. In contrast, Pakistan, says the SBP report:

. . . hit by the global commodity price shock and given the delays in (the) pass-through of this price effect, witnessed a growth in its fiscal and external current account deficits that reached unsustainable levels and alarmingly high inflation. With stagnating tax to GDP ratio, this not only enhanced recourse to borrowings from the SBP but also resulted in a fall in foreign exchange reserves, triggering depreciation in the exchange rate. Since there are significant differences in 'diagnostics' among Pakistan and other countries it must be recognised that the policy solutions will also be different.[9]

The IMF pointed out in its press statement that 'the program and its conditionality is based on the targets and measures that the authorities have set for themselves for the next two years. The IMF is convinced that the best implemented programs are the ones that are homegrown and fully owned by the country.' Alongside the IMF's financial support, 'there is an urgent need to mobilise additional donor support to strengthen Pakistan's resilience to potential shocks, help finance the expanded social safety net, and allow for higher spending on development programs', said the statement.[10]

To be fair, the above 'conditions' have nothing to do with the current IMF loan and were on the government's agenda earlier. Nevertheless, the Fund's oversight will restore some confidence in the economy. At the moment, Pakistan's foreign credit rating has practically hit rock bottom. Standard & Poor has lowered Pakistan's foreign credit rating three times in the current year to 'CCC', eight levels below investment grade and it has kept Pakistan on the watch list. Both the IMF and the Pakistani authorities are hoping that investor confidence will be restored and foreign capital will start flowing in.

There has also been an intensive debate in Pakistan in favour of and against the expected IMF 'conditions'. Two such reported 'conditions' included the cuts on defence expenditure and the imposition of an agriculture tax. However, in reality, there were no discussions whatsoever on the defence budget in the negotiations with the Fund[11] while the tax on commercial agriculture was set as a medium- to long-term agenda. In fact, tax on commercial agriculture in Pakistan is less likely to hurt the poor than the feudal landlords. There have been calls for an agriculture tax for a long time but this has always been put down by the powerful landowners who also sit on the legislative benches.

Conclusion

Apart from the Musharraf regime, no other Pakistani government has been able to meet the benchmarks of economic reforms imposed by the Fund since the first agreement between the IMF and Pakistan was signed in the 1980s. This has resulted in the premature termination of these agreements. The Musharraf regime owed its performance to its undemocratic origins and to indirect (and direct) assistance from the United States.

It remains to be seen if Pakistan will abide by the IMF conditions this time around. How these measures would help or hurt the economy depends on several factors, including oil and food prices, the global financial crisis, and Pakistan's domestic security and its political situation. In the final analysis, much would depend on Islamabad's ability to quell militancy and keep Washington and other donors on its side by providing stable and secure business climate through good governance.

NOTES

1. All data, unless otherwise stated, is from the State Bank of Pakistan and the International Monetary Fund.
2. Oil prices surged from US $55 per barrel in January 2007 to US $140 per barrel in May 2008, a jump of more than 155 per cent. Similarly international food price index increased by roughly 40 per cent in 2007 and, in the first three months of 2008, prices rose by about 50 per cent. The prices of rice, wheat and palm oil also increased by 78 per cent, 120 per cent and 102 per cent respectively between April 2007 and April 2008. M. Shahid, Islam, 'Of Agflation and Agriculture: Time to Fix the Structural Problems', ISAS Insight No. 30, 5 May 2008—Quoted International Monetary Fund. http://www.isasnus.org/events/insights/31.pdf.
3. Iqbal Anwar (2008), 'IMF not Pressing for Defence Cuts', *Dawn*, 26 October, http://www.dawn.com/ 2008/10/26/top18.htm

4. The FoP was formed during President Zardari's visit to America in September 2008 on the margins of the United Nations General Assembly session. The FoP includes the G7 countries, plus Australia, China, Turkey, Saudi Arabia, the United Arab Emirates, the United Nations and the European Union.
5. The subsidies increased from a provision of Rs 114 billion (US $1.67 billion—1.1 per cent of GDP) in the FY 2008 budget to Rs 407 billion (US $6 billion—3.9 per cent of GDP).
6. The government also envisages, in the budget, to increase tax-to-GDP ratio from 10 per cent to 15 per cent within the next five to seven years.
7. The 20 per cent weighted trimmed measure of core inflation reflects steeper inflationary pressure as it rose to 21.7 per cent in October 2008 from 17.2 per cent in June 2008.
8. 'Pakistan's Plan C, Does the IMF have no Fresh Ideas?', *The Wall Street Journal*, 28 October 2008. http://online.wsj.com/article/SB12251339 7704572755.html?mod=relevancy
9. 'Interim Monetary Policy Measures', State Bank of Pakistan, November 2008. http://www.sbp.org.pk/m_ policy/MPS-MAY-FY08-EN.pdf
10. 'IMF Executive Board Approves US $7.6 billion Stand-By Arrangement for Pakistan', International Monetary Fund, 24 November 2008. http:// www.imf.org/external/country/PAK/index.htm
11. And rightly so, given the current security situation, it would be naïve to think that the IMF would cut defence expenditure.

27

Will the UPA Victory in the Trust Vote Result in Faster Economic Reforms?

AMITENDU PALIT

(29 July 2008)

AS THE CURTAINS came down on an action-packed two-day session of the Indian parliament with the United Progressive Alliance (UPA) government surviving a close trust vote, the stock market erupted with joy. On 23 July 2008, the day after the trust vote, the benchmark Sensex at the Bombay Stock Exchange gained 838 points (almost 6 per cent) in a single day's trade. The Nifty at the National Stock Exchange also responded in an equally robust manner. The signals emanating from the rally were loud and clear. Industry and business were ecstatic at the outcome of the trust vote.

Though many were expecting the markets to respond favourably to the outcome, the reaction was probably greater than anticipated. The spurts in the Sensex and Nifty marked significant departures from the prevailing market trend given that bourses have been largely bearish since early 2008. The euphoria indicated that the survival and continuation of the UPA government was a 'shot-in-the-arm' for a capital market that has been plagued by adverse sentiments following high inflation, withdrawal of short-term capital flows, worrying dips in industrial and core sector output, and warning signals from international rating agencies.

It is simplistic to assume that stock market movements capture the sentiments of all segments of the economy. The stock market reflects more of the immediate perceptions on risk-return payoffs. At the same time, there is no denying that it resonates the gut impulse of business and industry. So why did the stock market respond so positively following the trust vote? For industry and business, the continuation of the UPA government minus the Left implies the revival and constructive movement on a long-pending economic reform agenda. The Left was perceived to be the major roadblock to key reforms. During the last couple of years, there were several occasions when the government was forced to backtrack on policy measures on which the Left had taken radically different positions. These included reforms in vital segments of the financial sector such as pension, insurance and banking, and disinvestment of government stake in public sector undertakings.

Financial sector reforms have indeed suffered in recent years. Several bills mooting major changes in policies in different financial segments are pending passage in parliament. In insurance, for example, there is a proposal to increase the threshold limit of foreign equity in joint ventures from the current ceiling of 26 per cent to 49 per cent. The measure, whenever approved, is expected to encourage several global insurance service providers (both life and non-life) to tap the underexploited Indian market, where less than a tenth of the population is insured. The policy has obvious implications for incoming foreign direct investment in India. Similarly, in pension, there have been attempts to set up a regulator for the sector for quite a few years now. Once the legislation proposing the establishment of the Pension Funds Regulatory and Development Authority (PFRDA) is approved, it will pave the way for private fund managers to enter India's pension industry. This is an urgent and critical reform that has been pending for long. A functional PFRDA will not only help in creating a competitive environment in the pension industry, but will also help in making resources available for long-term investment purposes, particularly in infrastructure projects. Finally, in banking, the government has been trying hard to bring down its stake to below 50 per cent of the total equity base in public sector banks. However, sustained opposition from the Left has prevented it from doing so.

There is little doubt that, if in the few months left in its tenure, the UPA government is able to get these legislations cleared, it will provide a strong boost to the sagging morale of the capital market. The portfolio investment inflows from Foreign Institutional Investors (FII), which have been the strongest drivers of the Indian stock market and have been lukewarm in recent months, are likely to rebound with new vigour. The pension reforms can trigger an immediate recovery, which can derive further stimulus and strength from insurance and banking reforms.

At this juncture, however, it is probably important to think through the prevailing euphoria for assessing how much of reforms are possible in the coming months. Notwithstanding the expectations of stock market actors and agents and the benefits that can accrue from pending reforms, will these actually happen? And what about the reforms which are supposed to address deeper structural imbalances such as the privatisation of public enterprises and reduction of subsidies? With the Left out of the way, will these much-needed reforms also receive the desired attention?

As far as financial sector reforms are concerned, the passage of pending legislations depends on the success of the government in convincing its new allies. The Samajwadi Party has given the assurance that it will adopt an 'open mind' on reforms. Having said this, an important point cannot be overlooked. A consensus on economic reforms within the new political alliance will depend upon the perceived impact of such reforms on the electorate. Fortunately, regarding pension and insurance, barring the Left, there has not been much disagreement across the political spectrum. So these should go through, at most, with minor changes.

Unfortunately, the same cannot be said about more difficult and complex reforms such as privatisation and reducing subsidies. The possibility of these reforms occurring in the remaining months of the current government does not appear too bright. Regarding privatisation of public enterprises, the UPA government's policy, right from the beginning, has been soft and sedate. The privatisation of profit-making public enterprises was ruled out. So were strategic sales that involved the transfer of management control of public enterprises to strategic partners identified through competitive bidding. In February 2005, the government called off the process of strategic sales in 13 enterprises. Effectively, the disinvestment strategy of the UPA government emphasises the minority sales of government shares so that the 'public' character of these enterprises does not change.

One can argue that the thrust of the government's public sector policy, as documented in the National Common Minimum Programme, was a trade-off for the Left's support. But are there enough reasons to believe that this policy will now change with less than a year remaining before the next general elections? The government is unlikely to tread on sensitive toes so close to elections. Aggressive moves on privatisation will resume heated debates and widespread protests. Privatisation in India continues to be an emotive issue with sharply diverse views. Thus, the possibility of any progress on public sector reforms looks remote.

What about subsidies? Again, the tendency to avoid ruffling feathers is likely to result in inaction in this sphere too. Food, fertilizer and oil are the three main categories of subsidies. Cutting food subsidies at a time when food prices are high and elections are close is out of the question. Rather, there might be increases in such subsidies through the announcement of higher procurement prices if some crops do not fare well. Bringing down fertilizer subsidies will increase the costs of production for farmers. Given the inflationary conditions, such a step can prove self-destructive. Finally, the oil subsidies—considering the public outcry at the last round of subsidy cuts and price revisions (June 2008), the government will be averse to burning its fingers again. That will be unfortunate since the current moderation in global oil prices offers a wonderful opportunity for rationalising subsidies in a relatively 'painless' manner. Inaction on this front will imply a rare chance foregone.

Thus, the hopes of 'big-ticket' reforms in the coming months might actually turn out to be an anti-climax. There is unlikely to be progress in critical areas since the government will aim to avoid confrontations. So will its allies. These political considerations will inhibit precipitate actions to a large extent. As a result, the government is likely to become more circumspect for avoiding political setbacks. For example, the spectre of the current downward trend of global oil prices reversing, however, unlikely it may be, will continue to haunt policy makers and prevent them from pursuing action on oil subsidies. With inflation being where it is (the latest estimates put inflation measured by the wholesale price index at 11.59 per cent), the government will be doubly cautious about the inflationary and 'political' impact of all policies.

So it will actually be a significant achievement if the financial sector reforms, particularly pension and insurance, go through. A couple of months ago, nobody had thought that they would actually have any chance of going through. Achieving these, therefore, will be unforeseen gains. But expecting anything more will be irrational. After all, the trust vote was only a capsule edition of the much larger countrywide exercise that is in the pipeline. Having won the battle, the focus of the government will now be on winning the war. Reforms can certainly wait. The message seems to have gone out to the stock market too. Otherwise, in spite of global cues, the market should have remained largely up and uncorrected during the later sessions of last week. However, it did not.

28

Some Approaches to Pricing Controls for Patented Drugs in India

S. NARAYAN

(1 December 2008)

INTRODUCTION

IN 2006, THE Indian government announced that it would adopt a National Pharmaceutical Policy, and circulated a draft policy outlining its intentions. To finalise this policy, a Group of Ministers (GOM) was set up by the government in 2007. The GOM has met several times, and the National Pharmaceutical Pricing Authority (NPPA) has also made a presentation to the GOM in April 2008. One of the elements of the proposed policy is that patented drugs (formulations under the Product Patent protection) that were launched in India after 1 January 2005 would be subjected to price negotiations before approval is given for them to be marketed. The government set up a Committee (hereafter called the Committee) to explore the possibility of Price Negotiations for Patented Drugs and Medical Devices. Chaired by the Deputy Secretary (Pharmaceutical Industry) the Committee would propose a system of reference pricing/price negotiations/differential prices which could be applied for price negotiations of patented drugs and medical devices before their marketing approval in India.[1] It should be noted that only a few medicines in India are patented, with the vast majority not covered by any patents.

Under the Drug Prices Control Orders, the government has been regulating prices of drugs and formulations since 1970. Initially, there was a 100 per cent control on all drugs and formulations. However, progressive liberalisation reduced it to 74 bulk drugs in 1995. An attempt to reduce it further to 25 bulk drugs in 2002 was unsuccessful, with litigation against the move. The United Progressive Alliance government that came to power in 2004 has been leaning towards greater controls over pricing and, of late, the NPPA has been fairly stringent in monitoring retail prices of drugs and has attempted to levy fines on manufacturers that have transgressed. These issues are in dispute at various forums and relate entirely to generic drugs and formulations. However, it is clear that the government is concerned about the availability of drugs at reasonable prices and this is a key issue for the Committee that is considering approaches to the pricing of patented drugs.

The approach of the Committee in its deliberations so far has been towards finding a suitable model of pricing control to apply to patented drugs. This is based on the basic premise that the absence of controls would subject the availability as well as the use of these drugs to market forces which may set prices at unaffordable levels. The Committee has been examining drug price regimens in use in several countries such as Canada, France, the United Kingdom, Australia, Egypt, Brazil, South Africa, Philippines, etc., to find a model that would be replicable in the conditions prevailing in India. An important element in India is the fact that the majority of the drug costs are privately paid for, in the absence of an effective health insurance system that provides access and availability to all. As per the World Health Organization data, only 21.3 per cent of the total expenditure on medicine in India is accounted for by the government or insurance, with the balance of nearly 78.6 per cent paid for privately. In the United Kingdom, public health and insurance takes care of 83.4 per cent of the spending on medicine, and in Germany, it is 78.5 per cent. Price regulation in most countries is, therefore, oriented towards the determination of prices at which governments purchase the medicine for delivery through the public health system or to fix the reimbursement rates against insurance claims, but seldom to fix prices prevailing in the open market. The task of the Committee is made more onerous by the need to work out a policy and a process that would be easy to implement in India and, at the same time, be monitorable, effective and efficient.

PRICE CONTROL OF PATENTED DRUGS—CONSIDERATIONS

Several countries have adopted a model for arriving at pre-determined prices for drugs and pharmaceuticals, and at the forefront are those that have a well established national health system such as the United Kingdom, Australia and Canada. However, the determination of prices that manufacturers would be entitled to is invariably arrived at through a transparent, public process, and there is recourse to remedy decisions through appellate forums. Prices in general reflect an understanding of the need to reward innovation and the critical nature of research and development (R&D).

At the same time, it is important to examine some of the concerns that have been expressed about the concept of price control for patented drugs in order to take note of the limitations to this approach. In academic literature as well as industry analyses, there is a consensus that there is no acceptable way to set prices to reward innovation in life sciences and that those who set prices do so with a focus on reducing costs rather than providing incentives for innovators to continue their R&D endeavours.[2]

There is a wide body of published literature[3] whose conclusions can broadly be summarized into four major themes.

First, R&D investment in the pharmaceutical industry is motivated by the size of the potential market, as determined by volumes and prices, and the opportunities of risks and rewards on proposed investments. This has led to facile complaints that the industry only seeks to maximize profits and does not have improved health outcomes as a primary concern. It is also maintained that where the size of the market is small, in terms of volume as well as ability to pay, there is little incentive for innovation, and non-government organisations (NGO) have been quick to point out that there is very little R&D in respect of several known so-called 'neglected' diseases. The answer perhaps is in treating R&D in these diseases as a public good and providing for public expenditure through government-supported institutions such as the Council for Scientific and Industrial Research and the Indian Council of Medical

Research. This would have two positive consequences. One, there would be a national mission to develop drugs that are considered a priority for a country. Two, the costs of R&D would become open and transparent, and thus subject to public scrutiny.

Second, there is sufficient evidence to show that the combination of regulation and economic disincentives, for example, mandatory price reductions, tend to discourage both rapid entry of generics as well as price cutting after entry. Controls[4] appear to affect openness of competition as well as the availability of alternatives.[5]

Third, evidence from European Union (EU) markets indicates that the EU drug price controls have brought a reduced number of drugs to the market, and that these markets offer significantly lower rewards for R&D.

Finally, there is adequate evidence to indicate that the introduction of new drugs tends to yield important offsets in the form of savings in health care expenditure elsewhere in the system through reduced hospitalisation, after-care, doctor's fees and the like.

In addition to the above are the worries that the future of new discoveries may be less in the realm of chemicals and much more in the area of biotechnology. This is because the biopharmaceutical industry is not in the business of catering to the tastes of the market looking for the next-generation cell phone, but rather it is trying to decipher the intricacies of complex diseases such as diabetes and cancer which require ever more sophisticated scientific techniques. It is not impossible to imagine region-specific and even patient-specific drugs in the future, all of which would be hard put to fit into any standardised price discovery mechanism.

Any policy on price controls over patented drugs is, therefore, fraught with the above concerns. Ostensibly, the government and public policy initiatives are focused on providing cutting-edge drugs at affordable prices. At the same time, there are strident media and NGO comments[6] about the supposed profits that multinational corporations (MNC) are making, that is to say, that there is a justification for controls simply because, according to the writers, MNCs make huge profits. It is fervently hoped that the Committee recognises these arguments as being particularly uninformed and that the sale of patented drugs will, in the foreseeable future, constitute a miniscule proportion of all drugs sold in India and a small fraction of the total sales worldwide. Any form of government pricing controls needs to be justified only on the basis of improving affordability for the majority of Indians and there must be mechanisms to ensure that prices finalised are implemented in the form of availability of drugs in the general market, outside government purchases, at these prices. Without this, the entire exercise would be futile.

Pricing of Patented Drugs—Suggested Approaches

The mandate for the Committee, therefore, comes down to a determination of how prices might be negotiated, who would be responsible for the negotiations and how to monitor the availability of the drugs in the open market at the negotiated prices. Arising from this are several issues that need to be addressed:

- Who would constitute the decision-making group?
- Are price controls to apply to all patented drugs or only selected ones? Can those below a certain threshold level be left out?
- What inputs would the group need?
- What criteria are to be adopted?
- What should be the principles for arriving at the pricing?
- What will be the period of controls? When would they take effect and how often would they be negotiated?
- If using an international reference pricing system, which should be the comparator countries?[7]
- How are the prices and volumes to be monitored post-introduction?

In this context, the Committee has been studying the practices prevailing in several countries, including Canada, the United Kingdom, France, Germany, Egypt, South Africa, Brazil, Malaysia, Vietnam, Pakistan, etc. As already pointed out, in almost all the countries, price controls apply to those drugs that are purchased for delivery through the public health systems and as a benchmark, for insurance, reimbursement claims, and there is no clear methodology available for ensuring the monitoring of open market prices. In that respect, the initiative is likely to be unique to India.

Constitution of the Group

The approach of the Committee has been to examine the practices prevailing in several developing and developed countries to identify approaches that would be relevant for India. The common feature of all the countries is that there is a body or group, duly constituted, either by law or by executive orders, that is authorised to act on this. The constitution of the group varies but the Canadian concept of the Patented Medicines Prices Review Board[8] appears to be relevant. In the case of France, the United Kingdom and in most European countries,[9] the concerns are primarily with reimbursement of medicine costs through insurance and the public health system.

In India, pricing is approached as a direct intervention in the market and is likely to affect supply and demand. Therefore, the constitution of the group becomes important, for it has to be relevant, transparent and objective. The important constituents should include representatives from the NPPA and Drug Controller General of India. The Department of Pharmaceuticals, as such, may like to keep out of the group as decisions of the group are likely to be debated, discussed, and, sometimes, disputed. It would, therefore, lend greater credibility to the group if it were to be headed by an eminent public figure such as a scientist. The group should contain representatives of the medical profession as well.

Practices in other Countires

In brief, free pricing is available in the United States and in some European countries including Denmark.[10] Malaysia also adopts a free pricing system. In France,[11] there is an agency for market authorisation called the Comité économique des produits de santé (CEPS) that decides on the entry of new drugs after an expert-based examination of their therapeutic value. The CEPS sets the reimbursable medicinal costs which are adopted by all the insurers and the public health authorities. The CEPS ensures that prices set are similar to those in Germany, Italy, Spain and the United Kingdom which are taken as the comparator countries for this purpose. In the United Kingdom,[12] prices for patented products are set through a voluntary agreement between manufacturers and the Pharmaceutical Price Regulation System, and these prices remain in force for a period of five years. At the other end of the spectrum are Brazil and Egypt, where price controls are arbitrary. Brazil has introduced a price freeze for the last three years. In Vietnam,[13] the companies submit a price list to the Ministry of Health (MOH), that needs to be approved. There is a two-tier arrangement whereby government purchase prices are negotiated by the ministry separately, with an undertaking on volumes, while open market prices could be different, though they need the approval of the MOH. The prices of patented drugs in Canada are subject to capping and should not exceed the maximum price in seven reference countries, namely, France, Germany, Italy, Sweden, Switzerland, the United Kingdom and the United States. The Price Monitoring and Review Committee in Canada is committed to transparency, and publishes the prices every month on its website.

There are thus three different models. At one end are countries where there are no price controls and, at the other, where they are arbitrary price freezes from time to time. Among the countries that do try to apply principles to pricing of patented products, the overwhelming majority is concerned with costs of reimbursement for its own government insurance schemes, and not with market prices *per se*. In other words, companies are free to price their drugs as they see fit in the open market.

Evidence from a study of prices in nine countries (Danzon and Furakawa 2007)[13] indicates a range of between 6 and 23 per cent from the prices prevailing in the United States for the same drugs. As argued earlier, in the context of India, it is important to recognise that only 20 per cent of the drug delivery is through the public health system and that insurance is not yet widespread. Therefore, a substantial quantity of medicines are purchased directly from the market.

Isssues Before the Group

The basic issues that need to be settled *ab initio* are whether all drugs that are granted patents after 1 January 2005 would be subject to price negotiations, and what would be the criteria that would be applied. In the initial stages, it does not appear to be feasible for the group to engage itself in negotiations over a very large number of products—it would delay the introduction of the products and prolong the process. There may be drugs that would have only small volumes and of limited relevance. In most countries, the drug companies prepare estimates of the likely volumes of the drug in the market before its introduction. These could be used to determine whether price controls need to be applied or not. The deciding group could arrive at a threshold of forecasted sales of a particular medicine. If the sales are less than a specified threshold of volume, in terms of quantities sold (for example, one million doses a year), there is little purpose in bringing the drugs under control. Price control mechanisms could, therefore, work above a particular pre-set threshold in terms of volumes and revenues. The total volumes would then be monitored annually to ensure that the drugs move into the price control regime when the volumes cross the threshold. There could be a simple criteria for the applicants to submit anticipated volumes of sales in the first five years, and drugs that have a threshold of actual sales below a particular volume could be excluded,[15] with the stipulation that if the actual sales are higher than that threshold in any year, the companies would be up for negotiations in the following year.

The group would need inputs from the manufacturers that should include anticipated volumes of sales, the price and strength of formulations in other countries, details on dosages and clinical administration to determine the quantities required for treatment (this would help determine total patient cost). There is little purpose served in looking at company balance sheet data to arrive at R&D costs, overheads and profits—these would be subject to interpretation and dispute, and, in any case, vary from company to company and even from country to country. It is important to reiterate that the purpose of the price controls would be to ensure availability and affordability, not to question the commercial operations of the manufacturers. The group should be satisfied that the prices are lower than those in comparator countries and this could be a simple and straightforward approach to adopt. The Canadian example of using the seven reference countries and ensuring that the prices in Canada are not above any of those could be used in reverse to ensure that the prices offered are the lowest among the comparator countries. Once the price for a dosage is available, then alternate dosages or formulations could broadly be based on the per unit prices to ensure that they are not excessive. In short, since the focus is on costs to the patient, it needs only to be ensured that the costs are the lowest, as compared with the comparator countries. Any attempts at averaging, or mean or median pricing are likely to be difficult to interpret.

The group should always consider inflation or increases in prices on an annual basis, and this should be in reference to all drugs and formulations, and not to the patented ones alone.

An important consideration would be whether the drug is 'first-in-class', or whether alternative drugs or clinical regimens are available. The group would need to satisfy itself about this from medical experts. In the case of a 'first-in-class' drug, the price should be fixed simply as at the lowest prevailing price in the comparator countries, and in the case of drugs where alternatives are available, with reference to the price of the alternatives.

Comparator Countries

There has been an argument that the practices in developed countries such as the United Kingdom, France, etc., are not relevant in the Indian context. There have been some arguments in favour of the Canadian model, primarily because of its simplicity of approach—the manufacturers are required to give information about prices in other countries, the volumes expected and alternative formulations. As an approach, its simplicity is its elegance while, at the same time, the price levels arrived at may not be relevant for India. Perhaps a combination of the Canadian approach to the prices prevailing in similarly-placed countries could be considered relevant for comparison. The comparator countries need to be chosen carefully with reference to the size and state of the economy, the public health delivery systems, the size of the drug industry and the total volumes and sales. At the bottom end, there is no merit in arguing for price levels that are even lower than in other South Asian countries such as Pakistan and Bangladesh, for Indians pride themselves in being better off.

Post-price Fixing Activities

There are two issues here. The first is data collection on the efficacy of the drugs, volumes sold and comparable therapy, and the second is the monitoring and implementation of the prices set. In a large country such as India, with a federal set-up, this is possible only through the cooperation of state governments. It is important to include them as stakeholders in the exercise, though involving them at the level of price negotiations would be cumbersome and would lead to complaints of bias. It is possible to conceive of a mechanism whereby the notified prices are applicable all over the country, with only variations being due to local taxes. The concept of Maximum Retail Price-based pricing exists in many products and needs to be extended to patented products as well. Once this is done, it is important to see that the state governments do not engage in fresh discussions and negotiations with the manufacturers for their government purchases, for this would fragment the market and distort prices more than what they would be already.

Finally, a two-price format for government purchases as well as for the open market is still an option to be considered, with the pre-set prices being determined as per suggestions above. These pre-set prices would be applicable to all government purchases, state or centre, while the sale in the open market could be free from controls. A system modelled on that of Vietnam, where open market prices are not negotiated but intimated in advance to the government, could also be considered.

NOTES

1. Letter from Under Secretary, Ministry of Chemicals and Fertilizers, Government of India 5/80/2006-PI I dated 22 February 2007.
2. John Caffee, 'Pharmaceutical Market Competition Issues', American Enterprise Institute, Washington, June 2008.
3. For example, Danzon and Li-Wei Chao (2000), 'Does Regulation Drive out Competition in Pharmaceutical Markets?, *Journal of Law and Economics*, vol. 32, no. 2, pp. 311–57.
4. Danzon and Furakawa, 'International Prices and Availability of Pharmaceuticals in 2005', *Health Affairs*, vol. 27, no. 1, pp. 221ff.
5. Danzon and Furakawa, 'Prices and Availability of Pharmaceuticals—Evidence from Nine Countries', *Health Affairs Web Exclusive*; 2007.
6. For example, P.A. Francis, 'Pricing Patented Drugs', *Pharmabiz*; 19 November 2008.
7. A 'comparator country' is defined as one which has a standard or benchmark in a particular parameter that offers the facility of other countries being compared *vis-à-vis* the country in the same parameter.
8. Global Insight Report: Health Infrastructure; Canada; 2008 www.global insight.com.
9. Global Insight Report: Health Infrastructure, 2008 (relevant countries) www.globalinsight.com.
10. Pharmaceutical Pricing and Reimbursement and Information: European Union Reports, Directorate of Health and Consumer Protection, Denmark, February 2007.
11. Pharmaceutical Pricing and Reimbursement and Information: European Union Reports, Directorate of Health and Consumer Protection, France, October 2007.
12. Global Insight Report: Health Infrastructure, U.K., 2008 www.globa linsight.com.
13. Global Insight Report: Health Infrastructure, Vietnam, 2008 www.global insight.com.
14. Danzon and Furakawa, 2007, op. cit.
15. Similar approaches are available in other countries.

SECTION II

ECONOMIC DEVELOPMENT

B. Fiscal Policies and Financial Markets

29

The Sub-prime Crisis: Likely Consequences for the Indian Economy

S. NARAYAN

(*10 January 2008*)

IN THE LAST few weeks, the prime minister of India, the finance minister as well as the deputy chairman of the Planning Commission, Montek Singh Ahluwalia, have been expressing anxiety over the impact of the sub-prime crisis in the United States on growth in India. In fact, Ahluwalia has said that this is more worrying than the rise in energy prices. It is only the governor of the Reserve Bank of India (RBI) who has not expressed similar views, focusing his concern more on growing capital flows and the impact on the currency.

This brief attempts to examine the likely consequences of the sub-prime crisis for India in 2008.

Two articles in the *Financial Times*[1] and posts on the Martin Wolf blog site[2] offer an interesting overview of the debate, the causes, effects and consequences of the United States sub-prime crisis. There is the argument that over the past several years, the United States' trade deficit has persistently drained spending from the United States' economy. As a result, much of manufacturing failed to recover after 2001 which then prompted the Federal Reserve to push interest rates down to all time lows. This staved off recession but gave rise to the housing bubble—a house price inflation, a construction boom, explosive growth of non-traditional sub-prime mortgages, a debt-financed consumer spending scenario and, yet, larger trade deficits.

These gave rise to trade surpluses in the rest of the world, distributing the sub-prime holdings globally. The trade surpluses persisted as the Asian countries pursued export-led growth and they blocked appreciation of their currencies against the dollar to maintain their competitiveness. A great portion of the surpluses were re-invested in dollars. Therefore, long-term interest rates did not rise even when the Federal Reserve raised short-term rates in 2004. Artificially low interest rates prompted investors to increase risky lending at diminished risk premiums. In this conceptualisation, the failure to address problems in the area of trade deficits can trigger policy responses in the area of monetary policy that can ultimately create even bigger problems. More important for India, large trade deficits cause real distortions, the consequences of which are costly, though they may be slow to emerge. Most importantly, citizens have been encouraged to view their appreciated (bubble?) assets as a substitute for cash in the bank.

On the consequences for the global economy, there have been statements in the last week from responsible analysts and even the Federal Reserve that the United States' economy is likely to face a contraction in the second and third quarters of 2008, annualising about 1 per cent. The treasury secretary has promised slower growth rather than a contraction through a slew of measures and it remains to be seen whether the worrying United States' unemployment data of November 2007 is part of a monthly trend, or just a blip.

Against this backdrop, it is possible to look at likely consequences of the sub-prime crises for the Indian economy and impact, if any, on gross domestic product (GDP) growth.

At the top are concerns of a direct impact on financial institutions in India. The RBI has clarified that the exposure of Indian banks and institutions to the crisis is 'marginal'. There is a story in *Business Standard*[3] that claims that State Bank of India, ICICI Bank, Bank of Baroda and Bank of India are set to bookmark to market losses on their foreign offices to credit derivatives. The *Business Standard* has estimated the total of these losses to be around US $3 billion for the four banks put together, and has commented that the provisioning made by these banks so far has been quite small. Given the size of the banks and their balance sheets, even if these figures were accurate, there would be little impact on the overall performance of the banks. In short, the direct fall-out effect of the collapse of the sub-prime mortgages to institutions in India is likely to be quite insignificant.

Second, it is clear that there would be weak (or no) growth in the United States, and estimates by the World Bank[4] suggest that high-income countries would grow at just 2.2 per cent this year, as against 7.1 per cent for developing countries. (Estimates put China at 10.8 per cent, India at 8.4 per cent and South Asia at 7.9 per cent.) Given low inflation expectations in the United States, the World Bank suggests that emerging countries would pull high-income countries behind them. The benign part of the projection is that low growth in the developed countries would keep commodity price increases under control, lessening risks of inflation in the developing countries, and adding to stimulus for growth.

The other side of the coin is that contraction in the United States would lead to less demand for imported goods, impacting imports. There is the argument that the Indian economy is sufficiently decoupled from the rest of the world and that there is robust domestic demand and employment creation—this would cushion the economy from external shocks. But this may not be quite true. In 2002, trade was only 17 per cent of GDP but it is now close to 40 per cent. Thus, the trade dependency of the Indian economy has doubled in the last five years. The United States is the top trading partner for India (though China is catching up) and there would be the concern that exports to the United States may fall. The current monetary policy in India is battling with the need to control inflation, keep interest rates at a level that promotes growth while simultaneously attempting to prevent undue appreciation of the rupee—a task considered to be very difficult to accomplish together. Already, export orders for the textile sector have fallen significantly, and large job losses are being reported. The appreciation of the rupee is largely due to accentuated capital flows, and free and flexible financial markets and, hence, the concern of the RBI governor that this is likely to be exacerbated by the contraction in demand in the United States.

The likely policy response in India is to ensure that the rupee does not appreciate 'too much', a task that will entail active sterilisation operations by the RBI. These sterilization operations, through issue of market stabilization bonds, entail an additional fiscal burden on the government for the interest costs of these bonds. Energy costs have risen but adjustment of consumer prices has not been possible due to political compulsions of the coalition. It is likely that fiscal stresses on the government may increase. It is this total picture of rupee appreciation, lower exports and fiscal stress that is causing worries in the Indian Finance Ministry and Planning Commission.

On the positive side, data reveals that the quarter ending December 2007 has been quite good for Indian manufacturing as well as the services sector, asset prices in terms of equities and real estate remain firm, and revenue collections have been extremely buoyant. The Indian industry seems less than concerned about domestic demand growth. The measures by the RBI to curb liquidity have yielded positive results and inflation appears to be a lesser worry than in China.

The worry lies in two areas. The first is that capital formation, in terms of investments in plant and machinery, after reaching a peak in the middle of last year, appears to be stagnant and is likely to be going down. The effects of this slowdown are likely to be seen towards the end of 2008 or in 2009. This needs to be balanced by capital spending for infrastructure and it is likely that the government will come out with some initiatives, especially in the power, aviation and shipping sectors. The second is that trade deficit continues to be very high and is increasing, signalling the lack of competitiveness in the economy. The finance minister has already promised that he would consider sops to exporters in the forthcoming budget. He has also an election year ahead to factor in and cannot afford to see the economy slowing down. He is, therefore, wary of controls on capital flows and has been encouraging banks to reduce lending rates to spur consumption and growth. This is at variance with the task given to the RBI—that of controlling inflation and excess liquidity. Policy alternatives appear to be at cross-purposes.

The growth rates of 2005 and 2006 are unlikely to be repeated, and this is due to the unfinished reform agenda, as much as to external factors. The United Progressive Alliance government has not been successful in bringing about reforms in the financial sector as well as in labour markets and issues related to manufacturing competitiveness such as uniform tariffs. There have been several promises for reducing processes and procedures that have not been implemented. The reforms in agriculture, much needed and much announced, remain only on paper. There is thus, the need to find a peg to hang the lower GDP growth rate anticipated in 2008.

It is politic to blame it on global factors than on delays in infrastructure development, poor reforms in education, health and insurance, and flip-flops on monetary policy. The sub-prime crisis offers such an opportunity and, in the forthcoming months, one is likely to see enhanced explanations of how the Indian economy has been affected.

NOTES

1. Thomas Palley, 'The Subprime—Trade Deficit Connection', *The Financial Times*, 8 January 2008.
2. See posts at blogs.ft.com by Martin Wolf, et al.
3. 'Subprime Crisis to hit 4 Big Banks' Profits', *Business Standard*, 7 January 2008.
4. *World Bank: Global Economic Prospects*, 2007.

30

The Appreciating Rupee and India's Exports: Should Policy Makers Worry?

K.V. RAMASWAMY

(*18 January 2008*)

'INDIAN CURRENCY will sink if allowed to float'—this used to be the answer one would often get during classroom discussions in the 1980s on flexible and fixed exchange rates. However, with the remarkable Indian economic performance in the last few years, the Indian rupee has attained respectability and suggests strong underlying fundamentals. The current rupee price of the United States dollar stands at Rs 39.29 per dollar (as on 10 January 2008) as against Rs 44.53 exactly a year ago, indicating a 12 per cent appreciation. This is appreciation of the nominal exchange rate and one should perhaps look at Real Effective Exchange Rates (REER) that take into account relative price movement in trading partners. The Reserve Bank of India (RBI) estimates REER (based on 36-currency trade based weights) with different base years. Without going into details, it is suffice to note that REER, either based on five currencies or on a 36-currency basket, has also appreciated since September 2006.

So what has been the impact of the appreciation of the rupee on Indian exports? The answer would be that there has been no impact if one goes by the latest available data on export. The monthly economic report of the Ministry of Finance, India, October and November 2007, indicates that exports in dollar terms have risen by 22.1 per cent in the period April–November 2007, compared to the same period the year before.

Based on this scenario, should one then conclude that real

exchange rate does not matter in India's competitiveness? The answer is no, simply because an appreciating rupee will impact exports but there will be a time lag before the impact is visible. Further, one can already observe a deceleration in the growth rate of exports in 2007 relative to that in 2006. The growth rate of exports is lower by 10 percentage points in 2007 (April to September) relative to the growth rate achieved in the same period in 2006.

What caused the appreciation of the rupee? The reason can be found in the large capital inflows comprising foreign direct investment (FDI), external commercial borrowings (ECB), foreign portfolio investment and remittances. One just needs to examine recent information on each of these based on the latest quarterly balance of payments data released by the RBI to understand the appreciation of the rupee.

The net FDI into India during April–September 2007 amounted to US $9.9 billion and its impact was largely offset by outflows to the tune of US $6 billion. The emergence of India as an attractive FDI destination due to its growing and potential large domestic market is passé. One may add that the low penetration of consumer durables in India and the perceptions of improved conditions of doing business in India have also been positive factors in the increase in FDI into the country.

The net ECB reached US $10.6 billion between April and September 2007, double the amount from US $5.7 billion during the same period in 2006. This was due to lower interest rates on ECB and rising financing requirements of domestic capacity expansion. Indian companies have been able to raise capital abroad by taking advantage of lower cost via global depository receipts and American depository receipts. Portfolio investment recorded an absolute increase of US $16.8 billion in the period April–September 2007, reflecting India's better stock market performance in 2007. The average annual inflow of portfolio investment between 2003 and 2006 was around US $9 billion.

Also, investment and remittances from the large number of Indians working abroad are growing rapidly. Private transfers comprising primarily remittances reached US $19 billion in 2007 (April–September), recording a growth rate of 49 per cent over the same period in 2006.

Net short-term credit has also caught the attention of many market watchers in India—it recorded an increase of US $5.7 billion during April–September 2007 and included inflows under the heading 'Suppliers Credit up to 180 days' amounting to US $1.9 billion. Other capital receipts (such as leads and lags in exports, advances for share purchase, etc.) amounted to US $5.9 billion during April–September in 2007. The net addition to India's foreign exchange reserves is reported to be US $40.4 billion during April–September 2007.

Impact on Indian Exports

The rupee appreciated by 12 per cent between September 2006 and September 2007. Unfortunately, detailed commodity-wise trade data is not readily available corresponding to this period. Alternatively, let us consider export growth during April–September 2007 relative to that achieved during April–September 2006.[1] India's total exports increased by 17 per cent, in dollar terms, between the two periods. However, several individual industries experienced a decline in export growth. They were sports goods (-6.6 per cent), readymade garments (-3.3 per cent), natural silk textiles (-14.3 per cent) and wool manufactures (-4.9 per cent). Cotton textiles grew by only 1.2 per cent. The other products with negative export growth were coffee (-10 per cent), handicrafts (-38.2 per cent) and carpets (-6.8 per cent). Low value-added products and those with very low or zero import intensity were the ones that witnessed a decline in growth. Industries with high import content (for example, machinery, gems and jewellery) have been able to offset the negative impact due to the lower cost of imported inputs.

Between September 2005 and September 2006, when the rupee depreciated by 5 per cent, low value-added and price sensitive products grew quite well. Looking at the period April–September 2006 for which commodity-wise export data is available, India's total exports grew at 27 per cent—sports goods grew by 13.55 per cent, readymade garments by 10.8 per cent, coffee by 27 per cent, carpets by 12.6 per cent and cotton textiles by 12.9 per cent.

Thus, it is not wrong to state that low value-added and price sensitive export items have been adversely affected by the appreciating rupee. These products, already facing intensive competitive pressure from the United States and the European Union markets, are likely to be further impacted as world trade and output growth are likely to slow down. And in such a scenario, price renegotiation with buyers will provide a further nightmare for these exporters, especially in the case of buyer-driven industries such as sports goods, footwear, garments and textiles.

The competitiveness of a country depends on the cost of imported intermediates. Appreciating the rupee would make imported intermediates cheap. Consequently, it would not negatively impact import-intensive industries such as automobile and engineering. Low value-added products with zero or very low import intensity are likely to suffer. The profit margin in software-exporting firms is also likely to decline, reducing the dollar value of information technology (IT) software exports. The Indian stock market seems to have already taken this into account and stocks/securities of IT companies have undergone sharp price corrections in recent months.

One school of thought argues that the real exchange rate appreciation is productivity driven and reflects a natural evolution of the economy towards a long-run equilibrium. This emphasises supply-side factors such as technological change and labour mobility. At the same time, other demand-side factors such as transitory demand shocks like fiscal expansion and structural factors like rising real income growth, leading to higher services (non-tradable) demand, could cause appreciation. In the Indian case, the driving factor is capital inflows. This appreciation is more likely to negatively impact small and medium firms who are more likely to be credit constrained. They will have less back up, in terms of reserves and access to working capital, to sail through the difficult times as in the current case. Some of them may go out of business if they are not able to manage the declining rupee profit margins and competitiveness.

Indian exporters certainly need state support as they operate in markets with greater uncertainty and competition. How can Indian government help exporters? There are several ways. First, it could reduce import duty, excise and service taxes (domestic taxes) to compensate for the reduced export realisation of exporters in rupee terms. In simple words, it could facilitate the reduction of transaction costs of businesses and exporters. Second, it could speed up the implementation of the policy measures announced by the Ministry of Commerce and Industry in June 2007 such as the reduction of pre-shipment credit, mandated export credit disbursement by commercial banks and so forth.

It is often said that only a crisis will force the state to carry out certain reforms. One may anticipate that the current situation of the appreciating rupee, while it may not be a crisis, will compel the Indian government, both at the centre and state level, towards export facilitation measures. However, even with reforms, given the current state of global economic environment, the task of achieving export target of US $160 billion for 2007–8 has become all the more difficult for India.

NOTE

1. This is the most recent period for which commodity-wise data is available. One hopes that the trend changes for the better when more recent data trickles in.

31

Analysing India's Credit Policy: Keeping an Eye on Inflation and the Elections

S. NARAYAN

(4 February 2008)

THE RESERVE BANK of India (RBI) announced last week that it would keep interest rates unchanged, and chose to adopt a wait and watch policy. Markets and commentators in India had expected a reduction in interest rates, following the United States Federal Bank's decision to reduce rates in two tranches by 1.25 per cent.

There were two reasons that prompted the market watchers to expect a softening of interest rates in India. First, there have been significant inflows of capital into the financial markets since October last year, forcing the RBI to buy up the excess dollars in the market, and to sterilise the consequent liquidity through the issue of market stabilisation bonds. This approach keeps the strengthening of the rupee against the dollar within limits that can be managed by the RBI. The costs of this operation, in the nature of the interest burden of these bonds, is met by the Indian government from its budget and, therefore, the cost of keeping the rupee–dollar rate from appreciating is actually a burden on the government's fiscal position. In the face of the reduction of United States' interest rates, it was expected that the differences in interest rates between India and the United States would lead to accelerated flows into Indian markets that would strengthen the rupee even further and affect exports even more.

It was also the expectation of the corporate sector that interest rates needed to soften, given the apparent slow-down in the off-take of credit and the slow-down in consumption expenditure as well as in the stock markets.

The RBI chose to look the other way on these two. Two comments made by the RBI were interesting. The first was that inflationary pressures were lurking in the economy and that this was a matter for concern. The second was that banks had enough leeway to reduce borrowing and lending rates, and that money supply was already ahead of expectations and there was, therefore, sufficient liquidity in the economy.

Only a few weeks back, the RBI and the government had congratulated themselves on keeping a lid on inflation, having brought it down to less than 5 per cent. Further, the expected increases in petrol and diesel prices did not materialise and the consumer was cushioned from the burden of increased energy prices. On the agriculture front, there have been reports that winter wheat sowing has been above expectations and the recent steps taken by the government to stockpile wheat have yielded satisfactory results. The sudden concern over inflation, therefore, appears to be a little intriguing. The RBI's answer is that it is looking at a 3 to 4 per cent rate by next year and the finance minister, Chidambaram, has said that, between a high growth high inflation scenario and a somewhat moderate economic growth and low inflation alternative, choosing the former would be 'disastrous'. In fact, in Davos, he said that .5 per cent lower growth would still leave the country with a healthy 8 per cent rate of growth. A possible explanation is that there is a need to be extra careful in an election year and that while growth may not win votes, inflation will surely lose them. The future of oil and food prices beyond the middle of the year is still unclear and it may, therefore, be better to wait than to do something. Further, there is little evidence yet that credit deflation is happening and, hence, it is better to guard against inflationary pressures.

The RBI and the government have also been urging the banks to look at their borrowing and lending rates. The RBI, in particular, feels that the margins that the banks are making are quite a lot and can be reduced. There was, thus, need to put pressure on the banks to look at borrowing and lending rates—the finance minister had already said as much at a recent meeting with the bankers. It has been clear for some time that credit supply has been quite skewed. Corporate India has had access to all the credit that it needs and there are several cash surplus companies that have had access to credit limits that they have used for arbitraging the market. At the same time, interests on housing loans have been up and retail loans as well as small-medium enterprises have had to bear the brunt of high charges. The argument of the RBI on interest rates apparently was that there was enough scope for the banks to reduce rates by themselves. Coupled with the information that investment expenditure in projects and infrastructure continues to be robust, there was merit in the RBI taking the 'do nothing' stand.

The corporate and the media sectors have been critical for the same reason. The third quarter results of many of the firms were published last week and clearly show pressures on margins. It is interesting that several companies have reported considerable increases in 'other incomes'—possibly a euphemism for the incomes earned in the financial markets. These entrepreneurs would, therefore, have benefited most from an interest rate cut and, hence, have felt let down.

That the RBI and government have moved in the right direction is clear from the fact that the HDFC bank cut interest rates for home loans soon thereafter and the market is now expecting other banks to follow. If the effect of the RBI stance improves credit flows at lower rates for home loans and consumption, it would have achieved its purpose.

Finally, there was the need for the RBI to be cautious. The effects of the interest rate cuts in the United States and the efforts to revitalise that economy are not yet clear. If the interest rate arbitrage does indeed bring in greater flows to the Indian capital markets, then the costs of sterilisation by the RBI will go up. The Indian finance minister has already talked about the impact of the market stabilisation scheme (MSS) on the budget. The higher interest burden and the costs of MSS are likely to squeeze out all the benefits of buoyancy in tax revenues, leaving the government little room for populist schemes, without hurting the fiscal deficit. This being the last full budget before elections, there is likely to be great pressure on give-aways as well as pressure on subsidies for food, fertilizer and oil. If there is dampening of growth as well, then sops for exports and tax concessions will be pressed for by interested groups. The government and the RBI need room for manoeuvering in the next few months.

At the same time, if the effects of the decline in the United States economy do not translate into greater interest in the Indian financial markets, then there would continue to be a fall in equity values and, after a lag, in real estate prices. As it is, market analysts are predicting a fall of at least another 12 to 15 per cent in the stock markets over the next few weeks.

No wonder that the RBI did not do anything, and indeed, it was the best thing that they could have done.

The silver lining that everyone is looking for is a domestic upturn later in the year. The argument is that investment is robust, particularly in construction and infrastructure and, therefore, demand would be robust. Equity offerings and new mutual fund offerings in infrastructure have garnered huge investible resources that are waiting to be deployed in the financial markets, and soon. A good wheat crop would stabilise rural incomes and energise rural demand. Foreign investors, waiting in the wings, would also be ready to come in with their investments. If the opportunities arise, it would then be the right time for the RBI to pump-prime the economy through a rate cut later in the year. And then one would have a very smooth sailing into the election mode. There are several elections to state assemblies, including Rajasthan and Madhya Pradesh, that are very important for the Congress this year, and it is important that everything runs smooth in the eco-nomy.

The only risks in this scenario would be that of inflationary pressures caused by increases in energy and commodity prices. Even here, it is likely that these may not be passed on to the consumers in an election year. They would be absorbed as subsidies adding to fiscal strains and they could be tackled later.

It is obvious that investors, funds and the Indian government would be waiting expectantly for things to right themselves out and until then, markets may continue to be soft.

These are interesting times to live in.

32

India's Economic Survey 2007–2008: Impressive Growth and a Promising Future

K.V. RAMASWAMY

(29 February 2008)

ON 28 FEBRUARY 2008, India's finance minister, P. Chidambaram, released the Economic Survey 2007–8, the annual state of the economy report. This year's report is all the more interesting as one could examine India's economic performance in the Tenth Five Year Plan (2002–7) and sets the stage for the Eleventh Five Year Plan (2008–12).

Keen observers of India's economy would be surprised to note that the recorded gross domestic product (GDP) growth rate of 7.8 per cent in the Tenth Five Year Plan (2002–7) period has turned out to the highest so far, when compared to growth in the past five-year plans. This growth rate is very close to the 8 per cent target set for the tenth plan. This is indeed quite remarkable for the Indian economy which has, in the past, been accustomed to actual growth rates routinely falling short of set targets. The acknowledged, unexpected growth rate of 9.4 and 9.6 per cent in the years 2005–6 and 2006–7 respectively were chiefly responsible for this impressive growth rates during the tenth plan period. The survey also reported that India has moved on to a higher growth path—a point with which one is inclined to agree without reservation.

The key factor of India's creditable economic growth is the resurgence of the manufacturing sector. Manufacturing growth underwent a sharp acceleration from 3.3 per cent (average for 1997–2002 during the ninth plan period) to 8.6 per cent in 2002–7. As such, its contribution in the total economic growth increased from 9.6 per cent during the ninth plan period to 17.7 per cent during the tenth plan period. In the last three years (2005–6 to 2007–8), the manufacturing sector grew by 9.9 per cent. Indian policy makers may now feel more confident about the Indian manufacturing sector, in particular, and the economy, in general. The growth of the Indian manufacturing sector will certainly not spell good news for competitor countries such as China and others in the South-East Asian region.

Two other sectors which have made substantial contributions to India's overall economic growth are the construction and transport and telecommunications sectors. The former grew by nearly 13 per cent per annum and the latter by an astonishing 15.3 per cent during the tenth plan period. Again, this signals a welcome change as these sectors have the capacity to generate substantial employment opportunities for the Indian populace.

In view of the good performance in the last plan, Indian policy makers are extremely confident that the economy will continue to grow. They have, in fact, set a target of 9 per cent GDP growth for the Eleventh Five Year Plan (2007–8 to 2011–12). This appears to be an attainable target even after taking into account the projected growth slow-down of 8.7 per cent in 2007–8 largely due to global factors. The Survey notes that, if India achieves the target growth set for the eleventh plan, it would be among a select group of economies (such as China, Singapore, Japan, among others) which have averaged a GDP growth rate of 9 per cent or more for at least a decade during their growth trajectory.

Regarding the sources of economic growth, the Survey makes some revealing observations. It states that growth acceleration is driven by investment demand supported by growth in private consumption. The growth in investment demand is due to the acceleration of fixed capital formation. The first spurt of investment began in the early 1990s and lasted up until 1995–6. This largely reflects the vast improvement in the investment climate resulting from economic reforms of August 1991. The improved investment climate is attributed to the trade and industrial policy liberalisation. The former led to a reduction of tariffs and import decontrol of capital and intermediate goods. This had the salutary effect of providing access to machinery and intermediate goods required by Indian industry to achieve international competitiveness. The latter facilitated the entry of new firms and capacity expansion of existing firms. The second period of investment spurt began in 2002–3 as the Indian industry carried out structural adjustments in response to trade openness and the removal of quantitative restrictions on import of consumer goods in 2000.

The Economic Survey admits that external trade has played an insignificant role in this growth acceleration. Further, it goes on to state that the 'economy is likely to remain domestic demand driven in the medium run'. This would be seen by Indians and other external observers as an inherent advantage and will insulate the Indian economy from the uncertainties of global economic fluctuations generated by, say irresponsible behaviour of financial institutions in the West, as several recent events have shown.

In the last five years, India's economic growth has been remarkable and the eleventh plan holds much more promise for the country. What is indeed pleasing for the Indian policy makers is that the growth in the services sector has been broad-based. Both domestic trade (retail and wholesale) and the hospitality industry, as well as the financing services (banking, insurance and business services), have registered higher growth rates in the tenth plan period. Agricultural growth has continued to fluctuate as it is monsoon dependent. With elections in many states and at the centre soon to come, the Economic Survey has certainly provided Prime Minister Manmohan Singh's government and the Congress with some degree of confidence in overcoming the battles that lie ahead.

33

The Indian Budget 2008–2009: An Assessment

S. NARAYAN

(*3 March 2008*)

THE BUDGET proposals presented by the Indian finance minister in parliament on 29 February have provided a number of concessions for the middle class and the farmers. It was a well thought out document and there has been an attempt to control inflation and, at the same time, stimulate growth.

The Indian economy has been growing at over 8.7 per cent for the last 12 consecutive quarters. Per capita incomes have risen over 50 per cent at current prices in the last six years, and are over US $1,000 now. Savings, both public and private, have grown, and are close to 31 per cent of gross domestic product (GDP) now, and capital formation is growing at a even faster pace. Asset markets, represented by both financial and real assets, have been buoyant and this has resulted in a transfer of real wealth to even small landholders.

At the same time, there are real pressures. The increases in prices of oil and other commodities need to be adjusted into consumer prices. The Indian government has been cushioning the consumer from petroleum product increases through a mechanism that allows oil-marketing companies to float bonds in the market to offset cost increases. The government guarantees these bonds. There are also unpaid subsidies to the fertilizer industry, for which the government has issued bonds in favour of these companies. Finally, the large capital inflows force the Reserve Bank of India to purchase dollars to keep the rupee from appreciating too rapidly, and the excess liquidity is mopped up through market stabilisation bonds, the interest for which is borne by the government. All these are measures that prevent true costs of goods and services from being passed on to the consumer, and the costs of distorting prices and markets become a burden on the budget. With oil exceeding US $100 a barrel, these distortions and costs are likely to increase.

There is also a concern over food prices. With an economy growing at around 9 per cent and per capita incomes rising, whatever the food-GDP elasticity, consumption of food grains is bound to increase. Growth of agriculture is projected to be 2.6 per cent in the current year, and has been around 3 per cent in the last three years. Given the supply constraints, prices of wheat and rice are on the increase, as also those of edible oil and pulses. Prime Minister Manmohan Singh has said that an era of rising food prices is inevitable and is a corollary of growth and larger numbers of people getting out of poverty. During the current year, this is exacerbated by global increases in food prices. Wheat output is expected to be lower than last year and there are pressures on a number of crops, including coffee. Food price inflation is, therefore, a reality that the Indian government has to contend with.

There are worries of a slowdown in the global economy, led by the financial crisis in the United States markets. This slow-down would affect exports and investments into India as well as valuations in the financial markets. Though the Indian economy is less dependent on global trade than the Chinese economy, the effects of a slow-down in global growth would be felt in India too. There are estimates that this could reduce growth by up to 1 per cent.

Finally, this is the last budget of the current United Progressive Alliance (UPA) coalition government. The new parliament (Lok Sabha) has to be constituted before May 2009 and elections need to be held, latest, by March next year. Therefore, this budget has, of necessity, to cater to the aspirations of the people and to give a signal to the voters that the concessions are voter- and people-friendly, and appeal to as wide a section of the Indian populace as possible.

In dealing with these complexities, the budget is a carefully crafted document that takes a middle path of encouraging growth without adding inflationary pressures.

The primary focus is on agriculture. Rural India accounts for over 50 per cent of the population and most farmers are in subsistence agriculture. Crop yields are low by international standards and there has not been adequate capital formation in agriculture to encourage the use of higher technologies or mechanisation. Substantial areas are rainfall dependant and vagaries of the monsoon often decimate yields, leading to continuing indebtedness among poor farmers. There have been widespread incidents of farmer suicides in many regions—there is an estimate that, in the last four years alone, over 60,000 farmers have committed suicide due to their inability to repay short-term crop loans. The government has announced a waiver of agricultural loans in the budget of over Rs 60,000 crore (US $15 billion). This would benefit all small and marginal farmers with landholdings of three hectares or less. As banks and cooperatives disburse the loans, the government has promised to reimburse the liabilities to the lenders over a period of three years. The farmers would become eligible for fresh loans. Earlier this month, the government had announced a US $6 billion dollars plan for agriculture and food security that includes a package of seeds, fertilizer, irrigation and technology to help agriculture grow faster. In this budget, there is an emphasis on new irrigation programmes as well as measures of storing surface water and sustainable exploitation of ground water.

The next area of focus of the budget is education. The midday meals programmes (school meals) is to be extended to all schools. Six thousand high quality middle schools will be opened to provide skills and knowledge to primary school leavers. Three new Indian Institutes of Technology and three new Indian Institutes of Management are to be opened. Sixteen central universities are to be set up. Most importantly, there is recognition that there is a mismatch between the skills needed in the economy and the skills available, leading to structural unemployment and a pressure on wages of skilled personnel and managers. A major programme for improving skills has been formulated with public–private partnership.

On health, outlays have been increased 15 per cent, with a focus on enlarging rural health programmes. A tax holiday for entrepreneurs wishing to set up hospitals in Tier Two and Tier Three cities has been announced. There are concessions on the imports of vaccines and life saving drugs.

Turning to the large middle class, the budget announcements include a large number of concessions. The income tax exemption limit has been raised from Rs 100,000 to 150,000 and would result in a cascading benefit for all taxpayers. Concessions for women and the elderly have been enhanced. Excise duties on small cars, two wheelers and some consumer items have been reduced.

Corporate taxes have been left undisturbed. Reduction in corporate taxes helps the company, the promoters and the shareholders but a reduction in input taxes helps the manufacturing industry as a whole. This budget has reduced excise duties on manufacturing from 16 to 14 per cent, a reduction that would make manufacturing more competitive. It would also pave the wave for the integration of a national Goods and Services Tax in 2010. The Central Sales Tax, levied on interstate sales of goods, has been reduced to 2 per cent. The moderation in excise duties has been due for some time and the finance minister, P. Chidambaram, has taken advantage of the buoyancy in revenues to reduce duties. On customs duties, peak rates are unchanged, given that there has been a significant appreciation of the rupee that has made imports cheaper. Some selective concessions that are industry-specific have been granted.

In the financial sector, a levy on transactions in the commodity exchanges has been announced. Similarly, there is an increase in short-term capital gains tax from 10 per cent to 15 per cent.

There are also a number of programmes that are aimed at the Scheduled Castes and Tribes, the minorities and the Muslims. This is the first time that the budget speech carries details of such affirmative action programmes. It appears to be a measure to win the votes of these sections in the elections though it is not entirely clear whether these sections would be swayed by these give-aways. At least, on paper, the government appears to have managed to balance populism with fiscal responsibility, though the reality is much less forgiving (see Table 1).

However, the expenditure appears to be understated for three reasons:

Table 1: Tax Revenues

(Rs bn, fiscal years beginning April 1)

		2007–8		2008–9	%	
	2006–7	Budget	Revised	Budget	2007–8	2008–9
Gross tax revenues	4,735.1	5,481.2	5,854.1	6,877.2	23.6	17.5
Union excise duties	1,176.1	1,302.2	1,279.5	1,378.7	8.8	7.8
Customs	863.3	987.7	1,007.7	1,189.3	16.7	18.0
Corporation tax	1,443.2	1,684.0	1,861.3	2,263.6	29.0	21.6
Income tax	750.9	987.7	1,183.2	1,383.1	57.6	16.9
Service tax	376.0	502.0	506.0	644.6	34.6	27.4

Source: Ministry of Finance. Website: Budget at a Glance: Budget 2008–2009. The weblink is: http://finmin.nic.in/the ministry/dept eco affairs/dea.html

1. Expenditure to the tune of 2–2.5 per cent of GDP (on oil bonds and fertilizer subsidies) remains off budget;
2. There is no provision for the potential hit to fiscal finances from the Sixth Pay Commission's recommendations that are expected in April this year; and
3. The loan waiver of Rs 600 billion (1.1 per cent of the official full year GDP for 2008–9) is not reflected in government spending.

The finance minister has preferred to show rosy projections rather than be realistic and be fiscally responsible by including in the budget at least some estimate of the potential hit from the Pay Commission and the loan waiver.

The fiscal deficit for 2008–9 is forecast at 2.5 per cent of GDP, lower than the better-than-expected deficit outcome of 3.1 per cent of GDP for 2007–8, and lower than the 3 per cent of GDP mandated by the Fiscal Responsibility and Budget Management Act. It is highly unlikely that the government will achieve its forecast for next year's fiscal deficit owing to aforementioned factors that will cause actual spending to be higher than the budget forecast. The officially stated improvement in fiscal deficit appears to be an exercise in virtual reality.

Net borrowings for 2008–9 have been budgeted at Rs 1 trillion, lower than expectations of Rs 1.1 trillion. The gross borrowing estimate is also lower-than-expected at Rs 1.45 trillion. Critically, it does not include oil bond redemptions of Rs. 130 billion. It remains to be seen how the government finances maturing oil bonds. Moreover, the budget estimates do not provide for any outgo from anticipated salary increases owing to the recommendations of the Sixth Pay Commission. The debt waiver granted to farmers has also not been included in the government's expenditure and this lends upside risks to the fiscal deficit estimate. In short, it is unlikely that the finance minister's expectations on revenues would be met, leaving the next government with the unhappy task of cleaning up the deficits.

The debt waiver scheme is not without its perils. Periodic debt waivers set up incentives for farmers to be irresponsible in borrowing, knowing that they will get a waiver at a future date. They contaminate the opportunity to build a genuine financial ecosystem surrounding farmers, which can cope with the risks and requirements of these users. If the intent is to help 'poor people', then landholders are the wrong target audience; poor people are those who do not have land. While 80 per cent of holdings are covered in the debt waiver plan, the government has gone on to offer a 25 per cent write off even to the top 20 per cent of holdings. The UPA's agenda was to focus on a number of flagship welfare programmes. The spending is underway but it hasn't been delivering results. The 'flagship programmes of the UPA' are not working too well and the UPA isn't winning elections. This debt waiver programme appears to be an effort at trying somehow to get state money to some voters.

The Economic Survey, tabled in parliament a few days back, had indicated that, if growth were to pick up, the acceleration of reforms was necessary. Several areas, including reforms in banking, insurance, labour markets and privatisation initiatives, have been mentioned in the document. There is also an urgency expressed about the need to hasten the implementation of infrastructure projects. It is interesting that the budget speech makes no mention of any reform or even of infrastructure constraints and the need to address them. It is surprising that there is no effort to deal with the existing obstacles to growth.

Finally, several important initiatives have not been fleshed out. There is an urgent need to upgrade skills for ensuring employability but the details of this scheme have not been worked out. Irrigation is important but funding has not been provided. There is a mention of corporate bond and currency derivative markets but the road-map is not clear. The announcements outweigh the actionable programmes and it does appear as though a number of promises have been made only keeping the voter in mind and are not part of a clearly thought out government policy.

It is clear that there will be elections before the end of the year.

34

South Asia's Inflation Challenges

M. SHAHIDUL ISLAM

(*28 March 2008*)

Introduction

After recovering from the two oil shocks in 1974 and 1979, the global economy enjoyed fairly stable price levels till early 2000 (see Figure 1). It is widely viewed that globalisation has had a positive impact on prices for over one and a half decade by increasing competition both on the demand and supply sides. Central bankers, especially those that pursued inflation targeting monetary policies, have widely been credited for keeping inflation low. However, many economies (net commodity importing countries, in particular) around the world are now faced with exorbitant price hike in fuel and non-fuel commodities (see Figures 1 and 2). Since early 2007, oil and many agricultural commodities have been witnessing an abrupt price hike (see Table 1, and Figures 1 and 2). In the past year alone, prices of rice and wheat have gone up by 52 and 112 per cent respectively, and oil is now traded over US $100 a barrel.

In South Asia (excluding India), the current hikes have exposed the vulnerability of the low and middle income groups and the government exchequers. The price hike situation of primary commodities in most South Asian countries has further worsened due to low per capita agricultural production, the Central Bank's lax monetary policies (or lagged effects of earlier expansionary monetary policies), undervalued exchange rate polices (economies other than India and Nepal), and internal political instability.

South Asia's largest economy, India, is relatively less vulnerable to the current inflationary shock, thanks largely to its higher domestic production capacity of agricultural commodities and

Table 1: Actual Market Prices for Selected Fuel and Non-Fuel Commodities: 2004–February 2008

Commodities	Units	2004	2005	2006	2007 Q2	2007 Q4	February 2008
Wheat	$/MT	157	152	192	206	342	425
Rice	$/MT	246	288	304	323	357	481
Soyabean Oil	$/MT	590	496	551	751	965	1,308
Palm Oil	$/MT	435	368	417	711	862	1,109
Copper	$/MT	2,863	3,676	6,731	7,649	7,203	7,941
Aluminium	$/MT	1,719	1,901	2,573	2,768	2,445	2,785
Dubai Brent	$/bbl	33.5	49.2	61.4	64.7	83.2	90.0

Source: International Monetary Fund's Primary Commodity Price data.

Figure 1: Commodity Research Bureau Spot Index (1967=100): January 1947 to February 2008

Source: Commodity Research Bureau (http://www.crbtrader.com/)

Figure 2: Indices of Primary Commodity Prices: 1995–2007

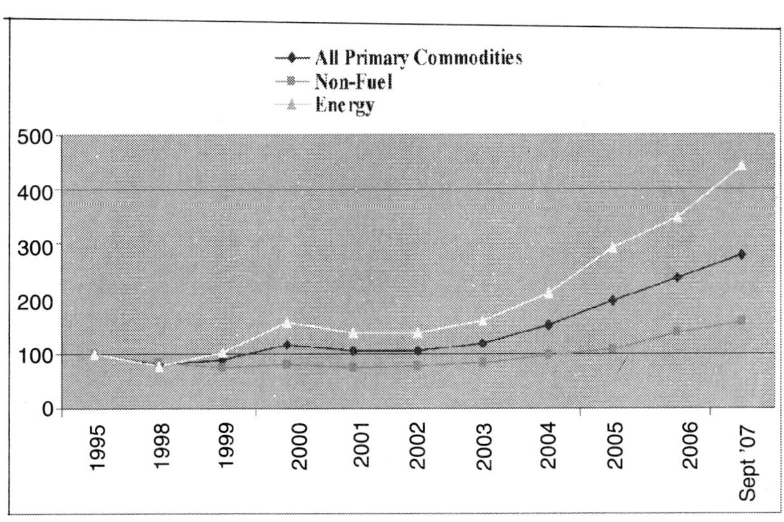

Note: 1995=100, Non-fuel commodities comprise of cereals, vegetable oil and protein meals, meat, sugar, bananas, oranges, Beverages, industrial inputs, agriculture raw materials, and metals.

Source: Based on International Monetary Fund's Primary Commodity Price data.

recent appreciation in its currency, *inter alia*. Nevertheless, oil price volatilities in the world market remain a worry for the economy. In *Macroeconomic and Monetary Developments* 28 January 2008, the RBI acknowledged that 'since pass-through of higher international oil prices to domestic prices remains incomplete, inflation has remained suppressed'.

The other major economies in the region, viz., Pakistan, Bangladesh, Sri Lanka who largely depend on international markets for fuel and, to lesser extent, for non-fuel commodities face much more daunting challenges than India to contain inflation. The inflation scenario in Nepal is likely to follow the price level in India, largely because the former's domestic currency is pegged to that of the latter.

According to the Economist Intelligence Unit (EIU), the Consumer Price Index (CPI) inflation in Sri Lanka recorded 17.5 per cent in 2007, followed by Bangladesh (9.1 per cent), Pakistan (7.6 per cent), India (6.4 per cent), and Nepal (5.3 per cent) (see Figure 3).

Figure 3: CPI Inflation in Selected South Asian Economies: 2007 and 2008 (forecast value)

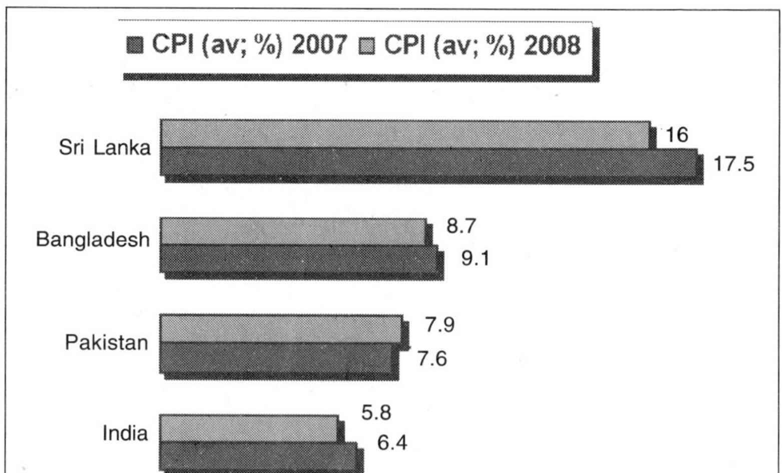

Source: Based on Economist Intelligence Unit.

For the South Asian countries, the challenges of inflation are two-pronged. Firstly, galloping inflation could significantly destabilise key macroeconomic variables, including gross domestic (GDP) growth. Higher oil import bills that most economies in the region absorb through subsidies could further swell their fiscal deficits. Secondly, price volatilities pose political danger. South Asia hosts the largest number of poor people in the world and the correlation between per capita income and food weight in total CPI is generally higher for low-income group consumers. Rising food prices are effectively a regressive tax. If the past is any guide, price volatilities of South Asian staples, rice and wheat, could result in political instability in the region. The World Food Programme cautioned that the rising prices of food items, especially rice, may cause political instability, since poorer households spend up to 80 per cent of their income on food.

Against this backdrop, this paper briefly analyses the ongoing inflation in South Asia. It also suggests some anti-inflationary measures for these economies.

Inflation Scenarios in South Asia

Among all South Asian economies, Sri Lanka is the hardest hit by the current price spiral. The New Colombo CPI reached 21.6 per cent in February 2008 while the annual average inflation moved up to 17 per cent, according to the Central Bank of Sri Lanka (CBSL). Unlike the other economies of South Asia, Sri Lanka has revised its administered energy prices upward in several stages since 2000. The country imports almost 100 per cent of its oil needs, and petroleum price hike in the international market is substantially being passed through to its consumers albeit the Exchequer absorbs diesel and kerosene price rise to some extent.[1] As a result, oil price hike has had a direct impact on the economy's CPI inflation. Secondly, apart from oil, price hike in most soft commodities in the international markets, has had an impact on the country's inflation. Thirdly, the real wage increase in the recent past has put additional pressure on prices.[2] Fourthly, due to a setback in Sri Lanka's agriculture sector, the prices of domestically-produced agricultural commodities, that account for 78 per cent of the total consumption basket in the CPI, have increased significantly. Fifthly, inflation has been exacerbated due to the distribution disruptions of agriculture produce following the adverse security developments in the Northern and Eastern provinces. Sixthly, imported inflation has soared as the Sri Lanka rupee has weakened in recent years[3] (see Figure 7). Last but not least, between May and September last year, the CBSL issued currency worth of Rs 49 billion (US $457 million). The extra cash injection in the economy, along with high government spending and rapid growth in credit, has also been exerting pressure on the price rise.

Consumers in Bangladesh have been observing an exorbitant price hike of primary commodities. The Bangladesh Bank, the Central Bank of Bangladesh, reported that inflation was 11.43 per cent on a point-to-point basis in January 2008 whereas food-inflation hit 14.20 per cent in the same period. The price hike of fuel and non-fuel commodities in the international markets is widely blamed for the current inflation in Bangladesh. Secondly, Bangladesh faced two major natural disasters (summer floods and cyclone *Sidr*) in 2007 which damaged standing crops, among others, and escalated food prices. Moreover, in recent years, growth in the agriculture sector has been sluggish. Thirdly, the recent ban on exports of some essentials such as rice, wheat, lentil and onion by neighbouring India has been a major supply shock for the economy. Fourthly, the current caretaker government's drives against corruption have exacerbated the supply-side problem. The actions against the so-called unscrupulous business people have greatly handicapped the country's business, including commodity trading. Consequently, there has been a supply-side constraint in the food grain market. Fifthly, the depreciation in the country's currency unit, the Bangladesh taka against its major trading partners, the expansion of broad money and credit have also played a part in raising prices. In its latest Monetary Policy Statement, the Bangladesh Bank acknowledged that the lagged effects of higher than programmed monetary expansion during fiscal year 2007 and excess liquidity played a part in raising prices.

The inflation scenario in Bangladesh could have been much

worse had the Exchequer not absorbed a substantial portion of the oil import bills as subsidies. The country imports 90 per cent of its oil requirements from international markets but does not pass through the full oil import bill directly to its consumers. The Bangladesh Petroleum Corporation (BPC), the state-owned energy entity, sells petroleum products at much lower prices in the domestic market than its actual import costs, and the difference (import price minus local market price) is being absorbed by the government of Bangladesh as subsidies. The BPC's losses are estimated at US $794 million or 1.1 per cent of GDP in the fiscal year 2008, according to the Asian Development Bank (ADB). The Bangladesh government is under severe pressure from the World Bank and the International Monetary Fund to pass through the oil prices instead of increasing its fiscal burden. The economy's fiscal deficit is projected to expand to 5 per cent of its GDP in 2008 from 4.4 per cent in 2007 (see Figure 4).

Figure 4: Fiscal Deficit in Selected South Asian Countries (% of GDP): 2007 and 2008 (forecast value)

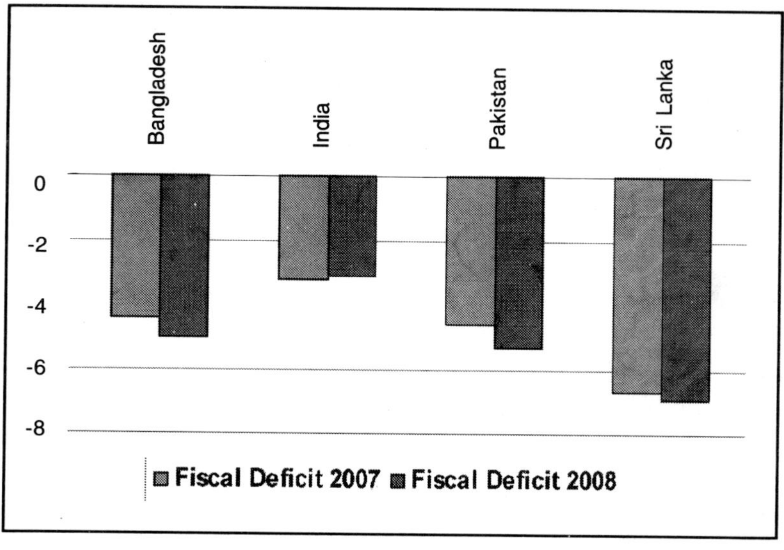

Source: Based on Economist Intelligence Unit.

In Pakistan, the year-on-year consumer price inflation reached 11.3 per cent in February 2008, largely owing to the extraordinarily high food prices, apart from higher energy prices. The food inflation reached 18.3 per cent—the fifth consecutive month with a double-digit increase, according to the EIU. Pakistan is an oil producer but relies on imports for more than 80 per cent of its consumption. The oil price hike in the international markets is absorbed partly by the government and partly by the consumers. As a result, the recent oil price hike pushed the CPI upward as well as added an extra burden on the government's fiscal health. The energy prices were revised upward in March 2008.[4] The government's domestic borrowing exceeded Rs 350 billion (US $5.7 billion) out of which Rs 150 billion (US $2.45 billion) went to the oil subsidies. Consequently, Pakistan's fiscal deficit is projected to increase to 5.3 per cent in 2008 from 4.6 per cent in 2007, according to EIU (see Figure 4). In its latest Monetary Policy Statement, the State Bank of Pakistan reported that inflation has been exacerbated due to high growth of money supply in the current fiscal year. The broad money growth in the current fiscal year was 19.3 per cent which exceeded its target level (5.8 per cent). Further, like Sri Lanka and Bangladesh, the depreciating Pakistan rupee has contributed to imported inflation (see Figure 8).

In India, the CPI inflation was in the range of 5.1 to 5.9 per cent during November–December 2007. Inflation based on the wholesale price index soared to a 12-month high of 5.92 per cent as on 8 March 2008 which is above the 5 per cent limit set by the RBI for this fiscal year. India imports 70 per cent of its oil requirements, and the petroleum import bill is largely absorbed by the Indian government and its public sector energy entities through oil bonds so that oil price hike in the international markets do not hurt the consumers and the central government's fiscal book.

In his 2007–8 union budget speech, the Indian finance minister, P. Chidambaram, too reckoned that there is pressure on domestic prices of food articles in India. He contended that, 'Managing the supply side of food articles will be the most crucial task in the ensuing year and keeping inflation under check is one of the cornerstones of our policy.'

Growth in India's agriculture sector has been sluggish in recent years. However, the country is expecting a record harvest in 2008. The total food grains output in India in 2007–8 is expected to be 219.32 million tonnes. To avoid food price spiral in its domestic market, the authorities have banned exports of several commodities and fixed higher prices of exportable agriculture produces. Further, rupee appreciations since late 2006 have insulated the economy from imported inflation (see Figure 6).

The headline inflation in Nepal remains broadly in line with price developments in India. The appreciation of the Nepalese rupee had contained the imported inflation. However, food and oil prices continue to push the prices up. In January 2008, the authorities have increased energy prices,[5] and, since October 2007, the prices have been adjusted upward three times, as losses for Nepal Oil, the state-owned energy entity, have soared due to global oil price increase. The Nepal Rastra Bank expects that inflation will remain about 5 per cent in 2007–8, whereas the ADB projects that the figure will be 5.3 to 5.4 per cent.

Based on the above analysis, we can summarize the current state of South Asia's inflation as follows:

1. Sri Lanka, Bangladesh and Pakistan are highly vulnerable to fuel and food price hike.
2. The CPI figure in Sri Lanka is much higher *vis-à-vis* its neighbours, as the country adjusted oil prices upward instead of putting additional pressure on its fiscal sector. The reason is that the fiscal deficit in Sri Lanka has already exceeded the danger level (6.7 per cent of the country's GDP in 2007) as the government's expenditure outweighed its revenue income alarmingly. In Bangladesh and Pakistan, fiscal deficit has swelled due to petroleum subsidies, among others.
3. The Nominal Effective Exchange Rate (NEER) and the Real Effective Exchange Rate (REER), except for the Indian rupee, have been moving in opposite directions (see Figures 6 to 9). Generally, the NEER and the REER move quite closely together, with the exception being in high inflationary environments. In Figure 6, we see that in 2007, the NEER and the

REER of the Indian rupee moved in the same direction largely owing to low to moderate inflation in India. Though the rapid depreciation in the Sri Lankan rupee, the Bangladeshi taka and the Pakistani rupee against the United States dollar, in the recent past, has slowed down lately (the Bangladesh taka even appreciated slightly), it has to be remembered that the United States dollar has seen a sharp depreciation against major currencies, which is known as the United States dollar index of late. Consequently, India's exchange rate policies (so is Nepal's) have been of help in weathering imported inflation. In other countries, undervalued (competitive) exchange rate policies have exacerbated their domestic inflation. Economic theories too support that if the nominal exchange rate does not allow sufficient appreciation, real exchange rate adjustment only happens through increase in the price level over time, relative to trading partners. The Chinese economy also experienced a similar situation recently until its currency, the yuan, was allowed to appreciate.

4. Monetary policies in most economies have been lax which is reflected by the fact that money supply has increased steadily in these economies in recent years. Even if the broad money and credit growth have declined in Bangladesh in the recent quarters (see Figure 5), there is a lagged effect of these variables on prices.
5. In Bangladesh and Pakistan, the supply-side of the commodity market has been disrupted by the internal political unrests and emergency rules, and in Sri Lanka, the market is disturbed by ethnic conflicts.

Near Term Inflation Expectations

Although the global commodity prices worked predictably in line with the Prebisch and Singer (1950) hypothesis which states that the prices of commodities relative to that of manufactured goods will tend to decline over time, however, the recent trends show that the ongoing upturn in the global commodity markets has been large and rapid.

Figure 5: Broad Money Growth in Selected South Asian Economics (in %): 2006–7

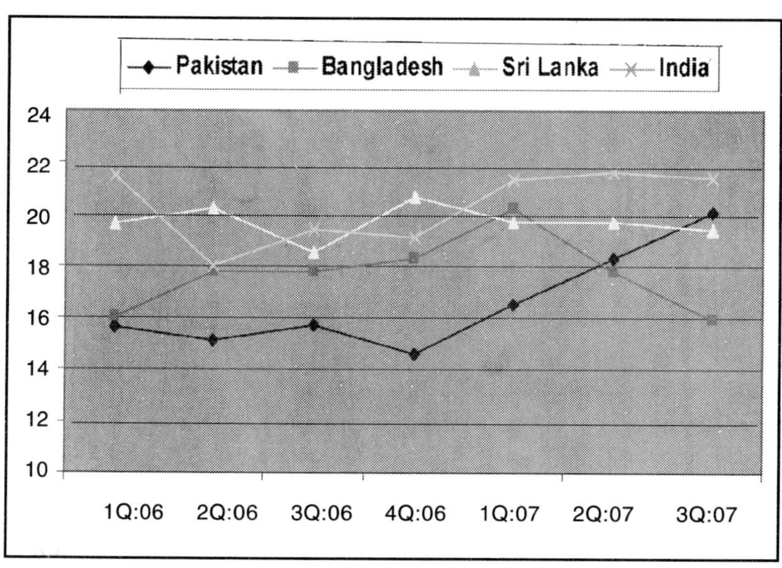

Source: Based on Economist Intelligence Unit.

Figure 6: NEER and REER Movements of Indian Rupee: January 2007–December 2007

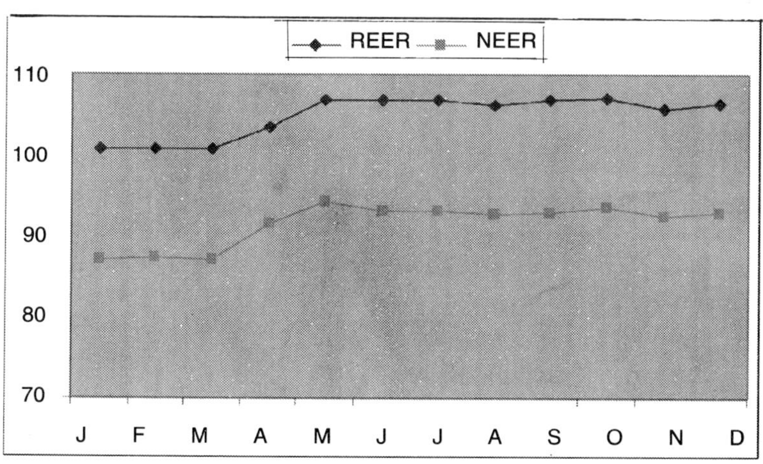

Source: Based on Reserve Bank of India.

Figure 7: NEER and REER Movements of Sri Lanka Rupee: October 2006–October 2007

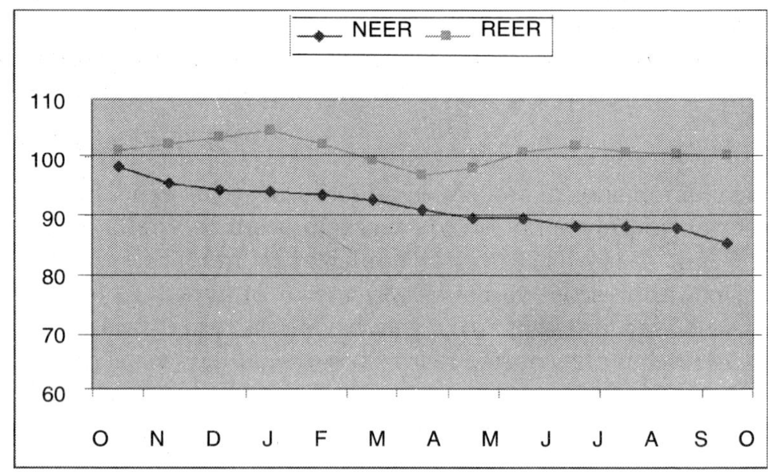

Source: Based on Central Bank of Sri Lanka.

Figure 8: NEER and REER Movements of Pakistan Rupee: January 2007–December 2007

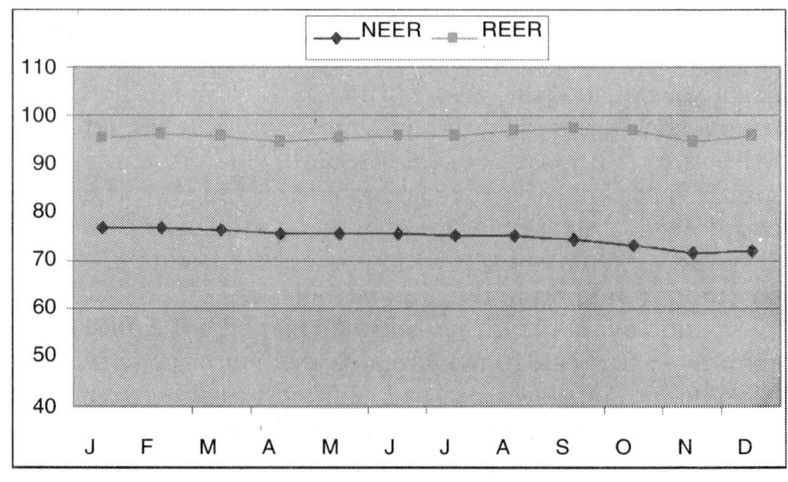

Source: Based on State Bank of Pakistan.

Figure 9: NEER and REER Movements of Bangladesh Taka: March 2005–June 2007

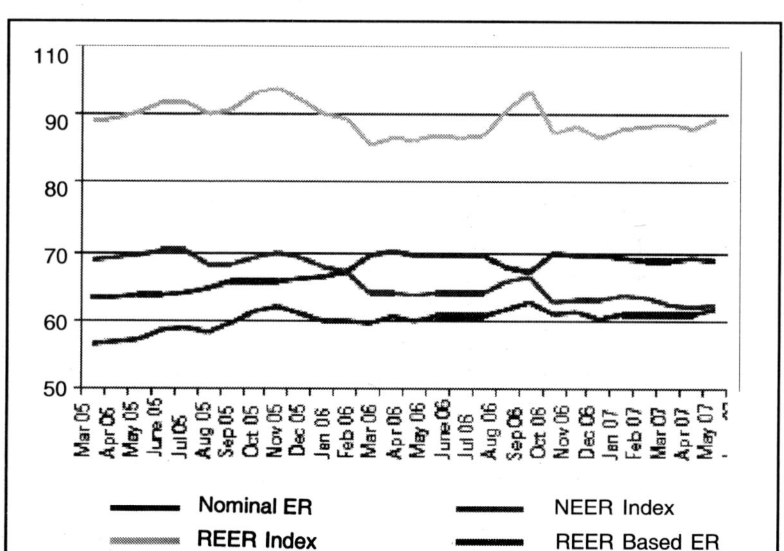

Source: Bangladesh Bank.

If the United States dollar continues to slide, oil prices remain high, strong demand for commodities (particularly from emerging markets) persists, and more and more oil-seeds, and staples channels towards bio-fuel production, the South Asian economies may observe even higher than the current level of inflation in the coming months.

Nevertheless, the flip side of this forecast is that the slow-down in the United States and some other major economies may have a dampening effect on prices. Moreover, if China and other major emerging markets prioritise inflation checks over growth, then the sky-rocketing trend of commodity prices might slow-down.

The EIU's inflation forecast for Sri Lanka, Bangladesh, India and Pakistan for 2008 shows that the prices in these economies are likely to follow the 2007 prices (see Figure 3). As discussed, India's inflation is still at a tolerable level. Moreover, the country is expecting a record harvest in 2008. To avoid food inflation, the authorities have banned exports of several commodities and fixed higher prices of exportable agriculture produces. Nevertheless, the potential risk of price hike in the economy may arise from three avenues. First, foreign portfolio investor's increasing appetite for the Indian market will continue to put pressure on the Indian rupee. If not fully sterilised, the economy will have excess liquidity that can induce inflation. Following the sub-prime crisis, the Fed cut interest rates a few times and this has put pressure on the RBI to revise its key interest rates downward. However, the dilemma for the RBI is that lowering interest rates will increase inflation. Secondly, roughly 10 million public sector employees in India are likely to get a 40 per cent pay rise this year. If wages go up, prices are also set to increase. Thirdly, the country is preparing for parliamentary elections early next year. Government expenditures and political parties' budget (both disclosed and undisclosed) tend to increase in election years. If all these issues are left unchecked, inflation might surpass the RBI's expectations in coming months.

Fiscal and Monetary Measures to Contain Inflation

Both fiscal and monetary policies have a role to play in containing inflation. Fiscal policy tools, including a reduction in import and excise duties, could be applied to contain imported inflation. Indeed, such tools have applied in Bangladesh[6] and, lately, import duties on a number of essential commodities, in particular, edible oil, have been reduced in India. Sri Lanka had earlier reduced import duties but later re-imposed them with the view that the revenues generated from this avenue are too important to forgo, even albeit temporarily.

Monetary- and exchange-rate policies in these inflation-hit economies should be applied prudently. Most emerging market economies are now fighting inflation either by appreciating their currencies or hiking policy rates or applying both, depending on their macroeconomic conditions. In India, currency appreciation continues to be used as a major instrument to contain imported inflation, though widening current account deficit is a concern for the policy makers (see Figure 10). Nevertheless, as most of India's

Figure 10: Current Account Balance in Selected South Asian Countries (% of GDP): 2007 and 2008 (forecast value)

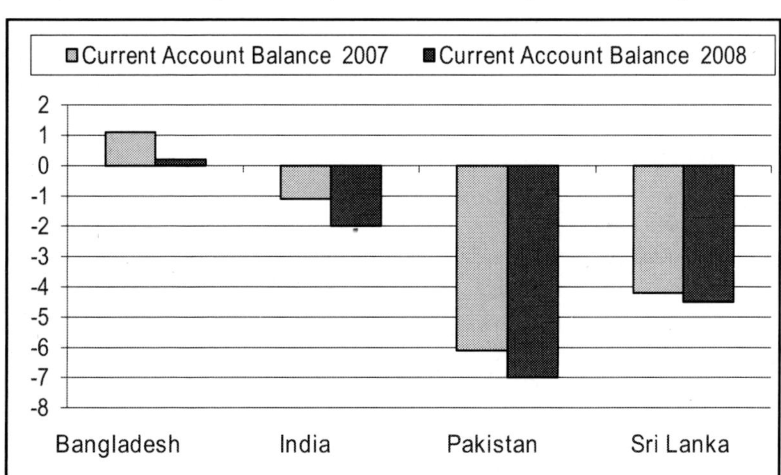

Source: Based on Economist Intelligence Unit.

competitor economies, including China, are now appreciating their currencies to contain inflation, the competitiveness concern for the economy is becoming a less pressing issue. Following the latest Federal rate cut, the RBI may increase its key policy rates slightly. In an election year, the current United Progressive Alliance government may prefer inflation check as a priority even if such a move (containing credit and money supply growth) slows down India's economic growth.

Bangladesh can afford to keep its currency slightly stronger, thanks to its favourable current account position, albeit the current account surplus in the economy is projected to decline in 2008 (see Figure 10). The Bangladesh Bank has already tightened the broad money supply and credit growth, though there is a lagged effect of its previous expansionary monetary policies. The monetary policy should be more contractionary even if it is at the cost of the country's economic growth. Sri Lanka and Pakistan have to rely on the interest rates hike, as the current account deficits in these economies have been widening (see Figure 10).

Apart from fiscal and monetary measures, it is important for the

South Asian states to address domestic supply-side bottlenecks. There is a need to tackle the supply-side constraints in the commodity markets, particularly in Bangladesh, so that international market prices can converge with the domestic prices.

The South Asian economies, other than India, may also need to rely on external aid if their agriculture sectors fail to provide a good harvest in the coming months.

There is a need for fuel cost economisation in most South Asian economies. However, automatic adjustment of oil prices in the midst of ongoing sky-rocketing inflation might bring countervailing results, especially in Bangladesh and Pakistan. At the same time, there is a high fiscal risk of petroleum subsidies in these economies. Gradual price adjustment for the high-end energy products might be a viable option. In the absence of a vibrant financial sector, bond markets in particular, India's strategy to cushion off the consumers and the fiscal sector from the ongoing oil price hike may not be a feasible solution for other countries in South Asia.

NOTES

1. In January 2007, the prices of petrol increased to Rs 127 (US $ 1.16) per litre from Rs 117 and the prices of diesel and kerosene rose to Rs 80 and 70 respectively. The gas price has also seen a similar trend.
2. Public sector wages were increased from January 2007.
3. The Sri Lankan rupee depreciated by around 5 by September 2007, compared with 1.6 in the same period of 2006.
4. The price of gas rose 6.9 per cent to Rs 62.81 (US $1.03) per litre. Diesel rose 7.2 per cent to a little over Rs 40 (US $0.65) per litre.
5. In January 2008, diesel prices were increased by 9 per cent to Rs 61 (96 US cents) and kerosene prices by 19.6 per cent, also to Rs 61. Liquid petroleum gas prices were also raised by 16 per cent to Rs 1,250 per cylinder.
6. The import duties on a number of essential commodities, including rice and wheat, have been withdrawn.

35

India's Annual Policy Statement for FY 2008–2009: Achieving a 'Neither Tight, Nor Liberal' Monetary Policy

AMITENDU PALIT

(7 May 2008)

THE RESERVE BANK of India (RBI) announced its Annual Policy Statement for FY 2008–9 on 29 April 2008. Given the high headline inflation in India, many had felt that the RBI would tighten monetary policy by increasing interest rates. It was, therefore, surprising to note that all the key policy rates (that is, bank rate, repo rate and reverse repo rate) were kept unchanged. Only the Cash Reserve Ratio (CRR) has been increased for arresting growth in liquidity.

It must have been difficult for the RBI to work out an appropriate monetary policy, given the complexities in the current macroeconomic environment. Price management, undoubtedly, is one of the biggest policy challenges facing the RBI now. With headline inflation based on the point-to-point wholesale price index at more than 7 per cent, maintaining price stability is of utmost importance. With elections to the Indian parliament drawing closer, much of the overall policy focus in the coming months will be on reducing prices. It was, therefore, imperative for the RBI to accord 'high' priority to price stability.

It is not only the RBI that is worried about maintaining prices. Price stability has emerged as the top priority for central banks in practically all major Emerging Market Economies (EME). High food and energy prices produced by wide demand-supply imbalances have led to a sharp increase in headline inflations in EMEs. Central banks in these economies are implementing a variety of measures to contain inflation. Some, such as the People's Bank of China and the Banco Central do Brasil, have tightened monetary policies by increasing interest rates. Other central banks, such as those in Mexico, Malaysia, and Thailand, have however, kept interest rates and the broader stance of their monetary policies unchanged. The specific monetary policies being adopted by different EMEs' central banks across the world are being determined by several factors. These include levels of capital inflows, liquidity positions, conditions of domestic financial markets, exchange rate movements, overall macroeconomic fundamentals and the current state of domestic prices.

In preparing its latest policy, the RBI has had to accommodate conflicting concerns and major trade-offs. On the one hand, it had to ensure that the monetary policy is strongly anti-inflationary. Anti-inflationary monetary policies are usually tight having relatively high interest rates. However, increasing interest rates at this juncture could have created other problems. The RBI has already come in for sharp criticism for increasing interest rates during 2007–8, which many felt, were not only unnecessary, but were also responsible for adversely affecting growth in industrial output.

With industrial growth during April–February 2007–8 coming down to 8.7 per cent, compared with 11.2 per cent in the corresponding period of 2006–7, concerns over moderation in industrial growth couldn't have been overlooked. Such concerns look graver if one takes into account the current performance of infrastructure industries. The six core infrastructure industries (electricity, coal, steel, cement, crude oil and finished petroleum products) show an overall growth of only 5.6 per cent in April–February 2007–8. This is more than 3 percentage points lower than the growth of 8.7 per cent recorded by infrastructure industries in April–February 2006–7.

The challenge before the RBI was to prepare a monetary policy that would ensure price stability without affecting industrial and overall growth. It also had to take note of the emerging concerns over a possible slow-down in industrial investment. This is reflected in the lower growth of non-food credit disbursed by scheduled commercial banks during 2007–8. Till the end of March 2008, non-food credit, which is essentially meant for industrial and commercial purposes, grew at a lower rate of 22.3 per cent, compared with 28.5 per cent in the previous year. Critics of the RBI's policies are quick to point out that lower credit flow to industry is a natural outcome of higher interest rates. Any further increase in interest rates might have worsened the industrial investment outlook for the coming months.

In developing the latest policy, the RBI has clearly refrained from adopting any measure that might adversely affect industrial performance and sentiments. However, by increasing the CRR, it has indicated its concern over the liquidity levels in the economy. The reserve money growth in the economy at around 30.9 per cent is probably much higher than what the RBI would like it to be. Such growth has taken place despite an earlier round of increase in the CRR. Much of the growth in reserve money is being contributed by net foreign exchange assets. As on 18 April 2008, India's foreign exchange reserves were US $313.5 billion, showing the continuing high rate of accumulation of foreign assets. Indeed, such accumulation during 2007–8 was around US $110.5 billion.

It is evident that despite the occasional setbacks suffered by the stock market in recent months, capital flows continue to come in. Such flows, if left 'unsterilised', affect the exchange rate. This is again another critical issue that the RBI could hardly have overlooked. A stronger rupee will erode export margins, particularly for textile and information technology exporters. After faltering during the first half of 2007–8, merchandise exports have recovered in the later months to record an overall growth of 22.8 per cent during April 2007–February 2008. This is, however, still lower than the growth rate of 23.2 per cent achieved during the corresponding period of 2006–7.

Thus, the RBI cannot afford to leave the capital inflows unsterilised. It would intervene in the market for picking up the foreign currency denominated inflows and releasing an equivalent amount of domestic currency in the process. Unless it does so, the exchange rate might move against the interests of exporters.

However, 'sterilisation' increases the money supply in the economy. In an economy, where despite high prices, the propensity to consume is yet to show signs of reducing, thanks mostly to higher middle-class disposable incomes, higher money supply can push up prices with a time lag. Inflationary concerns, therefore, call for reducing money supply and liquid balances at the disposal of the general public. In addition to usual open market operations involving buying and selling of government securities for mopping up liquidity, the RBI has also decided to force commercial banks to hold on to larger cash balances by upping the CRR.

The main objective that the RBI aims to achieve through the current policy is to bring down headline inflation from its current level of 7.14 per cent to around 5.5 per cent and closer to 5 per cent. It takes note of the monetary overhang in the system and emphasises the reduction of monetary expansion. At the same time, it is wary of the signals emanating from the industry and would like to maintain growth of non-food credit to at least around 20 per cent during the year. It must be noted that these objectives are conceived in the backdrop of a somewhat lower gross domestic product (GDP) growth during 2008–9. While the advance estimates for 2007–8 prepared by the Central Statistical Organisation show a real GDP growth of 8.7 per cent for the year, the projections for 2008–9 are range-bound, marginally lower between 8–8.5 per cent.

Only time will tell whether the RBI will be able to achieve its objectives or not. However, like almost all other EMEs' central banks, it is evident that the RBI is also caught in a policy dilemma. The dilemma is a result of its trying to manage several conflicting policy goals. Maintaining price stability is definitely its foremost objective. However, it cannot afford to engage in too much monetary tightening for curbing prices as that will have adverse impacts elsewhere in the economy. Industrial production in the short term and investment growth in the long term are likely to suffer from tight monetary policies and high interest rates. On the other hand, it cannot afford to liberalise the monetary policy too much. That will increase money supply and add to inflationary pressures. Thus, it needs to discover a 'neither tight, nor liberal' monetary policy. That is not an easy task. And to further compound its woes, it has to contend with jerky levels of capital flows, exchange rate fluctuations and problems of sterilisation. The latest policy has tried to address all these concerns with minimum fuss. It is time to wait for the results.

36

Of Agflation and Agriculture: Time to Fix the Structural Problems

M. SHAHIDUL ISLAM
(*5 May 2008*)

> If agriculture goes wrong, nothing else can go right.
>
> M.S. SWAMINATHAN

AGRICULTURAL COMMODITY prices have reached nosebleed levels in recent months.[1] The impact of the ongoing agflation across the world, especially on the low and fixed income groups, is so severe that the World Food Programme has described the phenomenon as a 'silent tsunami'.[2] The current food shortage is also seen as the first truly global food crisis since World War II. The Asian Development Bank thinks that one billion people in Asia are seriously affected by the surging global food prices.[3] As there is a direct nexus between access to food and poverty, it is feared that soaring food prices will push more people under the poverty line and this could jeopardise the progress towards the millennium development goals. The World Bank believes that the current food crisis imperils 100 million people in poor countries.[4] Nevertheless, the World Bank's explanation of extreme poverty (people who earn less than US $1 a day) underestimates the actual number of the poor in the world, as the sliding United States dollar and higher food and energy prices have made the definition somewhat obsolete. However, there are some winners of the current soft commodity boom too. Net food exporting countries have been enjoying improved terms of trade.

There are several explanations for the ongoing high food prices. Rising demand from emerging markets, sliding United States dollar, higher energy prices, excessively loose monetary conditions, commodity speculation, weather woes, and developments of bio-fuels, *inter alia*, are the drivers of the current agflation. Further, to fuel the fire, some Asian countries, including China, India and Vietnam, have banned or restricted several key cereal exports, which has created food shortages in many parts of Asia. These factors, mostly demand-driven ones, are pushing food inflation up. However, the ongoing agflation is also linked to some fundamental supply-side factors associated with agriculture. Nonetheless, the current global food crisis can be a tipping point for the civilisations' most primitive sector, if history is any guide.

New Dynamics in Food Supply-Demand

In the last four decades, cereal production has more than doubled largely owing to the Green Revolution in the late 1960s, exceeding the population growth.[5] However, these great achievements have been overshadowed by chronic hunger and malnutrition that still haunt over 800 million people, mostly in Sub-Saharan Africa and many parts of Asia and Latin America.[6]

After maintaining equilibrium in the food grain market for a long period, some important factors have emerged in the global food supply-demand scene in recent years.

First, there has been a sudden shift from demand-constraint to supply-constraint environment in the agriculture market. Despite a 3.5 billion increase in global population since 1960, world food supplies have been 20 per cent higher per person and real prices are 40 per cent lower than they were in 1961, according to the Food and Agriculture Organization (FAO).[7] As there has been a dampening effect on agricultural commodity prices, cereal and other food grain production have started to increase at a decreasing pace, especially in India, China and some other parts of the world.[8] Since early 1990s, agricultural productivity growth (particularly rice, wheat and maize) has shown a declining trend.[9] Since 2007, higher demand has been pushing the food prices up, as supply is not able to cope with it.

Second, as the per capita income increases, the demand for meat and dairy products tends to increase. In recent years, per capita calorie intake has been increasing steadily in developing countries, particularly in Asia. Since China and other emerging economies' higher gross domestic product (GDP) growth has lifted millions of people out of extreme poverty, the demand for high-protein diets has increased. As a result, meat consumption has increased tremendously. The end result is that more and more cereals have been diverted to produce poultry and other meat. For instance, in China, the 2005/1990 ratios of per capita consumption for cereals, meat, milk and vegetables were 0.8, 2.4, 3.0 and 2.9 respectively.[10] It is estimated that, for the production of 1 kg of meat, on an average at least 3 kg of cereals are needed.[11] Consequently, the world's cereal demand is likely to increase by 40–50 per cent, driven strongly by rapidly growing animal feed use and meat production.[12]

Third, climate change concerns have promoted the development of alternative energy market. For instance, the road to biofuel was paved with good intentions. But the end result—the diversion of food to fuel—is doing more harm than good. The European Union, the United States and some other countries subsidise farmers to grow crops for alternative energy. The United States farmers have shifted their cultivation towards biofuel crops substantially in recent years. It is estimated that, in 2008, roughly 30 per cent of United States' maize production will be diverted to ethanol production[13] and such transformation is largely at the cost of wheat and soyabean cultivation. The United Nations has dubbed this phenomenon as a crime against humanity. Though staples like rice and wheat are not used in biofuel production, if the use of maize in biofuel makes it more expensive, then the consumers might be forced to substitute maize for cheaper wheat and rice. As a result, the prices of rice and wheat would increase *in tandem* with the price of maize.

Last but not least, the world is depleting resources much faster than they are being replaced. There has been increasing damage to the ecological foundations of agriculture such as land, water, forests, biodiversity and atmosphere, among others. The higher energy and food prices are giving a signal that these commodities have been under-priced and the supply-demand mismatch could lead to even higher prices for non-renewable and quasi-nonrenewable commodities. For instance, oil is believed to be under-priced relative to the cost of carbon emissions. Similarly, biodiversity losses due to environmental degradation are not being replaced, which has had an adverse impact on agricultural productivity. Such a scenario could prove the Club of Rome right, which in 1972 predicted that, 'If present growth trends continued unchanged, a limit to the growth that our planet has enjoyed would be reached sometime within the next 100 years.'[14]

Structural Change in Asia's Agricultural Production

Asia accounts for 42 per cent of global cereal (91 per cent of global rice production) and 39 per cent of meat production.[15] China and India are the two largest homes to agriculture which constitute roughly 28 per cent (China's share 18 per cent and India's 10 per cent) share in the world cereal production.[16] These two economies, along with some other Asian countries, have shown tremendous success in terms of food production since 1970s. However, in the current decade, the portfolio of Asia's agriculture, particularly the Chinese, has changed significantly. The share of cereal in the total agriculture produce has declined both in China and India compared to the period of 1999–2000.[17] However, cereal production has increased in Vietnam, Indonesia and Thailand. In 2006, global cereal stocks, particularly wheat, were at their lowest levels since the early 1980s. Stocks in China, which consist about 40 per cent of total stocks, declined significantly from 2000 to 2004 and have not recovered in recent years.[18] Nevertheless, meat, vegetables, fruits and fish production have witnessed a tremendous growth in China, which comprise approximately 37 per cent and 29 per cent share of the world's vegetables and fruits, and meat production.[19] As a result, China's food production index increased from 59 per ent in 1990 to 127 per cent in 2006.[20]

India also witnessed a steady growth in its food production index until 2001 after which the country's food production has been less than stable.[21] India's agricultural sector grew by 1.66 per cent annually from 1996–7 to 2004–5, as compared to 3.29 per cent growth from 1980–1 to 1989–90.[22] Consequently, the share of agriculture to total GDP has declined without a commensurate decline in the number of agricultural workers. The country has been a major import source for cereal and numerous food items until recently.

Noted agronomists have studied the crisis in the Indian agriculture sector, both quantitatively and qualitatively. Generally, agricultural output is a function of rainfall, terms of trade between agriculture and non-agriculture, fertiliser, irrigation, crop intensity, institutional credit, public investment in agriculture, among others. In India's case, a study focusing on the aforesaid explanatory variables has found that, after 1996–7, almost all factors, except credit, turned unfavourable for the growth of agricultural output.[23] Increasing farmer suicides in India in recent years is an obvious reflection of the agrarian crisis in the country.

As the recent growth in the Indian agricultural sector has been below its population growth, the country has lost its position as a food surplus country. The food grain growth rate (1.2 per cent) in India was lower than its population growth rate (1.82 per cent) in 1990s, though the latter has declined in recent years. As a result, India's share in food export has declined from 16 per cent in 1990 to 9 per cent in 2005.[24] India's recent poor agricultural performance has caused food problems in many parts of Asia. For instance, one of the reasons for the ongoing high food-inflation in Bangladesh is due to india's ban on all but non-basmati rice and some other agriculture produce. Agriculture diversification in China, coupled with higher demand for protein meal, has forced the country to slash its food export steadily. Its share in food export has also declined alarmingly from 13 per cent in 1990 to 3 per cent in 2006.[25] The recent decline in cereal production in China and India has not been fully compensated by production increase in other parts of Asia, particularly in Vietnam, Indonesia and Thailand.[26]

Subsidy, Tax, and Market Access: Major Roadblocks for the Agriculture Sector

Traditionally, developed countries subsidise and developing countries tax their agriculture sector. Nevertheless, the developing countries' agriculture tax policies underwent some changes in the 1980s and 1990s, and both direct and indirect taxes were reduced.[27] Market access barriers and agriculture subsidies in the countries of the Organisation for Economic Co-operation and Development (OECD) are two major hurdles for the farmers in developing countries as well as the free-flow of agriculture commodities across the world.

Estimation shows that more than 90 per cent of the global costs comes from market access restrictions through tariffs rather than from export subsidies and domestic support.[28] According to the World Bank, the economic and social cost of today's trade, price and subsidy policies in world agriculture is large and they depressed international commodity prices by 5 per cent on an average and suppress agricultural output growth in developing countries.[29] The United States, the European Union and other industrialised countries' generous subsidies to their domestic farmers,[30] trade policies including dumping, among others, have kept agriculture commodity prices low. The developed nations' agricultural and trade policies have barred the developing countries access to the global agricultural market. Such distortions have made the developing nations' comparative advantage in agriculture redundant. Estimation shows that developed countries' agricultural policies cost developing countries US $17 billion a year.[31]

As the agricultural produce has been under-priced for a long period, developing countries' terms of trade have deteriorated *vis-à-vis* its developed counterpart. There has been less incentive to stay in the paddy field than rushing to metropolis for off-firm jobs or migrating to the Gulf and other booming economic zones. Indeed, one of the reasons for the Chinese move from cereal to vegetables, fruits and meat production in the late 1990s and in early 2000s is that oversupply caused the grain prices to fall.[32] Had there been no bar to send the surplus grain to other parts of the world, China (so as other developing countries) could have maintained its higher cereal production record. These market distortion policies have had adverse consequences on agriculture sector in developing countries.

Is the Era of Cheap Food Over?

Is the current agflation a signal to produce more food which could lead to a fall in food prices? Or are the higher food prices here to stay? Generally, when demand for a particular product goes up, the market reacts by producing more. As a result, the demand–supply interactions stabilise the prices in the medium to long term. If this is the case, then farmers will grow more crops in the coming seasons and the prices of agricultural commodities are expected to go down. Unfortunately, the scenario is not that straightforward for agricultural produce, as the agricultural sector has been suffering from some structural problems.

The global commodity prices, including agricultural commodities, work predictably in line with the Prebisch and Singer (1950) hypothesis[33] which states that the prices of primary commodities relative to that of manufactured goods will tend to decline over time. However, recent trends show that the ongoing upturn in the global agricultural commodity markets has been large and rapid.[34]

There is little reason to hope that food prices will return to their long-term trend soon unless there is a sea change in the agricultural sector. Even if all factors work favourably for the agricultural sector in the short run, it is a daunting task to shift the agricultural supply curve rightward. Higher food prices are, therefore, likely to stay in the next few years. After that, a greater involvement of the market and the state could augment cereal production and other food items.

To make change happen, there is a need for significant policy changes pertaining to agriculture both at the local and the global levels. Agriculture has been neglected both by the state and multilateral organisations for a long period. For example, the World Bank's lending to agriculture amounted to US $1.75 billion in 2006, just 7 per cent of the total bank lending, compared to more than 30 per cent in 1982.[35] A mere 4 per cent of official development assistance goes to the agricultural sector in developing countries.[36] According to Oxfam, overall global aid to agriculture had declined by two-thirds, from US $11.5 billion from 1987 to US $3.9 billion in 2005.[37]

Intensive research and development in the agricultural sector and more investment in irrigation, fertilizer and seeds, among others, could increase agricultural productivity, even if there is a constraint to expand the sector horizontally. For instance, it is estimated that 85 per cent of increases needed in global food production must come from agricultural land already under cultivation.[38] According to the FAO, some 80 per cent of future increases in crop production in developing countries will have to be generated from higher yields, increased multiple cropping and shorter fallow period.[39] Technology and economic forces can spur solutions. Recent developments in bio-technology could increase crop intensity and overall agricultural productivity substantially. But all these developments will take a long time to have an impact.

But there is a flip side too. The current export ban on key agricultural commodities by many agricultural commodity producing countries is giving a wrong signal to farmers to judge the actual demand and such actions are depriving them of getting the right price for their produce.

Further, climate change could emerge as a major barrier to increase food production, both vertically and horizontally, especially in Asia. Water shortage is another huge impediment increasing food production. In Asia, due to rapid industrialisation, water is increasingly being transferred out of agriculture to meet the growing demands from domestic and industrial sectors. Moreover, water is a major source of contention in many parts of Asia.

Besides, as many Asian economies are rapidly industrialising, the wage level is rising both in the farm and non-farm sectors. As a result, the cost of producing food and other agricultural produce is set to increase.

There is also a direct association between energy prices and agricultural production cost. As higher oil prices are likely to stay in the near term, so is agriculture input and output cost.

Last but not least, cheap food is a double-edged sword. High food prices are essentially a regressive tax on the poor, especially on those who are net food buyers. Asia is home to two-thirds of the world's poor with 1.5 billion people. At the same time, any attempt to keep food prices low will do more harm than good, as farmers should be properly compensated for their hard work and increasing uncertainties in food production. The world should search for an answer to the right food price.

The Way Forward

Asia is the largest home to agriculture and the region is also highly vulnerable to the ongoing agflation. There is a need for both short- and long-term solutions to address food scarcity in the region. The current food (and agrarian) crisis indeed is an opportunity to fix the structural problems in the agriculture sector. Food aid can help to avoid hunger and starvation in the short run. But higher cereal and other food production are the ultimate solution to stabilise the prices in the medium to long run.

Distortions in the agricultural sector and agricultural trade (through tax, subsidies and market access) should be addressed sooner rather than latter. Agriculture, among others, has brought the Doha trade negotiation round to a standstill. Chances are still bleak that the world leaders will reach a consensus over key issues concerning agriculture soon. Moreover, neither the United States nor the European Union has shown any sign that it would revise its current bio-fuel policies that are driving up food prices across the world, *inter alia*, as it is energy that affects developed countries' consumer price inflation greatly, not food.

As there is little hope that the OECD countries will address the longstanding agriculture trade policies or that the United States and the European Union will change their bio-fuel policies, an Asian solution is the need of the hour. Thailand's recent proposal to form an OPEC-style cartel with some of its South-East Asian neighbours will create further distortion in the grain market. Such an oligopolistic structure does not sound like a viable policy in the long run, as unlike oil, rice is a renewable commodity and has close substitutes.

Policy makers in this part of the world should rather address issues like research and development in agriculture, technology share, water sharing, market access and potential free flow of agriculture commodities within the region, among others. Asia needs to act now—any further delay could exacerbate the current food crisis and could lead to greater economic and political uncertainties, if not conflicts, in Asia.

NOTES

1. For instance, in the last one year, the prices of rice, wheat and palm oil have increased 78 per cent, 120 per cent and 102 per cent respectively, according to the International Monetary Fund Commodity Prices. In 2007, international food price index increased by roughly 40 per cent, and in the first three months of 2008 prices rose by about 50 per cent, according to the International Food Policy and Research Institute (IFPRI).
2. Press Release, The World Food Programme, available at http://www.wfp.org/english/?ModuleID=137& Key=2820
3. *International Herald Tribune*, 3 May 2008.
4. Robert Zoellick, the World Bank President, commented at the International Monetary Fund–World Bank Spring Meetings in Washington on 14 April 2008.
5. Norman E. Borlaug et al. (2003), 'Feeding a World of Ten Billion People: A 21st Century Challenge', Proceedings of the International Congress 'In the Wake of the Double Helix: From the Green Revolution to the Gene Revolution', 27–31 May 2003, Bologna, Italy.
6. Food and Agriculture Organization (2005), 'The State of Food Insecurity in the World' available at ftp://ftp.fao.org/docrep/fao/008/a0200e/a0199e.pdf.
7. Food and Agriculture Organization (2003), 'World Agriculture: Towards 2015/2020: An FAO Perspective', FAO, Rome.
8. FAOSTAT, available at <http://faostat.fao.org/ >
9. World Development Report 2008.
10. Joachim Von Braun (2008), 'High and Rising Food Prices', IFPRI, presented at a USAID conference on 'Addressing the Challenges of a Changing World Food Situation: Preventing and Leveraging Opportunities, Washington, D.C., 11 April 2008.
11. According to the Europa Bio, available at <http://www.europabio.org/Biofuels/PressBrief/Food_ March08.pdf >
12. Borlaug et al. (2003), 'Feeding a World of Ten Billion People: A 21st Century Challenge', op. cit.
13. 'Rising Food Prices: What Should be Done'?, IFPRI Policy Brief, April 2008.

14. The Club of Rome (1972), 'The Limits to Growth', available at www.clubofrome.org/docs/limits.rtf.
15. 'Reducing Poverty and Hunger in Asia', IFPRI Brief No. 6, March 2008.
16. FAOSTAT.
17. Ibid.
18. IFPRI (2007): 'The World Food Situation', Policy Report No. 18, available at http://www.ifpri.org/pubs/fpr/pr18.asp.
19. FAOSTAT.
20 Ibid.
21. Ibid.
22. Ramesh Chand et al. (2007), 'Growth Crisis in Agriculture: Severity and Options at National and State Levels', *Economic and Political Weekly*, 30 June 2007.
23. Ibid.
24. 'The World Development Indicators', available at www.worldbank.org/data.
25. Ibid.
26. FAOSTAT.
27. *World Development Report 2008*, Chapter 4.
28. Ibid.
29. Ibid.
30. Though the average support to agriculture producers in the OECD countries fell from 37 per cent of the gross value of farm receipts in 1986–8 to 30 per cent in 2003–5, the amount support increased over the same period from US $242 to 273 billion.
31. *World Development Report 2008*, Chapter 4.
32. OECD (2005), 'Agriculture Policy Reform in China', available at www.oecd.org/dataoecd/3/ 48/35543482.pdf.
33. Raúl Prebisch and Singer (1950), 'The Economic Development of Latin America and its Principal Problems', reprinted in *Economic Bulletin for Latin America*, vol. 7, no. 1, 1962, 1–22.
34. For details see the IMF Primary Commodity Prices, available at <http://www.imf.org/external/np/res/commod/index.asp> and Joachim Von Braun, (2008), 'High and Rising Food Prices', IFPRI, presented at a USAID conference on 'Addressing the Challenges of a Changing World Food Situation: Preventing and Leveraging Opportunities', Washington, D.C., 11 April 2008.
35. Third World Network, http://www.twnside.org.sg/title2/susagri/susagri 017.htm.
36. Agence France Presse, 20 October 2007.

37. Third World Network, http://www.twnside.org.sg/title2/susagri/susagri017.htm.
38. Von Braun (2008), 'High and Rising Food Prices', op. cit., n. 10.
39. Food and Agriculture Organization (2003), 'World Agriculture: Towards 2015/2020: An FAO Perspective', FAO, Rome.

37

Modifications of the External Commercial Borrowings Policy: Implications for Overseas Investments

S. NARAYAN

(5 June 2008)

OVERSEAS BORROWING rules for firms are governed by policy directives from the Government of India. The External Commercial Borrowings (ECB) policy is regularly reviewed by the government in consultation with the Reserve Bank of India (RBI) to keep it aligned with evolving macroeconomic situation and changing market conditions. On 29 May 2008,[1] a partial modification of the ECB policy was announced.

- The all-in-cost ceilings in respect of ECBs have been modified as follows:

Average maturity period	All in costs over 6 months LIBOR	
	Existing	Proposed
3 years and up to 5 years	150 bps	200 bps
More than 5 years	250 bps	350 bps

- Borrowers in the infrastructure sector will now be permitted to avail themselves of the ECB up to US $100 million for permissible end uses under the approval route.
- In the case of other borrowers, the existing limit of US $20 million has been enhanced to US $50 million under the approval route.

In August 2007, the ECB norms were tightened, to control money supply, aimed at controlling inflation and allaying fears of overheating. The move checked the rise of the rupee, considered responsible for eroding competitiveness of Indian exports and widening the current account deficit. The reduced credit availability reduced capital flows into the economy. The present notification attempts to relax this.

As a further measure, the government announced that Foreign Institutional Investors (FII) would also be allowed to invest up to five billion dollars in government securities and up to 3 billion dollars in corporate bonds. At present, they are allowed to invest up to 3.2 billion dollars in government securities and 1.5 billion dollars in corporate bonds.

Simultaneously, the Securities and Exchange Board of India (SEBI) has relaxed investment norms for investors from abroad allowing Non-Resident Indians (NRI) and overseas Sovereign Wealth Funds (SWF) to register as FIIs. In addition, international or multilateral organisations, foreign governmental agencies and overseas central banks can also register as FIIs now. Asset management firms founded by overseas Indians can also register as FIIs, which will enable them to buy and sell shares directly through a broker. Last year, the regulator had curbed the use of participatory notes, or P-notes, used by unregistered foreigners to take exposure in Indian stocks.

The new net worth required for registration would be US $2 billion for foreign corporates, and US $50 million for foreign individuals to operate in the Indian market. They can operate as sub-accounts, where FIIs registered in India manage the investments. Till now sub-accounts, on whose behalf investments were made in India by FIIs, had to be primarily broad-based—this meant that sub-accounts had to have at least 20 investors, and no one could hold over 10 per cent stake. Now a sub-account investor can have as much as 49 per cent stake, which would make it possible for just three investors to form a sub-account—two with 49 per cent stake each and one with 2 per cent.

NRIs, however, would continue to be prohibited from participating in the capital markets as sub-accounts of FIIs, and also from investing their proprietary funds in the market. Earlier, NRIs were not permitted to register as FIIs or invest through the sub-account route. SEBI has also clarified that unregulated university funds, endowments and charitable trusts can seek registration as FIIs.

SEBI has also allowed FIIs to invest in collective investment schemes. 'The type of securities in which FIIs are permitted to invest has been widened to include schemes floated by a collective investment scheme (CIS),' SEBI said. CIS, as per current rules, are those schemes in which payments made by the investors are pooled and utilised with a view to receiving profits. Under CIS, the profit received is managed on behalf of the investors who do not have any day-to-day control over the management and operation of such schemes.

At present, FIIs are allowed to invest in stocks through primary and secondary markets, mutual funds, government securities, derivatives and commercial paper.

Referring to offshore derivatives, SEBI said FIIs would not be able to invest in offshore derivatives like P-notes, equity linked notes, etc., unless such derivatives are issued in compliance with know-your-client (KYC) norms.

What's New

- More overseas entities can invest as sub-accounts of FII.
- Sub-account investor can have as much as 49 per cent stake; so just three investors can form a sub-account.
- Foreign portfolio managers can take exposure to collective investment schemes like art funds.
- FIIs can issue P-notes to entities like some hedge funds.
- NRIs can set-up their own advisory companies and get funds registered as FII with SEBI.

New Considered FIIs

- Sovereign Wealth Funds.
- NRI-owned/set-up asset management company/investment manager/advisor/institutional portfolio manager.
- Unregulated university funds.
- Endowments and charitable trusts.

- International or multilateral organisations.
- Foreign government agencies.
- Overseas central banks.

These relaxations come in the wake of a rupee that is weakening against the dollar. The rupee has lost nearly 8 per cent since January 2008, and is currently trading at around 42.4 to the dollar. FII flow has been negative since March 2008.

Background

The position in May 2008 is very different from that prevailing one year ago. At that time, the financial markets in India were buoyant, and returns in the equity markets in India were among the best in the world in 2007. This encouraged significant FII flows into the market,[2] and there was considerable investment taking place through venture capital and private equity deals. The rupee, which was around 42 to the dollar around March 2007, had strengthened by 12 per cent to nearly 39 to the dollar by October 2007. Inflationary pressures were starting to appear, but the government as well as the RBI were confident that these could be contained.[3]

At that time, there were two concerns. The first related to capital inflows and the ability of the economy to absorb these. It was evident that the pace of investment in infrastructure was not yet adequate to absorb these inflows. During 2007, the RBI had to resort to repeated interventions in the forex markets to purchase dollars and to sterilise the liquidity through issue of Market Stabilisation Scheme (MSS) bonds.[4] The total issue of bonds in 2007–8 exceeded Rs 130,000 crore (approximately US $35 billion). Between August and December 2007, the stock of MSS bonds increased by over US $10 billion.[5]

Apart from financial market investments, two other factors contributed to these inflows. The first was the growth of remittances by overseas Indians (termed 'invisibles' by the RBI), that grew to over US $22 billion in 2006–7, and to US $28 billion the following year. Second, there was an increase in ECBs by private sector that added to the available liquidity. Though the RBI had indicated a cap of US $23 billion for these borrowings, since a significant proportion happened under the 'automatic' route, the figure was exceeded substantially. Between August and December 2007, there was considerable comment in the media and among analysts that these flows needed to be monitored, and that a substantial quantity of funds was being used in the financial markets for speculation. There was also concern that the 'P-notes'[6] added an element of non-transparency to the markets and the identity of investors.

The stronger rupee led to some decline in the growth of exports to 22.6 per cent between April 2007 and February 2008, and the negative merchandise trade balance increased from around $50 billion in 2006–7 to US $72.5 billion in the same period in 2007–8.

At this time, the government took several steps to reverse these trends. There was an announcement that investments through P-notes would not be permitted, and that existing investors should unwind their positions within six weeks. At the same time, these investors could register themselves as FIIs, and procedures for these compliances were eased. A restriction on ECBs was imposed, most importantly, restricting access to the real estate and financial sector investments. ECB borrowings were to be parked outside the country until actually required for the purpose intended. The 'prior approval' route was tightened, with longer queues for approval. The RBI also stepped in progressively with a tighter monetary policy, hiking CRR and repo rates progressively, in an attempt to drain some liquidity from the economy.

In retrospect, it is possible to argue that these steps were somewhat belated, and did not yield the results intended. There were several reasons for this. First, the Indian policy makers did not fully appreciate the impact of the financial downturn in the United States. The policy makers were confident that a domestic demand-driven economy like India could weather the deflationary winds that were sweeping through the United States. The assessment was that though FIIs were strapped for liquidity overseas, they might cash out of India as there were enough funds waiting with domestic savings in their hands to step in and shore up the markets. This is true, but the extent of the meltdown in the financial institutions has been considerably more than anticipated, and the Indian markets have seen an exodus of capital since February 2008, leaving the markets very volatile.

Second, the impact of the global food crisis was not factored into calculations. The steep rise in prices of rice and edible oils, and most importantly, the concerns over global food production estimates, were factored in rather late. The government did an excellent job of managing the crisis by ensuring that the winter wheat was purchased by the Food Corporation of India as a buffer (a record of over 21 million tonnes), and that the ban on rice exports would temporarily hold the prices of rice until the next harvest came in, and finally, adopted some administrative measures to prevent hoarding and black-marketeering. These measures have mitigated food prices inflation to some extent.

Third and most important, has been the steep increases in prices of crude oil (35 per cent since January 2008). Consumer prices are subsidised, with the subsidies being borne by the balance sheets of the government-owned oil companies, and the issue of guaranteed bonds by the government.[7]

The outflow of FII capital, the drain of liquidity through additional working capital borrowings by the oil and fertiliser companies, and for the procurement of food grains, the announcement of waiver of farm loans to the extent of US $18 billion, are likely to cause interest rates to harden and credit availability for industry to tighten. The scramble for dollars by the oil companies for crude and product purchases, coupled with the withdrawal of P-notes' investments, has put pressure on the rupee that has declined by over 8 per cent against the dollar in the last twelve weeks. The current account deficit is likely to increase to 2.5 per cent of the gross domestic product this year, a manageable, though a worrying figure.

The hardening of interest rates is likely to affect the borrowings of the government, especially state governments and oil companies, and also make borrowings for industry and manufacturing more expensive. There are media comments that oil companies have put on hold capital investment programmes, which would have a downstream effect on machinery manufacturers.

At the same time, inflationary pressures continue. On the one hand, they are fuelled by commodity prices including those of steel and cement, and primary minerals. On the other hand, the high prices of crude would impact on prices of fertilisers, petrochemicals, industrial chemicals and plastics, thus impacting the input costs in several manufacturing sectors. High inflationary pressures prevent the easy option of reducing interest rates being exercised, and the country is likely to witness a slow-down of growth coupled with unacceptable inflation, a situation several countries are facing now.

The relaxations in the ECB and SEBI guidelines have to be viewed against the context of these developments. There is an attempt here to make credit available for genuine investors. It is interesting that the relaxations focus on those investors who have rupee investments to make, a clear indication that the government is focusing on improving capital investments in these sectors, most importantly, infrastructure. The attempt to woo hedge funds and NRI money is an attempt to shore up the equity markets through these inflows.

The worry is that these steps may not be effective and adequate. The relaxations are for borrowings that require prior approval of the RBI, and this has proved to be a long and tortuous process, with the RBI reluctant to open the gates. There are large numbers of applications pending before the RBI even now, and there is little indication that the process would speed up.

Second, secondary market activity is likely to be much more selective, focused on those sectors that would benefit from the current market situation. These could include oil exploration, petrochemicals, steel and cement, but one could easily argue that financial sector stocks, including banking sector stocks, would be under pressure.

Investments in infrastructure are a function of the costs and returns of the investment, and these depend crucially upon the extent to which oil price increases are passed on to the consumer. If the pass-through is significant, it would impact consumer costs and spending and saving patterns; if too little, it would have a serious impact on the government's fiscal deficits and on interest rates as public sector firms scramble for working capital.

In short, this appears to be a wait-and-watch time for the Indian economy, as the managers and the policy makers scramble for alternatives to keep the story of growth going, while at the same time putting out the flames of inflation.

NOTES

1. Press Release BSC/SS/GN-132/08 dated 29 May 2008 (website of the Press Information Bureau, GOI).
2. Institutional investment peaked to over Rs. 20,000 crore in December 2007; RBI.
3. 'Macroeconomic and Monetary Policy Developments 2008', RBI, 29 April 2008.
4. These bonds are off-budget instruments, with the interest commitment being borne by the government as a budgetary commitment.
5. RBI indicators, 29 April 2008.
6. Subscriptions by overseas investors to instruments for investments in Indian markets through an approved mutual fund or FII.
7. Public Sector Companies are permitted to issue bonds in the market that are guaranteed for repayment by the government, and hence, though an off-budget mechanism, it is part of the additional contingent liability of the government.

38

The Third Oil Shock: The Path Forward for Bangladesh

M. SHAHIDUL ISLAM

(*10 June 2008*)

OIL IS NOW TRADED at nearly US $140 a barrel.[1] The real price of oil is already at an all-time high.[2] Goldman Sachs, the United States-based investment bank, which correctly predicted three years ago that oil prices would exceed US $100, has recently forecasted that US $200 a barrel could be a reality in the not-too-distant future.[3] A 170 per cent price hike[4] over a three-year period (from US $47 a barrel in May 2005 to US $127 May 2008) and, more importantly, a relentless rise in fuel prices has resulted in the current scenario being termed 'the third oil shock'.[5] This is certainly true from the perspective of the least developed countries. The term was, in fact, used by Gordon Brown, the British prime minister, who, in a recent article, stated that the global economy is facing the 'third great oil shock' of recent decades.[6] *The Economist* has dubbed the phenomenon a 'slow-motion oil shock'. Worse still, Joseph Stiglitz, the current economics Nobel laureate, is concerned that oil is underpriced relative to the cost of carbon emissions.[7] Apparently, the price of the black gold will continue to swell until it finds equili-brium when alternative energy becomes viable.

Bangladesh, a least developed country with a per capita income of US $419 (US $1119 in purchasing power parity terms),[8] faces severe challenges in the wake of astounding oil price hikes. Like most economies in Asia, the domestic prices of petroleum products in Bangladesh are capped. In recent years, favourable developments in the country's external sector, particularly the steady growth of export and remittance, and its sizeable stock of natural gas[9] had cushioned the Bangladesh economy from the ongoing oil price hike until recently. However, the higher than expected level of oil prices, coupled with fertilizer and food subsidies, have pushed the economy to the brink of a fiscal problem, if not a crisis.

Natural gas constitutes 68 per cent of Bangladesh's energy basket, followed by oil (30 per cent) and hydro (2 per cent).[10] The country produces 10 per cent of its oil requirement while the rest is procured from international markets. It imports 3.8 million tonnes of oil annually, including 2.1 million tonnes of diesel. Bangladesh has had a long history of fuel subsidy and the exchequer absorbs a significant part of the price hike in international markets. In April 2007, the government raised diesel prices by about 21 per cent when crude oil was US $67 per barrel.

The Bangladesh government traditionally borrows from the state-owned banks and the Islamic Development Bank (IDB) to finance the Bangladesh Petroleum Corporation (BPC), the energy entity that imports fuels from international markets and distributes them in the domestic market at a subsidised price. The government has asked the IDB to double its annual loan to US $2 billion for the next year.[11] In the current fiscal year (2007–8) to June, Bangladesh will require US $4.5 billion for oil import and repayments of loans which are 30 per cent higher than the past fiscal year's oil bill.

A sharp increase in subsidies following the rise in oil prices, among others, is widening the country's fiscal deficit. The Asian Development Bank (ADB) forecasts that the fiscal deficit in the country in FY 2008 is likely to increase to 4.8 per cent of gross domestic product compared to 3.2 per cent in the preceding year.[12] The Economist Intelligence Unit has also projected a 5 per cent budget deficit for 2008 for the economy. But if oil prices continue to rise, the fiscal deficit will augment accordingly.

CRUDE MEASURES: WHO GAINS FROM FUEL SUBSIDIES?

Economic theories state that subsidies do not serve the purpose of efficient allocation of resources for such mechanisms distort the relative prices of goods and services. Subsidies compete with an economy's scarce resources that could be used for some other productive purposes. But reality is often contrasted with theory. From political economy perspectives, subsidies seem to be based on political expediency rather than economic considerations. Bangladesh is no exception.

According to the ADB, based on the average domestic and international prices of diesel, kerosene, and octane at the end of April 2008, the implicit subsidy for diesel in Bangladesh was US $0.52/litre, for kerosene US $0.51/litre, and for octane US $0.09/litre.[13] An estimate shows that the cost of subsidy is about US $730 million per year.[14] But this amount is also on the rise in line with higher oil prices. The ADB estimates that the BPC would lose US $1.1 billion this fiscal year due to soaring oil prices.

The question is who benefits from fuel subsidies. The traditional view is that poor people cannot afford higher oil prices and, so that, they should be protected through subsidy. But the real picture is different. An International Monetary Fund study of five emerging economies shows that the richest 20 per cent of households received, on average, 42 per cent of total fuel subsidies and the bottom 20 per cent received less than 10 per cent.[15] Further, in countries such as Bangladesh, the poorest of the poor in many instances use traditional bio-mass and do not have access to electricity and other public utilities. The increasing need of resources for fuel subsidies indeed hurts the poor people most. The ADB has cautioned the country of late that huge subsidies for fuel might be hindering the government's targeted interventions to protect the poor.

However, Bangladesh's agricultural sector that depends on energy-intensive irrigation, especially during the dry season, badly needs subsidised fuel. Over 70 per cent of Bangladesh's 144 million people depend on agriculture. Public transport is another area that relies on subsidised fuel. The apparel and other labour intensive manufacturing sectors that absorb millions of low-income people also depend on fuel subsidies. To remain competitive in this highly distorted global fuel subsidy regime, economies such as Bangladesh can ill-afford to pass the full oil bill to its consumers. For instance, petrol is sold for as low as 5 cents per litre in Venezuela and as high as US $2.35 per litre in Germany.[16] This means that the price of oil should be set keeping in mind the fact that the country's industrial output remains competitive while, at the same time, ensuring that the economy does not produce subsidised products for external consumers.

Cross-country Experience: Lessons for Bangladesh

Countries across Asia are adopting multi-pronged approaches to cope with higher oil prices. The Indian government raised retail prices of petrol, diesel and liquid petroleum gas by 8 to 17 per cent recently despite the inflation risk. Malaysia has also announced a 41 per cent fuel price hike. Sri Lanka, Indonesia and Taiwan have also increased their prices and more countries, including China, are expected to do so as well. The exchange rate policy, particularly domestic currency appreciation, is also widely used by Singapore and some other countries to manage oil price increases. Apart from these, fuel conservation and energy rationing are some other options that could be employed to address the problem.

The full or significant pass-through of oil prices poses huge political risk for the current caretaker government in Bangladesh as the economy is already in the midst of a double-digit inflation. Moreover, from food security perspectives, the government cannot afford to withdraw subsidy for the agricultural sector considerably.

The following measures can be considered for the Bangladesh economy to partly weather the oil shock:

(a) Gradual increase of oil prices should be the most viable policy at this stage. Full or significant pass-through could destabilise the country, both politically and economically.

(b) The concerned authorities should also devise an appropriate means to disburse the subsidised fuel to farmers so that the country's agricultural output is not affected. To offset the impact of fuel price hike on farmers, cash transfers through social safety-net programmes could be initiated.

(c) To discourage the use of private transport, a higher tax should be levied on private vehicles so that people find public transport a more economic and viable way to commute.

(d) The exchange rate policies should also be used prudently—an undervalued currency can import inflation from abroad. Bangladesh's domestic currency has remained fairly unchanged *vis-à-vis* the United States' dollar for a year but the latter has lost significant value against the Euro dollar and other major currencies, known as the United States dollar index, in the recent past. If undervalued, the domestic currency should be appreciated so that it can contain the currency-induced energy inflation.

(e) As Bangladesh's close neighbour, India, is adjusting its oil prices, it also needs to do so. In the presence of an underground economy in the India–Bangladesh border, some subsidised resources can benefit the wrong side of Bangladesh's border.

(f) The country needs to increase investment in its gas sector so that this relatively clean form of fossil fuel can be increasingly used as a close substitute for oil.

(g) Greater regional energy cooperation is needed in terms of clean energy, particularly hydroelectricity, as Bangladesh's neighbouring countries (India's northeastern region, Nepal and Bhutan) have huge hydro potential.

(h) Energy conservation should be another policy option that can economise Bangladesh's fuel cost.

(i) As oil prices are skyrocketing, alternative energy might become viable in the near future. The country should also invest in clean energy so that its energy basket is diversified.

Conclusion

As discussed, oil price hike in international markets poses a severe risk to Bangladesh's macroeconomic stability. If not tackled prudently, the oil shock could derail the country's hard-earned macroeconomic stability. In the short run, the economy needs to phase out fuel subsidies gradually. At the same time, there should be safety nets for low-income people, and the agricultural sector should be protected from fuel price adjustment. In the medium term, market and technology should be allowed to spur the solution with minimal state intervention. Following the two oil shocks in the 1970s, people changed their energy consumption pattern and industries were forced to enhance fuel efficiency. Both short-term and medium-term policies should be applied so that the economy is able to contain oil shocks. As many Asian countries, including its next-door neighbour India, are withdrawing fuel subsidies gradually, the region may witness a new consumption and production regime. Bangladesh needs to be better prepared to adjust its regime in the new environment.

NOTES

1. Light, sweet crude for July 2008 delivery settled at $127.35 a barrel on the New York Mercantile Exchange in May 2008, according to the *Wall Street Journal.*
2. Martin Wolf, 'The Market Sets High Oil Prices to Tell us What to Do', *Financial Times*, 13 May 2008.
3. 'Analyst Warns of Oil at $200 a Barrel', *Financial Times*, 6 May 2008.
4. Energy Information Administration <http://tonto.eia.doe.gov/dnav/pet/hist/wepcagsaw.htm>
5. The world economy observed two oil shocks in 1974 and 1979.
6. *The Guardian*, <http://www.guardian.co.uk/commentisfree/2008/may/28/gordonbrown.oil>
7. 'New Limits to Growth Revive Malthusian Fears', *Wall Street Journal*, 24 March 2008.
8. World Development Indicator Online.
9. Natural gas serves as close substitute of oil to some extent. Natural gas constitutes 68 per cent weight in Bangladesh's energy basket followed by oil (30 per cent) and hydro (2 per cent).
10. Based on data of Regional Energy Security for South Asia, Regional Report, South Asia Regional Initiative for Energy (SARI), 2006.
11. *The Economic Times*, 28 May 2008.
12. Asian Development Bank, *Quarterly Economic Update*, March 2008.
13. Ibid.
14. 'Subsidised Oil Prices: Are They Sustainable?' available at <http://www.doe.gov.ph/e per cent20summit/presentation/Mr. per cent20Neil per cent20Atkinson.pdf>
15. *The Economist*, 29 May 2008.
16. Ibid.

39

India's Employment Exchanges: Should they be Revamped or Scrapped Altogether?

BIBEK DEBROY
(*10 July 2008*)

There have been no attempts, so far, on collecting statistical material on employment and unemployment; the only published figures at present available are the registrations and placements of employment exchanges. These figures cannot, however, give an idea of the total volume of unemployment. Firstly, employment exchanges are confined to industrial towns and the figures of registrations and placements which they compile are restricted mostly to the industrial and commercial sector. Secondly, even in the industrial sector, there is neither compulsion for the unemployed, to register with the exchanges, nor is there any obligation on the part of the employer to recruit labour only through these exchanges. Even the information regarding unemployment among the industrial workers is, thus, inadequate. Thirdly, in the nature of the case, employment exchange statistics cannot indicate the amount of disguised unemployment which is otherwise believed to exist. This means that the extent to which qualified persons have to accept work which does not give them the income which persons with similar qualifications get elsewhere cannot be assessed from these data. There is also to some extent registration of persons who are already in employment and who desire to seek better jobs. This tendency is reported to exist in the more qualified section of registrants, but to the extent a region maintains these persons on the register of employment seekers, there is an overestimate of the number unemployed.

THIS WAS NOT written yesterday. It is a quote from India's First Five Year Plan (1951–6) document.[1] Nothing would substantially change if this were to be written now.

In September 2007, the National Commission for Enterprises in the Unorganized Sector submitted a report.[2] It estimated that in 2004–5, out of a workforce of 457 million, 92 per cent was in the unorganised sector, a workforce of around 394 million. However, since there are informal workers also in the organised sector, the total number of informal/unorganised workers was 423 million, and 256 million of them were in agriculture. Of the remaining 167 million workers who were unorganised, 100 million were self-employed. But this still leaves a relatively large figure of 67 million workers in non-agricultural wage employment. Till the National Sample Survey (NSS) large-sample data for 2004–5 became available, there were question marks about whether Indian reforms had led to an increase in employment. In December 2006, after the NSS 2004–5 became available, the Approach Paper to the Eleventh Five Year Plan (2007–12) stated that:

> Growth without jobs can neither be inclusive nor can it bridge divides. . . . Employment is an area which shows up where our growth process is failing on inclusiveness. The number of workers is growing, particularly in non-agricultural employment, but weaknesses appear in unemployment, the quality of employment, and in large and increasing differentials in productivity and wages.[3]

Pointing to the quality of employment (informal, low productivity, low wages and lack of protection) is one thing (as the National Commission for Enterprises in the Unorganized Sector did). Saying that there is an overall non-agricultural employment problem is another.

The industry's perception is unambiguous. Workers are not available. This is often a comment on the lack of requisite skills, but is also increasingly a comment on non-availability, regardless of skills. The broader point about the lack of skills and low educational attainments is well taken and is often talked about in reports emanating from within India and from without. For instance, it figures in a list of 10 things a recent Goldman Sachs report wants India to focus on.[4] What is, however, often missed is a regional-cum-spatial mismatch. Purely in passing, the Goldman Sachs report states that, 'As with other aspects of Indian life, there are considerable differences in organisational structures for education in different states, so broad generalisations are difficult.' The Approach Paper dismisses this mismatch issue in half a sentence and the

Economic Survey 2007–8 does not even mention it. There are geographical areas and segments where there is excess demand and ones where there is excess supply. The demographic dividend accrues in parts of the country. But that is not necessarily where jobs are being created. Earlier, public sector (and even private sector) establishments could be set up in locations where there was labour. But with de-licensing, this is no longer a possible option.

Unorganised sector male wage employment is primarily in manufacturing, construction, trading and transport. For women, trading and transport can be replaced by domestic services. Depending on how we count, the total is around 70 million. These figures are from 2004–5. They must have increased since then and it is a considerable number. Hence, one should ask the question: How do these workers find out jobs are available and decide on temporary or permanent migration? The answer is simple. Barring limited instances of job offers at factory gates, there are only two channels: informal (family, caste, community) networks and labour contractors. This kind of information dissemination cannot be efficient, apart from cases where commissions are paid to agents.

Clearly, one needs efficient clearing houses that match supply and demand. Is that not what employment exchanges were supposed to do? Not quite. First, the system started (in 1945) because of the need to resettle demobilised defence service personnel and later (1948) displaced persons from Pakistan. Second, the mandatory Employment Exchanges (Compulsory Notification of Vacancies) Act of 1959, applicable to public sector and private sector units (excluding agriculture) that employ more than 25 people, are not as compulsory as one may think. For the private sector, the mandatory requirement only applies below a threshold level of wages and these have not been revised for years. Whatever the law may say *de jure*, there is nothing mandatory about employment exchanges *de facto*. For the public sector, a Supreme Court judgement in 1996 said that appointments no longer had to be from the pool that was registered with employment exchanges, as long as job vacancies were suitably publicised. The public sector also set up channels like Staff Selection Commissions, Banking Service Commissions and Railway Recruitment Boards. The Directorate

General of Employment and Training's (DGET) website states that, 'Therefore Employment Exchanges are left with only stray cases that too at the lower levels of employment. Therefore in the placement side (regular wage employment) the role of Employment Exchanges is definitely going to be not very significant.'[5] One cannot be more honest than that. The aforementioned National Commission's report stated that, 'A few workers said they had registered at the Employment Exchange where they received unemployment allowance of Rs 50 per day. But they stopped going to the Exchange since it costs them Rs 80 each day to reach there.' The apparent attraction of employment exchanges is that they are free. Private placement agencies charge, and the DGET also tells us that these private ones may be fraudulent, besides being city-centric.

What do the 947 employment exchanges (82 are physically located in universities) do? There will be a song and dance about the training services they provide. But training is a separate issue. On matching supply and demand and providing employment, as on 31 December 2007, 39.97 million people were registered with employment exchanges to seek jobs. As far as employment exchange performance is concerned, in 2007, 263,540 people got jobs through employment exchanges and 7.3 million had registered themselves with employment exchanges in 2006. To reinforce the spatial point made earlier, most placements were in Gujarat (178,346), Tamil Nadu (23,757), Kerala (10,962), Maharashtra (8,207), West Bengal (5,304) and Rajasthan (4,544).[6] If one leaves out Gujarat, the numbers are insignificant. Most new registrations are in Uttar Pradesh (with most of the backlog in West Bengal). Administration and expenditure on employment exchanges are now state subjects, an earlier matching grant from the centre having run its course. In 1952, a committee known as the Training and Employment Services Organization Committee (popularly known as the Shiva Rao Committee) was set up and it recommended that the administration of employment exchanges should be handed over to state governments. Till 1969, funding came through central sources. However, once this system was scrapped, though the service *per se* continues to be a joint responsibility, expenditure comes out of state government budgets. Hence, it is difficult to get data on expenditure on employment exchanges, or on what it costs the budget to get people those 263,540 jobs. A back-of-the-envelope computation with the Delhi government's budget suggests that it costs the government (and, therefore, citizens) Rs 228,381 for a single placement.[7] An employment exchange exists in Chitradurga in Karnataka, staffed with bureaucracy. But it has not provided a single job in the last four years and Chitradurga is not an exception. This is not efficient use of scarce public funds and equally scarce infrastructure in those 947 exchanges.

The Mid-Term Appraisal of the Tenth Five Year Plan (2002–7) was fairly forthright about what should be done with the employment exchanges.[8]

> At present, the employment exchanges function as offices of the state governments, as is prescribed under the Employment Exchanges (Compulsory Notification of Vacancies) Act, 1959. These exchanges also collect data on the number of workers employed in establishments in their respective areas, which is used by the government for statistics relating to employment in the organised sector. The coverage of the establishments is very poor and the data fails to capture the changes in employment. A role for employment exchanges can be considered for providing employment-related information services for new initiatives like the National Food for Work Programme and the proposed employee guarantee scheme, in both of which work on projects in rural areas is to be assured at the level of the household. However, their functions will have to be restructured and they will have to be relocated to the rural areas. Currently, they are located at the district headquarters in most parts of the country. So far, very few states have set up web-based information systems on employment services. E-governance initiatives should be used for generating and maintaining information for providing employment services for the rural areas. The delivery of employment-related information services by private employment exchanges should be encouraged in urban areas. The Employment Exchanges Act should be amended to allow private employment exchanges to provide job placement services to both private sector and public sector/government establishments and to collect the data on the creation of employment opportunities at the level of the establishments.

This city-centric focus of the present employment exchanges is something the Communist Party of India (Marxist) also accepts. M.K. Pandhe, the president of Centre of Indian Trade Unions wrote,

'However, they collect data only for the organised sector while the vast area of unorganised sector is out of the purview of these exchanges. Moreover, these employment exchanges are only operating in the urban areas and have no centres in the rural areas.'[9]

The Ministry of Labour estimates that there are around 800 private placement agencies that are large and are not fraudulent. If one sets up a regulatory structure, fraudulent ones will be eliminated and informal networks (family, caste, community, contractors) will become large and formalised, ensuring economies of scale and scope in information processing, dissemination and intermediation. Some states have experimented with reforming employment exchanges. In 2002, an Administrative Reforms Commission (the Harnahalli Ramaswamy Commission) recommended that employment exchanges should be downsized. States like Gujarat[10] and Rajasthan[11] have experimented with allowing private placement agencies to get into the matching function. Even a state like West Bengal has permitted private training organisations to offer training at employment exchanges. However, no state has yet taken the logical step of winding down public employment exchanges and handing the assets over to private placement agencies for management. Since this has been contemplated for industrial training institutes, there is no reason why it should not be done for employment exchanges as well.

Instead, the wheel has turned in the opposite direction. For example, in the specific case of the labour market, the reform-driven thrust of the Mid-Term Appraisal of the tenth plan is conspicuously missing in the approach paper to the eleventh plan. This is in consonance with the mindset of the United Progressive Alliance (UPA) government. The argument is that public employment exchanges need to be revamped and computerised, not scrapped. 'The DGET, responsible for "National Employment Service" and "National Vocational Training" in the country, has taken initiatives to achieve widespread applications of IT in all possible areas of employment service and vocational training.'[12] As Indian budgets go, this computerisation plan does not involve a great deal of money—from Rs 6 billion to 7 billion and is expected to be completed by 2010. One-third of the 947 employment exchanges are apparently already computerised. However, such plans and talk of ISO certification should be considered against the backdrop of inefficient public expenditure and opportunity costs of those resources. An audit report for 2004–5 for West Bengal stated that,

> The Directorate of Employment, West Bengal, through its network of Employment Exchanges, caters to activities like registration of job seekers, renewal of registration and submission of list of eligible candidates to employers. Computerisation of 40 employment exchanges in the state was taken up along with network connectivity and the work was entrusted to the ET & TDC on a turnkey basis. However, even after spending Rs 6.52 crore, the computerised system installed in the employment exchanges have been lying inoperative for last 30 to 46 months, owing to a default timer-based lock implanted by the vendor, the non-completion of the creation of the database and the non-installation of the software due to the abandonment of work by the vendor, largely frustrating the basic objective of the scheme. The application software also lacked in data processing and data manipulation controls. Absence of data disaster recovery strategy led to substantial data loss.[13]

This is symptomatic of much that the UPA government has sought to do. With the UPA tenure coming to an end, perhaps one will get back to reforms. Since revamping is pointless, public employment exchanges should be scrapped. While this is fundamentally a state government subject, the centre does have a catalytic and triggering role to play.

NOTES

1. Chapter 39, 'Employment' in India's First Five Year Plan, 1951–6, New Delhi.
2. *Report on Conditions of Work and Promotion of Livelihoods in the Unorganized Sector*, New Delhi: National Commission for Enterprises in the Unorganized Sector, September 2007.
3. *Towards Faster and More Inclusive Growth: An Approach to the 11th Five Year Plan*, December 2006.
4. Goldman Sachs, *Ten Things for India to Achieve its 2050 Potential, Global Economics Paper No. 169*, June 2008.

5. http://dget.gov.in/
6. *Rajya Sabha Parliamentary Question*, 18 March 2008.
7. *State of Governance: Delhi Citizens Handbook*, Centre for Civil Society, 2006.
8. *Mid-Term Appraisal of the Tenth Five Year Plan*, Chapter 8, http://planning commission.nic.in/midterm/ english-pdf/chapter-08.pdf
9. 'The National Employment Service: A Hoax', *People's Democracy*, 6 June 2004.
10. These are called Rozgar Sahay Kendras in Gujarat, labelled as public–private partnerships. The public employment exchange provides a database of people on the register (the supply of labour, so to speak) and the private agency matches it with demand.
11. Job *melas* have been organised in Rajasthan.
12. *Annual Report of the Ministry of Labour, 2007–8*, Chapter 30, http:// www.labour.nic.in/annrep/annrep0708/ english/Ch-11.pdf
13. www.intosaiitaudit.org/hosted_external_publications/India_3WEST_ BENGAL.pdf.

40

For Illiberal Finance: Building Dams, Constructing Conduits

ROMAR CORREA

(*12 November 2008*)

Finance and Real Development

THE CONTEXT OF financial liberalisation in India was the inefficiencies created by the government's control of prices and quantities in the financial markets. One alleged legacy has been the stockpiling of non-performing assets in connection with funds requisitioned for given sectors. Here, as well as elsewhere, more discrimination must be exercised in passing judgement. In Appendix Table III.29 (A) of the *Report on Trends and Progress of Banking in India 2006–2007* by the Reserve Bank of India, 2007, it is stated that non-performing assets of public sector banks are 60 per cent in connection with the priority sector, and 40 per cent in connection with the non-priority sector. Reform has meant the cautious relaxing of these constraints. The recent worldwide conflagration has brought to the fore the inherent fragility of financially sophisticated economies. The dynamics of modern economies are written by real-financial couplings. Over good times, conservative postures give way to excessive risk-taking. Financial innovations abound, securitisation being a recent illustration. At some time during the euphoric upswing, there is a correspondence between securities and the underlying assets and then a downward cascade results. In the case of developing countries as well, the link between financial liberalisation and crises is quite robust.[1]

The response of societies in history has been twofold. Since banks have been the lynchpin of financial systems anywhere, firewalls were constructed between their different functions. The principle was to protect the items on their balance sheets that pertained to deposit taking and lending for productive purposes from investment activity. Thus, the bulwark of the New Deal Financial Reform in the United States was The Banking Act of 1933. The Glass-Steagall sub-sections separated commercial and investment banking on the sole criterion of systemic stability. The Act was repealed in 1999. The Indian trajectory has not been dissimilar, earmarking financial institutions such as the Industrial Credit and Investment Corporation of India, the Industrial Development Bank of India and others for developmental purposes. In the current dispensation of universal banking, the separation of functions is blurred. Perhaps, as a result, a slight downward trend since 2001–2 is to be found in financial assistance, both sanctioned and disbursed by all financial institutions (Tables 85, *Handbook of Statistics on the Indian Economy*, RBI, 2007).

The second response was to build in macroeconomic stabilisers in the form of monetary and fiscal policies. Countries in Asia that grew rapidly and in a broad-based fashion in recent times added direction to macroeconomic instruments by indicating the sectors such as exports which should be the focus of policy formulation. At any rate, the development of financial markets was never regarded as autonomous of the development of commodity and labour markets. The late Professor Sukhamoy Chakravarty, the architect of the Chakravarty Committee Report which laid the foundations of monetary planning in India, would have recommended an instrumental approach. In the similar modern language of backward induction, we specify the future states that the economy is expected to achieve and then work towards the present ensemble of institutions that must be constructed to deliver. There can be no question that, for a country with deep and extensive poverty, employment generation must be a fundamental objective.

However, the relationship between financial and real outcomes is less than clear. James Ang, 2008, *Journal of Economic Surveys*, 22, 2, 536–76, summarises the tensions in the econometric evidence. Two theses go back a long way. One is where growth leads, output follows; the other is the finance-leading-growth proposition. When financial development is specified as the dependent variable, some country studies show that economic development positively impacts financial development. Recently, Rajan and Zingales have pioneered panel studies, exploiting firm-level or industry-level data. However, the regressions are subject to uncontrolled variable problems or heterogeneity bias. When the unobserved country-specific effects are included in the error term,[2] the result is biased and with inconsistent estimates. Holding country-specific elements constant in panel regressions generates a spurious aggregate relationship as the reported relationship is due to inter-country differences rather than intra-country differences over time.

A conclusion is the danger of cross-country regressions. These studies construct a series by averaging out variables. Grouping countries carry more than the obvious dangers. For instance, when legal and social factors have been controlled the positive association between stock markets and growth in some exercises vanishes. Time series studies are no less inconclusive. The limitations here are short series and arbitrary choice of lag lengths. Demetriades and Luintel are pioneers. While they conclude that, in India and Malaysia, financial repression negatively impacted on financial development, the South Korean experience was the opposite. The reason is the solid institutional structures in South Korea. Finance, as an engine thesis, finds scant support in Mauritius, Pakistan and Thailand. Instead, financial and real development are joint products. In all instances, the neo-classical impetus for financial opening up finds little support as the effect of real interest rates was insignificant. In a study for India using annual data over the period 1951–95, financial aggregates are shown to have preceded increases in both investment and growth, while the financial sector has no influence on the total factor productivity of manufacturing industries. Annual data for 10 Asian countries reveals that finance pushes investment. At the same time, the influence of finance on output is weak. The explanation might lie in expectations. If businessmen forecast robust economic performance, they might be tempted into financial services-related investments in anticipation of future returns. Then financial development would be no more than a leading indicator. Granger causality would be a misleading conclusion.

The Dilemma of Regulation

It is well known that, despite over a decade of financial liberalisation, the appetite of the banking sector in India for riskless government paper has remained as strong. Correspondingly, the inducement to support private investment has been weak. The following numbers from Appendix Table 1 of the *Annual Report 2007–08* by the Reserve Bank of India, 2008, only underscore the familiar pattern.

Table 1: Scheduled Commercial Bank (% change)

Scheduled Commercial Banks (% change)	2005–6	2006–7	2007–8
Bank Credit	30.8	28.1	22.3
Non-Food Credit	31.8	28.5	23.0
Investments in Government Securities	−2.7	10.7	23.5
Dubai Brent	33.5	49.2	61.4
barrel per $	64.7	83.2	90.0

Source: International Monetary Fund's Primary Commodity Price Data.

The problem is that, even if Indian banks were to be suddenly seized by an inducement to lend to private enterprise brought about, say, by a spate of interesting projects, Basel I and Basel II norms will effectively stymie such a movement.[3] Almost all studies of the micro-effects of bank capital regulation report that the short-run effects are a reduction in individual bank lending and, in models that include endogenous loan-market adjustments, an increase in the equilibrium loan rate. The longer run effects are an increase in bank capital both absolutely and relative to bank lending. The interesting point is that there is no convincing evidence that the imposition of binding risk-based capital requirements contributed significantly to an increase in actual bank capital ratios. Pre- and post-regulation behaviour of banks remained almost the same.

Since the demand for credit and the supply of deposits varies positively with the level of economic activity, bank activity as well tends to be pro-cyclical. Regulation augments the cycle. The supervisory process obliges banks to constrict lending during contractions to protect bank bottom lines from the risks inherent in downturns. During upswings, on the other hand, regulators tend to adopt a *laissez-faire* attitude. Capital regulation reduces the ability of central banks to influence bank lending. Banks must employ onerous screening standards and, consequently, would be prone to respond to a monetary expansion by boosting deposits and security holdings, thereby operating like mutual funds. In the long run, however, an expansionary monetary policy stance will induce banks to expand equity which, under risk-based capital regulation requirements, would enable bank credit to expand.

Building Dams: Deposit-Creating Institutions

B. Bossone and A. Sarr[4] of the World Bank/IMF have devised a monetary scheme to initiate activity in a non-destabilising fashion in desperately poor economies. The proposal is to construct a firewall between the lending and the deposit-creating functions of banks. Deposit-creating institutions (DCI) would collect non-interest-bearing deposits and would distribute money on a non-lending basis, that is, with no condition to restitution. Their liabilities would be backed by the central bank's money. Every deposit balance would be augmented by a proportion of the depositor's own holdings calculated over a reference period. DCIs would not extend credit but would earn revenue from fees charged for payments services. They would not be permitted to distribute their liquidity to businesses or non-DCI intermediaries. The latter would fund their assets exclusively with non-debt instruments. The proposal is distinct from the institution of narrow banking which is concerned with deposit acceptance. At the same time, there are some resemblances. In both instances, the objective is to ensure the complete integrity of the money supply process and both innovations involve a firewall. Banks create the economy's medium of exchange while non-blank financial intermediaries transfer savings from surplus units to deficit units. Under the Bossone-Sarr scheme, these financial institutions would operate under securities' firm regulation. Their innovative impulses would not be impaired. Their non-monetary financial activities would be backed by non-guaranteed funds and they would be allowed to fail. The motive force behind the scheme is to kick-start activity from a position of near inactivity. We have extended the model to suggest that the money be disbursed as wages to workers in production.[5] The demand for food, clothing, and housing would rise. Production and production finance for these goods would be stimulated. Higher output would mean greater capital accumulation and so on in second and higher order effects.

Constructing Conduits: Monetary-Fiscal Coordination

The macroeconomic dynamics of the private sector of a relatively closed economy like India must be narrated in terms of savings and investment. The components of each of the figures in Appendix Table 11 of the *Annual Report 2007–08* by the Reserve Bank of India, 2008, show a tepid increase over 2004–5 to 2006–7. New capital issues by non-government public limited companies have displayed a steady downward trend from the latter half of the 1990s only to pick up over the last few years (Table 82, *Handbook of Statistics on the Indian Economy*, RBI, 2007). Table 83 shows that bonds issued by public sector undertakings have tapered off since the beginning of this century. Absorption of private capital issues has also been fluctuating in a downward direction since the latter part of the last century. One may recall that, over the 1970s, India recorded a trend break in savings and investment. Gross capital formation increased *in tandem*. Kaushik Basu (*Journal of Economic Literature*, 2008, XLVI, 2, 396–406) has noted that the cause of the increase in savings was the nationalisation of banks in 1969. Banks had to open branches in remote rural areas.

We regard it as incontrovertibly true that the purpose of financial liberalisation must be the generation of employment and growth. Furthermore, given the fact that the deceleration of employment has been particularly acute in the rural sector and that over 60 per cent of the labour force is sustained by agriculture, our task is cut out. The agenda must be to plan in terms of agriculture-industry linkages, between items consumed by the working class and those consumed by others. The macroeconomic counterpart of the requirement would be captured by reviving the 'employer of last resort' function of the Reserve Bank of India.[6] The notion dates back to the seventeenth century in the period after the Industrial Revolution when it was seen that existing enterprises were in no position to facilitate a state of full employment. In 1662, William Petty recommended a scheme for public employment for the purpose of building infrastructure. The government was to become a market maker for labour by building up a 'buffer stock of labour'. Thus, the government, in a sense, would purchase all the unemployed workers at a fixed price or sell them to the private sector at a higher wage. Counterpart government spending would increase commercial bank reserves. Excess reserves drive down interbank rates overnight. In order to keep them positive, the government would borrow from these reserves. As a borrower of the last resort, it can effectively set the interbank rate. Interest rates, then, are not constrained by the willingness of the private sector to buy government debt or by the size of the government deficit. Fiat currency absolves the government from borrowing or issuing debt to deficit spend. Governments can spend by crediting bank accounts and tax by debiting them. Excess reserves are drained as part of the interbank interest rate targeting procedure. This is the agenda of functional finance.

A proposal to direct credit into appropriate channels can be culled from a scheme of Asset Based Reserve Requirements (ABRR) proposed by Thomas Palley.[7] Under such a system, financial intermediaries would hold reserves against their assets. The reserve requirement for each asset class would be set by the monetary authority. In order to prevent regulatory arbitrage, the ABRR would apply to all financial intermediaries. Thus, a wedge would be created between interest rates on asset classes and the central bank's policy rate. By varying the size of the wedge, the authority would change relative returns across asset classes and, thereby influence portfolio and lending decisions. For instance, if the central bank wants to pierce a property bubble, it would impose reserve requirements on new mortgages. The cost of mortgages would rise without raising the general level of interest rates. Similarly, if the authorities want to channel investment to particular areas, it could impose zero or negative reserve requirements on loans directed at those sectors. Some merits in connection to our discussion are relevant. The ABRR are counter-cyclical. When asset prices fall, reserves would be released as the required reserves are based on the market value of the asset. Relatedly, the ABRR are automatic stabilisers. When asset prices rise, financial firms need to increase their reserve holdings, thereby putting brakes on the upswing. Finally, the ABRR restore the demand for central bank liabilities. Any process of disintermediation would be halted and the monetary transmission process strengthened.

The Spectre of Financialisation in India

We have indicated that the relationship between finance and growth is complex. One thesis is that financial markets are best described in the words of Charles Kindelberger as arenas of manias and panics. All regulatory measures that arise in response will suffer a version of Goodhart's Law, that is, financial entrepreneurs will arise to work around what we have called dams and conduits. Is India, then, condemned to financialisation? The term connotes the increasing role of the financial circulation relative to the real and the attendant atrophy of the real. Consider the former characteristic. In India, the lure of exotic financial fruits has not been tempting. All the same, it is worth noting in Appendix Table III.11 of the *Report on Trends and Progress of Banking in India 2006–2007* by the Reserve Bank of India, 2007, that bank group-wise lending to the sensitive sectors, exposure to the capital market by other public sector banks has increased from 2.8 to 4.16 per cent while the comparable figures for the new private sector banks are 2.3 and 2.19 per cent respectively. All banking groups display decent and increasing advances to real estate. The financial markets in India display the same flux as financial markets anywhere. For instance, the net resources mobilised by mutual funds display wild year-on-year fluctuations (*Handbook of Statistics on the Indian Economy*, RBI, 2007, Tables 78–80). As for the latter aspect, allowing for the qualifications about provisional, quick, and revised estimates, the following numbers do not paint a sanguine forecast of the economy by conventional standards.

Table 2: Economic Growth (Sectors)

Sector	2005–6	2006–7	2007–8
Agriculture & Allied Activities	5.9	3.8	4.5
Industry	8.0	10.6	8.1
Services	11.0	11.2	10.7

Source: *Annual Report*, RBI, 2008, Appendix Table 2.

The performance of the services should be noted particularly since its share in real gross domestic product continues to be high and increasing to around 60 per cent.

NOTES

1. P. Arestis and L.F. de Paula, eds., 2008. Introduction in *Financial Liberalization and Economic Performance in Emerging Countries*, New York: Palgrave Macmillan.
2. 'Error term' is a residual of repression.
3. D. VanHoose, 2008, 'Bank Capital Regulation, Economic Stability, and Monetary Policy: What Does the Academic Literature Tell Us?', *Atlantic Economic Journal*, 38, 1, 1–14.
4. B. Bossone and A. Sarr, 2005, 'Non-Credit Money to Fight Poverty', in *The Monetary Theory of Production*, eds. G. Fontana and R. Realfonzo, London: Palgrave Macmillan.
5. R. Correa, 2008, 'Heterodox Macroeconomics and the Design of Monetary Institutions', Working Paper 26/4/2008, Department of Economics, University of Mumbai.
6. D.B. Papadimitriou, 2008, 'Promoting Equality through an Employment of Last Resort Policy', Working Paper No. 54, The Levy Economics Institute of Bard College.
7. T. Palley, 2008, 'Asset Price Bubbles and Monetary Policy: Why Central Banks Have Been Wrong and What Should be Done', Macroeconomic Policy Institute Working Paper 05/2008.

41

National Treasury Management Agency Proposals: Implications for India's Financial Policies

S. NARAYAN

(27 November 2008)

THE RESERVE BANK of India (RBI) manages the borrowings of the Indian government. In almost all the years since Independence, the government has not had a fiscal surplus, and it has had to borrow from the market to meet capital requirements for planned schemes. In fact, the argument among the financial managers of the government was that there was no harm in running up a fiscal deficit if the funds were used for capital expenditure. By the 1980s, the government was borrowing for its current expenditure as well, and the resultant growth of debt threatened to take the country into a financial crisis. The RBI has managed these substantial borrowings from the market. It has managed government borrowing in a manner that the targets are fulfilled, without affecting credit flows to the rest of the economy. The RBI decides on tranches of government borrowing at different times of the year, the periodicity and the coupon rate, and 'persuades' the state-owned banks to pick up the bonds, which are then counted as part of their statutory lending ratio. Apart from this, the RBI manages the borrowings of the state governments as well, taking into account their needs and their capacities. In fact, the RBI has been the debt and treasury manager of the government.

There have been some problems with this. First, in order to be an effective bonds manager, it would like to keep interest rates low. However, this constrains the freedom of its monetary policy of setting short-term interest rates. Second, these bonds are illiquid, with trading taking place only between different public sector banks that hold these documents and, hence, it is non-transparent. It has also constrained the development of a bonds market where the public could buy and sell government bonds. It has also prevented corporates from accessing market for debt financing, as long-term bonds have not developed in the secondary markets. Finally, with a limited number of high credit-rated companies, there was little opportunity for the others to access the market, except at very high interest rates.

In the last decade, the situation has changed significantly. The equity markets have become world class and there has not been a single day, even in the current crisis, when the markets have not functioned and settlements not taken place. The markets have developed considerable depth, with a large number of companies being able to raise equity in the country, and equity as well as debt overseas. State government borrowings have been made independent of the central government's oversight on planned expenditure, after the Twelfth Finance Commission recommendations, and they can now borrow according to their creditworthiness, as needed.

It was against the backdrop to create a smooth, independent bonds market that the government announced in the 2007–8 Budget that the monetary and the debt management functions of the RBI would be separated. On 21 November 2008, the government released a draft bill to create a statutory corporate body called the National Treasury Management Agency (NTMA) to carry out debt and cash management, and the management of contingent and other liabilities of the centre and the states. The NTMA would help them to manage their debt so as to meet their financing needs. It would, over time, be able to extend the portfolio of debt instruments to include rupee-denominated bonds, foreign currency-denominated bonds and inflation-indexed bonds. This is a welcome move and will help create a vibrant bonds market, and also lend greater strength and depth to the financial markets.

At the same time, there are some moral hazards as well. First, the role of the RBI, which it has been ably executing for the last 60 years, is being curtailed. The NTMA, as the investment banker to the government, would work with the budget division of the Ministry of Finance, without oversight from the RBI. The NTMA would be an investment banker without any regulatory oversight. In the past, there have been several state governments which have been remarkably indiscreet in their borrowings, primarily to pay for subsidies and dole-outs. In the early part of this decade, the worsening of state finances was due to this profligacy. With the RBI in control, and the states needing overdraft and 'Ways and Means' facilities, the RBI was able to provide an effective oversight to the management of state finances. There have been several instances where the RBI has bailed out the states, through proactive advice and assistance. With the proposed NTMA, this role will cease to exist. There is no evidence to suggest that the states, and indeed even the central government (this financial year is a good example), have been able to rise above politics to manage their finances in an objective and prudent manner. The NTMA will be unable to prevent indiscreet borrowings by the states for it is slated to be an investment manager and not a fiscal regulator.

Second, the draft bill envisages that these government bonds would be available for sale in India and abroad. This would mean that, for the first time since Independence, India would be offering sovereign bonds to overseas investors. Earlier finance ministers and governments had shied away from this, for committing a sovereign to a debt that can be called outside the country, has been a very sensitive and emotional issue. This was the reason that, even at the height of the foreign exchange crisis, Resurgent India Bonds were in fact issued by the State Bank of India and not by the debt. It has been the principle so far that the sovereign, the State, would not issue debt overseas.

The worry is that the mere creation of the Debt Management Office in the Finance Ministry, without taking a holistic view of the problem, is likely to exacerbate the fiscal pressures that are being faced by the states and, eventually, the central government. Institutions need to be reformed as much as processes and it would have been better if both issues had been addressed simultaneously.

42

The Fall of the Indian Rupee and 'the Unholy Trinity'

M. SHAHIDUL ISLAM

(*10 December 2008*)

LET US BEGIN with an anecdote first—last year, Lehman Brothers predicted that the Indian rupee (INR) would appreciate to Rs 36 per United States dollar (US $) by the end of 2008. Ironically, the former investment bank did not anticipate that it would not be around to witness the reversal of its predictions. So much for the limitations of currency forecasting.

Following the volatilities in oil and other commodity markets, currencies around the world have had a roller coaster ride in recent months. The US $ surged to a 15-month high *vis-à-vis* á basket of major currencies. The Japanese yen (JPY) has been the strongest currency in the currency markets while commodity currencies such as the Australian dollar (AU $) and the Canadian dollar have witnessed a free fall. The INR, the South Korean won and the Indonesian rupiah have been the worst performing currencies in Asia in recent times.

This brief looks at the reasons behind the fall of the INR followed by an assessment of the economic implications of the currency depreciation on South Asia's largest economy. It also revisits the behaviour of the Indian currency (for the period of 2006–8) and contends that it is very likely that the INR fluctuations are here to stay, largely owing to the iron triangle of international finance.

THE FALL OF THE INDIAN RUPEE: CAUSES

The INR recently breached the psychological mark of Rs 50 per US $. The currency has lost its value substantially, both in nominal and real terms, notably against the US $ and the JPY. Only about one year back, the INR-greenback exchange rate was Rs 39.26 per US $. What has caused the marked downward spiral of the INR?

In recent months, fluctuations in low interest rate currencies such as the JPY[1] and high interest rate currencies such as the AU $ have been heavily subjected to carry trade.[2] In the case of the INR, the evidence is less sanguine.

The unexpected strength in the US $ relative to a basket of six major currencies, known as the US $ index, the outflow of foreign institutional investments (FII) from the Indian market, the country's widening trade deficit, and the significantly lower flow in external commercial borrowings (ECB) by Indian corporate houses, *inter alia*, have caused the depreciation of the INR.

The US $ index has strengthened 17 per cent over the past quarter.[3] As the financial crisis spreads to the emerging markets, the money is moving to the United States in search of a safe haven, despite mounting credit and other economic malaise in the world's largest economy.[4]

Moreover, there is an inverse relation between oil prices and the US $. As the developed world is in a recession and most emerging markets prioritise inflation check over growth, there is a big fall in oil and other commodity prices.

The Indian equity market has witnessed a rapid withdrawal of portfolio investments in the last few months that instigated, among others, the free fall of the Indian stock markets.[5] The Reserve Bank of India (RBI) reports that, during the first quarter of 2008–9, there were portfolio investment outflows by FIIs the order of US $5.2 billion, compared to a net inflow of US $7.1 billion during April–June 2007.[6] According to data from the Securities and Exchange Board of India, international investors sold a record US $13.5 billion in Indian equities this year as on 24 November 2008.[7] The net ECB was only US $1.6 billion during April–June 2008, as against US $6.9 billion a year ago.[8]

However, foreign direct investment (FDI) statistics show a different trend. India received US $19.3 billion in FDI as in September 2008. Inflows under the American depository receipts, global depository receipts and non-resident Indians deposits were higher during April–June 2008 than in the corresponding period last year.[9]

Although exports of both primary and manufacturing products recorded a higher growth in the current year than in the previous year, the trade data for the first quarter of 2008–9 showed a widening merchandise trade deficit, as the growth of imports (33.3 per cent) outpaced that of exports (22.2 per cent). Higher commodity prices, notably oil, have widened the export-import gap. Merchandise trade deficit widened to US $31.6 billion during the first quarter of 2008–9. However, the gross invisible receipts recorded US $37.7 billion, a year-on-year increase of 29.7 per cent. Nevertheless, the current account deficit amounted to US $10.7 billion in the first quarter of 2008–9, according to the RBI.[10]

The dynamics in the current and capital accounts resulted in a decline in India's foreign exchange reserve—it stood at US $245.8 billion as on 21 November 2008.[11] The reserve had reached more than US $313 billion at the end of April 2008. Moreover, the RBI had to intervene in the foreign exchange market by selling the US $ and buying the INR to curb the rapid fall in the INR.

All these factors placed huge pressures on the INR, and the currency depreciated by 18.9 per cent *vis-à-vis* the US $, 19.1 per cent against the JPY, and 0.4 per cent against the Euro in nominal terms during the current fiscal year (as on 22 October 2008).[12]

The Fall of Indian Rupee: Implications

The northbound or southbound of a currency is a common phenomenon in an economy such as India which is quite integrated with the global trade and finance.[13] Moreover, the RBI pursues managed float exchange rate policy.[14] However, what worries the stakeholders in the economy is the pace of appreciation or depreciation of the INR. Extreme volatilities in the currency market hurt exporters and importers who do not find adequate time to hedge against currency risk. For instance, a study shows that, in the period of 2004–8, 96 out of 124 industry indices exibited signs of a bet on the INR appreciation.[15]

Theoretically, the fall of the INR could benefit India's exports sector and discourage imports. Individuals (for instance, study loan) or corporate houses who have taken the foreign currency loans expect to be adversely affected.

There had been a hue and cry among Indian exporters last year when the INR appreciated markedly as they were worried that the country's currency appreciation could erode its export competitiveness. As the financial crisis spreads all over the world, Indian exporters are expected to experience negative price and revenue shocks. The INR deprecation is a welcome relief for them. However, the benefits of currency depreciation depend on how much it depreciates in real terms. For instance, the Real Effective Exchange Rate (REER) which is calculated by adjusting the Nominal Effective Exchange Rate (NEER) for inflation differentials with the countries whose currencies are included in the basket *vis-à-vis* the domestic currency is the actual measure of the rise and fall in a country's currency.

The RBI and the Bank for International Settlements data show that from October 2007 to September 2008 the INR has depreciated 14 per cent and 16 per cent respectively in nominal terms or NEER, whereas in real terms or REER, the depreciation has been only 7 per cent and 8.5 per cent respectively. These numbers are hardly surprising as India has been experiencing a higher inflation level *vis-à-vis* its major trading partners. The real benefits of the INR depreciations on the Indian exports are, thus, not as high as they sound.

Nevertheless, the INR depreciation is expected to have a positive impact on India's manufacturing and info-technology services sectors, among others. As India imports 70 per cent of its crude oil needs and follows an administered pricing, the INR depreciation has significant implications for the sector. The drop in oil prices has benefited, except for inventory losses,[16] the country's oil refining and marketing companies such as Hindustan Petroleum, Bharat Petroleum Corporation Limited and Indian Oil Corporation. However, the INR depreciation has affected them adversely. It is reported that although crude oil price corrected by roughly 57 per cent in dollar terms, it contracted by 52.5 per cent in real terms owing to the 9 per cent fall in the INR in the last four months.[17]

As a result, the breakeven point for the oil marketing companies has been pushed back further. With Rs 41–2 per US $, the crude oil's cut-off was US $67–8 per barrel which has been revised to US $59 as INR depreciated to Rs 49–50 per US $. It is estimated that for every Re 1 decrease in the value of the Indian currency against the USD, the annual under-realisations of these oil marketing companies' increases by around Rs 3,000 crore.[18]

It is expected, at least theoretically, that the fall in the INR will discourage the country's imports to some extent. However, the flip side of this fact is that it is not good news for the companies whose exports contain high-import contents. Moreover, the fall in capital machinery imports followed by currency depreciation indeed affects a country's productivity adversely. Further, the currency depreciation can countervail the RBI's fight against inflation, though the drop in oil price is a big solace for the country.

The INR Fluctuations and the Unholy Trinity

As India's financial markets have undergone significant liberalisation and the economy relies on international markets for capitals, gone are the days of a stable INR. The reason is that it is not possible for a country to have free international capital mobility, a fixed exchange rate and an independent monetary policy. Economists call the phenomenon 'unholy trinity' or 'impossible trinity', which essentially means that one of three things has to change, that is, either one reduces capital mobility, or adopts a flexible exchange rate policy; or abandons monetary control.

In the face of huge capital inflows in 2006–8, the RBI had to intervene in the foreign exchange market by sterilising the inflows through the market stabilisation scheme (MSS), increasing cash reserve ratio, etc. Now with the reversal of the capital inflows and widening trade gaps, the RBI faces the same unholy trinity. The country's central bank's dilemma is either to allow the currency to depreciate and maintain the current level of interest rate; or to intervene in the foreign exchange market (buy the INR and sell the USD) but to accept the tightening liquidity conditions in the market.

To ease the tight liquidity conditions, the RBI has responded several times in the last few weeks by reducing key interest rates, unwinding the MSS-liquidity stocks and relaxing the ECB norms. As the global liquidity condition is extremely tight and the outlook for India's current account remains bleak, it is expected that the liquidity conditions in India will remain stiff despite the RBI's several liquidity support measures. As the country's monetary authority has little choice but to intervene in the foreign exchange market, the liquidity support measures may not completely offset the tight liquid market which is a result of foreign exchange intervention, among others.

NOTES

1. Indeed, the impact of carry trade on the JPY has been so strong that it has broken down the long-standing strong positive correlation between USD/JPY and the Japanese trade balance.
2. This is a popular trading strategy used in the foreign exchange market. It consists of selling low interest-rate currencies (funding currencies) and investing in high interest-rate currencies (investment currencies).
3. *The Hindu Business Line*, 19 October 2008.
4. According to the Emerging Portfolio Fund Research, the United States equity funds witnessed an inflow of US $42 billion in the third quarter of 2008, the United States Money Market Funds attracted roughly US $40 billion, and the US Bond Funds drew US $8.9 billion in the same period. (*The Hindu Business Line*, 19 October 2008).
5. The BSE Sensex declined from the peak of 20,873 on 8 January 2008 to 10,170 in October 2008.
6. Statement by D. Subbarao, Governor, Reserve Bank of India, on the Mid-Term Review of Annual Policy for the Year 2008–09.
7. http://www.bloomberg.com/apps/news?pid=20601091& refer=india&sid=aHK4FwcVc2jM
8. Statement by D. Subbarao, Governor, Reserve Bank of India, on the Mid-Term Review of Annual Policy for the Year 2008–9.
9. Ibid.
10. Ibid.
11. Ibid.

12. Ibid.
13. Trade, one of the important indicators of global integration, has risen markedly as a proportion of GDP; net FDI has been growing at a good pace; and capital inflows, as a percentage of GDP, though volatile, have markedly increased during this decade.
14. The rupee exchange rate is neither completely free-float nor fixed, but is 'managed' by the Reserve Bank of India which is governed by broad principles of careful monitoring and management of exchange rates with flexibility without targeting a pre-announced rate on a bank, coupled with the ability to intervene if and when necessary.
15. Ila Patnaik, Ajay Shah (2008), 'One Way Bets on Pegged Exchange Rates', available at <http://www.nipfp.org.in/nipfp-dea-program/PDF/SP2008_onewaybets.pdf>, accessed on 3 December 2008.
16. As the crude oil prices in the international markets plunged, the worry emerged in the form of inventory losses. The reason is the companies' oil stocks were bought at higher prices that severely affected their financial health. It is estimated that the oil importing companies' combined losses stood at Rs 13,000 crore in the second quarter of FY 2009.
17. *The Business Standard*, 17 November 2008.
18. Ibid.

SECTION II

ECONOMIC DEVELOPMENT

C. Infrastructure Development

43

Urban Transport in India: The 'Nano' Effect

SHREEKANT GUPTA

(*5 February 2008*)

NANO, THE NEW low cost car unveiled by Tata Motors at the Auto India Expo at Delhi last month, has set the country abuzz. There has been considerable hype surrounding the car. Some commentators have declared the advent of this car as a transportation revolution, an event as significant as the launch of the Model T by Henry Ford. Others have argued that Nano will democratise car ownership, and have even called it a happening that may upturn the brahminical order in the country. On the technology front, Nano certainly epitomises India's progress in innovation, packed as it is with several firsts. Tata Motors has filed over 34 patents for the car. In particular, a great deal of innovation has gone into the drive train[1] and its placement, and half the patents filed pertain to the drive train alone. One of the key patents is the introduction of a balancer shaft to iron out the vibrations typical for a twin-cylinder engine. According to the company, Nano also meets all emission and safety norms, including (frontal) crash test norms in India. Its fuel efficiency is expected to be in the range of 18–20 km per litre.

Dubbed as a 'people's car' with a 623cc, two-cylinder MPFI engine delivering 33bhp, this rear drive vehicle is slated to cost Rs 100,000[2]/US $2,500 at current exchange rates. The car will be available in three variants—one basic version and two deluxe versions. The on-road price of the basic model (with manual transmission and without air-conditioning, electric windows and power steering) after registration, taxes and insurance will be around Rs 125,000 whereas the deluxe models will cost around

Rs 150,000. Thus, the round figure of Rs 100,000(++) is symbolic and the price tag is ostensibly meant to get India's two-wheeler segment into motor cars. Ratan Tata is quoted as having said he was motivated to develop an inexpensive car when he saw, 'the father (riding) the scooter, his young kid standing in front of him, his wife seated behind him holding a little baby'. Nano is expected to hit the roads in late October this year at the time of the festival of Diwali. It will be manufactured at the Tata Motors plant at Singur in West Bengal with an annual production capacity of 250,000 units. Given the ongoing local unrest, however (apparently due to the manner of land allotment to Tata Motors by the West Bengal government), the company may have to relocate production elsewhere. If this were to happen there could be a delay in the delivery schedule.[3]

This brief focuses on the economics of owning and operating a Nano and its impact on automobilisation in the country. Issues related to impact on air quality and congestion are addressed in a companion ISAS brief.

The implication of the impending advent of an inexpensive passenger car such as Nano on urban transport in India has to be seen in the context of overall trends in motorisation in the country. Auto sales (passenger and commercial vehicles, three-wheelers and two-wheelers) in India almost doubled in five years from about 5.23 million units in 2001–2 to 10.11 million units in 2006–7 (see Table 1). During the last financial year (2006–7) alone, sales of passenger cars grew at a scorching rate of 22 per cent. Over the same period, sales of two-wheelers went up by about 11.5 per cent. Thus, merits of the case aside, it is evident that the country is rapidly motorising. And with incomes rising in an economy growing at a rate of 8 per cent or more annually, there is no sign of this abating. But it is also true that the vast majority of vehicles sold in India are two-wheelers which currently comprise 77 per cent of market share—close to eight million two-wheelers were sold in 2006–7 (see Tables 1 and 2). It is, therefore, moot to what extent Nano, *per se*, will displace this segment in the near-term.

The demand for any product, including vehicles, is driven by two main factors—its price and the income of the buyer. The

Table 1: Automobile Domestic Sales Trends (Number of Vehicles)

Category	2001–2	2002–3	2003–4	2004–5	2005–6	2006–7
Passenger Cars	5,09,088	5,41,491	6,96,153	8,20,179	8,82,208	10,76,408
Utility Vehicles	1,04,253	1,13,620	1,46,388	1,76,360	1,94,502	2,20,199
MPVs	61,775	52,087	59,555	65,033	66,366	83,091
Total Passenger Vehicles	6,75,116	7,07,198	9,02,096	10,61,572	11,43,076	13,79,698
M&HCVs	89,999	1,15,711	1,61,395	1,98,506	2,07,472	2,75,600
LCVs	56,672	74,971	98,719	1,19,924	1,43,569	1,92,282
Total Commercial Vehicles	1,46,671	1,90,682	2,60,114	3,18,430	3,51,041	4,67,882
Three-wheelers	2,00,276	2,31,529	2,84,078	3,07,862	3,59,920	4,03,909
Scooters	9,08,268	8,25,648	8,86,295	9,22,428	9,09,051	9,40,673
Motorcycles	28,87,194	36,47,493	41,70,445	49,64,753	58,10,599	65,53,664
Mopeds	4,08,263	3,38,985	3,07,509	3,22,584	3,32,741	3,55,870
Electric Two-wheelers	–	–	–	–	–	7,341
Total Two-wheelers	42,03,725	48,12,126	53,64,249	62,09,765	70,52,391	78,57,548
Grand Total	52,25,788	59,41,535	68,10,537	78,97,629	89,06,428	1,01,09,037

Source: Society of Indian Automobile Manufacturers (SIAM).
http://www.siamindia.com/scripts/domestic-sales-trend.aspx

Table 2: Domestic Market Share for 2006–7

CVs	5
Total Passenger Vehicles	14
Total Two-wheelers	77
Three-wheelers	4

Source: Society of Indian Automobile Manufacturers (SIAM). http://www.siamindia.com/scripts/market-share.aspx

responsiveness of demand to each of these is known as price- and income-elasticity respectively. For most goods as incomes go up, demand goes up (these are known as 'normal' goods in the economic jargon). Vehicles certainly come under this category. Therefore, it is inevitable that as incomes go up, households move up the vehicle ladder graduating from bicycles to two-wheelers and from two-wheelers to motor cars. This happens, *ceteris paribus* (that is, other things being equal such as the price of vehicles). In addition, however, if the price were to decrease, demand undoubtedly would get a further fillip. But for an expensive product like a car, the strength of income-elasticity far outweighs that of price-elasticity, especially for marginal changes in price. The impact of Nano on automobile demand can be viewed within this analytical framework. It has been argued that the low price of Nano will galvanise demand. Is this true? One must bear in mind that the real price of any vehicle is its capital cost plus running costs, namely, fuel, insurance, service and maintenance. These are examined below, respectively, for Nano.

First, it is evident that the actual sale price of Nano will certainly exceed Rs 125,000 or 150,000 depending on the variant purchased. The reason is simple: demand will outstrip supply (at best 15,000–20,000 units per month) and the car will be sold at a premium officially or in the black market. When the first 'people's car' the Maruti Suzuki 800 was launched in India in the early 1980s, a similar phenomenon was observed. The car was sold against bookings made and a lottery determined who could buy it. Thus, while the price of the car was around Rs 60,000, letters of allotment were sold at a premium of up to Rs 30,000. This, in effect, validates another fundamental principle of economics: given the demand curve for a product one can either fix the quantity or the price, but not both. Given that production capacity is fixed, at least in the short- to medium-term, price has to give way since we cannot operate off the demand curve. In the case of Nano, a likely scenario is that the car will be sold at an (unofficial) price of well over Rs 125,000 and is likely to command a premium of at least Rs 30,000. The 'choke price', that is, the price at which demand is choked off will be set by the next most expensive option available, such as the Maruti 800 (now wholly-owned by Japan's Suzuki) which costs about Rs 215,000 on-the-road for a basic model. Thus, the premium for Nano is likely to be bounded upward by this price and will perhaps stabilise at around Rs 30,000–40,000. What this means in effect is that we are looking at a price in the range of Rs 155,000 to 165,000.

Two other factors that are likely to cause an upward drift in the price of Nano are cost escalation and production uncertainties. The latter has already been mentioned. With regard to the former, in a general inflationary scenario with a rise in the price of inputs such as steel, it is moot to what extent Tata Motors will be able to hold the ex-factory price at Rs 100,000, despite the appeal of this round figure.

More important, however, are the running costs of the car (or any car for that matter). According to Professor Dinesh Mohan, a transport expert at IIT Delhi, for an active commuter driving a small car in Delhi, expenditure on petrol is about Rs 3,000 a month and insurance and other expenses are a minimum of Rs 1,000 a month.[4] Also, according to him the typical monthly payment for a loan of Rs 150,000 (for a Nano) will be about Rs 2,700 whereas that for a Rs 200,000 Maruti is about Rs 3,400. In sum, it would cost a total of Rs 6,700 a month for owning and operating a Nano and Rs 7,400 a month for a Maruti 800, a saving of about 10 per cent per month which is not enormous. Professor Mohan, therefore, concludes,

A middle class family generally cannot spend more than 15 per cent of its income on transport. To spend about Rs 6,000 a month on Nano, your income should be more than Rs 40,000 a month. In Delhi, the richest city of India, only 30 per cent families earn more than about Rs 25,000 a month. Clearly, even with cheap cars available, less than 20 per cent of the families can own a car in Delhi and much fewer in other cities. That is why the motorcycle with its low maintenance and running costs will not get displaced by cheap cars.

Another point this statement substantiates is that it is growing incomes rather than lower prices that more strongly impact on the demand for a car.

Finally, another point against the price-elasticity view is that used cars in good condition are even now available for less than Rs 100,000. It does not appear, therefore, that breaching this symbolic barrier is the key to increasing car ownership and in getting people off scooters and into cars (even if that were a desirable policy objective).

In sum, it does not appear that Nano will lead to a spurt in car ownership in India. The symbolic price tag of Rs 100,000 is just that. The real cost of owning and operating it is likely to remain high enough for it not to be a 'people's car' in the true sense of the term in a country where two-thirds of the population still lives on US $2 a day or less.

NOTES

1. Drive train refers to all the moving parts of the car as a whole, including the engine, clutch, transmission, drive shaft, differential, axles and wheels.
2. US $1=Rs 40.
3. Tata Motors MD Ravi Kant on Tehelka.com: '. . . Kant made it clear that the Nano was no Houdini magic and agreed that its success would revolve around speedy production, an issue that currently hangs fire because of continued on-ground protests at the site of the newly created plant in Singur, West Bengal. A car plant generates economic boom in its surroundings. If people do not want jobs in Singur, it would not only be sad but also unfortunate. Visit our Pantnagar plant in Uttaranchal and see what it has done to the city and its people. *But if trouble lingers, we will have no option but to shift base.*' (emphasis added). http://tehelka.com/story_main37.asp?filename=Bu190108a_miracle.asp
4. 'The Nano Confusion', *Business Standard*, New Delhi, 20 January 2008.

44

Urban Transport in India: Beyond 'Nano'

SHREEKANT GUPTA

(6 February 2008)

A POSITIVE FALLOUT of the unveiling of Nano, a low cost (US $2,500) car by Tata Motors at Delhi last month (and slated to go into production later this year), is that it has re-ignited the debate about urban transport in India. Proponents of motorisation have argued that the advent of an inexpensive car will usher in a transport revolution in the country while critics have warned of impending chaos on the roads and of adverse impact on air quality, among other things. Further, several other auto manufacturers have also unveiled plans to introduce budget cars in the Indian market. Given that the penetration of cars in India is about seven per 1,000 people (as compared to 550 per 1,000 in Germany, for example), the potential size of the market is indeed enormous in a country of over a billion people. A larger issue, however, that the impending advent of low-cost automobiles has raised, is the direction in which urban transport in India is headed. This brief focuses on the current state and likely future of urban transport in the country and steps required to make it sustainable.

Urban transport in India has to be examined within the overall context of trends in urbanisation in the country. At present, India is about 29 per cent urban (second in South Asia behind Pakistan at 36 per cent, see Table 1). Also, contrary to popular belief, India's rate of urban growth has been and will continue to be relatively slow in the short run—about 2.3 per cent annually during 2005–10 (ranking behind Bangladesh, Nepal and Pakistan in South Asia alone). Nonetheless, at present, about 321 million Indians live in

Table 1: Urbanisation in South Asia and China

	Total population (millions) (2007)	Average population rate (%) (2005–10)	% urban (2007)	Urban growh rate (%) (2005–10)
Bangladesh	147.1	1.8	26	3.5
Bhutan	2.3	2.2	12	5.1
India	1,135.6	1.4	29	2.3
Nepal	28.2	1.9	17	4.8
Pakistan	164.6	2.1	36	3.3
Sri Lanka	21.1	0.8	15	0.8
China	1,331.4	0.6	42	2.7

Source: State of World Population 2007: Unleashing the Potential of Urban Growth, United Nations Population Fund.

towns and cities, a very large number in absolute terms. And this number is likely to double in the next 30 years (see Table 2). In fact, after China, India has the largest urban population in the world. Also, what the rate of urbanisation does not indicate is the growing size of existing Indian towns and cities—while the total urban population increased eightfold between 1901 and 1991, the number of settlements only doubled. In other words, urban expansion in India has been due to the enlargement of existing towns and cities.

All of this has important implications for urban transport. A large number of people living in large urban conglomerations enable economies of scale in urban transport. At the same time, if urban transport is not managed well, it has the potential to choke cities and bring economic activity to a grinding halt. Here lies the promise and peril of urban transport in India.

So far, the trend has not been encouraging. Factors that determine transport demand, namely, increase in population, household incomes and economic activity, have placed heavy demands on urban transport systems, a demand that most Indian cities and towns have been unable to meet. In the absence of an adequate and efficient public transport system, the number of private and

Table 2: Projections of Urban Population in India

Year	Total population (million)	Decadal growth rate (%)	Urban population (million)	Decadal growth rate (%)	% urban
2001	1,027	21.7	285	31.3	27.8
2011	1,220	18.8	372	30.5	30.5
2021	1,390	13.9	473	27.2	34.0
2031	1,534	10.4	583	23.3	38.0
2041	1,648	7.4	700	20.1	42.5
2051	1,732	5.1	820	17.1	47.5

Source: E.F.N. Ribeiro (2003), 'Urban India in 2051: An Emerging Transportation cum Settlements Interface', paper presented at the Annual Congress of the Institute of Urban Transport (India), New Delhi on India's Urban Transport Vision 2050.

intermediate public transport (IPT) or para-transit vehicles has increased to meet the travel demand. Nonetheless, the predominant modes of urban travel in Indian towns and cities are still walking, cycling and public transport, including IPT.[1] Despite the high growth rates of two-wheelers and cars, their penetration is still relatively low. Across different cities and towns car ownership ranges from 3–13 per cent of households and two-wheelers from 40–50 per cent, the latter being about the same as bicycle ownership. The dependence on bicycles and cycle rickshaws is higher in smaller cities which have lower incomes and are smaller in size. In medium-sized cities (1–3 million) such as Lucknow, Hubli, Varanasi, Kanpur and Vijayawada, IPT modes like tempos, cars and cycle rickshaws become important. This segment has little regulatory oversight and largely operates as a free for all by private operators, often resulting in serious safety and emission violations. Other than the metros, most other urban areas in India have skeletal bus services provided by the municipality. With regard to the urban poor who account for a third of India's urban population and many of whom live in slums, travel patterns are very different from residents in formal housing. Generally, cycling and walking account for 50 to 75 per cent of the commuter trips for those in the informal sector whereas the formal sector is dependent on buses, cars and two-wheelers. This implies that despite high risks and a hostile infrastructure, low cost modes exist because their users do not have any choice. They are the captive users of these modes.

With regard to modal split, in most urban areas, the share of mass transport is well below desired levels and that of personalised transport and para transit above the optimal level (see Tables 3 and 4). Moreover, a third of all motor vehicles ply in the seven metropolitan cities alone (cities with a population of 4 million or more, namely, Delhi, Mumbai, Kolkata, Chennai, Bangalore, Hyderabad and Ahmedabad) which constitute around 11 per cent of the total population. Delhi by itself, with 1.4 per cent of India's population, accounts for more than 7 per cent of all motor vehicles in the country. One consequence of this is heavy dependence on oil imports which were about 102 million tonnes in 2005, and of which over a third (35 million tonnes) was consumed by the transport sector alone.[2]

The policy response so far has been ad hoc and has had limited impact. The Report of the Working Group for the Eleventh Five Year Plan on Urban Transport, constituted by the Planning Commission of the Government of India in 2006 and chaired by the Secretary, Urban Development,[3] had stated in its review of government interventions on urban transport,[4]

Table 3: Desirable Modal Split for Indian Cities by Size

(*per cent of total trips by mechanical modes*)

Population (million)	Mass transport	Bicycle	Other modes
0.1–0.5	30–40	30–40	25–35
0.5–1.0	40–50	25–35	20–30
1.0–2.0	50–60	20–30	15–25
2.0–5.0	60–70	15–25	10–20
5.0+	70–85	15–20	10–15

Source: *Traffic and Transportation Policies and Strategies in Urban Areas in India*, Final Report, Ministry of Urban Development, Government of India, New Delhi, March 1998.

Table 4: Existing Modal Split in Indian Cities, 1994

(*per cent*)

Population (million)	Walk	Mass transport	Intermediate public transport, IPT		Car	Two-wheeler	Bicycle	Total
			Fast	Slow				
0.10–0.25	37.1	16.4	10.4	20.1	3.3	24.1	25.7	100
0.25–0.50	37.8	20.6	8.9	17.2	2.6	29.8	20.9	100
0.50–1.0	30.7	25.4	8.2	12.0	9.5	29.1	15.9	100
1.0–2.0	29.6	30.6	6.4	8.1	3.3	39.6	12.1	100
2.0–5.0	28.7	42.3	4.9	3.0	5.0	28.9	15.9	100
5.0+	28.4	62.8	3.3	3.7	6.1	14.8	9.4	100

Source: *Traffic and Transportation Policies and Strategies in Urban Areas in India*, Final Report, Ministry of Urban Development, Government of India, New Delhi, March 1998.

By and large, the following investments have been made in the past few years in an attempt to improve transport: (1) construction of flyovers in a large number of cities; (2) widening of roads; and (3) construction of the Mass Rapid Transit System (MRTS) in Delhi. The construction of flyovers and widening of roads have not produced the desired improvements in all locations. These policies have to be reviewed critically and best practices adopted taking into account the ex-perience of cities considered 'good' internationally. The construction of flyovers and widening of roads has, unfortunately, also been accompanied by the removal/reduction of pedestrian facilities. Considering that India has very high pedestrian mortality rates, this must be stopped immediately. It must be mandatory to provide at least a minimum of a prescribed area for pedestrian and bicycle facilities on all arterial roads (say, 4–5 metres combined in each direction). The MRTS in Delhi is operating at about 20 per cent of its projected capacity for December 2005 (4–5 lakh passengers per day *vs.* projection of 21.8 lakh passengers per day). The Kolkata MRTS is operating at 10 per cent capacity. *Therefore, the operating experience of metro rail systems in India should be taken into account in the proper planning and design of new systems.* It is also seen that there are considerable weaknesses in the proper planning of urban transport, which is a highly complex area. The skills and competencies required for urban transport planning are vastly different from those required for inter-city planning. Hence, a major capacity building initiative would be essential if meaningful proposals for improving urban mobility are to emerge from the state/city level authorities.

Of particular importance in the government review of its own interventions are its observations on the MRTS. It points to a careful of examination of the cost effectiveness of very expensive solutions such as monorail and underground metros. At-grade systems (those that run at ground level) such as light rail or bus-based rapid transport (with dedicated bus lanes) could work equally well and cost a tenth of an elevated system and a thirtieth of an underground system. With regard to the Delhi MRTS, even when the full system is in place with 200 km of track built at a cost of over 150 billion rupees at 1996 prices (approximately US $4 billion), about 80 per cent of the population of Delhi and about 70 per cent of its area will remain beyond walking distance (500 metres) of the Metro.[5] Researchers at IIT Delhi have estimated the system will be utilised at about 25 per cent of its capacity even when fully built, leading them to conclude, 'High capacity system does not necessarily generate high demand.'[6]

Looking to the future, the National Urban Transport Policy (NUTP), a white paper approved by the Union Cabinet in April 2006 provides a way forward if implemented effectively. The document rightly states that the key objective is to move people and not vehicles. Thus, it emphasises promotion of *cost effective* public transport as well as priority for non-motorised modes such as cycling and walking. Effective implementation of the NUTP, however, requires a concerted effort at the city level: *inter alia*, it requires preparation of integrated land use and transport plans. Another positive development is that the Indian government's ambitious urban renewal programme, the Jawaharlal Nehru National Urban Renewal Mission (JNNURM), has been coupled with the NUTP. To obtain approval for transport projects under the JNNURM, the guidelines require transport infrastructure improvement schemes to be in compliance with the NUTP. Since the focus of the NUTP is on public transport, pedestrians and bicycles, cities are modifying earlier road expansion projects to the Bus Rapid Transit (BRT) and bicycle-inclusive plans. The BRT and bicycle-inclusive plans have been approved by the central government for at least 10 cities.

In sum, the current trajectory of urban transport needs urgent correction. While some steps have been initiated, much still remains to be done to ensure sustainable urban transport so vital for viable urban growth in India.

NOTES

1. The discussion in this paragraph is based on 'Urban Transport in Indian Cities', by Geetam Tiwari, November 2007: http://www.urban-age.net/10_cities/07_mumbai/_reflections/india_Tiwari.html
2. This, of course, includes transport other than urban transport. Source: International Energy Agency, Energy Balances for India, accessed at: http://195.200.115.136/Textbase/stats/balancetable.asp?COUNTRY_CODE=IN&Submit=Submit

3. http://planningcommission.gov.in/aboutus/committee/wrkgrp11/wrk11_9b.htm
   http://urbanindia.nic.in/moud/programme/ut/utwg11plan.pdf
4. http://planningcommission.nic.in/aboutus/committee/wrkgrp11/wg11_MRTS.pdf (emphasis added).
5. 'Evaluation of Public Transport Systems: Case Study of Delhi Metro', by Mukti Advani and Geetam Tiwari, proceedings of START-2005 Conference held at IIT Kharagpur, India. Accessed at: http://web.iitd.ac.in/~tripp/publications/paper/planning/mukti_metro_kharagpur_05.pdf
6. Ibid. While the Delhi Metro is designed to handle 12.6 million commuter trips when fully completed it, is not likely to handle more than 3.13 million commuter trips.

45

India: Towards a Knowledge Superpower?: A View from Outside

GOPINATH PILLAI

(24 April 2008)

INTRODUCTION

FROM THE very dawn of history, whether it is for matters of the mind or material, India has always been a fertile land. The first references to astronomy are found in the *Rig Veda* which dates back to 2000 BC.[1] Mathematics has its roots in the nearly 4,000 years old Vedic literature. Indians developed many important mathematical concepts, including the base-ten decimal system.[2] India's Panini is well-regarded as the founder of linguistics, and his Sanskrit grammar is still considered to be the most sophisticated of any language in the world.[3] Even in manufacturing, India had an important position. According to the Yale historian, Paul Kennedy, India accounted for roughly 25 per cent of global industrial output in the 1770s.[4] India's tangible and intangible assets had always attracted external admirers and warriors alike.

Today, India's economic story is still impressive. The economy has been performing well, growing by an average 9 per cent in the last three years. Many high-tech industries have emerged and grown in India. These include information technology and communications, defence and space technology, pharmaceuticals and biotechnology. This rapid expansion of the Indian economy has resulted in gross domestic product (GDP) per capita increasing

*This paper was presented at the 1st IISS-CITI India Global Forum on 'India as A Rising Great Power: Challenges and Opportunities', held in New Delhi, from 18 to 20 April 2008.

from US $1,378 in 1998 to US $2,777 in 2007 (in purchasing power parity [PPP] terms).[5] Indian scholars have excelled in the areas of literature, physics, medicine, physiology, information technology (IT), and bio-technology, among others. The nation has half-a-dozen Nobel Prize winners to its credit.

Whilst one does not doubt India's economic rise, can one also then conclude that India has the potential to become a knowledge superpower? I shall discuss the question of whether India is a knowledge-based economy, as that will allow us to ascertain if it can become a knowledge superpower. I shall examine the key knowledge-based sectors in India as well as the advantages India has in pushing forward its knowledge-based industries. I shall then compare India with other knowledge-based countries. I shall also highlight the challenges facing India in this regard.

Definition of a Knowledge-based Economy

I think the first task of this paper is to define the term 'knowledge-based economy'. What is a knowledge economy? It is basically an economy that creates, disseminates and uses knowledge to enhance its growth and development. A country's success in the knowledge-based economy depends on the creation, acquisition, dissemination and application of knowledge.[6]

Knowledge creation depends on the the intensity of research and development (R&D) conducted in a country, and the availability of human resources needed for R&D.

Knowledge acquisition is reflected in the intellectual content embedded in imports from other knowledge-based economies (or through multinational corporations [MNC]). Linguistic skills will help to plug into the global knowledge network.

Knowledge dissemination depends on the resources allocated to develop information infrastructure, basic IT and linguistic skills to tap into the info-communication technology (ICT) network.

Finally, knowledge application is reflected in an economy's job market that demands and allows workers to apply knowledge extensively, and its ability to create new business models for generating, acquiring, diffusing and applying new ideas and processes.

The basic difference between a traditional and knowledge-based economy is that the former depends on quantitative factors such as labour, raw materials, premises and bulk transportation, among others, whereas the latter relies more on qualitative factors, namely, qualifications, R&D and good infrastructure. Resource-driven economies sometimes depend on a protectionist environment, whereas knowledge-based economies thrive in a friendly and open policy environment, and on innovation and qualified labour.

India's Key Knowledge-based Industries

The economic rise of India has seen Indian industries emerging as global players. I shall look at the development of several of the key knowledge-based industries in India.

Information and Communications Technology

The success story of India's IT and IT-enabled industries (ITES) is well documented. India's software industry grew at an average annual rate of approximately 50 per cent between 1992–3 and 2000–1.

The Indian IT-business process outsourcing (BPO) revenue aggregate is expected to grow by over 33 per cent and reach US $64 billion by the end of FY 2008. IT exports, (including hardware exports), are expected to cross US $40.8 billion in FY 2008 as against US $31.9 billion in FY 2007, a growth of 28 per cent. The domestic IT market (including hardware) is estimated to reach 23.2 billion in FY 2008 as against US $16.2 billion in FY 2007, a growth of 43 per cent. The direct employment in this sector is expected to reach nearly two million in FY 2008, an increase of about 375,000 professionals over FY 2007. The services exports, BPO exports and the domestic IT industries provide direct employment to 865,000, 704,000 and 427,000 professionals respectively.[7]

As a proportion of national GDP, the Indian technology sector revenue grew from 1.2 per cent in FY 1998 to an estimated 5.5 per cent in FY 2008. In 2007, there were more than 6,000 software exporting companies in the Software Technology Parks of India, spread over 21 cities, with a share of 73 per cent of the exports.

To reap the comparative advantages offered by the Indian software industry, about 250 of the Fortune 500 companies are now clients of Indian IT. As in December 2006, a total of 90 Indian companies have received the Software Engineering Institute Capability Maturity Model certificate. This is higher than any other country in the world.

India started by offering simple software solutions. It is now the favoured destination for high skilled, knowledge intensive activities. A majority of the Fortune 500 and Global 2,000 corporations are sourcing IT-ITES from India. HCL and Wipro carry out out-sourcing for innovation through MNCs like Boeing. IBM, Motorola, Hewlett-Packard, Cisco Systems and Google have set up R&D centres in Indian cities. General Electric's research centre in Bangalore is equal to its global research headquarters in New York. All the top 10 global fables design companies have operations in India. Fables designs are hardware devices implemented on semiconductor chips.

Having made an ineffaceable mark in the BPO business, India has now become an important Knowledge Process Outsourcing (KPO) destination. According to a recent report released by KPMG,[8] India will continue to be the preferred location for the global KPO destination and the industry is projected to be worth between US $10 billion and US $17 billion by 2010. However, the same report reveals that the shortage of skilled workers, rupee appreciation, and under-resourced and inadequately empowered legal framework and compliance within KPO providers are costing the competitiveness in this sector.

Defence and Space Technology

Although India has been starved of imported nuclear technology for almost three decades now, it has developed a competitive advantage in thorium-led nuclear technology. It has the world's second largest reserve of thorium just falling behind Australia. By producing the world's first U233-fuelled prototype reactor, Kamini, India has not only entered into Stage Three of its Nuclear Power Programme, it could also become the largest supplier of radioactive thorium by 2011. Incidentally, Kamini, with 30 kW capacity, is the only operating reactor in the world with U233 fuel.[9]

As the Indian Department of Atomic Energy progresses in the harnessing of fusion energy and in the development of thorium-based Fast Breeder Reactors, it is believed that India may well develop the capabilities to be nuclear self-sufficient. This has made it the world leader in thorium technology. The technology that has been used to operate the Canadian reactor CIRUS and to develop the 900 MW Pressurized Heavy Water Reactors is Indian as well.

India has come a long way in the development of nuclear technology. It began modestly with the commissioning of a Cirus 40 MW heavy-water-moderated research reactor from Canada in 1960.[10] Now, India provides the services of its scientists for expert assignments to other countries through the auspices of the International Atomic Energy Agency and through bilateral agreements for cooperation in the field of peaceful uses of atomic energy. This highlights India's leading position in nuclear technology in the world.[11] It also underlines India's self-reliance as it has mastered the expertise covering the complete nuclear cycle from exploration and mining to power generation and waste management.

In space technology too, India has developed advanced capabilities. Its seven communication satellites, the biggest civilian system in the Asia-Pacific region, now reach some of the remotest corners of the country, providing television coverage to 90 per cent of the population. The system is also being used to extend remote health care services and education to the rural poor.[12] For instance, it has already linked 69 hospitals in remote areas of India to 19 hospitals in India's main cities. This allows a health worker in a rural location to transmit a patient's medical information to a specialist in seconds and, as in many cases, a video consultation is sufficient for diagnosis. This reduces the need for the patient to travel long distances unless it is absolutely necessary.

India's space programme is a money-earner as the Indian Space Research Organisation (ISRO) sells infrared images from its remote-sensing satellites to other countries including the United States, where they are used for mapping.[13] Although India's initial few rocket launches ended tragically, its Polar Synchronous Launch Vehicles (PSLV) have been successful since September 1993. Three per cent of the ISRO's US $3.3 billion five-year budget is devoted to the planned moon mission. This features a reconfigured PSLV rocket which will lift the Chandrayan to 36,000 km, after which the craft's own engines will take it to the moon. The Chandrayan will create history by producing 3D maps of the moon's surface at a resolution of between 5 and 10 metres.[14] The Madras School of Economics estimates that the ISRO's projects have increased India's GDP by about three times the organisation's budget. As India becomes a model for its space programme, which meets its societal demands for the needy in a cost effective manner, developing countries around the world seek the ISRO's consultative assistance.

Pharmaceuticals

Today India is recognised as one of the leading global players in pharmaceuticals. It is internationally recognised as one of the lowest-cost-producers of drugs. India is the fourth largest producer of pharmaceuticals in the world.[15] The value of the pharmaceutical industry's output is reported to have grown more than tenfold from Rs. 50 billion in 1990 to Rs. 650 billion in 2006–7.[16] In 2005, there were 84 manufacturing units in India approved by the United States' Food and Drug Administration (FDA)—this was the largest number of FDA-approved manufacturing facilities in any country outside the United States. Indian companies are reported to be seeking more Abbreviated New Drug Approvals in the United States in specialised segments like anti-infectives, cardiovasculars and central nervous systems.[17]

In 2006–7, India exported drugs and pharmaceuticals worth US $1.3 billion. India exports pharmaceutical products to a large number of countries, including the United States, the United Kingdom, Germany, Russia and China. Several indicators suggest that this success is due to its excellent qualities.

In 2005, the Indian pharmaceutical industry consisted of 300 large to moderate firms and approximately 5,000 smaller firms. Some of the key players in this field are Biocon, Dr. Reddy's Laboratories, Ranbaxy and Piramal Pharmaceuticals. Leading pharmaceutical firms in India have been making higher allocations for R&D spending and trying to acquire patents abroad. In the case of Dr. Reddy's Laboratories, R&D charges, as a proportion of sales revenue, increased from 0.6 per cent in the three-year period ending in 1987 to 2.8 per cent and 11 per cent respectively in the three-year periods ending in 1994–5 and 2005–6. Ranbaxy made 698 patent filings in the first nine months of 2005, compared to 428 patent filings in the first nine months of 2004. Ranbaxy has set the target of becoming 'one of the top five generic drug makers in the world by 2012' and spends approximately 7 per cent of its global revenue on R&D.

Multinational companies have started outsourcing clinical trials to India as the cost reduction involved is substantial. Given the need for skilled manpower in this sector, the Indian government has decided to set up six new National Institutes of Pharmaceutical Education and Research.[18]

The R&D expenditures at the aggregate levels has recorded a 40 per cent increase from 2000–6.[19] But, in terms of innovation capabilities, even if firms develop new modules, the skills for advancing such modules to clinical trials and regulatory stages are limited. Hence, a major challenge for the Indian firms will be to focus on advanced research and to collaborate with developing markets.

Biotechnology

Biotechnology is an emerging knowledge-intensive sector in India. Within the biotechnology sector, the key opportunity segments are bio-pharmaceutical, bio-agriculture, bio-industry, bio-informatics and bio-services, namely, R&D, clinical trials and manufacturing on contract. According to the *Journal of Commercial Biotechnology*, the sector crossed the US $2 billion mark during 2006–7. While this figure accounts for roughly only 1 per cent share of the global biotechnology market, this sector has grown by over 35 per cent annually over the last five years. It could reach US $25 billion by 2015. As support for this sector, the Indian government increased the Department of Biotechnology's budget fourfold from US $30 million to US $120 million between 1999 and 2005. In spite of the increase in funds, fears have been expressed that the firms deal only with contract research, clinical trials and validation studies for MNCs and that adequate emphasis has not been given for the development of innovation skills.

The Indian biotechnology sector today comprises over 325 companies.[20] Many Indian biotechnology firms have achieved global reputation and have brought the cost of drugs and other life-saving medicines down significantly. For instance, Shantha Biotechnics of Hyderabad today supplies 40 per cent of the United Nations Children's Fund's global Hepatitis B vaccine supplies.[21]

The biotechnology sector is set to provide the next wave of opportunities in India. In recognition of its huge potential, some analysts have compared the Indian biotechnology sector to a baby elephant, which means that, when it matures, it will occupy much of India's economic space.

India's Ranking as a Knowledge-based Economy

Looking at these industries, one can safely conclude that India has made significant progress in its knowledge-based sectors. But how does India compare with other knowledge-based economies such as Ireland and Israel, or emerging knowledge-based economies like China? I must confess that the data is rather limited for some variables but I shall try to present an overview based on available data.

According to the World Bank's Knowledge Economy Index (KEI)[22] that takes into account the conduciveness of an economy's environment for knowledge to be used effectively for economic development, India ranked 101st out of 140 countries in 2007.[23] Ireland, Israel and China ranked 14th, 22nd and 75th respectively. The same source showed that, while China and other emerging economies have improved their position significantly, in terms of innovation, education and ICT, India's ranking remained the same in 2007 when compared to the 1995 figures. I have some doubts on the reliability of this figure. But it is possible that India lags behind the other countries in terms of R&D and education. India's position, in terms of the publication of technical journal articles, patents granted by the United States Patent and Trademark Office, gross tertiary enrolments, computer usage per thousand population, internet users per thousand people, and the number of telephone per thousand people, is still low when compared to other knowledge-based economies.

According to the Switzerland-based IMD World Competitiveness Yearbook 2007,[24] India is the 27th most-competitive economy out of 55 countries in the survey based on economic performance, government efficiency, business efficiency and infrastructure. It also showed that R&D expenditure in India (as percentage of GDP) declined in recent years. In 1998, India's R&D expenditure was 0.81 per cent of its GDP but declined to 0.61 per cent in 2005. China's R&D expenditure increased from 0.65 per cent (US $6,656.52) in 1998 to 1.33 per cent (US $36, 910.23) of its GDP in 2005. The same source also reported that, in 2005 Singapore R&D expenditure was US $2,752.74 equivalent to 2.36 per cent of the country's GDP. Israel's R&D expenditure was 4.53 per cent (US $6,440.31) of its GDP in 2006. In 2005, India's per capita R&D expenditure was US $4.41, whereas, China's and South Korea's per capita R&D expenditure were US $22.87 and US $1,537.57 respectively. The OECD Fact Book 2007 also painted a similar picture of India's expenditure in R&D.

However, in terms of availability of information technology skills, development and application of technology, the IMD World Competitiveness Center states that India ranks favourably *vis-à-vis* Israel and China, among others. The same source reports that science education in the Indian schools is being sufficiently emphasised when compared to Israel and China (see Table 1). In some areas, India is ahead of its peers. For instance, as mentioned earlier, in the pharmaceutical sector, India has the largest number of FDA-approved plants after the United States.

India's Strategic Advantages

The available data does not rank India as impressively as it does some of the other knowledge-based economies in the world. This is perhaps understandable, given that India's liberalisation efforts, when compared to other knowledge-based economies, are a recent

Table 1: Comparisons: Israel, India and China in the K-economy

	Israel	India	China
EDUCATION			
University education meets the needs of a competitive economy (score 0–10), 2007 data	7.33	6.07	4.98
Knowledge transfer between universities and companies (score 0–10), 2007 data	8.62	4.70	3.98
SCIENTIFIC INFRASTRUCTURE			
Total expenditure on R&D (% of GDP), 2005 data	4.53	0.61	1.41
Total expenditure on R&D per capita (US $ per capita), 2005 data	905.81	4.41	28.08
Basic research (score 0–10), 2007 data	7.08	5.30	6.56
Science in school sufficiently emphasised (score 0–10), 2007 data	533	6.63	5.98
Youth interest in science (score 0–10), 2007 data	6.10	6.73	5.94
No. of patents granted to residents, 2004 data	N.A.	695	11,798
No. of patents securing abroad, 2005 data	1633	710	716
Intellectual property rights are adequately enforced (score 0–10), 2007 data	6.79	5.29	5.40
ECHNOLOGICAL INFRASTRUCTURE			
Communication technology meets business requirements, 2007 data	9.08	7.63	7.67
No. of computers per 1,000 people, 2006 data	606.72	19.18	56.04
No. of internet users per 1,000 people, 2006 data	637.67	61.70	103.59
Information technology skills (score 0–10), 2007 data	9.28	8.75	5.81
Technological cooperation between companies (score 0–10), 2007 data	7.79	6.03	5.08
Development and application of technology (score 0–10), 2007 data	8.05	6.57	6.44
Funding for technological development (score 0–10), 2007 data	7.74	6.37	4.12
High-tech exports (% of manufactured exports), 2004 data	18.82	4.88	29.81

Basic Infrastructure			
The distribution infrastructure of goods and services (score 0–10), 2007 data	6.65	4.77	6.58
Maintenance and development of infrastructure (score 0–10), 2007 data	5.59	3.37	6.17
Quality of air transportation	6.67	6.83	7.38
Energy infrastructure (score 0–10), 2007 data	6.05	2.92	5.48
Engery intensity (commerical energy consumed for each dollar of GDP in kilojoules)	7,094.46	22,144.92	27,314.09
Productivity & Efficiency			
Overall productivity, GDP per person emplyed, US $, 2006 data	73,108.87	9,462.01	12,772.32
Productivity in services, GDP per person employed in services, 2006 data	71,105.44	20,257.29	14,795.88
Productivity of companies is sufficiently supported by global strategies (score 0–10), 2007 data	6.15	5.73	5.38

Source: *IMD World Competitiveness Yearbook*, various years.

phenomenon. However, India has several key advantages which could work in its favour in the 'knowledge-based economy' game. These are:

(a) *Young population*—India enjoys the advantage of having a young population. In 2004, the proportion of population below 15 years of age was 32.5 per cent in India, compared to 22 per cent for China. It is estimated that, in 2020, an average person will only be 29 years old in India, compared to 37 years in China, 45 years in Western Europe, and 48 years in Japan. Therefore, it is argued, India possesses the potential to benefit from the 'demographic dividend' many long years into the future. However, India will only be able to reap the benefits of its young populace if it is able to provide the education and skills needed to meet the demands of its high-technology industries. As will be discussed later, the education sector is a key challenge in India's push to becoming a knowledge-based economy.

(b) *Critical mass of English-speaking workers*—In 2001, India's English-speaking population was estimated to be between 30 and 50 million, which is almost as large as the population of a medium-sized country.[25] At present, it is estimated to be beyond 70 million. Such linguistic skills are important to allow Indians to connect with the rest of the world and to benefit from the opportunities in the global marketplace. Singapore opted for English as the main language for two reasons. First, it provided a level playing field for the different races to compete in. Second, it enabled the nation to plug directly into the science and technology sector without going through a translation. India must use the English language for the same purpose.

(c) *Large and fast growing domestic market*—Its relative domestic market size makes it one of the world's largest. This is true regardless of the conversion factor one chooses to use. Using the new conversion factor, India's GDP at PPP is estimated at US $3.19 trillion, making it the fifth largest economy in the world. At the nominal exchange rate (which means the value of a country's currency in relation to other currencies without adjustment for the inflation rate), India's GDP is projected to be US $1.16 trillion in 2007–8. India's per capita GDP at market prices (constant 1999–2000 prices) grew by at an average rate of 7.2 per cent per annum during the last five years (2003–4 to 2007–8). At this rate, India's average income would double in a decade. The growth rate of per capita consumption has also accelerated during the last five years to 5.1 per cent as against the average growth rate of 2.6 per cent in the 1990s.[26]

(d) *Large and impressive diaspora*—The Indian diaspora allows for invaluable knowledge linkages and networks globally. At the same time, the highly influential diaspora of Indian professionals and entrepreneurs have been instrumental in bringing high technology investments to Bangalore, Hyderabad and other Indian cities. The decision by the Indian government to allow for dual citizenship has provided further impetus to the diaspora to continue to stay rooted to India. India currently holds non-resident Indian (NRI) investments worth US $35 billion, with annual accretion of US $2–3 billion.[27] Remittances form nearly 3 per cent of India's GDP and have almost doubled over the last five years. The World Bank estimates have placed India as the largest recipient of remittances in the world and have predicted that India would receive more than US $200 billion remittances over the next five years.[28]

(e) *Emerging financial sector*—In recent years, India has attained macroeconomic stability and has made significant strides in institutional developments, including having a well-functioning financial sector. Currently, the Indian financial sector is more efficient at capital allocation than many other Asian countries. Small and medium enterprises account for 45 per cent of banks' business loans in India, compared to 26 per cent in China.[29] India continues to attract foreign investments and presence in its banking sector due to its sheer potential alone. The total asset size of the Indian banking sector was US $270 billion in 2006 while the total deposits amounted to US $220 billion. Revenues of the banking sector have grown at 6 per cent (compound annual growth rate) in recent years

> to reach US $15 billion in 2006. This has resulted in commercial banks no longer simply catering to short- and medium-term financing requirements, but also joining national-level and state-level financial institutions to provide project financing.[30]

The deregulation of the banking industry has contributed to improved capital access as it has increased the presence of foreign banks in India. In accordance with the first phase of this deregulation, between March 2005 and March 2009, foreign banks may establish a presence by way of setting up a wholly-owned subsidiary (WOS) or conversion of existing branches into a WOS. This has prompted some of the world's largest banks such as Citibank, ABN AMRO, HSBC, DBS and Standard Chartered Bank, among others, to have a significant presence in India.

KEY CHALLENGES

Whilst India enjoys significant advantages, it also faces several challenges which may impede or hinder it from becoming a knowledge superpower. I shall highlight the key challenges.

Education

India's premier technical institutions, namely, the Indian Institutes of Technology (IIT) and the Indian Institutes of Management (IIM) have been the source of entrepreneurship in recent years. India has emerged as an important player in the worldwide ICT revolution on the basis of the substantial number of skilled professionals in software and hardware. Over decades of planned development, India has built a fairly extensive system of higher education. This existing system is of varying quality. In March 2005, there were 343 institutes of higher education and 16,000 colleges. The total enrolment in higher education is estimated to be 9.3 million.

However, India's system of higher education suffers from several limitations.[31] First, the gross enrolment ratio in higher education is less than 9 per cent in India, compared to 15 per cent in China and more than 20 per cent in many developing countries such as Mexico, Malaysia, Thailand, Chile and Brazil. In the case of IT, the enrolment is 40 to 50 per cent more in developed countries.[32] Second, the enrolment ratios vary across Indian states, with the southern and western states faring better than their eastern counterparts. Furthermore, the share of students enrolled in science was less than 20 per cent in 2002–3 while the share of student enrolment in medicine and engineering/technology accounted for less than 12 per cent of total student enrolment.

In the case of youth literacy, India lags substantially behind all the other BRIC (Brazil, Russia, and China) countries. India's achievements are well below the average of all developing countries (See Table 2). In India, 93.4 per cent of all elementary-school-age children (6–14 year olds) were enrolled in school in 2006. Enrolment, however, is only the first step. A child must complete eight years of basic schooling. However, based on the Planning Commission Report of 2006, the drop-out rate in primary schools for the country as a whole was around 31 per cent in 2003–4 and it was much higher in many states. The picture is not very rosy for secondary education either, with gross enrolment ratio in 2003–4 estimated to be only 39 per cent.

The problem in the education sector is further compounded by the lack of proper teaching facilities and best practices, especially in the rural areas. According to the Third International Mathematics and Science study, 9th and 11th grade students in India

Table 2: Youth Literacy Rates (15–24 year olds): Latest available between 2000–4

Country	Total	Male	Female
India	76.4	84.2	67.7
China	98.9	99.2	98.5
Brazil	96.8	95.8	97.9
Russian Federation	99.7	99.7	99.8
World	87.3	90.5	84.1
Developing Countries	84.8	88.6	80.9

Source: Extracted from Table 1 in Kingdom (2007).

scored way below the international average.[33] Among some of the causes identified by education experts are a high teacher to pupil ratio, at 1:42 in some states and as high as 1:83 in others. There are also no standard teacher training processes in place, and accountability and benchmarking are almost absent. The outdated rote learning is also in practice, without sufficient conceptual understanding.[34]

Another challenge for the education sector is bridging the digital divide in the country. If India aspires to be a knowledge-based economy, it will have to ensure that most, if not all, of its people are equipped, prepared and ready to contribute to its development in this regard. At the moment, there is an urgent need to ensure affordable access to locally-relevant IT applications at a broad level. As it stands, less than 2 per cent of the population in India owns a computer, only 2 per cent of all schools have computers and about 6 per cent of the total population are internet users.[35]

A key development in the Indian education sector in recent times is the emergence of private schools. The Planning Commission reported in 2006 that private aided and unaided schools accounted for 58 per cent of the total number of secondary schools and 25 per cent of the student population. The proportion of private schools has certainly gone up in recent years. However, these schools have largely benefitted the relatively better-off sections of the Indian society. India needs to reduce this growing inequality in educational opportunity through state intervention and public investment in education.

The Indian government has been taking steps to address the challenges of the education sector. The annual budget allocation for education has been increasing over the years. The government allocation for education grew from Rs 18,337 crore in FY 2005–6 to Rs 28,674 crore in FY 2007–8. This accounted for 3 per cent and 4 per cent of the budget in FY 2005–6 and FY 2007–8 respectively. Expenditure on education will increase by 20 per cent over FY 2007–8 to Rs 34,400 crore in FY 2008–9, accounting for 4.5 per cent of the budget.[36]

Also, in the Budget of 2008, the Indian finance minister announced the establishment of three Indian Institutes of Science Education and Research (IISER) at Mohali, Pune and Kolkata while an IIT has started operations at Kanchipuram. At the same time, the government will to set up 16 central universities in each of the hitherto uncovered states; three IITs in Andhra Pradesh, Bihar and Rajasthan; two IISERs at Bhopal and Tiruvananthapuram; and two schools of Planning and Architecture at Bhopal and Vijayawada. The budget provided Rs 5 crore grant to Deccan College, Postgraduate and Research Institute, Pune while Rs 85 crore has been allocated for Innovation in Science Pursuit for Inspired Research which will include scholarships for young learners (10–17 years), scholarships for continuing science education (17–22 years) and opportunities for research careers (22–32 years). Also, Rs. 100 crore has provided for establishing the National Knowledge Network.

Over-regulated and Cumbersome Bureaucracy

India has more than 17 million state and federal government employees. 'About 20,000-odd federal officers control the collection and disbursement of over US $71 billion federal revenue every year.'[37] Transparency International, a global watchdog body on corruption, ranked India 72nd out of the 179 countries in its corruption perception index in 2007. One recent study by the Centre for Media Studies, New Delhi, on corruption in urban services revealed that 'nearly half of those who avail the services of the most frequently-visited public departments of the government in the country have had first hand experience of greasing palms at least once'.[38] At the same time, the 'Inspector Regime' or 'Licence Raj' has its inherent problems and, unfortunately, India has not done away with the old structures. A World Bank report ranked India 120th out of 178 countries in ease of doing business in 2006. The time to obtain a business licence in India ranges from 35 days in the financial hub, Mumbai, to 522 days in the eastern city of Ranchi. In contrast, a start-up takes five days in Singapore, and 17 days in the countries of the Organisation for Economic Co-operation and Development.[39]

In sectors where 100 per cent foreign ownership is allowed under the 'automatic route', NRI Overseas Corporate Bodies (OCB) have to get the Foreign Investment Promotion Board's permission to purchase even one share in an Indian company. And it takes a minimum of four to five weeks to get the approval of the Reserve Bank of India (RBI). The whole process for approval for a normal case for NRI OCBs can take between three to four months. In the interim period, the market conditions could change. It is estimated that investors setting up shop in India require up to 70 different approvals. The World Bank estimates that there are 47 national laws and 157 state regulations governing employment in India.[40]

Infrastructure Development

This is an oft-spoken subject in many forums. To develop a knowledge-based economy, the role of ICT, education and scientific infrastructure are necessary. However, equally critical is the need for supporting physical infrastructure such as railways, roads, ports, telecommunications and energy. A good infrastructure does not only enhance an economy's productivity, it is also a crucial determinant in attracting investments into the country.

India needs to develop its infrastructure. It remains one of the lowest per capita energy consuming countries, only ahead of the African countries. Only half of the total households have access to electricity. The IMD World Competitiveness Online database shows that, based on survey data, India graded poorly in terms of the distribution infrastructure of goods and services, the maintenance and development of infrastructure and energy infrastructure, among others (see Table 1).

As for education, scientific and technological infrastructure, India needs improvement in terms of R&D expenditure, enforcement of intellectual property rights, the number of computer and Internet users, and knowledge transfer between universities and companies, *inter alia*.

Role of Government in R&D

The state has an important role in transforming the economy from a traditional to a knowledge-based one, as the private sector may not always invest in areas like education, infrastructure and R&D,

if there is a mismatch between the firm's revenue and cost. In this context, Nobel Laureate and Economist Joseph Stiglitz's view is worth mentioning. Citing knowledge as a public good, Stiglitz expressed the view that the state must play some role in the provision of such goods.[41] Otherwise they will be undersupplied. To him, governments have pursued two different strategies in addressing the concern. The first is to increase the degree of appropriability of the return to knowledge by issuing patents and copyright protection. The second strategy for dealing with the appropriability problem entails direct government support. These two sets of issues are highly linked with an economy's basic, scientific and information technology infrastructure.

Cross-border cooperation in R&D is another way to enhance a country's scientific research. Countries in consideration can share their expertise based on comparative advantages. India has such an agreement with Israel, known as India–Israel Cooperation in Science and Technology. It could explore more of such collaborations, especially with countries which have made great strides in knowledge-based industries. In such matters, the government needs to take the lead.

Sharing the Singapore Experience

Before I conclude, I would like to share the experiences of Singapore in its push towards becoming a knowledge-based economy. One may argue that there is really no comparison between the two countries, given the size and complexities of India. However, I believe that we can draw some lessons from the tiny island state which could be useful and relevant to India.

First, the Singapore government takes the lead to promote sustained innovation as a driver of Singapore's economy. In this regard, it aims to increase R&D in three key areas. Based on their growth trajectory in Asia, the Singapore government anticipates biomedical science, environment and water technology, and media industries to be key economic drivers in the future. Intensive R&D will, thus, help these industries achieve their potential. Singapore's aggressive R&D pursuit includes a government commitment to increase research investment in these areas to 3 per cent of its GDP by 2010 from the current 2.1 per cent. This will increase Singapore's overall research expenditure by threefold from the current US $6.1 billion to reach US $19 billion in 2010.[42]

Each of these growth sectors contributes to the development of a knowledge-based Singapore. An extensive and reliable ICT infrastructure supports knowledge building in the country. In this regard, the info-communication authorities in Singapore have been instrumental in developing the Intelligent Nation 2015 masterplan.[43] This plan was hatched after a year-long consultation with the public and private sectors to develop Singapore as an intelligent nation. The main objective of this masterplan is to establish an info-communication infrastructure that will create the information superhighway to support the future generations of knowledge-based Singapore. This proposed infrastructure would consist of a wired and wireless network that would ensure the entire country is connected at home and everywhere.

Human capital is arguably the most valuable asset that India has. It is this strength that possesses the potential of propelling India into a knowledge-based economy if carefully nurtured.[44] Singapore, like India, also depends heavily on its human capital to facilitate this transition. Without any other resource, Singapore has relied heavily on human capital to drive its growth and, in doing so, has built up a resource base that is resilient enough to withstand shocks and flexible enough to meet the demands of globalisation.

Education has been a fundamental component of this process. Singapore has ensured that it provides the primary English, Mathematical and Science foundations needed to survive in this competitive environment.[45] However, this is insufficient for the society to transcend into an effective knowledge society and cope with the demands of a global workforce. The Singapore government introduced vocational education early on in its development history. This has helped to provide the talent needed for a skills-based section of the workforce. Further, by tapping on alternate talents other than strict academic education, Singapore has ensured that every spectrum of the society contributes positively to the overall knowledge attainment. In this regard, Institutes of Technical Education and Polytechnics plug this gap for a technically sound workforce.

Conclusion

The growth of a knowledge-economy is highly dependant on a robust policy environment. Countries aspiring to be knowledge-based economies must ensure a stable political and economic environment so that foreign direct investment and foreign expertise come in with their capital and other intangible assets. At the same time, local companies and talent will find it conducive to apply their knowledge and flourish in India.

In conclusion, India has progressed well since it initiated its liberalisation drive in the early 1990s. It has emerged to become an important global economic power and it will continue to witness good growth. Its key knowledge-based industries have also moved out of its borders to compete and collaborate with some of the best around the world. However, I would add that India faces several key challenges. These are, by no means, small but, at the same time, they are not insurmountable. They can be overcome but this would require a direct and more proactive approach from the Indian government and the large Indian.

NOTES

* The author would like to thank Hernaikh Singh, Head, Administration and Corporate Communications at the Institute of South Asian Studies (ISAS), and Mohammad Shahidul Islam, Indu Rayadurgam, Iftikhar Lodhi and Malminderjit Singh, Research Associates at ISAS, for their assistance in the preparation of this paper.

1. 'Mathematics and Science in Ancient India', available at <http://www.sfusd.k12.ca.us/schwww/sch618/India/ Math_and_Science.html>
2. 'History of Indian Science & Technology', available at <http://www.indianscience.org/>
3. 'History of Indian Science & Technology', available at <http://www.indianscience.org/>

4. Quoted in then Minister of External Affairs of India, K. Natwar Singh's address at McGill University and the Canadian Institute of International Affairs, Montreal, 27 September 2005.
5. Economist Intelligence Unit.
6. For details, see 'Mapping Singapore's Knowledge-based Economy', *Economic Survey of Singapore* (Third Quarter, 2002).
7. NASSCOM Strategic Review, 2008.
8. Available at <http://www.kpmg.co.uk/news/docs/ita_KnowPro Out sourcing 2008 per cent20web per cent20and per cent20links.pdf >
9. Bhabha Atomic Research Centre website [http://www.barc.ernet.in/webpages/technologies/home.html]
10. India Department of Atomic Energy [http://www.dae.gov.in].
11. Ibid.
12. *New Scientist Magazine*, Issue 2487, 19 February 2005.
13. Ibid.
14. Ibid.
15. *The Economic Survey 2006–7*, Ministry of Finance, India
16. *The Economic Survey 2007–8*, Ministry of Finance, India.
17. *The Economic Survey 2006–7*, Ministry of Finance, India.
18. *The Economic Survey 2007–8*, Ministry of Finance, India.
19. Compiled from Jayan Thomas (2007) and 'Where Will the Indian Drug Companies be in Five Years?—If they Innovate', prepared by Wharton and Bain & Company, www.bain.com/bainweb/pdfs/cms/hotTopics/Bain_ India_Pharma.pdf, accessed on 3 April 2008.
20. http://www.bangalorebio.in/biotechnology_show.html
21. Asian Science Park Association < http://cyberaspa.org/chi/board/sub02_view.php?page=21&id=233&no=& cid=1&code=asia_eco >
22. The World Bank's Knowledge Assessment Methodology consists of 83 structural and qualitative variables for 140 countries to measure their performance on the four Knowledge Economy pillars: Economic Incentive and Institutional Regime, Education, Innovation, and Information and Communications Technologies.
23. World Bank, 'Knowledge Assessment Methodology', available at <http://www.worldbank.org/kam>
24. Available at <http://www.imd.ch/research/centers/wcc/index.cfm>
25. *The Economist*, 2001.
26. *The Economic Survey 2007–8*, Ministry of Finance, Govt. of India.
27. P. Chidambaram, Pravasi Bharatiya Diwas 2007.
28. Anil Kapur, Pravasi Bharatiya Diwas 2007.
29. Reforming India's financial system, *Mckinsey Quarterly*, September 2005.

30. Indian Ministry of External Affairs Report on Financial Sector <http://meaindia.nic.in/indiapublication/ Financial sector.htm]
31. Kapur and Mehta (2004) and Hashim (2008).
32. See cited by Hashim (2008) based on PROPHE, http://www.albany.edu/dept/prophe/data/data.html.
33. World Bank (2006), Secondary Education in India, http://info. worldbank.org/etools/docs/library/235784/2 Amit%20Darsecondary. pdf
34. UNICEF (2006), 'Global Campaign for Education', http://www. unicef.org/india/education_1551.htm
35. 'India's Digital Divide May be Shrinking', Marketplace website, 22 March 2005.
36. These figures represent the central government's expenditure on education and were calculated by the Institute of South Asian Studies from the Indian budget for the respective years.
37. 'India tries to root out bureaucratic corruption', *Asia Times*, 7 August 2003, http://www.atimes.com/ atimes/South_Asia/ EH07Df01.html
38. Ibid.
39. 'The Investment Climate in Brazil, India, and South Africa: A Contribution to the IBSA Debate', World Bank, 2006.
40. 'Indian Bureaucracy as a Deterrent', Rediff Business Online, June 2003, http://www.rediff.com/money/2003/jun/27guest.htm
41. Knowledge as a Global Public Good <http://www.worldbank.org/knowledge/chiefecon/articles /undpk2/ index.htm>
42. Balaji Sadasivan, Speech delivered at The Pravasi Bharatiya Diwas 2008, New Delhi, 8 January 2008.
43. Ibid.
44. Shri Atal Behari Vajpayee, The Annual Singapore Lecture 2002, 'India's Perspectives on ASEAN and the Asia Pacific Region', Singapore, 9 April 2002.
45. Rear-Admiral (NS) Teo Chee Hean, East Asia Economic Summit Plenary Session, World Economic Forum, 'Building Competitiveness in the Knowledge Economy—How is Asia Facing up to the Task?' Singapore, 19 October 1999.

REFERENCES

Basu, K. and Annemie Maertens, 'The Pattern and Causes of Economic Growth in India', *Oxford Review of Economic Policy*, vol. 23, no. 2, 2007, pp. 143–67.

Dahlman, C. and A. Utz (2005), 'India and the Knowledge Economy; Leveraging

Strengths and Opportunities: Overview', Finance and Private Sector Development Unit of the World Bank's South Asia Region and The World Bank Institute, Washington, D.C. http://info.worldbank.org/etools/docs/library/145261/India_KE_Overview. pdf (accessed on 2 April 2008).

—— 'India as Knowledge Superpower', Planning Commission of India 2001.

—— 'Outsourcing to India: Back Office to the World', *The Economist*, 5 May 2001.

Kingdon, Geeta Gandhi (2007), 'The Progress of School Education in India', *Oxford Review of policy*, vol. 23, no. 2, 2007, pp. 168–95.

Hashim, S.R. (2008), 'State of Higher Education in India', in R. Radhakrishna (ed.), *India Development Report 2008*, Oxford University Press, New Delhi.

Kapur, Dives and Pratap Bhanu Mehta (2004), 'Indian Higher Education Reform: From Half-Baked Socialism to Half-Baked Capitalism' CID Working Paper No. 108, September 2004.

Planning Commission (2006), 'Towards Faster and Inclusive Growth: Approach to the 11th Five Year Plan: 2007–12', Yojana Bhawan, New Delhi. Available at www.planning commission.com. Accessed on 3 April 2008.

Thomas, Jayan Jose (2008), 'India's Rise in the New Economy: Implications for Labour', ISAS Working Paper 35, Institute of South Asian Studies, Singapore.

Thomas, Jayan Jose (2005), 'New Technologies for India's Development', in Kirit Parikh and R. Radhakrishna (eds.), *India Development Report 2004–5*, Oxford University Press, New Delhi, pp. 126–40.

46

Higher Education in India: Ducking the Answers

BIBEK DEBROY

(*16 May 2008*)

INTRODUCTION

IN 2005, THE World Bank published a report on India and the knowledge economy.[1] The thrust of the World Bank report was on the role of education as a fundamental enabler of the knowledge economy and the knowledge economy's requirement of a new set of skills and competencies. In a simple sense, a country's per capita national income is nothing but a measure of the average productivity of its citizens.[2] With ageing populations in developed countries, and even in countries like Russia and China, there has been talk of India's demographic dividend.[3] That the demographic dividend argument works, is known. For East Asia, several studies suggest that between 25 to 40 per cent of the East Asian miracle was due to the demographic dividend.[4] Other than East Asia, it has worked in Japan in the 1950s, in China in the 1980s and in Ireland in the 1980s and the 1990s.

Several factors explain the demographic dividend.[5] First, there is the obvious increase in working age populations, with a reduction in dependency ratios, and the direct impact of a larger quantity of labour input. To take but one dramatic number, between 2001 and 2026, India's total population is estimated to increase by 371 million and 83 per cent of the increase will occur in the age-group of 15–59 years.[6] Second, the quality of the labour input can increase and this is reflected in what economists call total factor productivity (TFP) growth, measured after netting out the contribution of increased labour and capital inputs.[7] Third, when dependency ratios decline, savings rates increase, leading to increases in investment rates and higher rates of gross domestic product (GDP) growth. Fourth, if the decline in dependency ratios is at the lower end of the age spectrum as a result of fertility declines, female work participation rates increase.

However, there is no automaticity about demographic dividend leading to sustained high growth rates. Among other things, one requires an improvement in health and education indicators, with a shortage in required skills already being felt. Nor should one forget the regional dimension, since high absolute and relative growths in population will happen in states like Assam, Bihar, Delhi,[8] Haryana, Madhya Pradesh, Rajasthan and Uttar Pradesh.[9] While the *National Human Development Report*[10] is now dated, it brings out these regional differences. When the education system has to adjust to tap the demographic dividend and opportunities thrown up by the knowledge economy, one must have in mind Bihar, Jharkhand, Madhya Pradesh, Chhattisgarh, Uttar Pradesh, Rajasthan, Uttar Pradesh and Orissa and India's 150-odd backward districts.[11]

The Education Report Card

In December 2006, the Planning Commission produced an Approach Paper to the Eleventh Five Year Plan (2007–12).[12] This has a sub-title on faster and more inclusive growth. The introductory chapter of this document states: 'It is important to recognise that better health and education are the necessary pre-conditions for sustained long-term growth.' There can be no quarrel with this generic statement.

Further down the chapter we have:

> A key element of 11th Plan strategy should be to provide essential education and health services to those large parts of our population who are still excluded from these. Education is the critical factor that empowers participation in the growth process but our performance has been less than satisfactory, both overall and in bridging gender and other divides. Overall literacy is still less than 70 per cent and rural female literacy less than 50 per cent with corresponding rates even lower among the marginalised groups and minorities. While the *Sarva*

Shiksha Abhiyan has expanded primary school enrolment, it is far from providing quality education. Looking ahead, we cannot be satisfied with only universal primary education; we must move towards universal secondary education too as quickly as possible.

This is also almost generic, though question marks can be raised about success indicators like increased primary school enrolment and the degree to which *Sarva Shiksha Abhiyan* can alone claim the credit.[13] Still further down the chapter, we have extensions of this argument:

While both education and curative health services are available for those who can afford to pay, quality service is beyond the reach of the common people. Other privately provided services are of highly variable quality. In this situation, access to essential services can only be through public financing. In most cases, this means public provision or partnership with non-profit and civil society organisations. A major institutional challenge is that even where service providers exist, the quality of delivery is poor and those responsible for delivering the services cannot be held accountable. Unless such accountability is established and cutting edge service providers trained, it will be difficult to ensure significant improvement in delivery even if large resources are made available.

Although this statement is about education at a very general level, some additional points have now been flagged. First, there is a question of access to the relatively poor. Second, flowing from the first argument, a case has been made for public financing, which is then equated with public provisioning, without making the jump from the one to the other at all clear. Third, an implicit argument has been made about regulation. Fourth, another implicit argument has been made about lack of accountability in public expenditure.

Let's go back to the afore-mentioned World Bank report on India and the knowledge economy. This sets out the main issues, as perceived by the Bank, in strengthening India's education system. Paraphrased, these issues are—(a) improving efficiency in the use of public resources; (b) making the education system responsive to market needs; (c) ensuring that access doesn't mean the crowding out of the relatively poor; (d) ensuring quality, relevance and practical skills; (e) in higher education, shifting the focus of the government from administrative management to regulation; and (f) relaxing entry barriers and accreditation systems for private players, including foreign ones. In its chapter[14] on strategic initiatives for inclusive development, the Approach Paper divides the education discussion into five segments—elementary education, secondary education, technical/vocational education and skill development, higher/technical education and adult literacy. Since education is a continuum and access to higher education is a function of access to school (elementary and secondary) education, such water-tight compartmentalisation doesn't always make sense. However, if the expression 'higher education' is used, most people would interpret it as technical/vocational education and higher/technical education, probably the latter. Once one has pinned down the expression, one should ask how the World Bank's six issues should be addressed.

If we interpret higher education as higher/technical education, to the exclusion of technical/vocational education and skill development, this is what the Approach Paper tells us:

> India has a well-developed and comprehensive higher education system which has served us well thus far but is now inadequate. The extent of access it provides is limited. Only about 10 per cent of the relevant age group go to universities whereas in many developing countries, the figure is between 20 and 25 per cent. There is an overwhelming need to undertake major expansion to increase access to higher education. The system also suffers from a serious problem of quality. While some of our institutions of higher education have the potential to become comparable with the best in the world, the average standard is much lower. High quality institutions are finding it difficult to get quality faculty given the enormous increase in private sector opportunities for the skills most in demand.

These are not the points that are being flagged for the first time. For instance, in 2002, the S.P. Gupta Special Group[15] constituted by the Planning Commission stated: 'It should be noted, however, that on the average the skilled labour force at present is hardly around 6–8 per cent of the total, compared to more than 60 per cent in most of the developed and emerging developing countries.' In 2001, the Montek Singh Ahluwalia Task Force,[16] again constituted by the Planning Commission, stated,

Only five per cent of the Indian labour force in this age category[17] has vocational skills whereas the percentage in industrial countries is much higher, varying between 60 per cent and 80 per cent, except for Italy, which is 44 per cent. The percentage for Korea, which has recently been categorised as an industrialised country, is exceptionally high at 96 per cent. The developing countries listed have percentages which are significantly lower than the developed countries but they are still much higher than India, for example, Mexico at 28 per cent and Peru at 17 per cent. Differences in definition may make inter-country comparison somewhat unreliable but the level in India is clearly far too low.

However, both these quotes have more to do with vocational education.

On higher education proper, the present regulatory and control structure is a maze. Although the Ministry of Human Resource Development is involved, directly or indirectly, there are multiple layers. First, there are 20 central universities, funded by the centre and, therefore, under direct central control.[18] Second, there are 109 deemed universities under the University Grants Commission (UGC) Act, five institutions established under state legislation and 13 institutes of national importance established under central legislation. Till 1976–7, higher education was in the State List of the Seventh Schedule. The 1976–7 amendment moved it to the Concurrent List. Third, in addition to central universities and deemed universities, there exist 222 state universities and colleges,[19] with the coordination function supposed to be exercised by the UGC and the Central Advisory Board of Education. There are 18,064 colleges, including 1,902 women's colleges. Fourth, some universities are affiliating, others are unitary. Some are single campus, others are multi-campus.[20] Fifth, several forms of professional education are regulated by statutory councils like All India Council for Technical Education (AICTE), Distance Education Council, Indian Council for Agriculture Research, Bar Council of India, National Council for Teacher Education, Rehabilitation Council of India, Medical Council of India, Pharmacy Council of India, Indian Nursing Council, Dentist Council of India, Central Council of Homeopathy and Central Council of Indian Medicine. This creates multiplicity and confusion, the artificial distinction between diplomas and degrees in the same subject and for the same duration being a case in point.

On the base that existed at the time of Independence, the numbers, including those of student enrollment and the number of teachers, represent an impressive increase. But a few uncomfortable questions need to be asked. How many of these institutes of higher education are of the requisite quality? Even if one ignores inter-national rankings of universities and colleges,[21] which can be subjective and, therefore, exhibit different rankings across different surveys, why is it that most of India's universities and colleges have excess and underutilised capacity while only a few have excess demand? Why is it that a large number of Indian students head abroad, and not just to the United States? Incidentally, this exit option is only available to the relatively richer segments of society. Why has there been a decline in the number of overseas students who come to India to study? From the World Trade Organization, there are no commitments right now in higher education. However, eventually, higher education is bound to be opened up. Are Indian institutes equipped to handle that eventual challenge and have the supply-side changes occurred? Why are legitimate and better foreign universities not allowed to operate in India while lesser known ones function through a grey area in the law? Why are Indian institutions of higher education more interested in setting up shops overseas (the Middle East, South-East Asia and even China) than in India?

The Policy Dead End

One looks to the Planning Commission to provide answers to these uncomfortable questions and address policy issues. Yet, if one reads the Approach Paper, all that one finds is concern over regional divides. The clichéd answer is that more colleges and universities must be set up, presumably through public resources. There must be reservation of seats for deprived segments (identified through collective identities like caste instead of individual identities like class) in institutions of higher education. This is in line with the standard prescription that public expenditure on education, including higher education, must be increased, a point that is also made by the National Common Minimum Programme (NCMP). The NCMP states that public expenditure on education must be increased to 6 per cent of GDP, a target that was originally articulated in the National Policy on Education (1986). Since half of this is to be spent on primary and secondary education, the remainder will be spent on other forms of education, including higher education.[22]

Before elaborating on these points, let us turn to the National Knowledge Commission (NKC), which elaborates on policy issues much more cogently than the Planning Commission does. The NKC prepared a note on higher education.[23] Part of this note is devoted to a description of the present malaise, which it is unnecessary to reiterate. On the philosophy behind concrete policy changes, we have:

> We recognise that a meaningful reform of the higher education system, with a long-term perspective is both complex and difficult. Yet, it is imperative. And we would suggest the following building blocks in this endeavour. First, it is essential to reform existing public universities and undergraduate colleges. Second, it is necessary to overhaul the entire regulatory structure governing higher education. Third, every possible source of financing investment in higher education needs to be explored. Fourth, it is important to think about pro-active strategies for enhancement of quality in higher education. Fifth, the time has come to create new institutions in the form of national universities that would become role models as centres of academic excellence. Sixth, the higher education system must be so designed that it provides access to marginalised and excluded groups.

Amplifying further, there are recommendations about the no. and size of universities (1,500 by 2015), curriculum, examinations, research, faculty, finances,[24] infrastructure, governance, the system of affiliation of colleges, regulation, incentives and access.

Of these, the section on regulation also deserves a quote:

> There is a clear need to establish an Independent Regulatory Authority for Higher Education (IRAHE). Such a regulatory authority is both necessary and desirable. It is necessary for two important reasons. First, in India, it requires an Act of Legislature of Parliament to set up a university. The deemed university route is much too difficult for new institutions. Entry through legislation alone, as at present, is a formidable barrier. The consequence is a steady increase in the average size of existing universities with a steady deterioration in their quality.

The absence of competition only compounds problems. Second, as we seek to expand the higher education system, entry norms will be needed for private institutions and public-private partnerships. . . . The present regulatory system in higher education is flawed in many respects. The barriers to entry are too high. The system of authorising entry is cumbersome. And there are extensive rules after entry, as the UGC seeks to regulate almost every aspect of an institution from fees to curriculum. The system is also based on patently irrational principles. . . . In higher education, regulators perform five functions: (1) Entry: licence to grant degrees; (2) Accreditation: quality benchmarking; (3) Disbursement of public funds; (4) Access: fees or affirmative action; and (5) Licence: to practice profession. India is perhaps the only country in the world where regulation in four of the five functions is carried out by one entity, that is, the UGC. The purpose of creating an IRAHE is to separate these functions.

To this, let's add a quote on financing of higher education:

There is no system of higher education in the world that is not based upon significant public outlays. And government financing will remain the cornerstone of any strategy to improve our system of higher education. The present support for higher education, at 0.7 per cent of GDP, is simply not adequate. In fact, over the past decade, in real terms, there has been a significant decline in the resources allocated for higher education, in the aggregate as also per student. In an ideal world, government support for higher education should be at least 1.5 per cent, if not 2 per cent of GDP, from a total of 6 per cent of GDP for education. . . . The time has come to rethink, as we have no choice but to rationalise fees. It is for universities to decide the level of fees but, as a norm, fees should meet at least 20 per cent of the total expenditure in universities. . . . In three professions—engineering, medicine and management—there has been a *de facto* privatisation of education so that two-thirds to three-fourths of the seats are in private institutions. But private investment in university education, where more than 70 per cent of our students study, is almost negligible. It is essential to stimulate private investment in higher education as a means of extending educational opportunities. We must recognise that, even with the best will in the world, government financing cannot be enough to support the massive expansion in opportunities for higher education on a scale that is now essential.

Barring one area, these quotes raise fundamental policy questions. The only area where the NKC ducks is on the question of allowing profit-making institutions of higher education. Let's restate the issues differently. First, contrary to what is sometimes felt, education, and certainly higher education, is *not* a public good.[25] Second, the message of the post-1991 reforms has been on ensuring competition and entry as drivers for better quality and choice. If that has worked for other areas, why should higher education be any different? The present regulatory system is not one designed for regulation, but for licensing and control, a phenomenon that has been discarded everywhere else. There is already *de facto* privatisation, not just in the three areas mentioned by the NKC but elsewhere too. Third, there is no reason why higher user charges should not be imposed, with actual user charges today typically lower for higher education than for school education. Fourth, cross-country evidence does not suggest that privatisation leads to crowding out of the relatively poor, since systems of scholarships and loans do exist. However, to the extent that such crowding out is a problem, no one argues against government financing through scholarships and loans. The argument is against the present inefficient system of public expenditure through salaries and pensions, so that colleges and universities do not face hard budget constraints that would have compelled them to reform. Public subsidies are perfectly in harmony with principles of choice, provided the subsidies are targeted towards those who actually need them, that is, students. It is because there is lack of clarity on these policies that courts have often stepped in, interpreting the law as it stands today, rather than creating it.[26] Whichever way one looks at it, higher education reform must begin with a complete revamping and replacement of the Department of Higher Education in the Ministry of Human Resource and Development, the UGC and AICTE.

NOTES

1. Carl Dahlman and Anuja Utz, *India and the Knowledge Economy, Leveraging Strengths and Opportunities*, World Bank, Washington, 2005.
2. Per capita national income is national income divided by population. More accurately, national income divided by the working-age population is a measure of the average level of labour productivity.
3. Vijay Kelkar, 'India: On the Growth Turnpike', 2004. K.R. Narayanan,

Oration, reprinted in Raghbendra Jha (ed.), *The First Ten, K.R. Narayanan Orations*, ANU Press, 2006; Shankar Acharya, *Can India Grow without Bharata?*, Academic Foundation, 2007; Gurcharan Das, 'The Indian Model,' *Foreign Affairs*, July/August 2006; *India Rising: A Medium Term Perspective*, Deutsche Bank Research, May 2005; 'Growing Old the Hard Way: China, Russia, India', Nicholas Eberstadt, *Policy Review*, Hoover Institution, April/May 2006; and Dominic Wilson and Roopa Purushothaman, 'Dreaming with BRICs: The Path to 2050', *Global Economics Paper No. 99*, Goldman Sachs, October 2003, are some instances.

4. See David E. Bloom, David Canning and Jaypee Sevilla, 'Economic Growth and the Demographic Transition', NBER Working Paper 8685, December 2001.
5. The empirical and theoretical literature is reviewed in *World Economic Outlook: The Global Demographic Transition*, IMF, September 2004.
6. *Population Projections for India and States 2001–26, Report of the Technical Group on Population Projections Constituted by the National Commission on Population*, Office of the Registrar General and Census Commissioner, May 2006.
7. Some skepticism of TFP estimation is warranted. However, one study that contrasted India and China in two sub-periods, 1989–95 and 1995–2003, is worth mentioning, since it found that the labour contribution to India's growth was driven more by quantity than quality. See Dale Jorgenson and Vu Khunog, 'Information Technology and the World Economy', *Scandinavian Journal of Economics*, vol. 107, no. 4, 2005.
8. For Delhi, this is primarily because of in-migration.
9. See, *India Labour Report: A Ranking of Indian States by their Labour Ecosystem*, TeamLease and Indicus Analytics, 2006.
10. *National Human Development Report 2001*, Planning Commission, Government of India, March 2002.
11. Of India's 600 districts, 100 are truly backward, by any criterion. The National Food for Work Programme had a list of 150 backward districts and the Rashtriya Sama Vikas Yojana (RSVY) increased the number to 167. The National Rural Employment Guarantee Act (NREGA) initially identified 200 backward districts, but has now been extended to all rural areas.
12. *Towards Faster and More Inclusive Growth: An Approach to the 11th Five Year Plan*, Planning Commission, Government of India, December 2006, http://planningcommission.nic.in/plans/planrel/app11_16jan.pdf
13. As opposed to the midday meal scheme.
14. Chapter 4.

15. *Report of the Special Group on Targeting Ten Million Employment Opportunities Per Year Over the Tenth Plan Period*, Planning Commission, May 2002, http://planningcommission.nic.in/aboutus/committee/tsk_sg 10m.pdf
16. *Report of the Task Force on Employment Opportunities*, Planning Commission, July 2001, http://planning commission.nic.in/aboutus/taskforce/tk_empopp.pdf
17. 20–4 age-group.
18. These figures are from the Ministry of Human Resource Development's *Annual Report for 2006–7*, http://www.education.nic.in/AR/AR0607-en.pdf.
19. 138 colleges are now autonomous.
20. This problem also renders cross-country figures on higher education institutes somewhat misleading.
21. Rarely do institutions other than the IITs and some business schools perform well in such cross-country rankings.
22. Public expenditure on higher education is around 0.7 per cent of GDP now.
23. *Note on Higher Education*, National Knowledge Commission, 29 November 2006, http://www.knowledge commission. gov.in/downloads/recommendations/HigherEducationNote.pdf.
24. 'In general, about 75 per cent of maintenance expenditure is on salaries and pensions. Of the remaining 25 per cent, at least 15 per cent is absorbed by pre-emptive claims such as rents, electricity, telephones and examinations.'
25. In terms of the classic definition of a public good used by economists.
26. For a brief review of this court intervention, see Devesh Kapur and Pratap Bhanu Mehta, 'Higher Education', in *The Oxford Companion to Economics in India*, ed. Kaushik Basu, Oxford University Press, 2007. Also see, 'Higher Education: Regulation and Control', Bibek Debroy, in the same volume.

47

Indian Management Education: The Regulatory Structure is still Confused

BIBEK DEBROY

(*27 May 2008*)

In recommendations submitted in December 2007, the National Knowledge Commission (NKC) has recommended that the All India Council for Technical Education (AICTE) should be scrapped and replaced by an Independent Regulatory Authority for Higher Education (IRAHE). These aren't recommendations specific to the AICTE or management education, but general and are based on arguments about multiplicity of regulating bodies, high entry barriers and lack of independence in regulation. However, if there is an IRAHE, roles of the University Grants Commission (UGC) and AICTE, and some other higher education councils, will change. Reacting to the NKC recommendations, Human Resource Development (HRD) Ministry has set up a 22-member committee chaired by Professor Yashpal to examine the future of both the AICTE and the UGC. Hence, nothing is going to change in a hurry. And lest one forgets, in 2003, there was a U.R. Rao Committee that went into the working of the AICTE. But this report was never made public.

The AICTE was originally set up as an advisory body in 1945. However, till 1987, it was only an advisory body, not a regulatory one. In the 1980s, especially in south India, engineering education was opened up to the private sector and, through a 1987 statute, the AICTE was actually set up to regulate it. The expression used was 'technical' education, but since this expression was never precisely defined, it came to mean management education, as well as engineering. This led to an odd situation. First, there are management institutions that are affiliated to universities and grant degrees. These are regulated, directly or indirectly, by the UGC. Historically, these have mostly been public, but now there are private ones also, except that profit-making is prohibited. Second, there are private management schools that offer diplomas (not degrees) and are accredited by the AICTE. In passing, in most business school rankings, if one leaves out the Indian Institutes of Management (IIM), degree-awarding public ones perform atrociously, while diploma-awarding private ones do well. Third, there are IIMs regulated directly by the HRD Ministry. Fourth, there are management schools run by deemed universities. Fifth, there are foreign degrees, sometimes in dual degree form. And sixth, there are programmes run without the AICTE accreditation, based on the perception that the market doesn't necessarily require such certification.

Typically, the AICTE approvals entitle a postgraduate programme to be called a diploma programme if it has a minimum duration of two years (15 months for executives). Any programme that has duration between one and two years will be called a certificate programme. Beyond what the NKC has said, there are several reasons why people complain about the AICTE. First, the AICTE approvals are based on formulae that are input-dependent and irrelevant, not on outcome variables. For example, indicators like faculty/student ratios, ownership of land, size of campus, built-up area, size of the reception office, capacity of the electricity generator, balance in the bank, mode of faculty recruitment, number of PhD degree-holders in faculty and number of permanent faculty are used. Each of these indicators can be individually questioned, even the number of PhD degree-holders, since it is argued that this may not be very relevant in a business school. But the more substantive point is that indicators should be based more on outcome variables, like data on placements. Second, there is the argument that insistence on minimum thresholds for these input variables amounts to licensing, not regulation. This licensing creates entry barriers which aren't realistic. For instance, a new business school can start with only 60 students per branch and this is too low a number to generate economies. Instead, regulation should manifest itself through disclosure norms on faculty, infrastructure, placement and fees. The AICTE already has such mandatory disclosure requirements. But they aren't exhaustive, especially on finances, and they haven't replaced the licensing. Disclosure norms can also operate *in tandem* with independent ratings. Today, such ratings do exist, usually undertaken by magazines. However, they aren't very credible.

Because of the multiplicity of regulation and because not all business schools are under the regulatory framework, often voluntarily, it is difficult to get a handle on how many business schools there are. The cited figure is around 1,000, with 75,000 annual seats. However, these figures are primarily for those that are under the AICTE framework. The All India Management Association's ranking, which is voluntary and not mandatory, covers around 200 management schools.

Despite clarifications, a few grey areas still remain in regulations. The government has clarified that foreign universities will have to seek recognition from the AICTE and accordingly, the AICTE has issued regulations (2005) for entry. Foreign universities and institutions will not be allowed to appoint franchisees. The foreign institution will have to give a declaration to the effect that the course offered in India is recognised in the parent country and is, therefore, equivalent to the degree or diploma awarded by the institution at home. The nomenclature will have to be the same as in the home country. A no objection certificate will have to be obtained from the Embassy to establish that the foreign institution is genuine. The AICTE will determine norms for admissions, the conduct of the course, modes of delivery, intakes and fees. Foreign institutions that already operate in India will have to seek fresh approvals from the AICTE within six months. The 2005 regulations superseded the earlier 2003 regulations.

On the face of it, judging by the AICTE Act, every business school should be under the AICTE's jurisdiction and should be covered through the AICTE's National Board of Accreditation (NBA). *De jure* accreditation should be mandatory. However, *de facto*, it doesn't work that way because of three reasons. First, universities and deemed universities are under the UGC framework and the UGC has the National Accreditation and Assessment Council (NAAC). The NBA and the NAAC have different approaches, procedures and norms for accreditation. To confuse matters further, the NBA is statutory, while the NAAC is not. Supreme Court judgements have clearly stated that deemed universities, and also universities, are autonomous and outside the AICTE's purview. And one shouldn't forget that some deemed universities were set up before the AICTE acquired statutory powers in 1987. But there are other High Court (Madras) judgements stating that deemed universities should be under the AICTE. In 2006, the HRD Ministry issued a notification to end the confusion and bring about some kind of compromise:

> It is not a prerequisite for an institution notified as a 'Deemed to be University' to obtain the approval of the AICTE, to start any programme in technical or management education leading to an award, including degrees in disciplines covered under the AICTE Act, 1987. However, institutions notified as 'Deemed to be University' are required to ensure the maintenance of the minimum standards prescribed by the AICTE for various courses that come under the jurisdiction of the said Council. It is expected that the institutions notified as 'Deemed to be University' maintain their standards of education higher than the minimum prescribed by the AICTE.

Second, there are programmes that don't fit into the AICTE's degree/diploma classification. That's one of the reasons why the Indian School of Business doesn't want to apply for the AICTE recognition. Third, the AICTE hasn't yet decided what it wishes to do about distance learning. Every once in a while, the AICTE publishes lists of institutes that run management programmes without the AICTE approval and this includes those with foreign collaborations.

Because of differences in methodology and subjectivity, it is difficult to list the best business schools. But regardless of criteria, the list of the 'best' is likely to include IIM Ahmedabad, IIM Bangalore, IIM Kolkata, IIM Lucknow, Xavier Labour Relations Institute (Jamshedpur), National Institute of Industrial Engineering

(Mumbai), Faculty of Management Studies (Delhi), S.P. Jain Institute (Mumbai), Institute of Rural Management (Anand), Management Development Institute (Gurgaon), Indian Institute of Foreign Trade (Delhi), International Management Institute (Delhi) and the two management schools in the Indian Institute of Technology (IIT) Delhi and IIT Mumbai.

48

A Brief Conceptual Note: Development of the Delhi–Mumbai Industrial Corridor

S. NARAYAN

(16 July 2008)

The Freight Corridors

The government of India has announced a dedicated freight corridor network between Delhi and Mumbai as well as between Ludhiana to Kolkata. The Delhi–Mumbai Industrial Corridor (DMIC) covers an overall length of 1,515 km and passes through the states of Uttar Pradesh, the National Capital Region (NCR) of Delhi,[1] Haryana, Rajasthan, Gujarat and Maharashtra, with end terminals at Dadri in the NCR of Delhi and Jawaharlal Nehru Port near Mumbai.

Each of the corridors will be dedicated to long-haul, fast movement of freight, at speeds up to 100 km per hour, and would free existing track space for short-haul freight as well as passenger traffic. The east-west corridor is expected to cater primarily to the movement of bulk commodities, particularly coal and steel, where there is substantial movement between the coal-fields and the steel plants in the east to the power stations and industries in the west and the north. As such, it is envisaged that this freight corridor would use open wagons with electric locomotives for traction. It would entail an expenditure of approximately Rs 12,000 crore.[2]

The north-west corridor, on the other hand, seeks to cater to industry, manufacturing and exports and, as such, would handle container traffic. The Indian railways and the Indian government have opted for flat wagons that can carry double stack containers.

This is the first time that such an alternative is being tried anywhere in the world. The only other two places that haul double stack containers by rail either use well-shaped wagons with electric traction (China) or flat wagons with diesel traction (United States). The attempt to use flat wagons with electric traction is, thus, an experiment, and pilot testing has started this week on this technology. The total cost of the project is estimated to be around Rs 16,000 crore (though the Japan International Cooperation Agency [JICA] estimates are considerably higher at Rs 28,000 crore). Tracks would be constructed for 25 tonne axle load and the project involves 745 road crossings, 200 new roads underbridges and 505 new roads overbridges. There would be nine junctions and three terminal stations along the route, and the ports of Mumbai, Navi Mumbai, Pipavav, Kandla, Dholera, Navlakhi, Dahej, Mundra, Mandvi, Mahuva, Rewas and Dighi would be served by this corridor.

The Japanese government has been involved from the beginning in the planning and feasibility studies, and has also come forward with concessional financing through its government-to-government programmes to assist this project. Japanese assistance for the portion in Rajasthan (Rewari to Palanpur) has already been assured, and the start and tail portion funding is under discussion. Some portion of the assistance would be tied to sourcing of locomotives and signalling equipment from Japan.

The Indian government has also decided to push ahead with the east-west corridor simultaneously, and some tenders have already been floated. The additional land involved for the project, over a 1,515 km line, is only about 5,300 ha, and not much difficulty is anticipated in putting this together.

DMIC Industrial Corridor

A memorandum of agreement was signed between the Indian Ministry of Commerce and Industry and the Japanese Ministry of Trade and Industry in December 2006 for the development of an industrial corridor along the freight corridor between Delhi and Mumbai. An inter-ministerial group was set up to work out the

Map 1: Delhi–Mumbai Industrial Corridor: Freight Corridor and Investment Regions

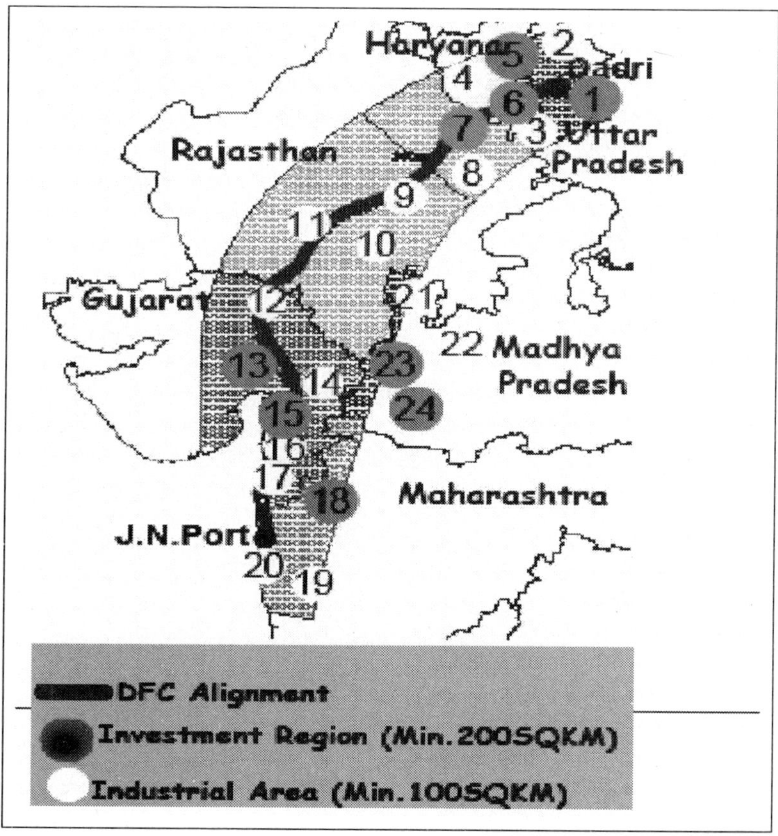

Source: Mumbai–Delhi Industrial Corridor—A Feasibility Study, Draft Report (Mimeo), Department of Industrial Promotion and Policy, Ministry of Industry and Commerce, Govt. of India, Feb. 2008 (for government circulation only).

project outline and an Indo–Japanese taskforce was set up to guide the process. The taskforce, after several meetings, came up with a concept paper for the development of an area of 150 km on either side of the freight corridor. The concept paper envisages the creation of a strong manufacturing and trading hub supported by world-class infrastructure.

High impact/market driven nodes-integrated Investment Regions (IR) and Industrial Areas (IA) have been identified within the corridor to provide transparent and investment-friendly facility regimes. These regions are proposed to be self-sustained industrial townships, with world-class infrastructure, road and rail connectivity for freight movement to and from ports and logistics hubs, served by domestic and international air connectivity, reliable power, quality social infrastructure, and they provide a globally-competitive environment conducive for setting up businesses. An IR would be a specifically delineated industrial region with a minimum area of over 200 sq. km (20,000 ha), while an IA would be developed with a minimum area of over 100 sq. km (10,000 ha). Twenty-four such nodes—9 IRs and 15 IAs spanning across six states—have been identified after wide consultations with the stake-holders, that is, the state governments and the concerned central ministries. It is proposed that six IRs and six IAs would be taken up for implementation in the first phase during 2008–12 and the rest of the development would be phased out in the next four years.

There are already several industrial belts along this region. These are:

(a) Uttar Pradesh: Noida/Greater Noida and Ghaziabad (General Manufacturing);
(b) Haryana: Gurgaon, Faridabad and Sonepat (Automobile, Electronics and Handloom);
(c) Rajasthan: Jaipur, Alwar, Kota, Bhilwara and Jodhpur (Marble, Leather and Textile);
(d) Gujarat: Ahmedabad, Vadodara, Anand, Bharuch and Surat (Engineering, Gems and Jewellery, Chemicals); and
(e) Maharashtra: Mumbai and Pune, Nasik (Auto/Auto Component, Textile, Pharma and Aluminium).

The development strategy of the DMIC is based on the competitiveness of each of the DMIC states. In this zone, several industrial regions, as well as industrial areas, have been identified for the first phase of development. The difference between the zones and the areas is that the latter is a smaller, more closely knit agglomeration of industrial units which is planned, while the former would

Map 2: Delhi–Mumbai Industrial Corridor: Industrial Nodes

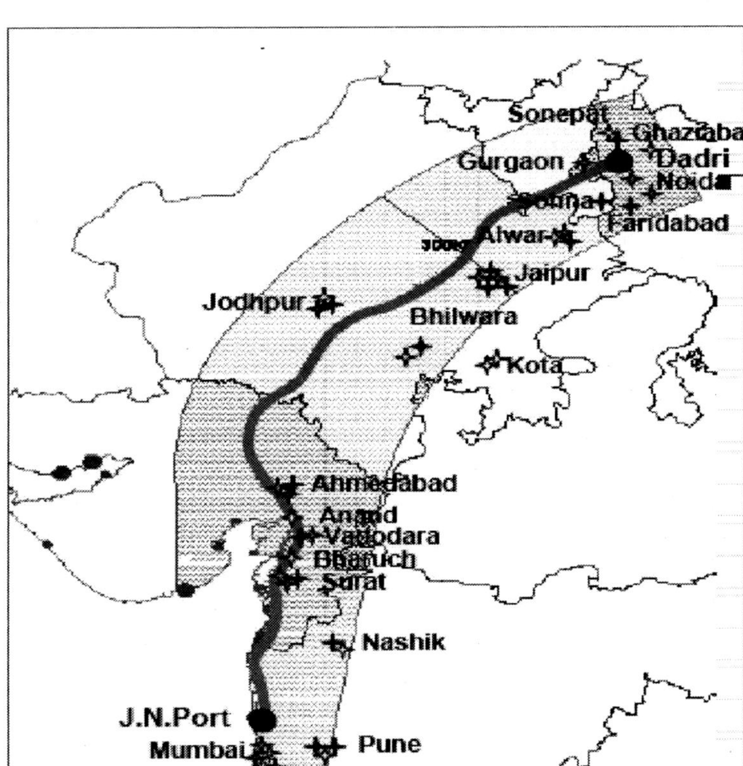

Source: Mumbai–Delhi Industrial Corridor—A Feasibility Study, Draft Report (Mimeo), Department of Industrial Promotion and Policy, Ministry of Industry and Commerce, Govt. of India, Feb. 2008 (for government circulation only).

represent a broader (approximately 200 sq. km) area development concept.

The identified IRs are:

(a) Dadri–Noida–Ghaziabad (Uttar Pradesh);
(b) Manesar–Bawal (Haryana);
(c) Khushkhera–Bhiwadi–Neemrana (Rajasthan);
(d) Ahmedabad–Dholera (Gujarat);

(e) Igatpuri–Nasik–Sinnar (Maharashtra); and
(f) Pitampura–Dhar–Mhow (Madhya Pradesh).

The identified IAs are:

(a) Meerut–Muzaffarnagar (Uttar Pradesh);
(b) Faridabad–Palwal (Haryana);
(c) Ajmer–Kishangarh (Rajasthan);
(d) Vadodara–Ankaleshwar (Gujarat);
(e) Dighi Port (Maharashtra); and
(f) Neemuch–Nayagaon (Madhya Pradesh).

Within these selected nodes, the activities would include developing new industrial clusters; upgrading existing industrial estates and clusters; and providing for efficient infrastructure and logistics. This would include road and rail connectivity to ports and markets; the development of new ports and port infrastructure; upgrading and modernising airports; power generation and transmission; and the development of integrated townships. An estimate of US $90 billion has been arrived at as the investment expectations of Phases I and II. The development is envisaged through public–private partnership models, and the large regions are sought to be developed as industrial hubs to make private infrastructure projects viable.

Organisational Structure and Project Implementation Framework

A four-tier system, as institutional framework, has been set up for the implementation of the DMIC. It is as follows:

(a) An apex body, headed by the Finance Minister with concerned central ministers and chief ministers of the respective DMIC states as members for overall guidance, planning, and approvals.
(b) A corporate entity, Delhi–Mumbai Industrial Corridor Development Corporation (DMICDC), specially envisaged to coordinate project development, finance and implementation, headed by a full-time chairman/managing director (C/MD) and having representation from the central government, state governments and financial institutions.
(c) A state-level coordination entity/nodal agency responsible for

coordination between the DMICDC and various state government entities and the project implementing agencies/special purpose vehicles (SPV); and

(d) Project-specific SPVs would actually implement the projects. These SPVs can be owned by the state governments in terms of governance structure, Board of Directors, etc. Some of these SPVs can also be formed by central/state governments and their agencies.

The apex authority has already been constituted under the chairmanship of the finance minister with the concerned central ministers and chief ministers of the DMIC states as members. The DMICDC has been incorporated with 49 per cent equity to the central government, 41 per cent to the Infrastructure Leasing and Finance Corporation (ILFC) and 10 per cent to the Industrial Development Finance Corporation. The ILFC has been appointed as the project management consultant. Enquiries have been floated for the appointment of consultants for one hub in each state. The Indian government has provided a budget grant of Rs 50 crore in 2008–9.

The implementation of the DMIC involves the DMICDC undertaking project development activity for various central government projects and also to assist the state governments, wherever desired. The DMICDC will be responsible for assisting state governments in raising finances on the basis of a sovereign guarantee. It will also act as a pass through entity for specific projects and raise a Project Development Fund (PDF). This will be used as a revolving fund and would specifically be used for undertaking project development activities, viz., identification of projects, preparation of feasibility reports, detailed project reports, etc., and its cost would be recovered from successful bidders. Creating a PDF will also ensure uninterrupted availability of funds for project preparatory activities. The representatives of the respective state governments and the DFC implementing agency could be represented as Directors on the Board of the DMICDC.

Looking at the cost of various projects likely to be implemented in Phase I and Phase II, it was estimated that US $2–2.5 billion might be required for project preparation alone. Taking 10 per

Figure 1: Delhi–Mumbai Corridor: Implementation Framework

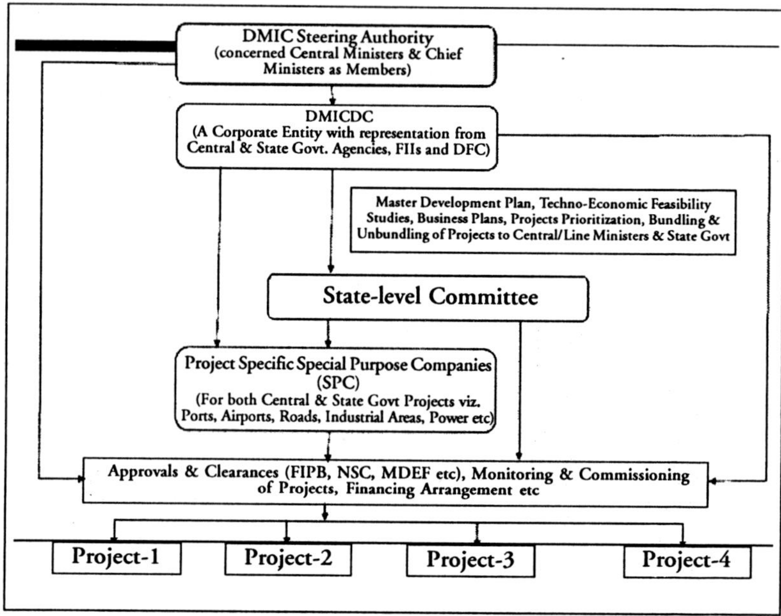

Source: Mumbai–Delhi Industrial Corridor—A Feasibility Study, Draft Report (Mimeo), Department of Industrial Production and Policy, Ministry of Industry and Commerce, Govt. of India, Feb. 2008 (for government circulation only).

cent of it as initial seed money, a reasonable size of project development fund would be US $250 million.

To start the entire process of project development, it is essential to undertake the preparation of detailed project reports along with master planning of nodes. Considering the importance of undertaking studies and meeting timelines and considering the fact that such resources from the state governments may take time to flow, the Indian government suggested that the Japanese side might consider special dispensation towards contributing 50 per cent of the initial requirement, that is, US $125 million to the PDF even if it might require deviations and special consideration in the existing arrangement of financing. It was, therefore, agreed that, looking at the importance of the project, a grant of an untied Japan Bank for International Cooperation loan to the DMICDC would be favourably considered by the Japanese government, which would like to consider building up partnership in the project from the very beginning.

It is envisaged that the funding for the DMIC project could be either through nodal agencies (budgetary/extra budgetary provisions) or through viability gap funding/long-term soft loans extended to the project SPVs. The DMICDC would facilitate this process by using a sovereign guarantee provided by the central government. Moreover, the SPVs could also borrow on their own balance sheets or project recourse basis.

Key Issues in Project Implementation

The complexity of implementing the DMIC would require rigorous detailing of all aspects of the project prior to implementation including engineering, environmental, social and financial issues. Given that there would be the involvement of several ministries and multiple state governments, an effective framework for coordination is essential.

The DMIC involves an investment of US $90 billion spread over 60 projects. An a priori strategy for the mobilisation of finances to cover each phase of the project is critical. The funding would need to be accessed from state and central governments, Indian and foreign investors, and bilateral and multilateral institutions.

It is a first of its kind project in India, and the record of interministerial coordination and project execution by state agencies in the past has been one of project delays and cost overruns. Quite apart from the financing and physical execution schedules, there are a lot of processes that involve interface with public concerns. These include land acquisition, rehabilitation of people and environmental safeguards. It is, therefore, likely that the pace of the implementation may be slower than envisaged.

At the same time, the construction of the freight corridor, which would happen within the next five years, would act a fillip to the industrialisation and development of this area, and one is likely to see a lot of initiative in the development of these industrial regions and areas. It is likely that the development of infrastructure and demand push would give a fillip to the execution of the projects.

ANNEXURE

Infrastructure Activities Required in the Corridor

- Twenty new/upgraded rail links, a total of 1,950 km.
- Five metro/suburban railway systems with route length of 330 km for inter-city connectivity.
- Twenty-seven road links covering 1,840 km to be built by state governments.
- Eleven road links covering 1,650 km to be constructed by the National Highways Authority of India.
- Eight multi-modal logistic parks, about 400 ha in size, with railway sidings to be developed for the DMIC at Dadri, Rewari, Palanpur, Ahmedabad, Gandhidham, Vapi, Navi Mumbai and Ludhiana.
- New ports at Dholera, Navlakhi, Dahej, Mandvi, Mahuva, Rewas and Dighi to be developed in Gujarat and Maharashtra.
- Existing ports at Mumbai, Jawaharlal Nehru Port, Kandla, Pipavav, Mundra and Bhavnagar to be enlarged and modernised.
- Nineteen rail links and 26 road links to improve port connectivity.
- Seven non-metro airports Agra, Jaipur, Udaipur, Indore, Ahmedabad, Vadodara and Pune to be upgraded.
- Four new international airports proposed at Jewar (near Delhi), Navi Mumbai, Chakan (between Mumbai and Pune) and near Ahmedabad.
- 492 km between Mumbai and Ahmedabad identified for high speed rail linkage.
- Development of electric power to meet the shortage of 75 billion units (kWh) in 2014.

NOTES

1. The NCR is the metropolitan area of Delhi which encompasses satellite cities like Faridabad, Gurgaon, Ghaziabad and Noida.
2. Rs. 1 crore is approximately US $2.4 million.

49

Locking in Private Investment in Indian Agriculture

ROMAR CORREA

(*12 November 2008*)

Private and Public Investment are Complements

Experience has conclusively established that investments in agriculture made by developing countries are pro-growth and pro-poor.[1] Agriculture continues to provide a labour-intensive source of employment, cheap food, raw materials, labour, savings, and the demand for non-agricultural goods. Yet, over the last three decades, there has been a significant systemic bias against the rural economy in the allocation of public resources. This scenario is inefficient because no developed economy of significant size became so without the agricultural sector recording substantial productivity gains. There is some historical evidence that a Green Revolution preceded the Industrial Revolution in Europe, its offshoots, and in Japan. Recent scholarship has excavated the importance of pre-war agricultural growth to the post-war industrialisation of Taiwan and South Korea. Cross-country studies which seek to track the sectoral sources of growth in developing countries unambiguously report that a dynamic agriculture has the strongest linkage to growth in other sectors and aggregate growth. India has a long way to go in this transition.[2] In the 1970s, India had a larger proportion of the workforce engaged in the organised sector in comparison to Thailand and Indonesia. By the early 1990s, the ratio was three times more, and in Indonesia, 2.3 times more. While the stagnation of output in agriculture can increase with improvements in infrastructure and technology, it is not clear that such changes lead to large increases in rural employment. The problem can only be addressed by generating demand for unskilled employment outside the agricultural sector. Here is where the labour absorptive capacity of organised manufacturing comes in. The evidence for India of the past few years, as given in the *Handbook of Statistics on the Indian Economy 2007* by the Reserve Bank of India, is unimpressive. Table 17 of the Handbook shows a flat trend of agricultural production of food grains. The pattern of land use and select inputs for agricultural production, including net and gross sown area, net and gross irrigated area in Table 24 of the Handbook, display anything but a dynamic agriculture. The following table, which is Table 18 of the Handbook on index numbers of area, production, and yield of food grains, non-food grains and all crops, is clear.

Table 1: Agriculture Production and Yield (2003/4–2006/7)

	2003–4	2004–5	2005–6	2006–7 (advanced estimates)
Production	155.1	144.2	152.5	158.6
Yield	121.0	115.6	120.8	123.2

Source: Handbook of Statistics on the Indian Economy 2007.

A ringing message from past and recent history is that public support programmes are a necessary precondition for growth in agricultural productivity. The large multiplier effects of agriculture mentioned above are externalities to the sector itself. Private investors will not be induced to invest. Besides, market failure is endemic. Consequently, a purposive 'industrial policy' towards agriculture is called for. In South Korea and Taiwan, for instance, the governments absorbed risks and invested in new agricultural technologies. Effete governments, in contrast, struggled with land reforms and kept prices low without the backing of sufficient public expenditure, particularly in research and development, and extension activities. The government, in the form of public sector and public institutions, would be the natural ground for the creation of jobs, given the objective of creating employment 'for the sake of employment'.[3]

While more employment leads to more demand, more employment requires a start-up of exogenous demand in the first place. Once some initial demand is created, say by an employment guarantee scheme, the production response creates income. Further demand is stimulated in a well-known multiplier process. Massive state intervention with budget deficits is not called for. All that is required is an initial push. With a savings rate of 25 per cent, the ultimate back-of-the-envelope increase in demand would be 400 per cent of the initial impulse. What is the record of India in this regard? In Table 111 on Public Sector Plan Outlay (at current prices) in the *Handbook of Statistics on the Indian Economy 2007* by the Reserve Bank of India, we ignore the figures from 2004–5 onwards as they are taken from the Economic Survey, 2006–7. The following figures (in rupees crores) for the earlier years speak for themselves.

Table 2: Agriculture and Allied Services Yield (2000/1–2003/4)

Year	2000–1	2001–2	2002–3	2003–4
Agriculture & Allied Services	7,577	8,248	7,655	8,776
Total	1,85,736	1,86,315	2,10,203	2,24,827

Source: Handbook of Statistics on the Indian Economy 2007.

The Objective

Small scale enterprises (SSI) are an adjunct to agriculture and require long-term and short-term capital. Long-term capital is provided by institutions such as the Small Industries Development Bank of India (SIDBI), State Financial Corporations (SFC), State Industry Development Corporations (SIDC), and so on while short-term capital is provided by the banking sector. SSI lending falls under priority sector lending. The overall picture which is an extension of earlier trends is not comforting. Under Non-food Gross Bank Credit, the figure for agriculture and allied activities has stagnated at 12.4 per cent (18 March 2005), the same for 31 March 2006 and 12.8 per cent outstanding as on 30 March 2007. Industry (small, medium and large) has steadily declined from 42.1 per cent to 38.2 per cent to 38.5 per cent recorded at the same time points. Priority sector advances have declined from 37.3 per cent to 36.4 per cent to 35.2 per cent. Outstanding credit to services, on the other hand, has shown an increase from 20 per cent to 22.8 per cent to 23.3 per cent, once again reported at the end of the financial years.[4]

Since the growth of small and medium enterprises (SME) cannot be regarded as inferior to the growth of other sectors in a transforming economy such as India, a subgroup on the flow of private investment to the SME sector was constituted. The definitions that were applied were provided by the Micro, Small and Medium Enterprises Development (MSMED) Act of 2006. Traditionally defined small scale enterprises (TDSSE) are units with investment in plant and machinery up to Rs 1 crore. The scope was broadened to include newly-defined SSIs (NDSSI) as units having investment in plant and machinery between Rs 1 crore and Rs 5 crore. The Act also introduced the concept of medium scale enterprises (MSE) as enterprises having investment in plant and machinery between Rs 5 crore and 10 crore. The methodology used was as follows. An average growth rate of gross domestic product of 8.5 per cent during the eleventh plan was assumed. Production data for TDSSEs in current prices was extrapolated assuming an average growth rate of 12 per cent and an inflation rate of 4.5 per cent. Data on NDSSIs is not easily available so the subgroup, after ex-perimenting with alternative econometric techniques, generated a series based on the proportionate share of the subsector in relation to the total. An average growth rate of 12 per cent was arrived at. The MSE sector partook more of the dynamics of the industrial sector. Hence the projected growth rate was 10 per cent.

Working Capital Requirements

A regression equation established a strong linkage between SSI production and bank credit. Outstanding bank advances to the TDSSE sector was estimated to be of the order of Rs 1 lakh crore at the end of the tenth plan to increase to the order of Rs 2 lakh crore in 2011–12, the terminal year of the eleventh plan. A similar regression equation for NDSSIs was run and the total working capital requirements were of the same order as above, the addition of the latter being slight. Another regression line for the MSE yielded an estimate of the order of Rs 18,000 crore at the end of the tenth plan to increase to the order of Rs 38,000 crore in 2011–12. The numbers were found to be consistent with the Government of India/Reserve Bank of India directives to public sector banks to double their credit to the SME sector between 2005–6 and 2009–10 with not less than a growth rate of 20 per cent.

Fixed Capital Projections

Here, along with regression analysis, the so-called institutional capacity was estimated. The numbers were of the order of Rs 72,000 crore for TDSSEs, Rs 20,000 crore for NDSSIs and Rs 9,000 crore for the MSE sector. It is worth noting that the requirements for the sector, as a whole, implied a growth of almost 40 per cent over the tenth plan estimate. Small and medium scale entrepreneurs approached SIDBI, the SFCs and the SIDCs with their business plans. Projections were made on the basis of this data, assuming a smartly growing industrial sector. It was found that the carrying capacity of these institutions was a disbursement of the order of Rs 1 lakh crore loans during the eleventh plan as against a disbursement of the order of Rs 45,000 crore during the tenth plan period, an increase of 130 per cent.

Towards New Private Initiatives

The share of priority sector advances in total non-food credit of scheduled commercial banks has been more or less constant at 37 per cent since 1999. According to Table 33 in the *Annual Survey of Industries—Principal Characteristics*, the number of factories have steadily declined over the last 10 years. The number of workers was less in 2004–5 than it was in 1997–8. Hardly any change can be noticed between fixed capital and working capital comparing

1997–8 and 2004–5. Wages have increased only slightly. Gross fixed capital formation is only slightly higher in the period which net fixed capital formation is lower.

Along traditional lines, there is a need to reinvigorate public investment.[5] There is a large public sector in India, huge portions of which are efficient as evidenced by their rising profitability. Many of them are in the infrastructure business, producing and generating power, in roads, railways, ports, and telecommunications. In addition, while funds are likely to continue being released through reductions in the cash reserve ratio, the Reserve Bank of India should return to the system of sector-specific re-finance facilities that induce banks to lend to agriculture and SMEs.[6]

We have recommended the encouragement of venture capital in order to finance entrepreneurial schemes in agriculture.[7] The motivation comes from the financial systems paradigm in microfinance. According to this view, microfinance providers should be resolved to covering their costs since anything less would undermine their ability to achieve the scale necessary to make any inroad into the unfulfilled demands of their clients. Their outreach is to be based on the offering of tailor-made products rather than eligibility rules or other measures denying access. Time should be spent on unearthing services that groups are willing and able to pay for rather than measuring the impact of their services on clients. Proponents of this perspective regard the reduction of poverty as a by-product of the numerous ways in which access to financial services helps poor households. The belief is that by reaching a massive scale, microfinance providers are likely to reach more of the very poor than many smaller agencies devoting their resources to reach them directly. A key problem with microfinance is sustainability, that is, the ability to withstand massive stochastic shocks. There might be a trade-off between lending to the very poor and sustainability. The ability to attract deposits is often taken to be an index of financial viability. However, while depositor funding may leverage donor funding to attain a large scale of operations, sustainability might be a casualty. Deposits can be withdrawn without notice in times of crisis. The central issue remains sustainability without the continuous infusion of external subsidies. The conclusion is that sustainable financial institutions by this criterion tend to have a low dependence on deposits.

Venture capitalists (VC) who finance and advise start-up enterprises can be regarded as an important adjunct to this perspective on microfinance. The case here is that a sophisticated venture capital industry makes young firms grow faster, increases value and creates more jobs. VCs screen projects, structure contracts and monitor firms. The joint inputs of both entrepreneurs and VCs interact to determine the long-term fortune of start-up enterprises. Entrepreneurs provide the novel technological inputs but tend to be inadequate financially. VCs support the firm with their financial expertise. They embody the best of principal-agent monitoring, thereby reducing risk. A special trait of VCs is that they are oriented towards exit. Thus, the infinite dependence on infusion of inputs like cash is obviated from the outset.

Yet another source of private investment in agriculture might be the routing of international long-run financial investors (LRFI) to India.[8] Mainly pension funds and insurance companies, LRFIs collect contractual savings and support long-run commitments on them but their contracts are founded on trust. Due to the sheer size of their portfolios, their strategy of divergence makes them universal owners. They are concerned with macro risks and returns over time. Importantly, they have an incentive to internalise external risks generated by venturing into strange pastures. With dynamic and not static portfolios, the base of diversification is the long-term bond, a riskless asset, not a short-term security.

In conclusion, the dramatic contrast between investment in India and China can be cited.[9] The growth of the capital stock in China is more than double that of India. During the period 1980–2003, investment in China grew at an annual average rate of 11.7 per cent in comparison to 6.8 per cent in India. The comparison is not odious as China's trajectory in this regards mirrors the experience of countries like Singapore and Korea.

NOTES

1. D. Bezemer and D. Headey, 2008, 'Agriculture, Development, and Urban Bias', *World Development*, 36, 8, 1342–64.
2. A. Bose, 2007, 'Employment', in *The Oxford Companion to Economics in India*, ed. K. Basu, New Delhi: Oxford University Press, 124–6.
3. Ibid.
4. RBI, 2007, *Report on Trend and Progress of Banking in India 2006–2007*, Appendix Table III.3.
5. A. Sengupta, 2008, 'A Monetised Deficit for Sustaining Growth amidst the Meltdown', *Economic & Political Weekly*, XLIII, 42, 10–11.
6. EPW Research Foundation, 2008, 'Paradigm Shift in Financial Policies: Need of the Hour', *Economic & Political Weekly*, XLIII, 42, 22–8.
7. A. Correa and R. Correa, July 2008, 'Microfinance: Debt and Equity Contracts', *Applied Financial Economics Letters.*
8. M. Agietta, 2008, 'Corporate Governance and the Long-run Investor', *International Review of Applied Economics*, 22, 4, 407–27.
9. J. Felipe, E. Lavina and E.X. Fan, 2008, 'The Diverging Patterns of Profitability: Investment and Growth of China and India During 1980–2003', *World Development*, 36, 5, 741–74.

SECTION II

ECONOMIC DEVELOPMENT

D. State Studies

50

Development Trends in Selected Indian States: Issues of Governance and Management

S. NARAYAN

(*28 April 2008*)

THE SOUTHERN and western states in India are regarded as high growth and high growth potential areas. This paper examines the management of government finances and expenditure in the states of Andhra Pradesh, Gujarat, Maharashtra, Karnataka, Kerala and Tamil Nadu.

Table 1 indicates that Gujarat has grown the most in recent years, considerably above the national average.

In terms of per capita net state domestic product current prices,

Table 1: Gross State Domestic Product (Current Prices)

(*Rs in crore*)

	2005–6	2006–6	2007–8 (E)	2008–9 (E)	Growth rate (%)
Andhra Pradesh	236,034	269,173	298,459	330,930	10.88
Gujarat	216,651	247,681	283,156	323,712	14.32
Karnataka	170,741	189,044	209,308	231,745	10.72
Kerala	118,998	132,739	146,952	162,687	10.71
Maharashtra	432,413	482,328	538,004	600,107	11.54
Tamil Nadu	223,528	246,266	274,378	308,136	9.08

Source: National Income Statistics, Central Statistical Organization (CSO); Estimates by Bureau of India (BIU).

Note: In the tables in this paper, Rs 1 crore is above US $250 million.

Tamil Nadu ranks 12th in the country (Rs 29,958), behind Haryana, Maharashtra and Punjab, among major states. Among the southern states, Tamil Nadu is just behind Kerala, but higher than the other three states. The estimates of gross state domestic product (GSDP) growth as well as population growth reveal that Gujarat could lead in per capita net state domestic product over the next two years (see Table 2).

An analysis of the budgets of these states for 2008–9 shows that Maharashtra and Andhra Pradesh have healthy revenue receipts, and are managing their revenue expenditures within the receipts. It may be recalled that, only a few years ago, these two states used to report massive revenue deficits. The lack of fiscal prudence and management is a function of governance. In Karnataka, ineffective and weak governments in the past five years have led the state into fiscal decline. In Kerala, the ruling coalitions have been unable to strategise a clear developmental path, and the budgets reflect these infirmities.

A similar trend is evident in the case of interest payments as well, with high commitments in the case of Karnataka and Kerala. Interestingly, Table 4 also indicates the overhang of past borrowings in the case of Maharashtra—there was a period when the state was even borrowing for salary payments. The high debt service burden is being slowly reduced through better management, but reflects the burden of poor governance on successor governments.

Table 2: Per Capita Net State Domestic Product
(Current Prices)

(*Rs in crore*)

	2005–6	2006–7	2007–8 (E)	2008–9 (E)	Growth rate (%)
Andhra Pradesh	26,226	29,582	35,879	36,100	9.18
Gujarat	34,157	43,324	50,400	57,048	10.63
Karnataka	27,101	32,447	36,058	39,548	8.59
Kerala	30,668	33,609	42,961	47,372	8.06
Maharashtra	37,081	32,733	49,579	54,863	8.13
Tamil Nadu	29,958	35,668	40,127	43,595	7.62

Sources: National Income Statistics, CSO; Estimates by BIU.

Table 3: Revenue Receipts/Expenditure and Deficit Position (Budget Estimates 2008–9)

(*Rs in crore*)

State	Revenue receipts	Revenue expenditure	Revenue surplus (+)/deficit(–)
Andhra Pradesh	70,927	70,218	709
Gujarat	38,278	38,226	484
Karnataka	46,189	31,787	–2,973
Kerala	24,936	28,303	–3,367
Maharashtra	79,911	78,946	965
Tamil Nadu	51,506	51,422	84

Source: State Budget Documents.

The fiscal indicators calculated in Table 5 indicate that the better governed states have had better performances. Tamil Nadu has been consistently a better fiscal performer among the key states. Both in terms of gross fiscal deficit and revenue deficit as percentage of GSDP, its ratios are better than that of other states in Table 5. This has been possible as tax revenues, as a percentage of GSDP, have been high in Tamil Nadu.

However, both Andhra Pradesh and Karnataka have better development expenditure/GSDP ratios. In terms of social sector

Table 4: Interest Payment *vis-à-vis* Revenue Expenditure (2008–9 BE)

	Interest payment (2008–9 BE)	Interest payment as % of total revenue expenditure
Andhra Pradesh	8,985	12.80
Gujarat	7,384	19.32
Karnataka	5,278	16.60
Kerala	5,144	18.17
Maharashtra	12,389	15.69
Tamil Nadu	5,957	10.82

Source: State Budget Documents.

Table 5: Key Fiscal Indicators (2008–9 BE)

	GFD/ GSDP	RD/ GSDP	OTR/ GSDP	*DEV/ GSDP	*SSE/ GSDP	CO/ GSDP
Andhra Pradesh	(2.92)	0.21	11.44	15.3	8.0	5.39
Gujarat	(0.15)	0.15	09.17	10.3	5.3	3.47
Karnataka	(2.31)	(1.22)	12.89	15.1	8.0	4.17
Kerala	4.26	(2.07)	09.70	10.4	7.2	0.96
Maharashtra	(2.19)	0.16	10.14	09.8	6.0	2.41
Tamil Nadu	(2.98)	0.03	10.10	12.7	7.8	3.01

GFD–Gross Fiscal Deficit
RD–Revenue Deficit
OTR–Own Tax Revenue
DEV–Development Expenditure
SSE–Social Sector Expenditure
CO–Capital Outlay

Note: Since estimates for all the states are not available for 2008–9, comparison has been made using 2007–8 figures.

Source: State Finances: A Study of Budgets of 2007–8; RBI*

spending, there is little to choose between Andhra Pradesh, Karnataka and Tamil Nadu. However, Andhra Pradesh and Karnataka have better capital outlay ratios in relation to the respective GSDP.

The pattern of growth strategies can be seen in the estimates of capital expenditure as well (see Table 6). Karnataka and Kerala have low growth (though in the case of Kerala, RE 2006–7 is an aberration due to a lumpy project commitment). Interestingly, fiscal prudence in Maharashtra is keeping capital expenditure growth low. There is focus in that state on more public-private partnership projects even for infrastructure, thus moving capital expenditure away from government budgets.

It is interesting to look at the focus on the social sectors in these states. All these states have spent more than 10 per cent of their outlay on education, with Kerala consistently allocating 15 per cent to 19 per cent (Table 7). It is possible to argue that, in Karnataka, Kerala and Maharashtra, there is continuing attention to and investment in education of a high order, whereas in the other three states, though attention has been given to education, there

Table 6: Capital Outlay

(*Rs in crore*)

	2005–6 (Accounts)	2006–7 (RE)	2007–8 (BE)	Growth rate (2006–7 over 2005–6)	Growth rate (2007–8 over 2006–7)
Andhra Pradesh	9,904	12,912	17,852	30.37%	38.26%
Gujarat	9,990	9,502	11,229	–4.88%	18.18%
Karnataka	8,900	9,330	10,169	4.83%	8.99%
Kerala	903	1,499	1,562	66.00%	4.20%
Maharashtra	11,591	13,406	14,471	15.66%	7.94%
Tamil Nadu	6,604	8,327	9,876	26.09%	18.60%

Source: State Finances: A Study of Budgets of 2007–8; RBI.

have been years where investments have lagged behind those made in the previous years.

The Indian National Planning Commission, and indeed the Common Minimum Programme of the United Progressive Alliance (UPA) have focussed on providing 3 per cent of all public expenditure for health. The selected states have been doing this on a regular basis (Table 8).

Three points are of note. First, Kerala and Tamil Nadu have been consistently high spenders and, surprisingly, allocations in Gujarat have been among the lowest in this set, as a percentage. Perhaps a per capita analysis might lead to a different picture, as population densities in Gujarat and Kerala are very different. A second point is that, in spite of four years of the UPA government and the announced emphasis on public health, there is little evidence of any sharp increases in public health expenditures. Third, as the fiscal situation in the states improves, there is evidence of greater attention to public health (and to education). This is a commentary on the fact that, when finances are stressed, allocations to these two sectors are under pressure. In an ideal situation of good governance, these two sectors should be the last to face the expenditure axe, but this does not seem to have been the case.

Table 7: Education Share in Total Disbursement

(per cent)

	2000–1	2001–2	2002–3	2003–4	2004–5	2005–6	2006–7 (RE)	2007–8 (RE)	Average
Andhra Pradesh	13.3	12.5	11.7	11.6	09.8	11.1	11.7	10.4	11.51
Gujarat	13.6	12.7	13.5	11.2	11.5	12.6	12.2	12.2	12.44
Karnataka	17.7	16.0	14.8	12.9	12.7	14.0	13.5	14.5	14.51
Kerala	20.0	19.0	17.6	15.7	16.2	16.6	17.2	18.1	17.55
Maharashtra	22.3	22.1	18.9	15.5	14.0	15.7	16.2	15.0	17.46
Tamil Nadu	18.0	17.3	13.8	12.6	11.2	13.6	13.2	15.1	14.35

Source: State Finances: A Study of Budgets of 2007–8; RBI.

Table 8: Public Health and Family Welfare Expenditure as Percentage of Aggregate Disbursement

(per cent)

	2000–1	2001–2	2002–3	2003–4	2004–5	2005–6	...... RE)	2007–8 (RE)	Average
Andhra Pradesh	4.7	4.4	4.0	3.7	3.2	3.4	3.4	3.3	3.76
Gujarat	3.4	2.8	3.2	2.7	2.8	3.1	2.9	3.1	3.00
Karnataka	5.1	4.9	4.2	3.4	3.0	3.3	3.6	3.9	3.93
Kerala	5.3	5.8	4.8	4.3	4.5	4.7	4.9	4.6	4.86
Maharashtra	3.9	4.3	3.7	3.2	2.7	3.2	3.3	3.3	3.45
Tamil Nadu	4.9	4.9	4.1	3.8	3.2	4.2	3.7	4.2	4.13

Source: State Finances: A Study of Budgets of 2007–8; RBI.

Tables 9 and 10 make interesting reading, and give an indication of the mindsets of the governments in power in the individual states. The government in Gujarat, for the last 10 years, has prided itself in being market-oriented, with consumers having to bear the costs of services. Electricity for agriculture and the price of products in the public distribution system reflect a philosophy of providing infrastructure and amenities at reasonable cost, and with little subsidy. The benefits have been in the form of a phenomenal growth and per capita incomes that the citizens of the state have benefited from.

The picture in Andhra Pradesh, Maharashtra and Tamil Nadu is different. The state governments need to protect election promises of subsidies and social welfare grants and the sharp increases in expenditure in the last three to four years is palpable. These are clearly crowding out other commitments in these states, as the percentage of amounts spent on the social sectors increases. Karnataka is a picture of politics, where, suddenly in 2007–8, there is a sharp increase in expenditure in the social sectors, as the government teetered into uncertainties and collapse.

It is possible to draw some broad conclusions from Tables 9 and 10. Along with Haryana and Punjab, the states chosen for study here are among the more progressive of the larger states of India. They are characterised by high growth rates of GSDP, and this is reflected in the steady increases in per capita incomes. The last three years have witnessed a steady attempt to increase state revenues, and to keep revenue expenditures within revenue receipts, an attempt at which most of these states have been successful. This has, in part, been possible through increases in revenue receipts, buoyed by the value-added tax introduced in 2005. Interest payments, as a percentage of expenditure, have fallen, and the state finances are on a sounder footing.

Within the environment of the overall improvements in the macro economy, the individual states have pursued somewhat different paths. These have been determined more by local political considerations of the governments in power in the state rather than by any perceived long-term strategy. Certain long-term investment trends, especially in Kerala in respect of education and health,

Table 9: Expenditure on Social Welfare

(*Rs in crore*)

	2000–1	2001–2	2002–3	2003–4	2004–5	2005–6	2006–7 (RE)	2007–8 (RE)	Average
Andhra Pradesh	10,006	10,876	11,179	13,367	13,821	14,900	21,119	28,247	15.98%
Gujarat	9,681	9,029	8,177	8,992	10,127	10,995	13,055	13,378	4.73%
Karnataka	7,541	7,642	7,570	8,315	9,764	11,675	15,479	19,225	14.30%
Kerala	5,242	4,932	6,338	5,924	7,344	7,524	9,768	10,472	10.39%
Maharashtra	15,429	15,452	15,704	18,877	20,433	24,268	29,928	31,307	10.64%
Tamil Nadu	9,618	9,190	9,662	11,586	13,617	14,297	18,778	21,221	11.97%

Source: State Finances: A Study of Budgets of 2007–8; RBI.

Table 10: Social Expenditure to Total Expenditure

(*per cent*)

	2000–1	2001–2	2002–3	2003–4	2004–5	2005–6	2006–7 (RE)	2007–8 (RE)	Average
Andhra Pradesh	35.6	35.0	32.5	33.3	29.3	30.8	34.8	36.1	33.43
Gujarat	35.6	35.2	30.4	27.3	29.0	32.1	33.6	32.1	31.91
Karnataka	38.3	34.8	31.4	28.4	28.5	33.4	34.9	39.1	33.60
Kerala	39.9	37.6	37.4	30.0	36.2	35.6	34.0	34.1	35.60
Maharashtra	36.6	36.4	33.3	30.9	28.1	35.3	38.2	37.9	34.59
Tamil Nadu	39.4	37.0	32.0	34.3	32.6	36.9	35.3	37.9	35.68

Source: State Finances: A Study of Budgets of 2007–8; RBI.

continue to be maintained but there are variations seen in the other states. The pattern in Gujarat appears to have stabilised towards a market-oriented liberal environment with the state taking the responsibility of providing public goods at a reasonable price in an efficient manner. The political compulsions of governance are considerably more apparent in Tamil Nadu, Andhra and Karnataka, where exiting governments are replacements of earlier political entities in power—the need to do something different is apparent in the patterns of expenditure. Typically, this is visible in additional allocations for social welfare. Outside of the presentation in the Tables, this has also been visible in the large announcements for subsidies for food grains in public distribution systems, freebies like television sets for all, and, in many ways, an attempt to ingratiate themselves with the populace through free gifts. Capital expenditure and plan expenditure have suffered, and it is possible to argue that the long-term investment gets crowded out through these ad hoc welfare measures.

It is difficult to argue, in the long term, which of these would have sustainable effects. Conventional arguments would say that a liberal market-oriented environment, coupled with investments in education and health, would lead to a long-term sustainable pattern of growth of per capita incomes, while grants and subsidies do not create wealth or employment. If this argument holds true, then, among these Indian states, perhaps Gujarat, Kerala, and even Maharashtra, appear to be on a more sustainable growth path than Tamil Nadu, Andhra Pradesh and Karnataka.

SECTION II

ECONOMIC DEVELOPMENT

E. International Trade and Business

51

Economic Slow-down in the United States: Importance of Domestic Market Leverage in South Asia

K.V. RAMASWAMY

(*13 February 2008*)

IS THE UNITED STATES' economy on the verge of a recession or is it already in one? How much of this (United States economic troubles) will spill over and impact the global economy? These are still much debated questions among economists and key policy makers. A recession, let us recall, is typically defined as a sustained period (two or more quarters) of negative growth in real gross domestic product (GDP). In the last quarter of 2007, the United States' real GDP grew by only 0.6 per cent. Therefore the jury is still out as far as the realisation of actual recession is concerned.

The central bank chiefs and finance ministers of the group of seven (G-7) industrialised countries in their recent meeting at Tokyo, Japan, have reportedly warned that the global economy could continue to slow-down. They, however, seem to have endorsed the view of Henry M. Paulson, the United States Treasury Secretary, by suggesting that the United States was likely to avoid recession. Closer home, the survey of American economists by the *Wall Street Journal* has raised their odds of the United States falling into recession to 49 per cent in February 2008 as against 40 per cent in the January 2008 survey. The suggested bottom line is an emerging scenario of growth slow-down in the United States' that will in turn pull down the global growth prospects.

This is reflected in the revised projection of the global growth by the International Monetary Fund (*Update on Global Economic Outlook*, 29 January 2008). According to the revised estimates, global growth is projected at 4.1 per cent in 2008, down from 4.9 per cent in 2007. The projected growth in the United States in 2008 has been lowered to 1.5 per cent on a year-on-year basis, down from 2.2 per cent in 2007. For the Euro area, growth has been lowered to 1.6 per cent in 2008 down from an estimate of 2.6 per cent during 2007. Will this slow-down have an impact on South Asia? If so, how intensive will it be?

Vulnerability of poor developing economies to external shocks can spring from many sources. The most common are terms of trade shocks due to volatility in primary commodity prices, commodity booms resulting in the Dutch disease, external aid reduction and natural disasters (floods, droughts and tsunami). Recession in rich countries that translates into fluctuation in GDP of high income countries (irrespective of the causes of the recession) that are the main markets for their manufactured products is certainly a key source. The intensity of the impact depends on the extent of external/export dependence of South Asian countries. The United States and the Euro area constitute the major markets for countries of South Asia and the predicted slow-down is bound to have some impact. The expected belt tightening by consumers in the United States in the face of higher food and energy cost (average United States inflation 4.1 per cent) is likely to put severe pressure on retail sales of manufactures. This, in turn, can be expected to lower imports into the United States of labour intensive manufactured goods of the South Asian countries. What is the extent of export dependence of South Asia?

A good measure of export dependence is the share of exports of goods and services in GDP. At present, the average export to GDP ratio for the five South Asian countries is 21 per cent (World Bank 2007). It ranges from a minimum of 15.5 per cent (Pakistan) to a maximum of 32 per cent (Sri Lanka). Nepal and Bangladesh have similar export to GDP ratios (18 per cent). India is closer to the average (20 per cent). On average, South Asia (except Sri Lanka perhaps) does not seem to suffer from a serious problem of export dependence.

The average conceals an underlying structural problem. This problem is with the structure of exports of South Asia which are heavily dependent on readymade garments and regional concentration of export markets. For instance, the share of garments, including textiles, is nearly 80 per cent in Bangladesh, with more than 70 per cent going to the United States and the European Union. Any slow-down in the United States (and global) economic activity will result in a decline in imports which, in turn, will have a negative impact on South Asian manufactured exports. This is likely to lead to reduction in South Asian growth rates but it will not necessarily derail the growth prospects.

According to the growth projections of *The Economist*, London, GDP growth rates in Pakistan in 2008 will be 5.4 per cent (against 7 per cent in 2007), 5.5 per cent in Bangladesh (6.5 per cent in 2007) and close to 8 per cent in India (9.4 per cent in 2007). Sri Lanka is estimated to have grown by 7 per cent in 2007 and one could expect a decline in growth rate in 2008. Sri Lanka may suffer more if tourism income also falls due to the global economic slow-down. It is important to note that these reductions in projected growth rates are due to a combination of domestic and external factors.

India, in particular, enjoys the advantage of an economy with a large domestic market (GDP of US $2.3 billion) and, is therefore, insulated from trade shocks to a greater extent. In other words, India can leverage its domestic market size and growth to stave off any adverse impact of global slowdown. The importance of a having healthy and growing domestic consumption-based economy is perhaps never driven home more than in these turbulent times. Recent reports indicate that India's information technology exports have also not been affected by the recent United States slow-down.

However, the other key countries of South Asia do not seem to be that blessed. These economies have the misfortune at present of suffering from serious domestic political and institutional problems. A combination of domestic conflict and the United States' (global) growth slow-down is not a happy set of events for these South Asian economies. The slow-down will inevitably create greater economic uncertainty in South Asia.

52

India's Trade Deficit: Increasing Fast but Still Manageable

AMITENDU PALIT

(*7 July 2008*)

INDIA'S TRADE DEFICIT, which reflects the excess of its merchandise imports over exports, has reached 7.7 per cent of its gross domestic product (GDP). According to the Balance of Payments (BOP) statistics for the year 2007–8 recently released by the Reserve Bank of India, the deficit has increased from US $63.2 billion in 2006–7 to US $90.1 billion in 2007–8. This increase of almost US $27 billion has resulted in the deficit swelling from 6.9 per cent of GDP in 2006–7 to 7.7 per cent in 2007–8.

Is this increase a cause for worry? The answer depends on the determinants of the deficit. For an expanding economy like India that is growing at more than 9 per cent per year, a trade deficit can arise from virtuous forces like heavy demand for raw material and intermediate imports from a robust domestic industry. This has indeed been happening in recent years, with capital goods leading the import rally. If industrial imports push the deficit, then there is little cause for concern. The deficit can also widen due to exchange rate movements. An appreciation in the value of the rupee *vis-à-vis* other major currencies can make Indian exports dearer and imports cheaper. Depreciation in the rupee will have the opposite effect. The eventual impact of exchange rate movements on the trade balance will depend upon relative price-sensitivities of Indian exports and imports. Adverse impacts of such exchange rate movements (if any) in a globalised world are usually short-lived as market forces tend to impact interest rates and capital flows in a manner that is self-equilibrating.

Enlarging deficits usually become a cause for concern if they are produced by chronic structural deficiencies. For developing countries, structural trade deficits can be difficult to finance, making them unsustainable after a point in time. This is because the chronic nature of the problems leaves little scope for policy intervention. The situation worsens if the deficiencies are accentuated by adverse circumstances. A typical example is the dependence on oil imports. The dependence on crude oil imports is chronic for most industrialising developing countries. The problem is also structural as their current resource utilisation pattern does not contain alternatives to imported crude. Furthermore, in a situation of unabated rise in oil prices, like now, the problem tends to get compounded.

Does this mean that high oil prices are making India's trade deficit unsustainable? Are there other structural factors contributing as well? A closer look at the recent BOP numbers reveals the following:

1. India's exports increased from US $128.1 billion in 2006–7 to US $158.5 billion in 2007–8. This year-on-year increase of US $30.4 billion was superceded by imports, which increased by as much as US $57.2 billion from US $191.3 billion in 2006–7 to US $248.5 billion in 2007–8. The sharp rise in imports impacted the final size of the trade deficit.
2. One of the possible reasons behind a progressively-widening trade deficit could be a decline in exports accompanied by an increase in imports. But this has not been so in India's case. Exports grew by 23.7 per cent in 2007–8, which was higher than their growth of 21.8 per cent in 2006–7. But the import growth of 29.9 per cent in 2007–8 was far higher than the 21.8 per cent growth in the previous year. So the rise in trade deficit can be attributed to a much faster rise in imports compared with exports.
3. What are the reasons behind the rapid rise in imports? Imports can be divided into two broad groups: oil and non-oil. The BOP statistics do not disaggregate oil imports as a separate category. According to the data made available by the Directorate General of Commercial Intelligence and Statistics of the Ministry

of Commerce, India's oil imports during 2007–8 were US $77.04 billion. This represented an increase of 35.3 per cent over US $56.9 billion in the previous year. Further, the year-on-year growth in oil imports in 2007–8 was higher than the growth of 30 per cent in 2006–7. In sharp contrast, non-oil imports, despite growing at a higher rate of 23.5 per cent in 2007–8, compared with 22.2 per cent in 2006–7, show a much lower rate of growth than oil imports. There is no doubt that high growth in oil imports has been the main factor behind the sharp rise in imports.

4. It's common knowledge that global crude prices are rising at an unprecedented rate. The prices have substantially inflated India's import bill. India's crude imports comprise a basket of three varieties—Brent, Dubai and Oman. Given the composition, even if one among the three experiences sharp increases in prices, the overall price of the basket does not get affected by the same extent. But during last year, all the three crude varieties saw their prices rising fast. The average price of the Indian basket varied between US $65.5 and US $99.8 per barrel, yielding an average price of US $79.5 per barrel for the year. This was a steep jump *vis-à-vis* US $62.5 per barrel in 2006–7. Interestingly, the volume of oil imports experienced a lower growth of 11.8 per cent in 2007–8 *vis-à-vis* 14.5 per cent in 2006–7. Thus, the increase in oil imports was primarily value-driven and not volume-driven.
5. Excluding gold and silver, among other non-oil imports, capital goods registered the fastest growth in 2007–8. Edible oil, fertilizers, iron and steel, chemicals, textile and coal were the other leading imports. It must be noted that along with crude oil, global prices of most of these imports too have gone up. Thus, the impact of the world commodity price boom has been felt across the board by Indian imports.

High crude prices, therefore, have been the main determinants of India's rising trade deficit. Given India's chronic dependence on oil imports, with the latter accounting for almost one-third of the country's total imports, the Indian economy's import bill and trade balance will continue to remain sensitive to movements in world oil prices. With global crude prices inching close to US $150 per barrel, the import bill and trade deficit are likely to increase further. Data for the first two months of 2008–9 clearly shows this happening. During April–May 2008, oil imports amounted to US $16.5 billion, showing a 48.5 per cent increase over US $11.1 billion during April–May 2007. The trade deficit has also increased to US $20.6 billion during April–May 2008, whereas it was only at US $13.9 billion during April–May 2007.

Assuming that oil prices will continue to rise in the near future, will the trade deficit become unsustainable? This depends on the Indian economy's capacity to finance the deficit. The high trade deficit has resulted in an increase in the current account deficit as well. From 1.1 per cent of GDP in 2006–7, the current account deficit has increased to 1.5 per cent of GDP in 2007–8. However, the balance of payments is yet to come under stress, due to a healthy capital account surplus. The current account deficit of US $17.4 billion in 2007–8 was more than compensated by a capital account surplus of US $108 billion. The result was net addition of more than US $90 billion to India's foreign exchange reserves, which have now risen to more than US $300 billion.

If capital flows continue to remain as robust as they were in 2007–8, then despite widening, the trade deficit will continue to be financed and is unlikely to create any adverse impact on the BOP. Sustaining the deficit should not be a problem even if it increases to much higher levels. The only downside risk that can be perceived is a reversal in the direction of short-term capital flows. India's large capital account surplus in 2007–8 had much to do with heavy portfolio investment inflows. However, latest trends suggest that the capital market is passing through a relatively bearish phase and foreign institutional investor (FII) inflows have significantly moderated. This, however, might be a temporary phase, with the flows reacting to alignments among global foreign exchange markets. A more stable outlook following adjustment of inflationary expectations can very well see resumption in FII investment.

As of now, notwithstanding India's chronic dependence on oil imports and the fact that such imports underline a structural deficiency in India's natural resource utilisation pattern, the economy looks capable of managing the trade deficit. Notwithstanding the prospect of oil prices zooming to untouched highs!

53

Pakistan's New Trade Policy Initiatives: Implications for India and Pakistan

IFTIKHAR A. LODHI

(*30 July 2008*)

IN A SIGNIFICANT policy shift, Pakistan has opened its doors to Indian investments and imports. As a result, India could become Pakistan's second largest trading partner after China at the end of this fiscal year.[1] The landmark directional change could have long-term political implications for the two nuclear rivals and the South Asian region.

The new trade policy, announced by the Pakistan Peoples Party (PPP)-led coalition government on 18 July 2008, sets a US $22 billion export target, up from the achieved target of US $19.2 billion last year, reflecting a 13 per cent growth. However, the government has sidestepped the question of soaring trade deficit that reached US $20.7 billion last year.[2] Nevertheless, it did emphasise increasing exports and diversifying export products as well as markets.[3]

The Pakistan government, recognising structural problems in export growth, plans to increase the country's competitiveness by removing bureaucratic bottlenecks, increasing market intelligence, establishing a Trade Dispute Settlement Organization and special economic zones, improving infrastructure and building capacity, instead of providing subsidies. It will also provide tax and duty exemptions on all inputs for exports, including machinery under the Duty and Tax Remission Export (DTRE) scheme. On the diplomatic front, it has also decided to participate in re-negotiations on the South Asian Free Trade Agreement and the Regional Agreement on Trade in Services among the South Asian Association for Regional Cooperation countries.

India-Specific Measures

The new trade policy of the Pakistan government allows Indian investors to establish compressed natural gas (CNG) bus manufacturing units in the country. It also allows imports of 10 CNG buses as test consignments from each manufacturer committed to investing in Pakistan. Islamabad has also enlarged the positive list of items by including another 136 commodities. Now, a total of 1,938 items can be imported from India. These include mining and agriculture machinery, stainless steel, cotton yarn, books and petroleum products, among other raw materials and capital goods. More significantly, virtually any product, whether it is on the positive list or not, can be imported from India under the DTRE scheme.

Although Pakistan has a more liberal trade and investment policy *vis-à-vis* India, both countries systematically restrict cross-border investments and trade through tariff and non-tariff barriers. Economic relations between the two south Asian neighbours have been mired by political conflict, particularly the territorial dispute over Kashmir. While India has accorded Pakistan the Most-Favored Nation (MFN) status, maintaining a negative list of items, Pakistan has declined to extend the MFN status to India, maintaining a positive list of items. However, there now seems a directional shift in Islamabad. Pakistan's commerce minister, Ahmed Mukhtar, while talking to press reporters after announcing the new trade policy, hinted at according India MFN status, provided 'India removes tariff and non-tariff trade barriers inhibiting Pakistani exports to India'.

Economic and Political Implications

Official trade between the two countries has increased manifold in the recent past, reaching US $2 billion in 2008, while estimates suggest a three times higher unofficial trade. However, the trade balance remains substantially in favour of India which has a trade surplus of about US $1 billion. With the new policy of allowing entry to Indian imports, the trade volume between the two countries is expected to double. Nevertheless, Pakistani exports to India are less likely to increase unless India lowers trade barriers. Pakistan's trade deficit with India is, therefore, expected to double.

The 'India-centric' trade policy stirred a storm in Pakistan. While the conservatives accused the PPP of giving into India, more serious criticism came from policy experts and business lobbyists who seem to be wary of the 'Indian tilt' in the new policy. Their criticism stems for their concern over the growing trade imbalance and the threat to Pakistan's domestic industry. The fact, however, is that Pakistan has a trade imbalance with all its major trading partners, not just India. Furthermore, if the domestic industry is threatened by cheap Indian imports, it would also be the case with cheap Chinese imports that have flooded Pakistan's market. Why should India then be viewed and treated differently? The answer lies in politics rather than economics. Rather than resisting Indian imports, perhaps Pakistan should look towards enhancing the competitiveness of its domestic production (and exports) while constantly ensuring its comparative advantage.

Despite the fact that India stands to gain more, the new trade policy undoubtedly holds promise for Pakistan as well. Most capital and intermediary goods that Pakistan imports from other countries are relatively cheaper to acquire from India. In addition, the transport cost is much lower. Pakistan stands to save about 15 to 30 per cent in cost by importing from India, according to a study published by the State Bank of Pakistan two years ago. This would help Pakistani manufacturers cut down the cost of production and enhance the competitiveness of their exports. A case in point is India's flourishing petroleum products industry, which has the potential to become Asia's largest refining industry. Pakistan would be better off by tapping into the Indian petroleum industry and saving payments on its soaring petroleum import bill. The price differential will also certainly offset some of the feared trade imbalance.

Cold Shoulder from India

However, New Delhi, overwhelmed by political and security concerns, has failed to appreciate these major steps by the new democratic government in Islamabad. India's Foreign Secretary, Shivshankar Menon, avoided any comments when asked about Islamabad's initiatives during a press briefing at the end of the first day of the fifth round of Pakistan–India Composite Dialogue held in New Delhi on 21 July 2008. The lack of any response from the Indian side seems to convey the message to Islamabad that, unless India's security concerns are taken seriously, it would not be impressed by the economic opportunities available.

According to the Indian foreign secretary, the dialogue was happening at a 'difficult time' and 'several events have vitiated the atmosphere between India and Pakistan'. He was referring to the suicide attack on the Indian embassy in Kabul on 7 July 2008 and the recent uprising in Indian-administered Kashmir. India has accused Islamabad of 'incitement to violence' in Indian Kashmir and the Inter Services Intelligence (ISI) agency of Pakistan for the attacks in Kabul. Unlike the national security advisor, M.K. Narayanan, the Indian foreign secretary avoided directly accusing the ISI but he echoed a similar view by referring to 'elements in Pakistan' for being responsible for the violence. Another reason for the lukewarm response from India could be that Prime Minister Manmohan Singh's UPA government was pre-occupied with the more pressing issue of its own political survival, after having to go for a trust vote following the withdrawal of its Left partners over the United States–India nuclear deal issue.

Opportunities Ahead?

In a relevant development, Islamabad has reportedly invited at least three Indian companies (Tata, Reliance and Essar) to a meeting of potential investors in the power sector to discuss the development of the Thar Coal Power Project. Pakistan has been planning to use its enormous 175 billion tons of coal reserves in Thar (the Sindh province) for power generation.

There is no denying that an integrated economy will have a trust dividend, currently lacking so much in Islamabad and New Delhi. If political will and economic rationale prevail, there are enormous possibilities for the two countries. For example, Pakistan, by successfully wooing Indian investors in the Thar power project or some other projects of strategic importance, could win sympathies of influential lobbyists in India. Perhaps an effective way to create interest groups in both countries is to engage in private sector joint ventures. Also, some of the projects (and groups) may reduce tensions between the two countries over Afghanistan by catering to the Afghanistan and Central Asian markets. Similarly, public sector joint ventures will definitely carry the integration process a step forward. A case in point is the Iran–Pakistan–India gas pipeline and a potential India–Pakistan petroleum pipeline.

Thus far, the elite in Pakistan and India have long kept their people and economy hostage to their own aspirations and prejudices. There are no breakthroughs and short-cut solutions to the decade-old problems. However, maintaining the tempo of the dialogue, slow and steady economic cooperation, and a gradual increase in people-to-people contact certainly point to a bright and prosperous future for the region.

NOTES

1. Pakistan's fiscal year is from July to June.
2. The policy does not give any import projections, citing the uncertainty in the international and domestic market. The total imports in the last fiscal year were US $9.4 billion higher than the targets, giving rise to a trade deficit of US $20.7 billion. Almost 70 per cent of this increase was due to high oil and food prices and a shortfall in cotton crop.
3. This would be done by incentivising leather, sports, surgical instruments, pharmaceutical items, jewellery and processed food products, and by reaching new markets of Latin America, Africa and Eastern Europe. Presently, the textile group (bed wear and apparel) constitutes two-thirds of total exports, with half of the total exports destined for only seven countries (the United States, Germany, Japan, the United Kingdom, Hong Kong, United Arab Emirates and Saudi Arabia).

54

It is Getting More Difficult to Do Business in South Asia

AMITENDU PALIT

(*15 September 2008*)

THE WORLD BANK released its latest 'doing business' rankings (2009) for 181 countries on 10 September 2008. The results reflect South Asia in a rather poor light. Not a single South Asian country figures among top business 'reformers' for 2008. What is more worrisome is that, except for Sri Lanka, individual rankings of all economies from the region have declined in year 2009, compared to 2008.

The 'doing business' rankings have been published annually for the last six years. These rankings order countries according to the ease with which investors can do business. The rank of a particular country changes every year, depending upon the reforms that it undertakes (or does not) for facilitating business. The rankings are determined on the basis of scores obtained in several indicators. Each of these indicators reflects important steps in starting, operating, sustaining and closing businesses. The indicators include the time taken to start a venture, ease with which workers can be employed and retrenched, protection available to shareholders, enforceability of contracts, procedures involved in registering property and obtaining credit, ease with which operations can be wound up, etc. Improvements in each of these indicators through policy reforms resulting in simpler procedures and less time influence overall scores and ranking in a positive manner. There are occasions when improvements in one indicator are accompanied by deteriorations elsewhere. The final impact on scores and ranks are determined by the net gains or losses achieved.

No South Asian country figures among the top 50 out of the

181 economies ranked by the World Bank. Maldives (69) has the highest global ranking in South Asia. Apart from Maldives, Pakistan (77) is the only other South Asian country to figure among the top 100. Sri Lanka (102), Bangladesh (110), Nepal (121), India (122), Bhutan (124) and Afghanistan (162) follow thereafter. The average global rank of a South Asian economy is 111.[1] This is better than only Sub-Saharan Africa, which has a global rank of 138, and is worse than all other regions of the world. Clearly, South Asia is lagging far behind other regions in introducing reforms that can make it a better place for doing business.

How do the South Asian economies fare in different business indicators? Table 1 provides a snapshot of the global rankings of South Asian countries in different indicators.

Table 1 reveals a complex scenario marked by sharp contrasts. Different economies from the region have contrasting situations in different parameters. Afghanistan, for example, has the highest rank in the region in starting a business. Kicking off a venture involves only four procedures in Afghanistan and can be done in nine days. Doing the same in India involves 13 procedures and 30 days. Interestingly, more procedures do not necessarily imply more days or vice versa. In Bangladesh, starting a business involves seven procedures but requires 73 days, while in Sri Lanka it takes 38 days for four procedures. In contrast, in Pakistan, 11 procedures get completed in only 24 days.

The four large economies from the region—India, Pakistan, Sri Lanka and Bangladesh—share some common problems in doing business. These are labour and land market inflexibilities, persistence of licenses, irrational tax structures and poor contract enforcement. Inflexible labour laws make both hiring and firing difficult for employers in all four countries. These are reflected in the ranks for employing workers (Table 1), which are particularly low for Pakistan and Bangladesh. Opaque procedures result in heavy costs of property registrations in all these four economies. In Bangladesh[2] and India, such costs are reported to be as much as 10.35 per cent and 7.49 per cent of the total value of property, while they are slightly lower at 5.11 and 5.29 per cent in Sri Lanka and Pakistan respectively. Poor ranks in dealing with licenses

Table 1: Rankings of South Asian Economies in 'Doing Business' Indicators for 2009

	India	Pakistan	Bangladesh	Sri Lanka	Nepal	Bhutan	Maldives	Afghanistan
Starting a business	121	77	90	29	73	63	38	22
Dealing with licenses	136	93	114	161	129	116	8	140
Employing workers	89	136	132	110	150	13	4	30
Registering property	105	97	175	141	28	38	177	174
Getting credit	28	59	59	68	109	172	145	178
Protecting investors	38	24	18	70	70	126	70	181
Paying taxes	169	124	90	164	107	82	1	49
Trading across borders	90	71	105	66	157	151	121	179
Enforcing contracts	180	154	178	135	121	37	90	160
Closing a business	140	53	106	43	103	181	123	181

Source: http://www.doingbusiness.org

(Table 1) underline the proliferation of multiple construction permits in all the four countries. The number of such permits and time taken to obtain them are quite similar in India (20 in 224 days), Pakistan (12 in 223 days), Bangladesh (14 in 231 days) and Sri Lanka (21 in 214 days).

Tax structures continue to create problems for businesses in South Asia. Pakistan has the lowest effective tax rate of 29 per cent (as a proportion of total profits) among the four economies, which is as high as 72 per cent in India. But it takes a total of 560 hours (more than 23 days) to pay up all taxes in Pakistan, which is more than double of 256 hours (10.5 days) that it takes in Bangladesh. In this regard, Bangladesh has emerged more efficient than India (11.2 days) and Sri Lanka (12.6 days). Finally, contract enforcement remains a serious concern for all the four economies. India and Bangladesh are the worst performers with enforcement requiring almost four years in both. Pakistan has been able to bring this down to 2.6 years, while for Sri Lanka it is 3.6 years.[3]

There are two aspects where the major South Asian economies have performed reasonably better. First is access to credit. Information about credit, its availability and legal rights of creditors have improved and are now much better in the South Asian economies compared to several other developing countries. India's banking reforms seem to have paid particular dividends as it scores higher than Pakistan, Bangladesh and Sri Lanka[4] in the credit indicator. The second aspect is investor protection. This essentially pertains to some fundamental corporate governance reforms entrenching rights of shareholders and protection of retail investors. Both Pakistan and Bangladesh have done commendably in this respect, followed by India. Sri Lanka is still some distance behind the rest.

The 'doing business' rankings appear to confirm the impression that South Asia remains a relatively difficult place for doing business. This is not to suggest that South Asian economies are not reforming at all. But the pace of their reforms seems to be much slower than those in other parts of the world. There are also some critical segments where reforms appear to have got stuck. These include land and labour markets. While capital market reforms appear to be on track, land and labour market measures are lagging behind. Heavy transaction costs associated with land and labour market inflexibilities are overweighing gains achieved from capital market reforms. These costs are increasing further due to regressive tax structures and poor enforceability. The fact that most South Asian economies have gone down in the latest rankings shows that the region has not endeared itself to investors.

The business outlook of South Asia depends significantly on India, the largest economy of the region. India is ranked below all in the region except Bhutan and Afghanistan. The 'doing business' report highlights only one major reform by India last year. This was the introduction of electronic data interchange for facilitating exports. But the lack of reforms elsewhere in the Indian economy for reducing transaction costs is surprising. Compared to Pakistan, Sri Lanka, Bangladesh and Nepal, India did not witness political turmoil or instability last year that could have deterred reforms. While the Left might have held up banking, insurance and pension reforms, much has not happened even after the departure of Left. The more difficult reforms such as privatisation, subsidies, land and labour markets, and contract enforcement have been left untouched for long. Though some of these require states to be active, the lack of coordinated efforts is disappointing. The inability to cut business costs can damage India's reputation of being one of the most attractive emerging markets for foreign direct investments (FDI). Strong reforms for improving business climate will not only 'pull' more FDI, but will set examples for the rest of the region and improve the regional outlook.

NOTES

1. The average ranking improves to 104 if Afghanistan is excluded.
2. Bangladesh has been able to reduce the time taken for registering property from 425 days to 245 days.
3. Bhutan has taken a significant step of creating a Land Commission to look into property disputes. This is expected to reduce time for contract enforcement by about 50 days.
4. The new Companies Act introduced by Sri Lanka is expected to significantly improve the legal rights of creditors.

55

Crisis in the United States Markets and Consequences for the Indian Markets

S. NARAYAN

(*16 September 2008*)

THE DECISION of the United States Treasury not to guarantee the debts or the bailout of Lehman Brothers, one of the four major investment banks in the United States, resulted in the institution going into bankruptcy yesterday. Merrill Lynch, whose share value has halved in the last few weeks, has merged with Bank of America, to ward off a similar fate. And next in line could well be AIG, another major international finance company. The total write-down in the United States alone, since the credit crisis began, exceeds US $500 billion, with possibly as much more to come.

It is interesting to examine the policy responses to the crisis in the United States and elsewhere, and to draw some conclusions on the likely future of financial markets policies in India. The origins of the crisis and the initial consequences are well known and do not need repetition. It is the policy response of the governments that bears some scrutiny. The first bank to be affected was Northern Rock in the United Kingdom. Over two days, the Bank of England did not come up with funds to bailout the liquidity crisis in Northern Rock and the bank collapsed. After a week, Northern Bank was taken over by the Bank of England, which changed the management, appointed an oversight committee and provided access to sovereign funds (actually public funds). When the Bank of England was criticised for the initial delay, it clarified that, after parliamentary amendments in 1999, the Bank of England was responsible primarily for inflation targeting and that it was not its domain to enter into the management of individual banks. Clearly, the subsequent turnaround was dictated by public outcry and the concerns in the British government about the fallouts of similar bank implosions. In effect, there appears to be an unstated commitment in the United Kingdom that retail banks would not be allowed to fail, a commitment to the depositors and the creditors, though not necessarily to the shareholders.

In the European Union, the crisis in the UBS and Deutsche Bank was handled by the banks themselves, through fresh infusion of equity, without any government guarantees or support.[1]

It is in the United States that there has been a gradual evolution of the government's response to the crisis. As long as the damage was limited to retail housing markets, regulators were willing to allow the markets to function in that the initial losses were borne by the creditors and the mortgage banks. The secondary effects in the financial system arose out of the instruments that these mortgages had generated, and that were being traded by the large investment banks. As the underlying assets collapsed, so did the value of these instruments, and the first major institution to be affected was Bear Stearns. Over a weekend, the United States Fed and the Treasury negotiated a bailout through J.P. Morgan. A financial special purpose vehicle was created, into which the Fed transferred funds.[2] J.P. Morgan used these funds to buy out Bear Stearns; the shareholders were punished, and got only around US $4 a share.[3]

The second major intervention happened last week. Freddie Mac and Frannie Mae, the two largest mortgage finance companies, with over US $1 trillion in debt, were formally taken over by the United States government, who provided a US $100 billion credit line, changed the management, and assumed control. The argument was that these were government-backed entities in the first instance and that their collapse would lead to large scale effects in the financial system. The next to go was Lehman Brothers, whose shares fell from over US $80 last year to around US $4 last week. In the case of Lehman Brothers, the Treasury and the Fed have categorically refused to provide any government guarantees and the bank had to file for bankruptcy.

One sees a lack of coherence in the Treasury policy here, among the different approaches to the crisis adopted in the last one year. It is easy to understand that, initially, given free market considerations, the United States government was reluctant to intervene. It is possible to argue that the Bear Stearns rescue was characterised by its timing. Northern Rock had just collapsed, and non-intervention was being criticised; there were implosions in Europe, and the domino effects in the United States were not fully known. In some sense, it was a quick pragmatic reaction to provide a safety net for the creditors and the depositors. In the case of Freddie Mac and Frannie Mae, it could be argued that the government had an inherent responsibility, having encouraged these institutions in the first instance. In the latest case, it is possible that the Treasury decided that it could go down the road of supporting or bailing out all the affected banks and that the market must indeed find its own solutions. In the forthcoming weeks, these will have some profound influences on the Asian scene.

Free market and state intervention concepts need certainly to be revised. It is clear that, even in the most open of economies, the need to intervene, on behalf of the larger citizenry, becomes both an economic as well as a political necessity. The state exists for the well-being of its citizens; any aberration that significantly affects that welfare and well-being needs to be corrected and cannot be left to the market forces alone. This single lesson would be drawn by many countries, some, like India, to justify continued interventions and regulation, and others, to arm themselves for intervention.

The distinction is likely to be in the transparency of the decision-making process. In all the examples cited earlier, the scene has been played out in full public view, with the stock markets factoring in each development. On the other hand, in Asia, there is still opacity about the extent of damage to the financial institutions and the banks as a result of this meltdown. Little is known about the losses suffered by Indian and Singapore banks[4] or about the damage to banks in China and Japan. This lack of transparency would, at one extreme, distort asset values, with share prices not reflecting the true nature of the stressed assets, while, at the other end providing leverage to governments to intervene ad hoc without explanation. One is arguing here that in many senses, the governments in South Asia could well see these events as a license to intervene in institutions at will and also to regulate them at will. As an example, the moves of the Reserve Bank of India (RBI) to control non-banking financial companies and the bill to regulate microcredit enterprises come to mind. In India, certainly, one is likely to see greater regulatory oversight in insurance, financial markets, commodity exchanges and in the RBI. As a consequence, it is possible that policy reforms are continuously hedged in by regulations and processes.

The next question relates to the category of participants to be protected. In the instances so far, there has been an attempt to protect the depositors and the creditors, but the shareholders have had to take the brunt of the asset losses. The picture would be somewhat different in the South Asian countries in a similar scenario. It is likely that the shareholders, being small investors and public sector banks, get some protection as well. The actual creators of the crisis, the investment managers and chief executive officers, who put together most of the instruments, have gotten away quite free so far: it is likely that regulations may change to bring them to account as well.

Indian Markets Cannot be Isolated from these Considerations

Currently, there are two reports on financial sector reforms that are under consideration in India—the High Power Expert Committee (Percy Mistry) report on making Mumbai an international financial centre, and the Committee on Financial Sector Reforms under the chairmanship of Raghuram Rajan. Both the reports advocate faster reforms in the financial sector, capital account convertibility, and a restriction of the RBI's role to inflation targeting. Equally, there are critics of this approach,[5] who argue that inflation targeting in India is unlikely to be effective or to guard against a balance of payment crisis. These critics argue on behalf of a more gradual approach and feel that there is little advantage to be had by rushing in.

Financial sector reforms meet with relatively little political resistance and are, thus, easy to push through and, in India, the financial sector represents crucial command over resources. In particular, indigenous industry seeking creation of equity capital would be keen on an open architecture that enables it to access debt and equity globally—a demand that suits the advocates of the open architecture.

In the circumstances, the progress in the financial sector in India is likely to be mixed. The new Governor of the RBI is a mature economist, a reformer who would read the reports carefully, but would be guided by objectivity. One could expect some of the recommendations of the committee reports to be followed through, but not the more major ones on inflation targeting and capital account convertibility. At the same time, it is likely that the RBI's and the government's oversight over the financial institutions may actually increase, as also result in a greater caution on the part of regulators on new instruments. It is likely that even some of the bolder reform pronouncements from the government get hedged in by regulatory processes during implementation. There would be a significant effort to ensure that the United States-like situation does not replicate in the Indian institutions. The new initiatives at the Securities and Exchange Board of India (SEBI) are likely to lead to greater transparency and accountability, and to keep the small investor in mind.

The markets, of course, are likely to be guided by global concerns and are likely to be quite soft. Foreign institutional investors, having already exited to the tune of nearly US $10 billion, are unlikely to stay invested in India except for short spells. The activity, therefore, could be in the new instruments introduced by the SEBI, rather than in secondary markets directly.

The growth story, supported by domestic demand and infrastructure investment, is still robust, but the impact of the global slow-down will continue to be felt, most importantly, in the financial markets.

NOTES

1. Interestingly, Northern Rock, UBS and Deutsche Bank are still to come out of the woods even after a year, with negative returns for the investors so far.
2. The exact amount is not public knowledge, but estimates place it around US $20 billion.
3. Bear Stearns is not doing well either.
4. This is estimated to be around US $4 billion and US $1 billion respectively so far.
5. See D.M. Nachane, 'Committee on Financial Sector Reforms: A Critique', *Economic and Political Weekly*, 9 August 2008.

56

Global Economic Slow-down: Can Bangladesh Remain Resilient?

M. SHAHIDUL ISLAM

(25 November 2008)

THE FINANCIAL crisis that originated in the United States and Europe is now hurting the real economies, and the crisis has spread to most parts of the world. Virtually no country has been spared from the shock, apart from countries such as Zimbabwe and Myanmar which are highly isolated from the global economy. Many developing countries, including Pakistan, have had to seek the International Monetary Fund (IMF) bailout to weather the external shocks. The Bangladesh economy, which is moderately integrated[1] with rest of the world, has shown significant resilience in the wake of the global economic crisis. The country's key macroeconomic and financial variables, particularly gross domestic product (GDP) growth, balance of payment, broad money, credit growth, exchange rate, remittances and foreign exchange reserves, registered either a positive growth or showed minimal fluctuations in recent months *vis-à-vis* the preceding period. Nevertheless, the economy still faces a double-digit inflation.

This brief looks at Bangladesh's ability to weather the global economic slow-down. At the same time, it assesses the ability of the economy to maintain its growth momentum in the face of external shocks.

In some ways, the financial crisis has been a boon for the Bangladesh economy. First, let us look at the impact of the financial crisis on commodity prices and inflation. Following the financial crisis, the fall in actual demand and market speculations have lowered commodity prices. Since the Bangladesh economy depends on external markets for many food and non-food commodities, the imported inflation has been declining in the country, albeit not at a dramatic pace. The price difference of commodities between the international and domestic market remains high due to the sticky nature of prices. The point-to-point inflation that reached 11.59 per cent in December 2007 came down to 10.19 per cent in September 2008.[2]

The external shocks generally emanate through equity markets and trade channels that are being captured broadly in a country's current account balance. As foreign equity investment accounted for only 3 to 4 per cent of market capitalisation, the shocks through the stock markets in Bangladesh have been limited. The index in Dhaka Stock Exchange, the country's major bourse, declined 12.62 per cent in November 2008, compared to June 2008.[3] As the major Asian bourses are in a free fall, the money is moving to the United States in search of a safe haven. Nevertheless, some funds are now looking for opportunities in economies such as Bangladesh which have shown less volatility in the wake of the financial crisis and offer growth potentials. For instance, Sweden's largest hedge fund manager, Brummer & Partners, plans to grow the fund in Bangladesh by about US $500 million in the next five years, from its current US $53 million.[4]

The Bangladeshi banks and other financial institutions had limited exposure to banks and investment firms in the United States and Europe. As a result, the country's banking sector is largely insulated from the banking sector troubles in the West. Nevertheless, these also show that Bangladesh's financial sector is still highly autarkic.

Bangladesh's external sector has maintained a positive growth when most economies have experienced a contraction of trade and of other sub-sectors in their current accounts. The growth in Bangladesh's imports and exports has been positive. The textile and readymade garments (RMG) sector which drives the country's exports has not, to-date, been affected by the recessions in the United States and Europe. This is reflected by the fact that knitwear garments received roughly 12 per cent higher export orders in October 2008 than in the corresponding period last year.[5] The textile and the RMG sector grew by 42.9 per cent in August 2008 *vis-à-vis* the corresponding period last year.[6]

The current economic crisis in the United States has increased the demand for Wal-Mart products as consumers switch from high-end fashioned clothes to low-end apparels. Wal-Mart, one of the world's largest retail shops, procures roughly US $1.7 billion worth of apparel products from Bangladesh every year.[7] Bangladesh's labour cost is one of the lowest in the world. Similarly, IKEA, a Sweden-based international home products retailer, plans to raise its purchases from Bangladesh, mainly home textiles.[8] It is expected that demand for Bangladesh's RMG is not likely to fall, if not increase, during this downturn period, owing to the 'Wal-Mart' effect.

Wage earners' remittances, which are the second most important foreign exchange earners in Bangladesh, registered 17.34 per cent growth in October 2008, compared to the corresponding period last year.[9] As a result, the country's current account posted a surplus worth of US $672 million in FY 2007–8, and it is projected that it will maintain a surplus, though by a relatively lower margin, in the period on July–August 2008–9.[10] The reason for this is that Bangladesh's import payments have registered a much higher growth than exports in recent months. As a result, its foreign exchange reserves reached US $5,095.57 million on 18 November 2008, which was slightly higher than the corresponding period last year, though it reached US $6,148.82 million in June 2008.[11]

The strength in the current account balance and foreign exchange reserves are reflected in the country's exchange rate which faces virtually no pressure unlike many of its South Asian neighbours. In recent months, most South Asian currencies, particularly the Indian rupee and the Pakistani rupee, have witnessed a free fall, whereas the Bangladesh taka has remained stable against the United States dollar, and it has experienced modest to significant appreciations *vis-à-vis* some major currencies, including the euro, the pound sterling and the Singapore dollar.

Further, as the oil and other commodity prices have declined significantly, the authorities in Bangladesh are under less pressure to continue accommodative monetary policies and expansionary fiscal measures so that the economy maintains the target GDP growth without worsening its inflation. According to the Bangladesh Bank, the central bank of the country, the Bangladesh economy grew at 6.63 per cent, 6.51 per cent and 6.20 per cent respectively in FY 2005–6, FY 2006–7 and FY 2007–8.[12] The same source projects that the economy will grow at 6.50 per cent in 2008–9, while the IMF, Citigroup and the Economist Intelligence Unit's forecasts have shown that the country's GDP growth will slow down to 5.5 per cent, 5.7 per cent, and 5.5 per cent respectively.[13]

Can Bangladesh Remain Resilient?

The above data and analysis show that Bangladesh has been coping well with the current global economic crisis. The question is whether the economy will be able to maintain its growth momentum in the coming months. What are the downside risks for Bangladesh?

As the financial crisis turns into an economic shock, the Bangladeshi economy's resilience will depend on a few factors.

The first factor is the outlook of the country's export sector. Bangladesh exports low-end labour-intensive manufacturing products and they are mostly related to people's basic needs such as apparel, frozen food and pharmaceuticals. A significant demand contraction for these products is less likely.

Second, the vulnerability in the country's current account will also depend on the inward flow of remittances. The lion's share of its remittances comes from the Middle East, followed by the United States. It is expected that the flows of remittances from the United States will slow-down. However, the pace of inflows from the Middle East will depend on the stabilisation of crude oil prices. If China implements its new stimulus package and developing Asia maintains its growth momentum, the current oil price drop may see a trend reversal. Even if oil prices consolidate to below the US $50 mark, it would help Bangladesh's balance of payments, as import payments are also expected to fall in line with the drop in oil price.

However, the Bangladesh Bank should monitor the country's exchange rate movements. As its major export competitors experience a sharp drop in the value of their currencies, a significant appreciation in the Bangladesh taka may erode the country's competitiveness to some extent, though it must be noted that the exchange rate is not the sole determinant of a country's export competitiveness. Further, though the currency appreciation is not highly inelastic to remittances, significant appreciations in the Bangladesh taka could affect the remittance flows moderately.

The domestic factors concerning the downside risks of Bangladesh's growth are no less important than the external dynamics. Natural calamities and political unrests are the two critical issues that could destabilise the growth. If a new democratic government takes over in early 2009 following the parliament elections, the political uncertainties could contract significantly. If so, the country could receive sizeable foreign direct investment (FDI) flows—these are currently very low. FDI projects that are in the pipeline also seek a stable political environment in the country.

Natural disasters that often cause crop failure and infrastructure damage in Bangladesh are persistent risks and these are very difficult to predict.

Private consumption is the main driver of growth in Bangladesh. As long as the global economic crisis does not deteriorate further, it is very likely that Bangladesh will remain resilient and will be able to maintain a 6 per cent GDP growth rate in the short-run.

Bangladesh's resilience and some South Asian economies' vulnerability in the wake of ongoing economic shocks are hardly surprising. The country has one of the highest trade-GDP ratios in the region and it remains a low-cost producer of low-end manufacturing output. Its financial system is rather protected through various measures. As a result, the economy has blissfully avoided the shock that has emanated through the global equity markets. External shocks that originate through trade, remittances and other components of current account are generally less vulnerable and take substantially longer time to have an impact. Moreover, policy makers get enough room to fine-tune macroeconomic variables to weather the current account shocks.

NOTES

1. One of the determinants of an economy's integration with the rest of the world is Trade-GDP ratio. For Bangladesh, the ratio is 45 per cent (World Trade Organization, available at http://stat.wto.org/Country Profile/WSDBCountryPFView.aspx?Language=E&Country=BD, accessed on 20 November 2008. Moreover, millions of Bangladeshis work abroad, and the remittances are the second most important determinants of the country's current account after trade.
2. Governor Secretariat, Bangladesh Bank, Dhaka, 19 November 2008.
3. AT Capital Weekly Update, Asian Tiger Capital Partners, Dhaka, 16 November 2008.
4. www.bloomberg.com, accessed on 19 November 2008.
5. AT Capital Weekly Update, Asian Tiger Capital Partners, Dhaka, 16 November 2008.
6. Ibid.
7. http://www.tg-supply.com/article/view.html?id=26524, accessed on 20 November 2008.
8. *The Daily Star*, 20 November 2008.
9. Governor Secretariat, Bangladesh Bank, Dhaka, 19 November 2008.
10. Ibid.
11. Ibid.
12. Ibid.
13. AT Capital Weekly Update, Asian Tiger Capital Partners, Dhaka, 16 November 2008, and Economist Intelligence Unit.

SECTION III

REGIONAL AND INTERNATIONAL RELATIONS

A. South Asian Regionalism

57

India–Pakistan Composite Dialogue: Towards a 'Grand Reconciliation'?

S.D. MUNI

(*26 May 2008*)

THE MESSAGE emanating from Islamabad after two days (20 and 21 May 2008) of meeting between foreign ministers and foreign secretaries of India and Pakistan to review the 'composite dialogue' and the 'peace process' between the two adversarial South Asian neighbours appears to be reassuring, at least on the face of it. Pakistan's foreign minister, Makhdoom Shah Mehmood Qureshi, assured that a 'grand reconciliation in resolving all outstanding issues' was Pakistan's promise, adding that 'we are ready to solve all the issues with self-respect and dignity for peace, stability and the development of the region'. Endorsing the sentiments of his hosts, the Indian foreign minister, Pranab Mukherjee, said: 'I found a strong willingness and desire on Pakistani side towards full normalisation of relations. . . . Secure, stable and prosperous India and Pakistan are in our mutual interest and good for our relations.'

One concrete basis of this optimism can be seen in the reiteration of the principal that while conflictual issues are being tackled, the two sides will continue to build on convergences and agreed areas of cooperation. The Indian side has been consistently pursuing this principal by repeatedly referring to the pattern of the Sino–Indian normalisation process where the unresolved border dispute, which, at times, becomes acrimonious, has not been allowed to come in the way of advancing cooperation and understanding in the areas of trade, commerce, investments, cultural contacts and international issues of mutual concern. The Pakistani side accepted that economic cooperation and conflictual issues, particularly the 'core issue of Kashmir', were mutually complementary and progress in one can positively influence the progress in another. Foreign Minister Qureshi said: 'Core issues will remain but talks will continue. The Line of Control (LOC) ceasefire is still in place and the peace process is back on the track.' One can also interpret it negatively, meaning that if no progress is made on the Kashmir issue, economic co-operation and mutual confidence building will also suffer.

Confidence-building Measures across the Line of Control

To keep up the momentum of cooperation and confidence-building, especially across the LOC, the two sides agreed to increase the frequency of the movement of people and goods across the border through rail, road and air. Accordingly, it was decided that the frequency of bus services should be increased from a fortnightly to a weekly basis, and to finalise modalities for 'intra-Kashmir trade and truck services'. Working and expert groups to explore more confidence-building measures were also to be facilitated, including in the nuclear and conventional fields. The questions of trade volume and imbalance were also considered and it was agreed that railway official from the two sides would meet in June 2008 to remove technical difficulties experienced in freight movement. To expand economic engagement, the two sides agreed to open the branches of each others' banks and agreed to work through the South Asian Association for Regional Cooperation to promote South Asian regional cooperation and development. Both sides also agreed seriously and sincerely to address the humanitarian aspects of persons of one country detained in another. An agreement was signed in Islamabad during the meeting for consular access to such detainees. There would also be release of such detainees by both the countries. The liberalisation of the visa regime between the two countries was also reiterated. The review meeting also looked at the issues of territorial disputes in Siachen and Sir Creek. While there was satisfaction on the progress made on Sir Creek through joint surveys, exchanges of maps and discussion of technicalities, no significant progress was visible on the icy heights of Siachen, apart from a 'commitment to seeking an early amicable solution'. Pakistan presented a new proposal on Siachen which would be considered and responded to by India.

The Kashmir Question

The main issue of contention between the two countries is Kashmir. A ceasefire agreement on the LOC has been in place since November 2003 and this agreement still holds generally, minor violations notwithstanding. However, there was a major violation of this agreement when missiles were fired from the Pakistani side on Indian security forces. India raised serious objections to this violation. The importance of ceasefire was accordingly reiterated in the Joint Statement issued after the Islamabad talks. Unfortunately, there was another similar instance of firing in the Poonch sector in Jammu & Kashmir within hours of the Pakistani assurances on ceasefire. The two sides will take up this question at the level of border security forces to ensure that such violations are not repeated. The Indian security forces are also of the view that, lately, there has been an increase in cross-border infiltration from the Pakistani side, as explosives and fake currency have been recovered in the border areas of Kashmir.

While India may accept the new Pakistani leaderships assurances and good intentions on the face value for the time being, its concerns on Kashmir arise on two counts—the changing tone of political stance of the new and democratic leadership in Pakistan on Kashmir and the approach towards Taliban and Islamic extremism of the post-election political and military establishments in Pakistan.

The new leadership, while projecting the vision of 'grand reconciliation' has sharpened its rhetorical stance on Kashmir, calling it a 'core' issue and bringing back the reference to United Nations Resolutions. On both these aspects, Pakistan's president, Pervez Musharraf, had diluted the Pakistani position significantly. When asked to state the democratic government's position on President Musharraf's four-point formula on Kashmir which included 'self-governance' and 'joint-supervision', Foreign Minister Qureshi said:

'The Kashmir issue should be addressed with the United Nations Resolution and taking into account the aspirations of the Kashmiri people, but we are open to all innovative ideas.' This is in conformity with the position of all the parties in the ruling coalition. It may be recalled that Kashmir was not an electoral issue in Pakistan's recently held elections, but the leaders of both the major parties, Benazir Bhutto and Nawaz Sharif, had been urging Indian leaders not to deal with President Musharraf on the Kashmir question. Both had, however, also affirmed their support for peace process with India, but not under President Musharraf's leadership. Reacting to President Musharraf's formulation on Kashmir, Prime Minister Syed Yousaf Raza Gilani said: 'They were half-baked things that did not have the mandate of Parliament'. Sharif was of the same view in his response to an Indian newspaper, saying:

> This gentleman Musharraf announces very very important things off-the-cuff. He has the habit of taking decisions in a very casual manner. . . . He is also erratic, a little impulsive. I don't agree on a lot of things with Mr Musharraf. But then one has to look into this. One will have to study this. We don't have to go by what Musharraf says. Let us sit down and see how best we can resolve this issue.

A benign explanation of the new Pakistani leadership's return to a harder stance on Kashmir could be seen in the compulsions of domestic politics; to distinguish its position from that of President Musharraf and also to keep the extremist groups, who had joined them on anti-Musharraf platform, in good humour as they provided electoral support to the political groups in the new coalition.

Reinforcement of Islamic Extremists

However, the evolving dynamics of Pakistani politics and gradually building political buoyancy of the extremist forces need to be watched carefully. Some of the die-hard extremist leaders, such as Masood Azhar of Jaish-e-Mohammed, have been released and they are freely mobilising support for their cause among the Pakistani masses. There are reports of greater resource flows to Hizbul Mujahideen, and Lashkar-e-Taiba, a banned extremist formation since 2002, is preparing to appeal for legal relief. While opening talks with India on the peace process, Islamabad also invited the separatist Hurriyat Conference for talks in June 2008, and the Hurriyat Conference is asking for talks to be held in Jammu & Kashmir. Some of the Kashmiri extremists, such as Salahuddin and Islamic jihadi groups in Pakistan, have been threatening the new democratic regime with agitation against any softening in its position on Kashmir, or even against any advance in the peace process with India. Mohammad Yusuf Shah, who heads both the Hizb-ul-Mujahideen and the United Jihad Council, declared in Muzaffarabad, the capital of the Pakistan-held Kashmir, in April 2008, that jihad in Kashmir will continue until the area is 'liberated from Indian occupation'.

Linked to the domestic political dynamics is the overall approach of the new establishment towards the global war on terror. There are increasing reports of the Pakistani army under its new leader General Kayani being soft on Taliban and Islamic extremist forces in the frontier areas. They are cutting out deals with the militant groups in order to buy peace in the frontier areas, much to the irritation and annoyance of Washington. The day India was concluding its Islamabad round of 'Composite Dialogue', Pakistani government concluded a 15-point deal with the militants in Swat, ending operations launched in October 2007. Under the deal, troops will be withdrawn and Islamic *Sharia* law will be imposed in the Swat Valley. Such deals seen in the context of reinforced jihadi activism and ceasefire violations in Kashmir are clear signs of rebuilding army–jihadi nexus that suffered a bit of a setback under President Musharraf's approach.

No one expected any major breakthrough at the fourth round of composite dialogue held in Islamabad. The Pakistani government is in a political flux, not only in relation to its evolving approach towards the extremist groups but also on other issues of coalition survival. There are areas of ambivalence not only in the relationship between the coalition government and the President but also between the mainstream political parties and the new leadership in the army on critical issues of governance, as well as peace and security. The Indian government is also bracing itself for the elections next year and does not seem to be in a position to radically shift its stand on critical issues of relationship with Pakistan, be it Siachen or Kashmir. Under these circumstances, the best that can be done bilaterally is to keep the dialogue alive and going. This dialogue is extremely vulnerable to the reinforced confidence and activism of the militant groups in Pakistan, notwithstanding the resolve on the two sides that they will keep the dialogue insulated from acts of terrorism and extremism. It will take considerable time, effort and political courage on the part of the two countries to work out the contours of the 'Grand Reconciliation' seriously.

58

Bangladesh–China–North-East India: Opportunities and Anxieties

M. SHAHIDUL ISLAM

(*8 September 2008*)

A RECENT WORKSHOP[1] in Kolkata on 'Southern Silk Route: Historical Links and Contemporary Convergences' explored the historical connections between Bangladesh, China,[2] India,[3] and Myanmar (also known as BCIM). These countries were believed to have been connected via the Southern Silk Route for centuries.[4] The workshop that drew nearly 30 academics and diplomats from different parts of the world also examined how century-old economic and cultural linkages could be re-exploited for economic and other benefits for the region's roughly 300 million people.

The gathering also drew substantive attention to India–Bangladesh relations and China's growing interest in Bangladesh, *inter alia*. There has been some exasperation among Indian scholars and diplomats regarding Bangladesh's position on transit facilities to India, gas exports to India, and its possible involvements with the insurgency in north-east India, among other matters. China's increasing influence over Bangladesh in recent years also caused some anxiety among some Indian participants at the workshop.

Against this backdrop, this paper attempts to explore some key Indo–Bangla bilateral issues, particularly those critical to north-east India's potential engagement with Bangladesh and other countries through the Kunming Initiative.[5] It also examines whether China's engagement with Bangladesh goes beyond economic interests.

Integration Prospects of Bangladesh and North-east India: Major Hurdles

Both Bangladesh and north-east India share a long history, culture and a long border.[6] The historic ties between Bangladesh and the north-eastern part of India date back to centuries. North-east India was integrally linked to the mainland India through what is now Bangladesh. Its passage to the sea was through Chittagong port in Bangladesh and via Bangladesh's rivers to Calcutta port. The region shipped tea and other exportables by inland water transports through the rivers of Bangladesh for overseas shipment from Calcutta.[7] However, with the Partition of India the region was cut-off from its hinterland, formerly East Bengal.

North-east India, which consists of eight states[8] is geographically more aligned with Bangladesh (see Map 1), Myanmar and China than its own mainland. It is an economic imperative for the landlocked region to seek benefits for itself through greater regional integration. Bangladesh too has an abiding interest in north-east India as it sees that the region can be its natural trading partner due to geographical proximity and historic linkages, among others.

However, less than friendly relations between Dhaka and New Delhi have been an impediment to increase trade, business and transportation networks between north-east India and Bangladesh. Owing to several factors, notably non-tariff barriers and high transaction costs (due to poor infrastructure and communication networks), north-east India–Bangladesh trade and other economic relations have not been developed despite their close geographical proximity. Moreover, a myriad of bilateral issues that have been a major bone of contention between New Delhi and Dhaka equally hinder the prospects of Bangladesh–north-east India economic integration.

Further, to integrate north-east India with its mainland, New Delhi is consistently seeking transit facilities from Dhaka that the latter is reluctant to allow unless the former provides a similar opportunity to Bangladesh to access the landlocked Himalayan countries.

In this paper, we will focus on two issues—trade and trans-

Map 1: Map of South Asia

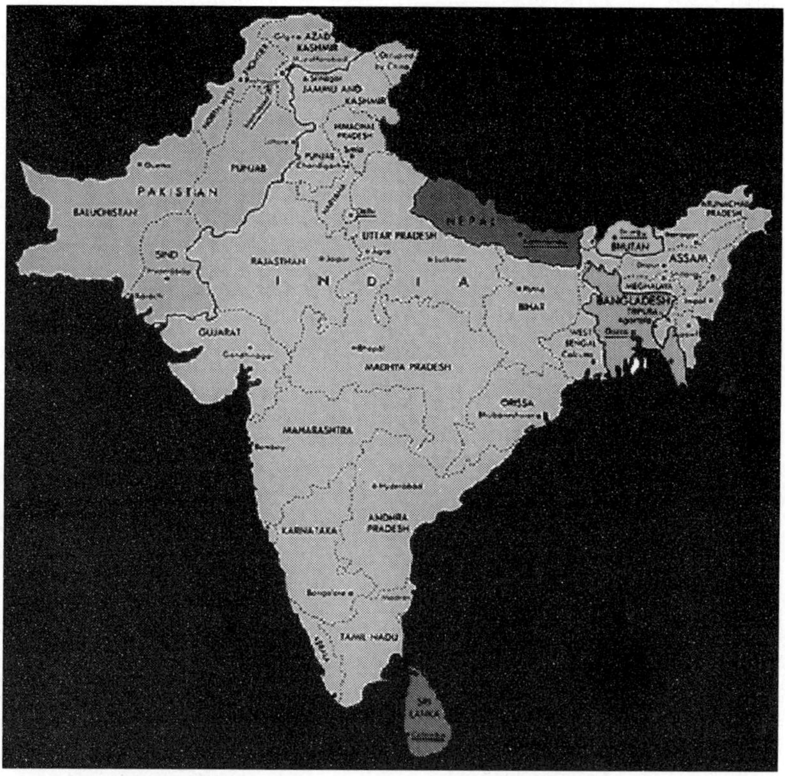

Source: http://www.sgs.utoronto.ca/sas/images/large-map.gif

portation—that are critical for both countries' economic engagements.

In recent years, trade barriers have declined, both in Bangladesh and India, in line with their commitments to World Trade Organization and South Asian Preferential Trade Arrangement (SAPTA). Moreover, India has given preferences to Bangladesh on approximately 2,925 tariff lines under SAPTA. Nevertheless, Bangladesh's export to India accounts for less than 7 per cent of its total import from the latter. As a result, it has a massive trade deficit with India.[9] Moreover, large volumes of informal imports from India cross the land border avoiding Bangladesh import duties. There are allegations from Bangladesh that its products often face India's non-tariff barriers and other bureaucratic hurdles.

It is a very common experience that two neighbouring countries can have trade imbalances. One needs to see whether Bangladesh has not been able to improve its trade imbalances with India only due to the latter's non-tariff barriers. One way of examining the case is how much complementariness they have in terms of trade. Trade Complementarity Index[10] shows that trade complementarity between Bangladesh and India is very low (5.42).[11] This low level of trade complementarity between these two neighbours is hardly surprising as (a) Bangladesh's export basket is not very diversified; and (b) it is highly concentrated on readymade garment product which is not a significant import item for India.

One of the reasons why India remains Bangladesh's second most important import destination is due to India's broad export basket and its close geographical proximity which, in turn, have helped Bangladesh to source for many commodities and final products with comparatively cheaper price, at least until recently. New Delhi's close attention to its non-tariff barriers and its bureaucratic bottlenecks can augment Bangladesh's trade to India to some extent but policy makers in Bangladesh should understand that this is not a panacea to redress the imbalances. Bangladesh does have similar trade imbalances with China also, but one observes fewer hue and cries in the Chinese case as we do in Indo–Bangla trade deficits.

Another issue that has been affecting Indo–Bangla relations is India's demand for transit facilities through Bangladesh. In the absence of a land transit link between India and Bangladesh,[12] the traffic between Kolkata and Assam is mainly carried by rail and road links through the Siliguri Corridor[13] and the requirements of additional transport costs for carrying goods is staggering. To transport goods to and from the north-east through the corridor the Indian government provides 25 per cent transport subsidy.[14] It is estimated that Rs 7 billion are being spent as additional costs to transport goods and services to and from north-east India.[15] The figure was estimated for the 1990s and it is expected that the cost has increased *in tandem* with economic growth both in north-east India and the rest of India. Thus a transit route through Bangladesh can integrate north-east India with its mainland and this can reduce transportation cost significantly.

However, an inland waterway transit exists between these two neighbours. After gaining independence, Bangladesh restored the 'Protocol on Inland Water Transit and Trade' in 1972, which was suspended by the then-Pakistan following the Indo–Pak war of 1965.

Now the question is: Why is Bangladesh reluctant to permit such facilities to India? It wants similar transit facilities from India to access Nepal and Bhutan. These landlocked Himalayan countries are geographically quite close to Bangladesh but they are surrounded by India. Nepal and Bangladesh are separated by a narrow piece of Indian territory of about 15 km in the south-east (see Map 1). Had there been transit facilities (Nepal–India–Bangladesh), landlocked Nepal (as is Bhutan) could use Chittagong and Mongla port of Bangladesh that could cut down its transportation cost dramatically and one could see better trade and tourism relations between these two countries. But New Delhi is unenthusiastic to respond to such calls. India keeps close eyes on these Himalayan countries, largely due to the China factor, and it is apparently less enthusiastic in wanting to see their integration with their close neighbours.

Another roadblock in solving Indo–Bangla transit problem is that Dhaka wants to solve all bilateral issues with New Delhi in a single package. Indeed, this is one of the reasons why the tripartite gas pipeline project (Myanmar–Bangladesh–India) has not been implemented finally.

So, it is not entirely true that Bangladesh is reluctant to allow India to use its territory to access north-east India but what it wants is a continental transit facility, especially in the southern part of the SAARC region (Bangladesh–India–Nepal–Bhutan) which does make more economic sense.

The deadlock on transit issues has been costing India and Bangladesh's transport and other communication links a great deal. There is an overwhelming consensus that, to integrate South Asia with south-east and other parts of Asia, there is a need for greater transport network across Asia. But India and Bangladesh have significant differences on the selection of routes of the Asian Highway Network (AHN). Bangladesh opposes the proposed route (India–Bangladesh portion) that enters into Bangladesh from India and goes back into India (see Map 2). Bangladesh wants to initiate a route that connects it with South-East Asia as well going through Chittagong and Myanmar (see Map 3), as otherwise the proposed route, it argues, will virtually become a transit route for Indian goods between rest of India and north-east India.

Bangladesh wants to link the AHN with transit issues (to north-east India through Bangladesh and to Nepal and Bhutan through India) that has handicapped Dhaka–Delhi relations greatly in recent years. If Bangladesh does not join the AHN, the length of the final route (see Map 4) will be much longer than either the proposed route or the route Bangladesh has suggested. As a result,

Map 2: The Asian Highway Network: The South-Asian Segment of the Road Network

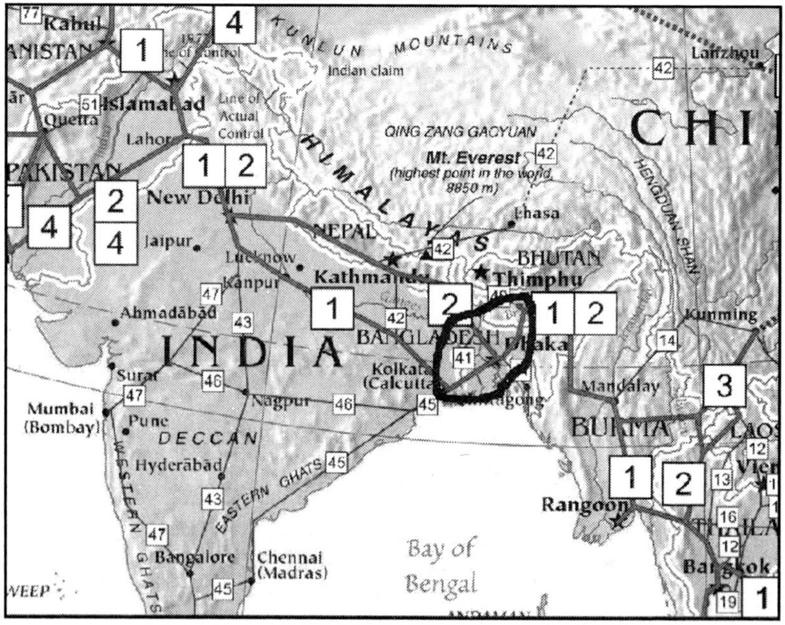

Source: http://horizonspeaks.wordpress.com/2005/12/15/asian-highway-the-past-and-future-maps/

Map 3: The Asian Highway Network: Bangladesh Government's Proposed Route

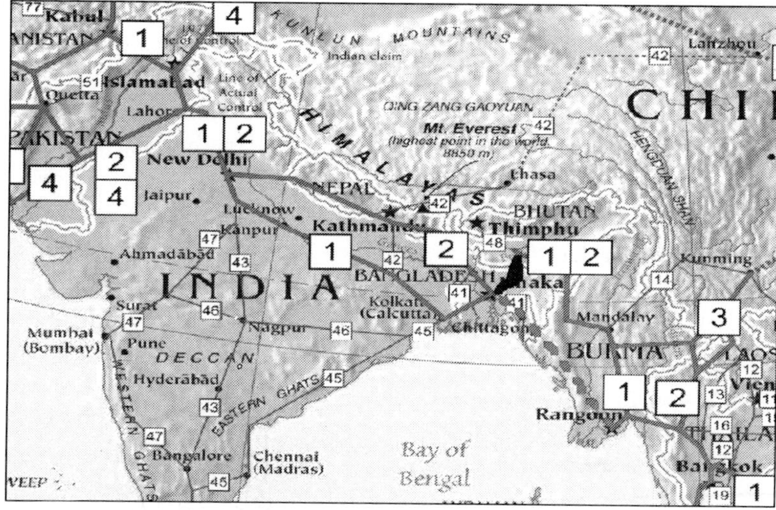

Source: http://horizonspeaks.wordpress.com/2005/12/15/asian-highway-the-past-and-future-maps/

Map 4: The Asian Highway Network, Excluding Bangladesh

Source: http://horizonspeaks.wordpress.com/2005/12/15/asian-highway-the-past-and-future-maps/

an AHN that excludes Bangladesh will make both north-east India and Bangladesh worse off.

The others issues, especially Bangladesh's reluctance to export gas to India and its involvements with the insurgency problems in the north-east India, have largely been muted in recent times. With regards to gas exports, it has become very evident that Bangladesh itself could become an energy scarce country in the near future if it continues to maintain its current gross domestic product growth rate.[16] New Delhi believes that some Bangladesh-based Islamic terrorist groups collaborate with the north-east separatist movements with the help of Pakistan Inter-Services Intelligence. There is no clear evidence that the Bangladesh state itself fuels the insurgency problems in north-east India, but it is true that some north-east insurgency groups find a safe haven in Bangladesh. This is not because the state itself patronises them but Dhaka does not have much control over north-east India–Bangladesh border. The current caretaker government has taken some genuine steps to control Islamic fundamentalism in Bangladesh, including hanging some terrorist leaders.

China–Bangladesh Relations: India's Concerns

As mentioned earlier, another important issue that has caused some anxiety to Indian policy makers is China's growing interest in Bangladesh. China and Bangladesh are old friends. However, in recent years, Dhaka–Beijing relations have reached new heights as China has become Bangladesh's number one trading partner, replacing India, and there has been a remarkable increase in Chinese investment in Bangladesh. The total trade between China and Bangladesh was around US $3.5 billion for 2007. Further, Beijing has become a key source of funds for Bangladesh's infrastructure development, having already funded the construction of six friendship bridges. Further, Bangladesh–China Cooperation Agreement on the Peaceful Usage of Nuclear Energy, that was signed in 2005, among eight other treaties when the Chinese Premier paid a state visit to Bangladesh, is aimed at assisting Dhaka in the peaceful development of nuclear energy for power generation and other development purposes.

The ties between China and Bangladesh are even more comprehensive when one looks at security cooperation. Being the largest supplier of military hardware and training to Bangladesh's armed forces, Beijing plays a key role in moulding Dhaka's security apparatus. Indeed, in 2002, Bangladesh signed a Defence Cooperation Agreement with China which is the first such agreement ever signed by Bangladesh in its history.

All these developments indicate that China has both economic and strategic interests in Bangladesh. Does it mean that China's strategies and interests are designed to contain India, especially when one also views its engagement with Myanmar and Pakistan, in addition to Bangladesh? Why is Bangladesh aligning more with China in recent years? Can Bangladesh afford to engage China and strategically ignore India's concerns? To understand the dynamics of Sino–Bangla relations, especially from Bangladesh's perspectives, one needs to understand three crucial areas—Bangladesh's economic aspirations, its relations with India and the dynamics of its domestic politics.

First, on the economic front, Bangladesh is an untapped market and China understands its significant economic potential. Bangladesh too has an abiding interest in China's rising economic prowess. Increasing Chinese export and investment in Bangladesh, especially in telecommunications, manufacturing, RMG, mining, power and agriculture, and the Chinese government's incentives to import Bangladeshi products have made China Bangladesh's number one trading and an important economic partner.

Second, as discussed, Bangladesh's and India's economic engagement has not been developed *in tandem* with their engagement with the outer world. Like many neighbouring countries, they have some outstanding issues to resolve. This has prompted Bangladesh to seek closer ties with China. Moreover, as Bangladesh's bilateral ties with India are less than friendly, and being a small state in the Indian neighbourhood, it faces a psychological threat. So apart from economic reasons, its security concerns are another motivating factor behind this alignment, and we can see such trends elsewhere in the world—perhaps more vividly in the Caucasus.

Third, one needs to look at Bangladesh's two major political parties' relations with New Delhi in order to understand the dynamics of Sino–Bangla and Indo–Bangla relations. The Bangladesh Awami League (AL), left-winged and relatively secular, is branded as a pro-Indian, whereas the Bangladesh Nationalist Party (BNP), right-winged and closely associated with Islamic parties, utilises anti-Indian sentiment to achieve its political objectives.

The AL does not publicise its close ties with New Delhi. However, during Sheikh Hasina's tenure (1996–2000), Dhaka–New Delhi relations witnessed a marked improvement and Bangladesh and India signed two important treaties—the Chittagong Hill Tract Peace Treaty and the Ganges Water Sharing Treaty—which had seemed a distant reality during her predecessor Khaleda Zia's premiership in the period of 1991–5. After a brief pause, less than friendly relations between these two neighbours re-emerged when the BNP-led four-party alliances returned to power in 2001. Dhaka–New Delhi bilateral relations again reached the pre-Hasina era.

On the other hand, the BNP's association with Beijing is just the reverse of its relations with New Delhi. China–Bangladesh relations gained momentum from 2002 when the BNP-led four-party alliance adopted a 'Look East' policy. Further, the then-Bangladeshi prime minister's visit to Beijing was a significant landmark in shaping the Sino–Bangla relations.[17] A Dhaka–New Delhi standoff on some key bilateral issues, little progress in South Asian regionalism and the psychological threat it perceives from its largest neighbour had convinced the then-government of Bangladesh that it should take advantage of the rise of China. The latter's reciprocal interest, especially Bangladesh's market potential and its geopolitical importance, has given the Sino–Bangla relation a big thumbs up.

Bangladesh's engagement with China is, therefore, partly driven by its economic interest. The long-standing mistrust between Dhaka and New Delhi has also prompted Bangladesh to align itself with China. Moreover, the dynamics of Bangladesh's domestic politics, particularly its two major political party's relations with New Delhi, and India's hegemonic attitude have helped China to increase its engagement with Bangladesh.

Despite these facts, good relations with India are equally important for Bangladesh, owing to its economic dependency, people-to-people connections and cultural linkages. It is believed that several millions Bangladeshis have found their shelter, mostly illegally, in different parts of India. Moreover, Bangladesh's dependency on India became very visible in the recent past when India imposed export ban on several agricultural commodities in the wake of its burgeoning food crisis. But India too failed to utilise the opportunity to alleviate the mistrust between two countries. One noticed a huge frustration among Bangladeshis when India made an extraordinary delay in delivering rice to Bangladesh (Dhaka was even ready to pay the international market price) when the country badly needed it.

There are growing concerns that India is losing Bangladesh to China, as we observed in the case of Myanmar, or that Bangladesh's relations with China will slowly emulate the Sino–Pak relations which are believed to be designed to contain India. But Bangladesh is no Myanmar, as it is culturally more aligned to India, and the geo-political dynamics of Pakistan are far more diverse than that of Bangladesh.

Even though the common people in Bangladesh have some suspicions about India, they are not hostile towards it. Moreover, it is true that a section of people, particularly the ultra-rightists within the establishment of BNP take an anti-Indian stance but the liberal section of the party believes in peaceful coexistence with India. The civil society in Bangladesh too sees the Sino–Bangla relations as largely driven by economics. Though security is another building block in this regard, they think it is designed to protect the country from any external aggressions. However, if the BNP's central command falls into the ultra-rightists' hand, they might resort to India bashing to gain their political objectives.

Further, Bangladesh's relations with the United Sates is another critical factor as both the AL and the BNP keep close relations with Washington which has significant influence over Dhaka. So no matter which party assumes power, the degree of Chinese influence over Bangladesh is not absolute.

India Needs to Make a New Case

As discussed earlier, two issues, trade and transit, which have handicapped Indo–Bangla bilateral ties, can be solved if both countries look at these issues afresh. New Delhi's close attention to its non-tariff barriers can give some comfort to Dhaka. It is clearly noticeable that the mere correction of non-tariff barriers will not significantly improve Bangladesh's trade imbalances with India but a serious attempt can prevent India from becoming the perfect scapegoat for Bangladesh's own problems in this regard. On transit issues, unless India offers similar opportunities to Bangladesh, any breakthrough on it is a distant reality. The real downside risk pertaining to transit is that if Bangladesh finally remains isolated from the AHN, it could make both countries worse off.

Bangladesh's alignment with China is not necessarily a barrier to forge plausible Indo–Bangla ties. Indeed, a growth quadrangle comprising Bangladesh, the Yunnan province of China, Myanmar and north-east India can change the economic geography in this part of the world. The region is blessed with diverse natural resources, rich biodiversity and enormous hydro-electricity potential, among others.

However, with regards to north-east India's integration with Bangladesh and South-East Asia, New Delhi should first make up its mind to what extent it wants its north-eastern part to get integrated with the rest of South Asia, as it has both economic and security concerns pertaining to the region. It has some fear that opening up of north-east India can soon turn it into a readymade market for Chinese goods, and the north-eastern states that are fighting for autonomy from the centre or even for sovereign states might go out of New Delhi's control. Indeed, one of the speakers at the workshop identified India as a rather reluctant participant in the BCIM due to these concerns, *inter alia*.

The differences over bilateral issues between two close neighbours are very common elsewhere in the world but most countries have prioritised their economic benefits even while keeping their political differences alive. In the case of India and Bangladesh, both parties need to revisit their bilateral differences. Being a big economic power and the largest country in the South Asia, India, in this case, has the upper hand. New Delhi needs to make a new case for its neighbourhood policies and it needs to act fast to change the course of Indo–Bangla relations.

NOTES

1. The workshop was held in Kolkata on 2–4 August 2008.
2. Particularly, Yunnan province of China.
3. Mostly north-eastern part of India.
4. Historical evidence shows that a south-west silk route was in use between India and China long before Marco Polo established a silk route over the Karakoram in the thirteenth century (Sobhan 2000). According to Verghese, the southern-most route passed through Mytkynia, the Hukwan valley and into the Paktai and Nagai hills to Assam (Verghese 1998). In more contemporary times the southern silk route or Burma road which was possibly used by Chinese emperor Kublai Khan's armies to conquer Burma, was resurrected as an important logistical artery by General Joe Stilwell, the US officer commanding allied forces on the Indo–Burmese front and designated to liaise with the Chinese forces resisting the Japanese occupation of China during World War II (Tuchman 1977).
5. The Kunming Initiative is a byproduct of the conference on 'Regional Cooperation and Development among China, India, Myanmar and Bangladesh' held in 1999 in Kunming, the capital of Yunnan province located in the south-western region of China. Over 100 officials and scholars from BCIM countries have called for forging a long-term relationship of friendship and joint efforts to accelerate economic development in the region.
6. Bangladesh is geographically surrounded mostly by north-east India except for small border with Myanmar to the far south-east and the Bay of Bengal to the south.
7. Sobhan, 'Rediscovering the Southern Silk Route: Integrating Asia's Transport Infrastructure', 2000.
8. Arunachal Pradesh, Assam, Manipur, Meghalaya, Mizoram, Nagaland, Sikkim and Tripura. Also often cited as seven sisters (except Sikkim).
9. For instance, in 2006, India's exports to Bangladesh were US $2230.77 million, whereas the latter's exports to the former were only $146.93 million (IMF, *Direction of Trade Statistics Yearbook*, 2007).

10. The trade complementarity (TC) index can provide useful information on prospects for intraregional trade in that it shows how well the structures of a country's imports and exports match. The TC between countries k and j is defined as: $TC_{ij} = 100 = sum(|m_{ik} - x_{ij}| /2)$. The index is zero when no goods are exported by one country or imported by the other and 100 when the export and import shares exactly match.
11. This figure is taken from Rahman et al., 2007.
12. It is worth noting here and as discussed earlier, there has been a developed transportation infrastructure between particularly rail and riverain links, between India and East Bengal until 1965. Following the Indo–Pak war these links were disrupted.
13. The total amount of inward and outward traffic is estimated at 10 million tonnes a year, of which only about 50,000 tonnes passes through Bangladesh, mostly by river transit.
14. Verghese, 'India's Northeast Resurgent', 1998.
15. Sobhan, op. cit., 2000.
16. For details see Wood Mackenzie and Petrobangla, 'Revised Interim Report on Development of Gas Sector Master Plan', 2005. Available at <http://www.energybangla.com/pdf/WM%20GSMP%20Rev%20Interim%20Report.pdf>
17. Three important treaties and a Memorandum of Understanding were signed between two countries on military cooperation, economy and technology and China promised interest-free loans to built infrastructure in Bangladesh.

REFERENCES

CIA Fact Book 2008.

http://hei.unige.ch/sas/files/portal/spotlight/country/asia_pdf/asia-india-2004.pdf>

http://horizonspeaks.wordpress.com

Census 2001, Government of India, Registrar General of India.

De, Prabir and Biswa N. Bhattacharya (2007), 'Deepening India-Bangladesh Economic Cooperation: Challenges and Opportunities', Research and Information System for Developing Countries, Discussion Paper No. 130.

Economic Survey, 2007–8, Planning Commission, Government of India.

International Monetary Fund, *Direction of Trade Statistics Yearbook*, 2007.

Rahman et al. (2007), 'BCIM Economic Cooperation: Prospects and Challenges', Centre for Policy Dialogue Occasional Paper No. 64.

Rehman, Sobhan (2000), *Rediscovering the Southern Silk Route: Integrating Asia's Transport Infrastructure*, The University Press Limited, Dhaka.

Statistical Pocket Book Bangladesh 2007, Bangladesh Bureau of Statistics.

'Strategic implications of Bangladesh-China relations', *The Daily Star*, 15th Anniversary issue, <http://www.thedailystar.net/suppliments/2006/15thanniv/bangladesh&theworld/bd_world12 .htm >

South Asian Enterprise Development Facility, SEDF (2004), 'Northeast India-Bangladesh Initiatives Map'.

Tuchman, Barbara W. (1977), 'Stillwell and the American Experience in China, 1911–45, McMillan.

Urvashi, Aneja (2006), 'China-Bangladesh Relations: An Emerging Strategic Partnership?', Institute of Peace and Conflict Studies, Special Report, 2006.

Verghese, B.G. (1998), *India's Northeast Resurgent*, Konark Publishers, New Delhi.

World Bank (2006), 'India-Bangladesh Bilateral Trade and Potential Free Trade Agreement', Bangladesh Development Series Paper No. 13.

Wood Mackenzie & Petrobangla (2005), 'Revised Interim Report on Development of Gas Sector Master Plan', 2005. Available at http://www.energybangla.com/pdf/WM%20GSMP% 20Rev%20Interim% 20Report.pdf

SECTION III

REGIONAL AND INTERNATIONAL RELATIONS

B. South Asia–China Relations

59

India and China: Towards Slow and Steady Cooperation

S.D. MUNI
(*18 January 2008*)

INDIAN PRIME MINISTER Manmohan Singh's visit to China from 13–15 January 2008 was a step in the direction of keeping the momentum of building incremental and evolutionary cooperation between the Asian giants. No breakthroughs were expected and none happened. There was no bilateral free trade agreement (FTA) which China, sitting on a comfortable and increasing trade surplus of about US $10 billion, was keen on. Nor was there any conclusion of a 'Framework Agreement' on the resolution of boundary issue that India has been looking forward to. The Chinese side was not forthcoming on endorsing the Indo–United States Civil Nuclear Cooperation, nor in assuring India that its request to the Nuclear Suppliers Group (NSG) in the context of Indo–United States nuclear deal would be supported by China.

And yet the visit was 'positive' and 'successful' in whichever way one looked at it. The two countries signed 11 documents of mutual understanding and cooperation on subjects ranging from the railways and planning to agriculture and rural development. The most important of these agreements was the vision statement signed by the two prime ministers that promised to build 'a harmonious world of durable peace and common prosperity' through the 'strategic and cooperative partnership' between their countries. In this statement, they talked about an open, inclusive and democratic (not multipolar) international system based on the famous principles of *Panchsheel*—about regional integration of Asia; about 'an international energy order that is fair, equitable, secure and stable';

about 'working together and with the international community' against terrorism in 'all its forms and manifestations'; and also about bilateral matters like 'defence dialogue'; and the resolution of 'outstanding differences, including on the boundary question, through peaceful negotiations'.

In substantive matters of bilateral interest, there was considerable focus on enhancing economic cooperation. The trade between the two countries has really been making the most impressive growth surpassing the targets already set. The target of US $20 billion bilateral trade by 2008 had been surpassed in 2006. By the end of this financial year, bilateral trade is expected to go beyond US $38 billion, as against the target of US $40 billion set for 2010. Therefore, the trade target was upgraded for the year 2010 from US $40 to US $60 billion, notwithstanding the Indian fears that, by the end of the current financial year, its trade deficit may touch a whopping US $14 billion mark.

India's hesitation in concluding a bilateral FTA arises from this fear of fast growing deficit trade. The concerns of the Indian business community arise from the fact that the flood of imports from China may threaten Indian manufactures in the long run instead of just replacing imports from third countries. The Indian business community also fears the lack of a level playing field in trade competition with China because of the 'opaque pricing mechanism' of the Chinese goods and 'massive subsidies to capital through huge non-performing assets in their banking system'. Dr Singh took a 40-member strong business group with his delegation to raise relevant and pressing issues with the Chinese business counterparts at the 'India–China Economic, Trade and Investment Summit' during the visit. Addressing this summit on 14 January 2008, Dr Singh encouraged the business community to 'acquire insights into each others markets, business customs and management styles'.

On the sensitive border issue, there was an informal exchange of views between the designated special representatives, National Security Adviser M.K. Narayan from the Indian side and Vice-Minister Dai Bingguo from the Chinese side. India realises the complexity of the issue but is not happy with increasing intrusions and encroachments numbering 140 last year, and is keen that a framework agreement is finalised soon to start demarcation of the Line of Actual Control (LAC). India has been asking for the next meeting of the expert group to clarify points on the LAC in view of encroachments and troops movements. It is learnt that two drafts of such an agreement—an Indian and a Chinese—have been prepared and will be reconciled by a taskforce set up by the two special representatives. Until this taskforce completes its job, border talks cannot move forward. However, the Chinese side is most reluctant in exchanging its version of the LAC map. The Chinese side feels that such exchanges of maps may be taken as a step towards formalisation of boundary along the LAC. There are also differences on interpreting displacement of populated areas. While India does not want any such displacement in the process of 'give and take', China wants to categorise such points so that the least populated places can be factored in for the displaced, if need be.

Looking at India's major foreign policy goals at the moment, two deserve mention here. One is to seek liberation from international nuclear restraints imposed in the aftermath of its 1998 nuclear explosion and to secure a place of respect in the United Nations Security Council as a permanent member. The question seems to have come up in the discussion between the two prime ministers during the visit. India would need China's support in the NSG as and when it has concluded an agreement with the International Atomic Energy Agency. The Chinese side is also not unaware of coalition tensions within India on the whole question of civil nuclear cooperation with the United States. In their response to the Indian aspirations, the Chinese made a subtle distinction. Without directly assuring India of the NSG support, China offered bilateral cooperation in the field of civil nuclear energy. This suited Dr Singh as well to use in his domestic coalition political dynamics to show that all the nuclear eggs of his government are not in the United States basket. China also assured its Indian guests that it would not do anything to block India's enhanced role in the United Nations and its Security Council. This does not really mean a Chinese support for India's permanent membership of the United Nations Security Council, as some in Indian media and official circles have interpreted. But China would like to avoid being blamed for India's difficulties in this respect. One may recall here that Indian candidature for United Nations Secretary General's contest was not vetoed by the Chinese, contrary to apprehensions about it in India.

Both India and China are also acutely concerned about the deteriorating regional environment. The spectre of instability in Pakistan, Myanmar, Nepal, Bangladesh and Sri Lanka haunts both of them because they will be affected directly and adversely by the spill-over of this instability. The two prime minister discussed this regional situation, including Iran, where the United States belligerent stance can precipitate serious turmoil. They both appealed for defeating extremism in these countries.

The real dynamics of Sino–Indian relations is governed by four 'Cs', if one were to put it metaphorically. These four 'Cs' are: co-operation, competition, conflict and containment. The present phase through which this relationship is evolving is dominated by the first two 'Cs' because neither India or China can afford to alienate each other. Both are seeking their due places in the emerging structure of global power; both are rising economic powers and they need peace and stability to realise their aspirations. They cannot let the areas of their conflict intervene and dominate to derail their long nursed aspirations. But underneath the thrust of cooperation, prospects of conflict are not overlooked and, therefore, there are quiet and contrived moves for containment too. India has always resented China's support for Pakistan's military and nuclear capabilities and seen it as a move to counterbalance and undermine India's position in the South Asian region. China's growing economic and strategic engagement with India's other South Asian neighbours has also always remained a cause of unease for India.

The expansion of this engagement that includes reinforcing of infrastructure links, and economic and defence cooperation is being watched closely in New Delhi. For China, India's cultural and political association with Tibet, and the presence of nearly 250,000 Tibet refugees and their spiritual head, the Dalai Lama, in India has always been a source of anxiety and concern. The Chinese fear that its international adversaries, with India's help, can use Tibet to destabilise China's rise. In this context, as also in relation to the emerging Asian balance, China is also concerned about India's increasing strategic proximity to the United States. China would like to see India as much distanced as possible from any anti-Chinese moves, like the 'quadrilateral' strategic group involving the United States, Japan, and Australia. Understanding Chinese sensitivities in this regards, Dr Singh had made it clear on the eve of his visit that India would never join any move aimed at containing China. The Indian government had also restrained its employees from attending any function to felicitate the Dalai Lama. Such gestures have been appreciated in Beijing and perhaps reciprocated in the form of keeping contentious issues like that of Tawang from delaying the border negotiations. But China will surely not sign the border agreement with India unless its concerns on the Tibetan question and the growing Indo–US strategic engagement are set at rest.

One hopes that the domination of the cooperation and competition 'Cs' over those of conflict and cooperation, so clearly evident during Prime Minister Singh's visit, will continue for at least a decade or so in Sino–Indian relations. One may also hope that the confidence and mutual trust built during this phase of compulsions and incentives for cooperation will lead to the development of such mutual stakes that they will always take conflict and mutual containment as counter-productive. India and China not only have stakes in their mutual cooperation but the whole of Asia's stability and prosperity depends upon coexistence and collaboration of the two emerging Asian giants.

60

Sino–Indian Trade Relations: Understanding the Bilateral and Regional Implications

DEEP K. DATTA-RAY
(*22 January 2008*)

WHEN INDIAN Prime Minister Manmohan Singh spoke in Beijing, during his visit from 13–15 January 2008, of a 'historic need' for India and China to work together, he was looking beyond the border dispute that has plagued relations for half a century to freeing millions of the world's poorest from disease and economic deprivation. Paradoxically, this goal, and not any misplaced nationalistic or protectionist sentiment, forced him to decline Chinese requests for a free trade agreement (FTA).

The implications for the Association of South-East Asian Nations (ASEAN) and, in particular, Singaporean economic and security concerns are significant. Once expected to weave India, China and the region into an inextricable economic web that rendered conflict unthinkable, trading relations are now under threat from a growing imbalance which directly affects India's hinterland. Between January and November 2007, India's trade deficit with China widened to US $9.02 billion, compared to the US $843 million surplus New Delhi enjoyed as recently as 2005. India exports primary products, mainly, iron ore. Nearly half of Chinese exports to India are manufactured goods which New Delhi fears will affect incipient local industries that would otherwise have absorbed India's rapidly growing educated young. New Delhi fears unemployment might lead to civil unrest. The 'deficit is tolerable only for a finite period, beyond which we risk seeing a "positive" of the relationship assuming negative tones', warns India's Ambassador to Beijing, Nirupama Rao.

For all its size and population, India, like ASEAN, might also feel it is coming under the looming shadow of a vast economic power. Singapore Minister Mentor Lee Kuan Yew's explanation of why he attempted to engage India long before India expressed an interest in the region is revealing in this context. China threatened regional security in the 1950s, 1960s and 1970s by supporting guerrilla movements. From the 1980s onwards, China has been burgeoning into an overpowering economic force. 'We don't want to be overwhelmed and become like Laos or Cambodia!' Minister Mentor Lee said in a recent conversation. The statement echoed his earlier comments that India alone had the girth and weight to balance China. No other country can hold the other end of the see-saw, he said as long ago as 1962. Other ASEAN leaders may be less forthright, but this is the only reason why Indonesia's former President Suharto so readily agreed in 1995 to India becoming a full ASEAN dialogue partner.

Indian diplomacy is not, however, designed to balance China. Dr Singh allayed fears of a trade war when he invoked a phrase familiar to ASEAN and said problems would be solved in the 'Asian way'. His definition of 'avoiding confrontation and building trust, confidence and consensus' almost reiterates what ASEAN calls the *musyawarah dan muafakar* (consultation and consensus) process. India expects its discussions in the East Asian Summit and other fora to result in an open and inclusive economic architecture in terms of trade in goods and services and the flow of investment and human capital in an area encompassing India, China and ASEAN. The impetus is local—in terms of creating infrastructure and jobs in the Indian hinterland—but the realisation depends on India getting further integrate into Asia's economic and security architecture.

The talk of 'multifaceted' relations has been translated into a remarkable shift in military relations. For the first time last year, both countries held joint anti-terrorism exercises and India will host the second round of exercises this year. The Manmohan Singh–Wen Jiabao Joint Declaration points to greater cooperation with spillover effects for the region. The Declaration says: 'The two sides take a positive view on each other's participation in sub-regional multilateral cooperation processes between like-minded countries, including the South Asian Association for Regional

Cooperation, the Bay of Bengal Initiative for Multi-Sectoral Technical and Economic Cooperation and the Shanghai Cooperation Organisation.' That points to regions like South-East Asia where Sino–Indian interests not only touch but overlap, repeating the historical process that gave Indochina its name.

Singapore could become a key player in this interaction between the Asian giants. In terms of business, Singapore could be a facilitator for the rapidly expanding Sino–Indian trade. This year's US $20 billion target was reached two years ago and the revised target of US $40 billion by 2010 is also likely to be achieved two years ahead of schedule. As an established player in China, Singapore is strengthening trading links with India. Negotiations are currently underway to revise the groundbreaking Comprehensive Economic Cooperation Agreement (CECA) which has played a major role in India outstripping even China to become Singapore's fastest growing trade partner amongst the major economies. Post-CECA, exports from India to Singapore increased to US $5.4 billion, a growth of 35.6 per cent. Exports to Singapore accounted for 5.26 per cent of India's total exports during 2005–6, which meant a more than a twofold increase from 2.3 per cent in 2002. Singapore is well positioned to facilitate trading links between the regional giants. With its special links with China, Singapore might even be able to convince Beijing not to allow trade to join the contentious border question as a 'negative' in the surging relations. After all, by his own admission, Minister Mentor Lee succeeded in convincing Deng Xiaoping that it was not good politics to export revolution to South-East Asia.

Admittedly, questions of nationalism rule out a quick resolution of the border dispute. But this does not affect Indian consumption patterns. The share of Chinese imports in India's global import basket rose from 4 per cent in 2001 to 9.4 per cent in 2007. That China's exports to India today amount to 10 per cent of India's entire industrial gross domestic product indicates China's ability to sell cheap and the openness of ordinary Indians to foreign goods. From under 1 per cent in 2001–2, today China supplies nearly 75 per cent of India's tubes and pipes. Similarly, in the area of transmission apparatus for radio and telephony, imports from

China have jumped from 12 to 50 per cent in a few years. In the case of automatic data processing machines, China's share in India's imports has risen from 12 to 35 per cent. Pragmatic and practical, Indians spurn, without a second thought, locally made goods for cheaper Chinese alternatives. The fact that these are allegedly 'dumped' on India does not stop anyone from buying them. 'Dumping', defined as selling goods abroad at a cost lower than production, is only possible with state complicity as it involves a complex transfer of profits from a successful sector to a failing industry. It should be welcomed by Indians because, in effect, the Chinese government is indirectly subsidising a rise in Indian living standards!

Nevertheless, shrill cries for a tax on imports from China, amounting to a tariff barrier, pierce the Sino–Indian discourse. Respected national daily newspapers warn darkly of a 'dependency syndrome' in 'critical areas'. Indian trading associations complain that India occupies a miniscule 1.3 per cent of China's global imports. But these are the voices not of India's poor who welcome Chinese products by buying them but of pampered and protected industrialists who see with alarm their long-captive markets now slipping away. India's elite is learning that globalisation does not discriminate against anyone. It bestows free choice on consumers. The migration of industries to the underdeveloped world checks price inflation in the rich world—a phenomenon that is being replicated within the underdeveloped world.

As an economist, Dr Singh is well versed in the theories and practices of free trade. He demurred about an FTA not because he opposes free choice, but because China has not reciprocated in opening its market to Indian goods. That might deprive Indian exporters of a market but the real losers are China's consumers and manufacturers. If the Chinese government does indeed subsidise cost-inefficient industries with profits earned in other sectors, then it is setting a dangerous precedent. Such practices skew the market and rob it of its fundamental virtue—the ability to convey information about choices efficiently to all quarters. If there is a shock in one sector of the Chinese economy—as is likely with the slow-down of the United States economy and the falling Western consumer spending—then shock waves will reverberate throughout the Chinese economic system.

Only the political courage to let the market run its course can contain the damage. Pharmaceuticals are a case in point. India boasts of the largest number of United States Food and Drug Administration-approved plants outside the United States. Pharmaceutical is a core Indian competency and exports to Western markets have grown by 19 per cent year-on-year for the last three years, racing ahead of the world average growth rate of 6 per cent. Yet, India's pharmaceutical exports to China have grown by just 3 per cent from US $94 million in 2002 to US $109 million in 2005.

This failure to penetrate China is due to 'non-tariff barriers' that manifest themselves in long and complicated registration procedures, prohibitively expensive drug import licences and inordinately protracted customs checks. Ultimately, even if a foreign firm enters China, the drug distribution system operates mainly through hospitals which, in practice, give preference to locally-produced drugs. The ultimate sufferer is the Chinese patient who is denied inexpensive, world class medicine.

As the nineteenth-century British politician, Richard Cobden, wrote, 'Free trade is God's diplomacy and there is no other certain way of uniting people in the bonds of peace.' Nationalistic Indian voices which risk upsetting a relationship on which the future of one-third of humanity depends can be silenced if China matches India and lowers trade barriers. That would pave the way for the FTA Beijing wants. The ultimate beneficiary would be the common man. The goodwill generated by a booming economic relationship might even prove a solvent for seemingly intractable problems like the border dispute. South-East Asia's trade, investment and security only stand to benefit from closer Sino–Indian cooperation.

61

The Third Tibetan Uprising: India's Response

S.D. MUNI

(*24 March 2008*)

TIBET REMAINS a complex issue in India's relations with China. It has a historical context, a sensitive humanitarian dimension and contemporary political imperatives. All these impinge on the unresolved, conflict-prone border issue between the two Asian giants. Keeping this in mind, India has been diplomatically correct and politically cautious in responding to the 2008 Tibetan uprising. This uprising has gone much beyond the arson and rioting in the Tibetan capital Lhasa, affecting not only other parts of Tibet but also other regions of China such as Gansu, Qinghai and Sichuan. In its scale, the uprising is comparable to the one in 1959 which led to the Dalai Lama's flight and it is much bigger than the one in 1988 which was strongly suppressed by Hu Jintao, who was then in-charge of Tibetan affairs.

In the statements made by India's minister of external affairs, Pranab Mukherjee, and the official spokesman of the Ministry of External Affairs, India felt 'distressed by the reports of the unsettled situation and violence in Lhasa and by the deaths of innocent people. We would hope that all those involved will work to improve the situation and remove the causes of such trouble in Tibet, which is an autonomous region of China, through dialogue and non-violent means'. On the attempts of the Tibetan refugees organising a march to Tibet to protest against the hosting of Olympic Games by China, the official Indian position was that the 'Tibetan refugees are our guests in India. All those in India, whether Indian citizens or foreigners, are subject to the law of the land regarding the crossing of our borders, marches or demonstrations. Like our other guests, Tibetan refugees, while they are in India, are expected to refrain from political activities and those activities that affect our relations with other friendly countries.' Even before the outburst in Lhasa, Indian police had, on 10 March 2008, disallowed the Tibetans organising demonstrations and launching marches to Tibet. About a hundred Tibetans were arrested.

There has clearly been an attempt on India's part to separate the humanitarian support to the Tibetan refugees from their political and anti-Chinese activities. At the same time, there has also been an attempt to disapprove of the violent means both by the Tibetan protesters and the Chinese authorities in Lhasa. India even asked the authorities to get the cause of disturbances and violence 'investigated independently'. New Delhi's position on the Tibetan protest has not pleased the Tibetans. The Dalai Lama, in his 'constructive criticism', called it as 'overcautious'. Tibetan agitators strongly disapproved it saying, 'India supports China too much. We are struggling but they don't let us. It's because India is afraid of China'.

India's stand was however, appreciated by the Chinese Prime Minister Wen Jiabao who expected India to 'follow the agreements reached between the two countries and handle this issue in a correct way'. This was done while blaming the 'Dalai clique' for 'Tibet independence' activities. The Chinese Ambassador in New Delhi, Zhang Yang, went even further in cautioning India against any 'irresponsible words or acts' on the evolving Tibetan situation. After explaining the Chinese account of arson, looting and violence in Lhasa, he said that there was no 'crackdown' and added, 'we hope that the Indian friends can see clearly the nature of those instigating and conspiring activities of the Dalai clique, which aim at splitting China and disrupting the Beijing Olympic Games'.

India's official position is in conformity with the broad political consensus that exists in India on the Tibetan issue. The opposition Bhartiya Janata Party's (BJP) strong reaction and parliamentary walkout on the Tibetan question, with isolated demands for raising the question in the United Nations, need not be taken as a breach of this consensus. While in power before 2004, the BJP had also followed a similar approach and its current deviation in this respect seems to be a reflection of its 'oppositional role' in the (expected) election year. Foreign Minister Mukherjee even taunted the BJP on its parliamentary antics by saying, 'What have they done to change this policy?' The United Progressive Alliance government's left supporters are obviously in agreement with this.

The evolution of India's Tibet policy can be traced back to its pre-Independence perspective, inherited in a large measure from the British. In the first Asian Relations Conference convened by India in March 1947, prior to its formal Independence, Jawaharlal Nehru invited Tibet as an independent country. He accommodated Chinese objections to the flying of independent Tibet's flag at the venue of the conference, but in his speeches, Tibet was equated with other independent countries like Nepal, Afghanistan, Sri Lanka (then Ceylon), Myanmar (then Burma), etc. But the Indian position started shifting after this conference, perhaps in response to the Chinese arguments against Tibetan independence. In a position paper prepared in the foreign office on India's stand on Tibet, it was underlined that India 'could not afford to prejudice her relations with so important a power as China by aggressive support of unqualified Tibetan independence'. India opposed Chinese military intervention in Tibet in October 1950 but refused to sponsor Tibet's appeal to the United Nations against this intervention. Dictated by India's incapability to challenge the Chinese militarily in Tibet, Nehru decided to follow the British formulation of 'Tibetan autonomy under Chinese suzerainty'. This was the basis of the April 1954 Agreement with China on Tibet under which India agreed to withdraw all its extra-territorial rights in Tibet enjoyed by the British during the colonial period. In this agreement, the Chinese side had committed itself to respect Tibetan cultural and religious autonomy.

Even while endorsing Dalai Lama's flight from Tibet and accepting not only Tibetan refugees, that number around 120,000 now, but also a Tibetan government in exile, India sought to differentiate between Tibet's political rights and its cultural and religious identity, with the Dalai Lama as its spiritual head. India has also kept itself discreetly distanced from efforts by other countries to harass China militarily in Tibet from the Indian territory, like the arming of Khampas by the United States.

India has, however, been sore that the Chinese have neither sincerely respected the Tibetan autonomy nor made genuine and sufficient efforts to resolve the Tibetan issue through dialogue with the Dalai Lama. The Chinese leadership has not fully honoured its own 17-point Agreement of May 1951 to 'Liberate Tibet Peacefully' which was imposed on the Tibetan delegation. A dialogue between the Dalai Lama and the Chinese authorities was encouraged by India and others during 2002–5 wherein Dalai Lama had gradually shifted his position from 'independence' to 'meaningful autonomy'. In 2005, there were even hopes that China may let the Dalai Lama visit Tibet, at a place other than Lhasa, to pave the way for gradual resolution of the issue. However, the hardliners in Beijing prevailed.

The thrust on 'Tibetan autonomy' in India's position has been gradually diluted under the imperatives of improving relations with China and the compulsions of Chinese assertive stance. During the suppression of Tibetan uprising in 1988, India's reaction was mild as the then-prime minister was planning a visit to China to break the ice in bilateral relations. Rajiv Gandhi's visit in December 1988 opened up the dialogue on the border issue. India's reaction to the Tiananmen Square pro-democracy protests in 1989 in China was also cautious and politically correct. Subsequent developments led to confidence-building measures between the two countries, through the agreements in 1993 and 1996, to ensure that the border issue would be resolved through dialogue and without recourse to force. In 2003, when Prime Minister Atal Behari Vajpayee visited China, even the word 'Chinese suzerainty' was dropped, accepting Tibet as a part of 'Chinese territory'. During Prime Minister Dr Manmohan Singh's visit to China in January 2008, Tibet did not even figure in the official documents or speeches. China was happy with India's reiteration of 'one China' policy. Not only that, in preparation of this visit, the government of India restrained its ministers from attending Dalai Lama's felicitation ceremony in November 2007, as such an attendance would be 'not in conformity with the foreign policy of the government'.

With smoothly growing economic engagement and expectations of China's support for Indo–US nuclear deal as well as the United Nations Security Council membership, New Delhi finds it prudent to avoid irritating the Chinese with the Tibetan question. More so, the international community is also moving cautiously on Tibet. Both the United States and the United Kingdom have asked China to start negotiations with the Dalai Lama. Both the Dalai Lama and the Chinese Premier Wen Jiabao have, in principal, agreed to talk, though one wonder if and when the talk would really take place. No other Asian country has come out strongly against China on the suppression of the third Tibetan uprising.

While New Delhi has not rejoiced over Beijing's huge embarrassment and not sought to take any political advantage of it, the third Tibetan uprising cannot be resented as an unwelcome development. Any dusting-off of the so-called Tibet card, howsoever blunted it may have become, is advantageous to New Delhi in border negotiations with China, particularly at a time when the Chinese leaders have chosen to reassert their claims on Arunachal Pradesh.

Tibet is a party to the 1914 Simla Agreement between India and China that drew the McMahon line. China refuses to accept that line but Tibet and the Dalai Lama's government-in-exile continues to endorse it. Following the recent controversy on Arunachal Pradesh and Tawang, India's foreign secretary had gone to Dharamshala to brief the Dalai Lama. The prime minister of the Dalai Lama's exiled government in India, endorsing India's position, said in an interview after the current Tibetan uprising,

> We have continued the legitimate government of the Dalai Lama, which is now 367 years old. That government has agreed to McMahon line and Tawang and other issues were agreed on the basis of the watershed principles. The watershed principle said that whatever water comes to this side belongs to India. It was very clear demarcation. . . . If Chinese say that because the sixth Dalai Lama was born in Tawang, it belongs to Tibet then if one Dalai Lama was born in Mongolia, can I say Mongolia is a part of Tibet?

No one in India can afford to fritter away such a strong support by abandoning the Tibet issue altogether. Indian media has taken a much stronger position against China on the Tibetan issue. They have criticised India's position as being too soft to please the Chinese and asked for an urgent and serious review of its Tibet policy. There is no indication of the government thinking of reviewing its Tibet policy at this moment, but New Delhi may not be averse to the positive side of the Tibetan question. That is why India continues to host the Tibetan cause, in howsoever a diluted manner under the prevailing political constraints. It is to keep the Tibetan issue alive that India pays Rs 10 crore (raised from the earlier amount of Rs 1 crore [Rs 1 crore are equivalent to Rs 10 million]) annually for the upkeep of the Tibetan refugees and for the running of the Dalai Lama's government. Even in the heat of the present controversy, India has allowed the United States Congresswoman and speaker of the House of Representatives, Nancy Pelosi, to visit the Dalai Lama in Dharamshala on 21 March 2008, ignoring the Chinese displeasure and discarding the risk that such a visit may invite the charge of Indo–US collaboration against China on Tibet. She is the third highest ranking United States official and a staunch supporter of the Dalai Lama and the Tibetan freedom.

India has also looked with disapproval at the Chinese charge of 'conspiracy by the Dalai clique' in Tibet, because the uprising indeed seems to be beyond the Dalai Lama. The Chinese blame on the Dalai Lama is self-defeating as it exposes the fragility of the Chinese control in Tibet and their inability to anticipate such a development. On his part, the Dalai Lama has publicly confessed his inability to stop the violence and even offered to 'resign' if disturbances did not stop. The third Tibetan uprising is a serious indication of the ground slipping from under the Dalai Lama's feet with regard to the Tibetan issue. The Chinese refusal to deal with the Dalai Lama, and his as well as the international community's helplessness in forcing China to change its stance has frustrated Tibetans and led to the rise of militancy among the Tibetan youth, both inside and outside Tibet. Tibetan youth organisations in India have been carefully studying the South Asian militant movements like the Maoists of Nepal and the Liberation Tigers of Tamil Eelam of Sri Lanka for the past couple of years. India certainly does not look forward to the militarisation of the Tibetan movement and irrelevance of the Dalai Lama's 'middle path'. Any isolation of the Dalai Lama from the Tibetan movement will force India to review its present position. It may be desirable for China seriously to proceed with moves to engage the Dalai Lama in seeking a negotiated and peaceful solution of the Tibetan tangle.

The Chinese government may succeed in putting the present uprising under its boot, but the issue will not disappear. Who knows then, what would be the form of the fourth Tibetan uprising?

SECTION III

REGIONAL AND INTERNATIONAL RELATIONS

C. South Asia–South-East Asia Relations

62

Developing India–Malaysia Relations: Managing Issues of the Diaspora

MALMINDERJIT SINGH

(27 February 2008)

THE LATEST round of demonstrations by Malaysian Indians in Kuala Lumpur on 16 February 2008 dealt a huge blow to the country which had anticipated the end of domestic instability. In fact, the reverberations of the recent racial tensions in Malaysia could be felt all the way to New Delhi. India, which has acted quickly to repair any damages in its bilateral relations with Malaysia thus far, would be concerned about the implications of the latest round of Malaysian–Indian discontent on ties with its South-East Asian partner.

In clear efforts to deliver a positive signal, Indian chief of army staff, Deepak Kapoor visited Kuala Lumpur on 4 February 2008 in a bid to strengthen the defense cooperation between India and Malaysia. This diplomatic intervention by India came at a time when its bilateral relations with Malaysia were shaky, due to earlier protests by Malaysian Indians and the call for intervention from some quarters in India.

Although there have been some outstanding issues between both countries that need to be resolved, the Hindu Rights Action Front (HINDRAF) issue has become the main catalyst in the deterioration of their relations. This issue came up when the HINDRAF led a demonstration of almost 10,000 people in Kuala Lumpur on 25 November 2007. The crowd protested against the poor economic conditions, lack of education, religious and racial discrimination as well as social and political marginalisation against Malaysian Indians. Outraged by the demonstration, the Malaysian government invoked the Internal Security Act and labelled the protestors as a threat to peace and stability in the country.

India became embroiled in the issue when some HINDRAF leaders, including its head, P. Waythamoorthy, fled to Tamil Nadu to escape the Malaysian authorities. Painting a somewhat distorted and grim picture of the state of Malaysian Indians, these HINDRAF activists managed to stir the emotions of the Indian society. This prompted several Indian government officials and the Indian media to criticise the Malaysian government's treatment of Malaysian Indians openly. The chief minister of Tamil Nadu, M. Karunanidhi, has been most vocal in expressing his concern for the plight of Malaysian Indians and has pushed the Indian government to take some form of action. There have also been some initial statements of concern from key Indian government figures, including External Affairs Minister Pranab Mukherjee. The Malaysian government did not react positively to these comments. The Indian government soon realised that it had to refrain from interfering in this matter if it did not wish to jeopardise its relations with Malaysia.

The Indian Congress party has been facing pressure from its coalition partners such as the Dravida Munnetra Kazhagam as well as groups of the public who accuse the government of turning a blind eye towards the ill-treatment of its diaspora in Malaysia. The issue has placed the Congress in a dilemma. If it interferes in the issue, it could endanger its ties with Malaysia. And if it remains silent on the matter, it risks facing the wrath of its coalition partners and segments of the Indian society. With elections on the horizon, the latter may not necessarily be a wise option.

The Indian government feels that it has some form of moral responsibility in ensuring the welfare of its diaspora. India is one of the few countries in the world, that actively engages its diaspora in matters pertaining to the country. The previous government of the Bharatiya Janata Party launched the Pravasi Bharatiya Divas (Indian Diaspora Day) which has been carried on by the current government. The objective of this platform is to allow foreigners of Indian origin to bond with Indians and India so as to establish some form of synergy in economic, cultural and social ties. Further, the government has also decided to allow dual nationality for overseas Indians by offering them the Persons of Indian Origin (PIO) cards. Through these policies, India intends to attract overseas Indians and their investments back to their 'motherland' to bolster its development and growth. This was most recently reiterated by Prime Minister Manmohan Singh at the 6th Pravasi Bharatiya Divas meetings in New Delhi from 7–9 January 2008 when he called for greater participation of PIOs in the social development of India's key sectors. In this context, not only does an economically poor diaspora in Malaysia constrain this policy, it also highlights the moral duty of India towards the Malaysian Indians.

India's relations with Malaysia, on the other hand, are more valuable the international context. As historical allies in the Non-Aligned Movement during the Cold War period, Malaysia and India had a dip in their relations during the 1990s as New Delhi's economic reforms brought it closer to the Western countries. However, as India increases its engagement with South-East Asia as part of its 'Look East' policy, it has worked hard to mend ties with Malaysia. Indeed, political, economic, trade and defense cooperation between both Malaysia and India has increased over the last decade. Bilateral trade surged to US $5.7 billion in 2006 from US $2.25 billion in 1998. In addition, as facilitator to the India–ASEAN Free Trade Agreement negotiations, Malaysia plays a key role in India's integration with the ASEAN economies. Moreover, India and Malaysia are negotiating a Closer Economic Cooperation Agreement that will see both sides aiming to seal a free trade deal, involving trade in goods and services, investment and economic cooperation, by March 2009. Bearing these factors in mind, it will be economically and politically too costly for India to sacrifice its relationship with Malaysia.

India realises the benefits of maintaining strong and deep ties with Malaysia. Even as it is no wonder that the most recent demonstrations in Malaysia should have caused some anxiety amongst Indian policy makers. With Malaysia preparing for elections, domestic stability becomes an important matter and the last thing that Malaysia needs is external interference. India, for one, has benefited greatly from Malaysia's leadership under Prime Minister Abdullah Badawi who has been keen to develop a close relationship with New Delhi. It is, thus, in India's interest that Badawi's government is voted back into power. Although a segment of the Malaysian Indian community, which is only 7 per cent of the country's population, is unlikely to be able to wield sufficient power to change the political fortunes in Malaysia, it could continue to remain a thorn on the Malaysian government's side.

If India feels that it has an obligation to empower Malaysian Indians, then it should adopt strategies to carry this out in a subtle yet non-obtrusive manner. First, India has to realise that not all Malaysian Indians are economically starved. In comparing Gini coefficients, the coefficient values among Indians have increased from 0.413 in 1999 to 0.425 in 2004. This shows that there is growing inequality among the Malaysian Indian community itself. Therefore, any assistance should be targeted at the lower-income Malaysian Indians and not at the entire community itself. Next, India should have specific strategies for improving the lives of these less well-off Malaysian Indians. India, fast becoming an education hub especially for information technology, management and medicine, could offer scholarships for low-income Malaysian Indians. The Indian government could also rally the Indian trade and business associations to offer some form of financial assistance or training in specific employable skills.

However, the Indian government would need to put into perspective the extent of its assistance to its diaspora, given the plight of a significant segment of its own population. The Malaysian Indians, and other diaspora, have to realise that they cannot turn to India to support them on issues of their adopted country. Doing so will only place India and its government in a precarious position with other countries and endanger the global rise of India. A few years after India's Independence, India's first prime minister, Jawaharlal Nehru, told the Indian diaspora that they had to integrate themselves fully into the countries of their adoption as their loyalties should lie primarily with the countries of their choice. It is timely that the current Indian administration reiterates this mantra to its expanding diaspora the world over.

63

Inter-Regionalism and its Possibilities

ONG KENG YONG
(*19 September 2008*)

SOUTH-EAST ASIA has the Association of South-East Asian Nations (ASEAN) and South Asia has the South Asian Association for Regional Cooperation (SAARC). Both regional organisations were founded to minimise and settle disputes without the use of force, and to maximise growth through economic development and trade. In other words, peace and prosperity are the goals of ASEAN and SAARC. There will be security and stability. There will be benefits for the people. Other nations outside South-East Asia and South Asia will desire stronger relations with the two regions, which means greater links with the world, and the multilateral international system will therefore be more open and be further strengthened.

Put simply, we will have a vast region of cohesive and progressing nations externally-oriented and committed to peace, prosperity and a people-centered future. Are we there? If not, what can be done to bring us there?

There is now a closer network of regional cooperation between South Asia and South-East Asia. We see a range of overlapping structures, from the ASEAN Regional Forum (ARF) to the Bay of Bengal Initiative for Multi Sectoral Technical and Economic Cooperation (BIMSTEC), shaping the framework of cooperation of our regions. India and Pakistan are Dialogue Partners of ASEAN. India, Pakistan, Bangladesh and Sri Lanka are also members of the ARF. India is a member of the East Asia Summit (EAS) process. India has also proposed an iconic cultural project—the Nalanda University. This project has the potential to bring South Asia and South-East Asia even closer together and revive the old civilisational links. Nalanda is also meant to bring us closer to the North-East Asian nations—

China, Japan and Korea—through its core action of rejuvenating Buddhist studies and reinforcing inter-faith understanding.

Throughout ASEAN and SAARC, influences originating from the Indus civilisation are prominent. This is not just about the great religions and their inclusiveness. It is also about how the magnanimity of power through the centuries before us created new culture, life and zeal for the flourishing of the human spirit. Mother India is omnipresent and so we need to see how the India of today fares in the cooperation of our two regions.

India is an important neighbour and stakeholder. A strong ASEAN–India partnership is the key to tackling current and future challenges. Among South Asian countries, India's relations with ASEAN are the most entrenched. Singapore believes that, as a major power, India can play a positive role in South-East Asia with others like the United States of America, China and Japan, and India has a critical stake in ASEAN's peace and prosperity. That is why Singapore has always encouraged greater engagement of ASEAN by India and why Singapore pushed strongly for India's inclusion in the EAS process. Over the past decade, with India's economic opening up and its 'Look East' policy, ASEAN and India are increasingly partaking in each other's growth.

Prime Minister Manmohan Singh has articulated India's 'Look East' policy in his vision of an 'Arc of Advantage'—an Asian economic community consisting of an integrated market, linked closely by rail, road, air and sea. Prime Minister Singh's commitment to the expeditious conclusion of two key building blocks in this architecture—the ASEAN–India Free Trade Area and the ASEAN–India Open Skies Agreement—is a signal of the resolve of today's India to become a key player in shaping the regional architecture.

Underpinning the thriving ASEAN–India relationship is the convergence in our strategic outlooks that view each other as natural extensions of strategic and economic space. It is likely that this geo-strategic logic provided strong impetus in driving the recent conclusion of the Goods chapter in the ASEAN–India Free Trade Agreement (FTA), even if the negotiations might have been a drawn-out process. The conclusion of the investment and services chapters, aimed for 2009, will further anchor the strategic and economic relationship between ASEAN and India.

In 2007, ASEAN's trade with India grew to US $38 billion. This figure represents just 2 per cent of ASEAN's global trade. The ASEAN–India FTA has the potential to catalyse economic linkages between the two regions, even as it acts to further anchor ASEAN–India relations.

During his visit to Indonesia in April 2005 for the 50th anniversary of the Bandung Conference, Prime Minister Singh stated that India intended to stay engaged by sharing experiences gained from its own development process with the Asian nations. He said: 'Human resource development holds the key to employment and wealth creation, particularly in this age of globalisation. This has been our strategy and we have laid particular emphasis on training and skills development as we globalize. . . . ' Indeed, India has set up training centres in ASEAN member states to impart technical knowledge, skills in English as a language of international communication and commerce, and foundation learning for the youth of South-East Asia.

India has thus strengthened economic ties, pursued educational cooperation and reinforced strategic relationships. This combination of hard and soft power is still in its infancy. A consolidation of this approach will lift India's engagement to an unprecedented level. It is important to bear in mind three things that India can offer South-East Asian nations which no other Asian power is able to do likewise. These are English language skills; management of 'unity in diversity' (that is, a multi-ethnic and multi-cultural society); and capacity building for a democratic governance (for example, an independent and functioning Election Commission).

The emerging assessment is quite positive for India's role in advancing cooperation between South-East Asia and South Asia. The challenge is to sustain this good progress. There is no doubt that domestic politics in India will draw attention away from this endeavour. Perhaps, the way forward is to get SAARC to carry the task into the future through an institutionalised partnership between the two regional organisations. Is this possible? Let us see what has happened in ASEAN–SAARC collaboration.

ASEAN and SAARC have been stepping up their engagement in recent years. Officials from both sides have met to exchange information and best practices in areas ranging from trade to tourism, and to tackling HIV/AIDS and Avian Influenza. Looking ahead, we can expect cooperation to increase in scope and intensity as the two regional bodies continue to mature and develop, and as we find more areas of common interest.

ASEAN is moving purposefully towards the ASEAN Community by 2015 based on the three pillars of political/security cooperation, economic integration and sociocultural cooperation. The ASEAN economic integration will create a single market and production base in South-East Asia. Many small and technical steps have been undertaken by ASEAN. Economic integration may not be very obvious to the layman but it is therefor real. In any case, ASEAN cannot stop this or move backwards because the geopolitical, economic and strategic drivers are in motion.

SAARC has also started its own free trade agenda and is moving on with small and technical steps. ASEAN and SAARC can share experiences, in the spirit of what Dr Singh stated during his visit to Indonesia in April 2005 for the Bandung Conference commemoration. The trade liberalisation initiatives in South Asia and South-East Asia will create new opportunities to forge stronger economic and political ties.

Some experts and scholars have been depressed by the slow progress and minimal developments to date. They argue that the huge size of India and its devotion to the maintenance of India's advantage in the subcontinent have been the drags on SAARC's own evolution and transition. Their contention is that the South Asian nations are in a continuous state of fire fighting, managing one crisis after another arising from hubris and political manoeuvres. As such, this region is not well connected with external actors and cannot do much with ASEAN in a common endeavour of regional cooperation and collaboration.

However, in my view, there is enlightened leadership in the South Asian nations and it has been shown to exercise statesmanship and manifest a regional ego. Political will can be delivered if mutual interests are articulated and demonstrated well. Globalisation and its attendant consequences, particularly the increased interdependence, require all governments and leaders to seek new policy options and competitive designs. In any case, the challenges looming ahead, such as climate change, environmental degradation, natural disasters, and rising cost of energy and food, are all transnational in nature and would need multilateral strategies to manage. Working together with ASEAN and South-East Asia gives the extra wherewithal.

I hold the view that India and SAARC have contributed to inter-regional partnership. They are supported by the positive attitudes of the other South Asian countries, especially Pakistan, Bangladesh and Sri Lanka. It is a real treat to see these four partners of ASEAN working constructively for the regional good at ASEAN-led forums. ASEAN's trade with Pakistan reached US $3.3 billion in 2006. Pakistan is attracting more investments from ASEAN member states such as Malaysia, Singapore and Thailand. Bangladesh's and Sri Lanka's trade with ASEAN individually totalled more than US $1 billion in 2005. There is also a large workforce from Bangladesh and Sri Lanka in ASEAN consisting not merely of manual labour but high-skilled professionals as well. Enhanced cooperation in the field of transnational crime has taken place, notably in the exchange of information on drug and human traffickers, and international terrorists.

What else can be done to obtain more benefits from inter-regional cooperation? Let me suggest the following possibilities:

1. Educational exchanges between 10 universities from ASEAN and 10 from SAARC;
2. Twinning 10 cities in ASEAN with 10 in SAARC;
3. Starting dialogues between Track II parties and inviting them to observe ASEAN/SAARC official meetings;
4. Connecting youth bodies via the e-net and other technological innovations;
5. Linking up parliamentarians through intellectual pursuits and sports;
6. Harnessing the latest technologies in increasing productivity, especially at the SME-level and in agriculture and aquaculture;
7. Improving transportation links to facilitate movements of people and tourists;
8. Working together in international bodies and forums which have

programmes and projects for the protection of children, women and the elderly and helping them to contribute in their own ways to society;

9. Those South Asian countries in the ARF can initiate more confidence-building and conflict prevention activities for ARF participants, especially joint training of relevant personnel; and
10. Foster a general atmosphere of good neighbourliness and positive governance where all ASEAN and SAARC member states contribute to the preservation of peace and security in the entire region.

In conclusion, while we cannot claim to have a rosy picture, there is cause for optimism. The potential is huge. ASEAN is committed to the ASEAN Community where political cooperation is buttressed by a solid single market based on economic integration and assisted by a salubrious socio-cultural milieu. South Asia can leverage on this to reach a new height in its own vision of peace, prosperity and people-centred future sooner than later.

SECTION III

REGIONAL AND INTERNATIONAL RELATIONS

D. South Asia–United States Relations

64

India's Nuclear Dilemma: To Drop the Deal or to Drop the Left

S.D. MUNI

(*30 June 2008*)

THE FATE OF the Indo–US nuclear deal is on the brink. The 9th meeting of India's ruling United Progressive Alliance (UPA) and its Left supporters, held in New Delhi on 25 June 2008, drew the parting line but ducked the final verdict. This was done in the interest of buying some more time to work out the least painful way of separation. After unusual hectic political activity for at least a week preceding the meeting, in a cold statement, the convenor of the meeting and minister of external affairs, Pranab Mukherjee, said, 'The Committee completed its discussions on all aspects of the India–United States Nuclear Cooperation Agreement. The next meeting of the Committee, to be convened in due course, will finalise its findings.'

THE DIFFERENCES AND THE ISSUES

Behind this vague statement are sharp differences on the issue. The Left parties, supporting the UPA government from outside with their 59 members in parliament, are adamant in not allowing the deal to go through. Their objections are at two levels; one, at the policy level, against India's growing strategic proximity with the United States and; two, with regard to the contents and implications of the deal. In their view, the deal, besides forcing India to compromise on further nuclear tests and reprocessing of the spent nuclear fuel, will also impose constraints on its relations with countries such as Iran, due to the overall Hyde Act of the

United States Congress, which governs the bilateral agreement. The Indian government, particularly Dr Manmohan Singh, is strongly committed to the deal as it promises to break India's nuclear and hi-tech isolation and offers an additional source of energy at a time when hydro-carbon dependence looks costly and grim. The government does not accept the objections raised by the Left and claims to be confident that it can deal with the foreign policy constraints as they are more notional than real. The government side circulated a 'Note' at the meeting underlining the competitive nature of the nuclear power.

There is more to the Left–Congress policy and ideological differences on the Indo–US nuclear deal. There exists a serious trust deficit between the two sides. The Left is annoyed at the Congress for cosying up to the United States on foreign policy issues and the Congress suspects that the Left is toeing the China line on keeping India away, not only from the United States strategically, but also from its legitimate status as a major international player. Media and overall political opinions are also divided along these lines. The Left accused the prime minister of not taking them into confidence while negotiating the deal with the United States and the prime minster had challenged the Left to withdraw support to his government if they want to (so be it) on the nuclear issue. The prime minister is personally convinced that the deal is in India's supreme national interests and has made a personal commitment to the United States president, George Bush, to deliver this deal from India's side.

The issue at stake in the 25 June 2008 meeting was to let India go ahead and sign the nuclear safeguards agreement with the International Atomic Energy Agency (IAEA). The negotiations on this issue have been finalised between India and the IAEA and a draft agreement has been prepared. These negotiations were carried out after seeking support of the Left under the condition that the government would get back to this Committee to brief the Left and other alliance partners on the outcome of these negotiations before signing the agreement with the IAEA. The government's 'Note' in the meeting clarified that, 'The safeguards will be restricted to the facilities that India identifies as civilian and such facilities will be eligible for international cooperation.' The 'Note' further said that, 'All externally-supplied items will come under the IAEA safeguards'. Once the government signs this agreement, the United States will follow it up, first, by getting the necessary waiver from the Nuclear Suppliers Group (NSG) on the Indo–United States deal and, then, by finally approving it in the United States Congress. The Left's opposition to the government signing the safeguards agreement was explained at the 26 June 2008 meeting by the Communist Party of India (Marxist) [CPI(M)] leader, Prakash Karat, who, after reiterating the Left's position on the deal and the Hyde Act, said that, once the IAEA agreement has signed, the deal would go on 'auto-pilot' where only the United States would carry it through and India (and the Left) would not be left with much scope to have any say. The Left also grumbled that the government had not shared the full text of the proposed IAEA agreement with them.

The Congress party's UPA allies are also in favour of the deal as they find it in India's national interests but they do not want the government to fall over the differences with the Left. In fact, no one wants the government to fall, except the Bhartiya Janata Party (BJP)-led National Democratic Alliance (NDA), which is in opposition. All the components of the ruling party combine are hesitant to plunge into elections at a time when inflation is more than 11 per cent and rising. The combined impact of the sky-rocketing oil prices and implications of the global sub-prime crisis have put heavy strains on the economy and, hence, on the common man in India. A heavy political price may be extracted by the voters if the government goes to polls without softening the economic burden. Rashtriya Janata Dal (RJD) chief and minister for railways in the UPA government, Lalu Prasad Yadav, cryptically remarked: 'The country needs energy and for that the deal is important. But inflation is a much more pressing issue affecting the common masses. It has to be reined in.' Yadav's concern is more specific because in his home state, where his party's government was defeated in the last elections, his electoral base has eroded and his rival provincial government headed by Nitish Kumar is doing much better. The Congress has also suffered electoral reverses in the recently-held state assembly elections, the latest being in the

Karnataka in June 2008. In these elections, the BJP and the NDA allies made gains.

Even the Left has electoral worries both in West Bengal and Kerala, their strongholds. In West Bengal, issues such as the Nandigram Special Economic Zone have dented their electoral hold in nearly 10 constituencies, including Kolkata, Barrackpur, Jadavpur, Sreerampur, Tamluk and Haldia. In Kerala, the Christian votes that favoured the CPI(M) in the last elections have been alienated. Muslim-dominated Malappuram and Kozhikode are also unhappy with the Left front on a textbook controversy. The Christians (20 per cent) and Muslims (25 per cent) in Kerala together constitute a decisive factor in six parliamentary constituencies. As a result, though the Left leader, Karat, put up a brave face by being prepared to go to elections, he pleaded with other UPA allies such as Dravida Munnetra Kazhagam leader, M. Karunanidhi, and the Nationalist Congress Party leader, Sharad Pawar, to persuade the Congress to avoid the split. No one in the ruling coalition is looking forward to immediate elections.

The Options

The opinions in the UPA and, the country as a whole, are polarised along three policy options. One is to drop the deal as is being suggested by the Left and develop India's indigenous civil nuclear power through thorium (which India has in abundance) cycle, even if takes time; or renegotiate the deal with the United States, if necessary, with the next administration. India is of as critical a value to the United States as the United States is to India in the emerging dynamics of global power equations. This will spare India from making any compromises with the United States in the freedom of its foreign policy and strategic options, though it may delay its nuclear energy programme. In any case, according to a section of the scientific community in India, the Indo–United States deal will also not deliver energy any time sooner. For energy security, the nuclear option is not the only way out. A vast potential of hydro-power lies unharnessed within India as also in the neighbouring countries and Indian scientists are working hard to develop the thorium cycle to generate power. Besides, renewable and newer sources of energy should also be harnessed. Thus, dropping the deal will help cement UPA–Left alliance, not only during the coming elections, but also in the post-election process of government formation.

The second option is to drop the Left and sign the deal. This will ensure India's credibility in the international community, and that of the Indian prime minister and the Congress within India. The prime minister and the UPA have given enough margin to the Left without effecting even the slightest change in the Left's attitude. The Left has seldom let a chance to embarrass and oppose the government go without taking full advantage of it. The Left refuses to see the positive aspects of the deal regarding energy and global access to strategic technologies and material. The UPA can no longer continue to be dictated by the Left on issues of vital national concern. This option is against any delay in the decision because there is a serious need to ensure a continuing supply of uranium for the currently-operating reactors. The prime minister has also to attend the G8 Summit in Tokyo in early July 2008, where he is likely to meet world leaders, including President Bush, and apprise them of India's progress on the nuclear deal. Moreover, a delayed decision will only buy the government four more months in power because, if the government falls now, elections will have to be held by November/December 2008; but if it does not, elections have to be held in April 2009, when the term of the present government comes to an end. These extra four months may not offer any great political advantage to the government.

The third option is to avoid any of the above precipitate actions and buy as much time as possible. In this period, efforts should be made on various fronts namely: (a) finding a mutually acceptable compromise between the UPA and the Left on the deal; (b) improving the economic situation with the help of good monsoon, bold monetary initiatives and in the hope that the global economy will show signs of improvement; and (c) pleading with the United States to cooperate in getting the deal finalised in November or December 2008 rather than in the forthcoming session of the Congress. This may be somewhat technically difficult but not impossible, and politically still feasible for the Bush administration. The Bush administration becomes a lame duck only after the presidential elections. In fact, the United States administration has assured India that it will work for the deal until 20 January 2009. The State Department spokesman, Tom Casey, said on 19 June 2008: 'From now until January 20, we'll continue to work to support this agreement. We will continue to encourage the Indian government to approve it.' He further hoped that the next administration would 'move forward' with the deal. It is argued under the third option that a precipitate action will surely provoke the Left into withdrawing its support. This would make the government either a lame duck, if a vote is carried against it in the parliament or a minority government if a parliamentary vote can be avoided.[1] In both these cases, the government's bargaining position *vis-à-vis* the United States will be compromised at the two pending stages of the NSG waiver and the Congressional endorsement. There are elements opposed to the deal at both these stages within the NSG and in the United States Congress.

The third option appeals to the core political instinct of survival among the political parties. It also gained acceptability in the given context of economic hardships and the BJP's recent political gains. To some extent, hectic political manoeuvres by the Left to scare the Congress and the UPA allies from taking a precipitate action of going ahead with the deal also whipped up this option. But this option does not have a longer life span, for it has already been in operation for the past more than one year. The possibility of the UPA exercising the first option is least likely as that will tarnish the image of its prime minister and the Congress, while sacrificing what it considers as in India's national interests.

The UPA seems to be gradually gearing towards the second option. There are indications that the Congress president, Mrs Sonia Gandhi, has already asked the Congress to rally round the prime minister. She has discounted the exaggerated fears that going with the Indo–US deal would necessarily result in the alienation of the Muslim votes, a threat branded by the Left. There are also signs of the Congress support among the other smaller parties that have remained out of the UPA and NDA and formed another grouping in the name of the United National Progressive Alliance (UNPA), led by Samajwadi Party (SP) of Mulayam Singh, to represent the 'third force' in Indian politics.[2] In the event of the Left pulling the rug, these parties may come forward to offer the necessary numbers for the survival of the UPA government. The SP has 39 members in parliament and with the addition of other smaller parties support (Rashtriya Lok Dal of Ajit Singh with three seats, Janata Dal (S) of Deve Gowda with three seats and some floating votes), the UPA may retain majority after the Left pulls out. The effective strength of the parliament is 542 and the UPA needs the support of 272 to win the confidence vote. Will the Congress succeed in creating counter-balances against the Left and mustering the political will of its allies and along with its own to exercise the second option, however, remains to be seen, as the UNPA will decide only on 3 July 2008.

Both the Left and the Congress are also trying to make their parting as less painful as possible. For achieving this, the Congress and the Left are in touch with each other. The Congress party's plea with the Left would be that when the government goes to the IAEA to endorse the safeguards agreement, the Left may politically distance itself but avoid writing to the president that they have no confidence in the government. In that situation, it will be upon the BJP/NDA to move the motion of no-confidence against the government in parliament. If and when the BJP moves such a motion, the Left may criticise and oppose the government during the debate on the no-confidence, short of voting with the BJP. It can walk out or abstain at the time of voting. The government may then survive either with the help of the SP and other smaller parties or it will be turned into a minority government without being voted out of office. The possibility of postponing the monsoon session, scheduled for July to August or September 2008 to keep any possibility of a no-confidence vote on hold is also being actively considered. Both the Left and the UPA, notwithstanding their sharp differences on the nuclear deal seem to be of the view that no political advantage should accrue to the BJP. The CPI leader, A.B. Bardhan, has already gone on record to say that his party will not vote with the BJP to oust the government.

The Indo–US nuclear deal is, perhaps, the first foreign policy issue in the past decades that has polarised Indian politics so sharply and precipitated a crisis of survival for the government. In 1962, Jawarharlal Nehru's China policy had come close to this in view of China's war on India. That political crisis was quickly diffused by Nehru by sacrificing his friend and then defence minister, Krishna Menon, to silence the critics of his China policy. Mrs Sonia Gandhi does not seem to be contemplating the possibility at all of re-inforcing her grandfather-in-law's precedence by sacrificing Prime Minister Manmohan Singh in the interest of UPA–Left alliance. She herself is committed to the Indo–US nuclear deal. India has now entered a phase of coalition politics which has eroded the broad foreign policy consensus prevailing for a long in the country. This is not a very happy development for a country that is still struggling to secure its rightful place in the global community. The world will naturally monitor closely the evolving interface between the coalition regimes and critical foreign policy issues in India.

NOTES

1. A legitimate minority government can continue to function even after the withdrawal of support by the Left if the Left or the opposition NDA does not force a confidence vote on the floor of the parliament.
2. The Congress has been actively pursuing Mulayam Singh for support as both the parties stand to gain even in Uttar Pradesh where Congress has fallen out from its erstwhile ally and the SP rival, Mayawati's Bahujan Samaj Party.

65

India–United States Relations under the Obama Administration

SANJAY BARU
(10 November 2008)

What would an Obama Administration in Washington D.C. mean for India and for India–United States Relations?

UNITED STATES President-elect Barack Obama's most recent and most detailed comment on relations with India is contained in the personal letter he addressed to Prime Minister Manmohan Singh when the latter visited Washington D.C. in September 2008. Obama said, 'I would like to see United States–India relations grow across the board to reflect our shared interests, shared values, shared sense of threats, and ever burgeoning ties between our two economies and societies.'

As a 'starting point', Obama said, 'our common strategic interests call for redoubling United States–Indian military, intelligence, and law enforcement cooperation'. He went on to add that 'the recent bombings (in New Delhi) remind us that we are both victims of terrorist attacks on our soil, and we share a common goal of defeating these forces of extremism'. He wanted the United States and India to work together

> to promote our democratic values and strengthen legal institutions in South Asia and beyond. We should also be working hand-in-hand to tap into the creativity and dynamism of our entrepreneurs, engineers and scientists to promote development of alternative sources of clean energy. Imagine our two democracies in action—Indian laboratories and industry collaborating with American laboratories and industry to discover innovative solutions to today's energy problems. That's the kind of new partnership I would like to build with India as President.

India's relations with the United States have evolved considerably during the past decade. The turning point was President Bill Clinton's visit to India in 1999. The foundation for the transformed India–United States relationship was laid in the last year of the Clinton Administration and the first term of the Bush administration. The conclusion of the historic India–United States civil nuclear co-operation agreement marked the high point of that transformation. Obama takes charge at a time when there is bipartisan support in the United States, and the dominant parties' support in India, for a stronger and deeper bilateral relationship.

Two sets of factors have shaped this transformation. These can be classified as 'real' and 'ideological'. The 'real' factors include India's economic growth and openness, the growing influence of the Indian American community in United States political and economic life, a shared concern with jihadi terrorism and for greater energy security. The 'ideological' factors include a shared desire to ensure a multipolar Asia, with the rise of China, and a shared commitment to democracy and pluralism. While George Bush may not have been interested in a multipolar world, Obama has shown greater willingness to work even at the global level with other 'major powers', including India. On the other hand, Obama may be less wary of a rising China than Bush was.

All these factors will endure and continue to work for improved India–United States relations in the foreseeable future. The two countries will, however, have differences on issues such as climate change and multilateral trade policy. While differences are likely to persist on other issues such as nuclear non-proliferation and while some expect old differences to crop up on issues such as 'Kashmir', these are by no means unmanageable. Thus, there is no reason to expect a reversal of the recent trend of improved bilateral economic, political and strategic relations, evolving in the direction of a full-fledged strategic partnership.

President-elect Obama's 'First 100 Days' in office will coincide with the 'Last 100 Days' of Prime Minister Singh's present term. However, for both of them economy and terrorism will remain the main preoccupations.

The Economy

While domestic economic issues will remain the major pre-occupation for both heads of government in these 100 days, both will remain equally focused on the global economic situation. These issues will dominate the agenda at the first meeting that Obama and Dr Singh will have on 15 November 2008 in Washington D.C. Dr Singh is likely to find a more sympathetic listener in Obama than President Bush. India and the United States have the potential to work together to address global economic management issues. They should.

Indo–US economic relations are poised to enter a new phase with the conclusion of the civil nuclear cooperation agreement. The possibility of increased high-technology trade and trade in defence, space, nuclear and other strategic areas has the potential sharply to increase bilateral trade, especially United States exports to India. Faced with the task of pulling the United States economy out of a potential depression, Obama is unlikely to harm this process by reversing any of the initiatives taken by the Bush administration that have opened up new business opportunities for United States companies in India. However, renewed protectionism in the United States could harm Indian business interests. India will have to be proactive in ensuring that any economic rescue package in the United States does not harm Indian trade interests.

Obama's two key economic advisors, Paul Volcker and Lawrence Summers, are personal friends of Prime Minister Singh. They have high professional regard for him and deep interest in closer economic relations with India. Both are likely to favour a larger role for India in global economic management as well. Prime Minister Singh's positive approach to finding consensual global solutions to the global economic crisis, his focus on improved regulation and strengthening of multilateral institutions, and his commitment to stay the course on domestic economic policies will add resonance to India's voice at the forthcoming G-20 heads of government meeting.

India would watch closely what position Obama adopts on the Doha Development Round of multilateral trade negotiations. More specifically, India would be interested in his administration's approach to outsourcing and to investments by United States firms in India. It is likely that the Obama administration would restrict H1-B visas. However, this is no longer a major issue in India, given the skill shortage within India and the emergence of other destinations for software engineers. However, outsourcing and services export opportunities remain important for India as its merchandise trade deficit grows.

War on Terror

India would welcome the tone of Obama's reference to terrorism in the region in his letter to Prime Minister Singh. Obama said:

> I deplore and condemn the vicious attacks perpetrated in New Delhi earlier this month, and on the Indian embassy in Kabul on 7 July. The death and destruction is reprehensible, and you and your nation have my deepest sympathy. These cowardly acts of mass murder are a stark reminder that India suffers from the scourge of terrorism on a scale few other nations can imagine. I will continue to urge all countries to cooperate with Indian authorities in tracking down the perpetrators of these atrocities. My thoughts and prayers are with the victims and their families.

It is not often recognised that the Indian view on the so-called 'war on terror' is closer to the Obama view than the Bush doctrine. Prime Minister Singh has not been given adequate credit for speaking out openly against the war in Iraq. Even in July 2005, on the very day the decision to seek a civil nuclear cooperation agreement was announced in Washington D.C., Prime Minister Singh said at the National Press Club in Washington D.C., 'it was our sincere view that it (invasion of Iraq) was a mistake. . . .'[1]

Equally, India has always sought more focused global attention on the situation in Afghanistan. India had been critical of the decline in the North Atlantic Treaty Organization's focus on Afghanistan. Hence, Obama's renewed focus on Afghanistan would be welcomed by India. However, concern has been expressed by some commentators about Obama's statements linking the situation in Afghanistan and Pakistan to that in Kashmir and the possibility of a revival of the 'hyphenation with Pakistan' in the India–United States relationship.[2]

One of the great achievements of the Bush administration has been the 'dehyphenation' of the India–Pakistan equation from the India–United States relationship. India would hope that Obama does not reverse the clock on this. Pakistan may well seek a re-hyphenation for its own political and diplomatic reasons, especially at a time when it is desperately seeking an economic lifeline. On the other hand, such a re-hyphenation could jeopardise progress at the India–Pakistan bilateral level. Moreover, Indian and Pakistani public opinion would favour a bilateral solution to the Kashmir issue rather than one actively mediated by the United States. Some elements in Pakistan army may favour United States involvement to divert United States attention away from the real battle against terrorism in the subcontinent, but no United States interest would be served.

One of the significant developments in India–Pakistan relations has been the enormous progress made through the 'back channel' in bilateral diplomacy. This bilateral diplomacy was initiated, on the Indian side, by the then-Prime Minister Atal Behari Vajpayee and sustained, widened and deepened by Dr Singh; and on the Pakistan side by the then-President Pervez Musharraf. President Asif Ali Zardari has also walked the same path so far and 'credible' options for 'solving' the 'Kashmir problem' exist. Indian, Pakistani and 'Kashmiri' political leaderships have shown remarkable maturity in developing such options. Concrete progress has been delayed by political developments in Pakistan during 2007–8 and could be resumed once the political leadership in Pakistan feels more settled and confident.

Obama would have to resist attempts by his advisors or other self-proclaimed do-gooders to get the United States back into this equation. The United States knows well that no India–Pakistan bilateral agreement can survive without its blessings. The Bush administration was wise to restrict its involvement to 'blessing' the Manmohan–Musharraf and the Manmohan–Zardari dialogue. That is exactly what Obama should do as well.

Nuclear Issues

Several analysts have pointed to the influence of the so-called 'Ayatollahs of non-proliferation' within the Democratic Party, in general, and among Obama advisors, in particular. While Obama was responsible for a key, aborted, 'killer amendment' to the Hyde Act, he subsequently recanted and supported the 123 Agreement. In his letter to Prime Minister Singh, he wrote,

> I also want to take this opportunity to express my great admiration for the courage you showed in shepherding the civil nuclear cooperation agreement through your Parliament, the IAEA, and the NSG. I was pleased to vote by proxy for the agreement in (Senate Foreign Relations) Committee today, and I very much hope we can vote on this agreement before the US Congress goes out of session. As you know, there are some procedural obstacles that may prevent a vote this year, . . . when it does come up for a vote, however, I will of course vote in favour. If time should run out in the current Congress, I will resubmit the agreement next year as president.

Obama said:

> I strongly support civil nuclear cooperation, because I believe it will enhance our partnership and deepen our cooperation on a whole range of matters. Importantly, it will help India to meet its growing electricity demands while aiding in the important effort to combat global warming. But I see this agreement only as a beginning of a much closer relationship between our two great countries.

What New Delhi would want elaboration of and clarification on, presumably, would be Obama's statement that the 'civil nuclear cooperation agreement can open the door to greater collaboration with India on non-proliferation issues', as well as his assertion of commitment to the Comprehensive Test Ban Treaty. India would, however, welcome Obama's statement that he is 'committed to the goal of a world without nuclear weapons, and will make this a central element of US nuclear weapons policy'. India has already welcomed the Kissinger, Nunn, et al's proposal on this.

The Obama Team

Individuals matter in the United States system. In the Bush administration, for example, the approach towards India changed markedly after Condoleezza Rice replaced Colin Powell as secretary of state. Hence, India will wait to see who the key officials will be in an Obama administration.

India would expect strong support for good India–United States relations from Vice-President-elect Joe Biden. He played an influential role in securing the Democratic Party's support for the civil nuclear cooperation agreement. India also enjoys a good equation with John Kerry, who could become secretary of state. Biden, Summers and Kerry would be influential members of an Obama administration favourably disposed towards India. Biden and Kerry visited India and publicly endorsed the civil nuclear agreement, helping forge the strong bilateral support that it received in the United States Senate and House.

John Hamre, head of the Center for Strategic and International Studies (CSIS), has been mentioned as a possible secretary of defence. Hamre chaired the first 'track two' United States–Japan–India Strategic Dialogue in Tokyo in 2007 and, under his leadership, CSIS has taken keen interest in the United States–India strategic and defence relationship. Others named as possible senior cabinet officials in the Obama administration such as Chuck Hagel, Richard Lugar, Richard Danzig and Richard Holbrooke have visited India in the past year and have had meetings with Prime Minister Singh.

The last United States president to visit India in his first term was Jimmy Carter in 1979. Both Clinton and Bush visited India only in their second term. A first term visit by Obama to India, perhaps in early 2010, a year after a new government takes charge in Delhi, would ensure that the momentum gained in the bilateral relationship in the past four years is sustained.

NOTES

1. Dr Singh recalled this fact while speaking in parliament during the debate on the vote of confidence in July this year. He said, 'We have differed with the USA on their intervention in Iraq. I had explicitly stated at a press conference at the National Press Club in Washington D.C. in July 2005 that intervention in Iraq was a mistake.' Prime Minister Manmohan Singh's speeches at www.pmindia.nic.in
2. C. Raja Mohan, 'Barack Obama's Kashmir Thesis', *Indian Express*, 3 November 2008. Also see Barack Obama, 'Renewing American Leadership', *Foreign Affairs*, July/August 2007.

SECTION III

REGIONAL AND INTERNATIONAL RELATIONS

E. South Asia–Russia Relations

66

Russian Premier Victor Zubkov in India: Reinvigorating Relations

S.D. MUNI

(*18 February 2008*)

WITHIN THREE months of Indian Prime Minister Manmohan Singh's state visit to Russia, his Russian counterpart, Prime Minister Viktor Zubkov, visited New Delhi for three days from 12 to 14 February 2008. The purpose was to deepen and expand multifaceted bilateral cooperation between the two countries, particularly in the areas of defence, energy and trade.

Defence has been the strongest sector of bilateral engagement between the two countries where India receives almost 70 per cent of its critical requirements from Russia. There have been, of late, irritants on issues related to the transfer of technology, supply of spare parts, and the cost and time scales of equipment and their upgrading. These irritants include the spill-over into public of the issue of the supply of the 44,570-ton upgraded aircraft carrier *Admiral Greshkov*—Russia was not only unable to meet the delivery deadline of August 2008 but it also asked for an increased cost of US $1.2 billion. India's navy chief publicly criticised Russia for this late last year. As in the case of SU30 Sukhoi fighter aircraft, the Russians plea for cost escalation has been that they had grossly underestimated these costs while signing the agreements and due to the fund crunch, there is no way they could underwrite the added costs. There are reports that Russia is resorting to price escalation and delays in delivery of critical weapon systems to show its displeasure against India's growing strategic proximity towards and defence acquisitions from the United States. Some of these issues were sorted out during Zubkov's visit. Prime Minister Singh, after an 'extremely productive and comprehensive discussion on all aspects of our relationship', said, 'We reaffirmed our commitment to build our defence relations which is an important pillar of our Strategic Partnership.' The mutually agreed cost escalation level has been worked out and Russia has also agreed to look into the question of technology transfers to manufacturing of the T-90s main-battle tanks.

Energy cooperation between India and Russia has two components—civil nuclear energy and the hydrocarbons. The highlight of the visit was the signing of an Inter-Governmental Agreement for the construction of additional four nuclear plants in Kudankulam in south India. The memorandum of intent for these plants was signed in January 2007 during Russian President Vladimir Putin's visit to India but the follow-up agreement could not be initialed during Prime Minister Singh's visit in November 2007. This agreement cannot be executed until the Nuclear Suppliers' Group (NSG) removes sanctions imposed on India after 1998 which will happen only after India's agreement with the International Atomic Energy Agency (IAEA) related to Indo–US civil nuclear deal. Accordingly, India was hesitant in initialing this agreement in November 2007. India thought this could unnecessarily offend the United States and the Western members of the NSG.

On its part, Russia has been keen to get the issue clinched as it wants to establish its presence in India to compete for the potential civil nuclear market of US $40 billion. Dr Leonid Bolshov, Head of the Russian Academy of Sciences' Institute for Safe Atomic Energy, was quoted in the media as having said, 'First come, first served. . . . To be sure, US Westinghouse and France's Areva will eventually come to India because it is a vast market. Meanwhile, Russia is expanding its presence on the Indian nuclear energy market, thereby also improving its competitive edge on other markets.' Russia, of course, has significant experience in building commercial nuclear reactors. It is already building two light water reactors in Kudankulam as the agreement for that was concluded by India before the 1998-sanctions were imposed. According to Russian journalist Vladimir Radyuhin, while the reactors under construction are of VVER-1000 type, the additional four to be built will be VVER-1200 type, an advanced version of the former. India has relented on the issue in the interest of the overall relationship with Russia. Possibly, the recent round of talks with the IAEA makes India more confident of concluding the deal. India's agreement with Russia and recently obtained assurances from France, according to analysts, may also put some pressure on those NSG members who are still reluctant to endorse the Indo–US deal.

Russia has a great advantage as a producer of hydrocarbon energy. India's experience of collaboration with Russia in Sakhalin-I oil and gas fields has been very satisfying. Russia's prime minister was very 'positive and sympathetic' towards India's desire to have major stakes in Sakhalin-III and other oil and gas projects in Russia. India is also pleading with Russian oil and gas companies to invest in India and conceive of joint projects with Indian companies in third countries. Negotiations in this respect have already been initiated between the companies of the two countries.

The real bottleneck in Indo–Russian relations has been in the area of trade and investments. The Indo–Russian trade stood at an abysmal level of US $1 billion a few years ago. It has grown to little more than US $4 billion now. This is pathetic in view of the fact that both India and Russia belong to the fastest growing BRIC (Brazil, Russia, India and China) group of countries. The two sides have now agreed to work towards a target of US $10 billion by 2010. The economic and trade relations between the two countries since the beginning of the 1990s have been marred by many procedural and institutional impediments. They include an ineffective payments system, credit risks, insurance cover, Russian ban on imports of farm products like tea, rubber and tobacco, registration of pharma products, expensive East Caribbean Group of Companies coverage, etc. If these impediments are removed, the Federation of Indian Chamber of Commerce and Industry estimates that trade can reach US $20 billion by 2015. While the Russian side has shown interest in India's oil, gas, mining, technology, transport and energy sectors, the Indian side has pleaded for the inclusion of services, transport, investments and high technology in the trade basket. A joint taskforce of the two countries is exploring the possibility of a Comprehensive Economic Cooperation Agreement between them.

While focusing on the substantive aspects of the relationship, Premier Zubkov's visit also enabled the two sides to rejuvenate people-to-people contacts between the two countries. The Russian guest inaugurated the celebrations of the 'Year of Russia in India' where impressive glimpses of the cultural diversity of the two countries were on display. These celebrations will have a year-long spread and, then in 2009, a similar 'Year of India in Russia' will be launched. In order to bridge the information gap between the two peoples, Zubkov also launched a Russian Information Centre in India in the presence of his Indian host. He said on the occasion, 'At the negotiations yesterday (with the Indian prime minister), we have noted repeatedly that our two societies are not getting enough information on each others' life, and the present customary mode of getting news from each other does not correspond with the rhythm of rapid developments of our two nations.'

It is hoped that, with this visit, the two countries have removed the mutual irritations and disinterest that marred their relations over the past few years. It cannot be otherwise because basically there has never been any clash of interest or source of conflict between the two countries. Imperatives of the Cold War led them to develop a pragmatic, interest-based (not ideology-based) mutually advantageous engagement with each other. The end of the Cold War and the disintegration of the Soviet empire prompted Russia to gravitate towards the United States and Europe in search of democracy and economic prosperity. It lost interest in the rest of the world, including Asia and India. However, as the strategic dimensions of a unipolar world started impinging on Russia, it tried to look for other options. Thanks to its swelling oil wealth and President Putin's resolve to follow a strategy of 'innovative modernisation of Russia by 2020', Russia is seeking a place and role of respect in the arena of global power politics. India has always found a strong Russia in the overall interest of a multipolar world and its own strategic interests in Asia.

The Indo–Russian relations for the past 60 years have been shaped by their respective relations with the other two global players, the

United States and China. As the Cold War suspicions creep back into the United States–Russia relations and, as the inherent sense of unease persists underneath the tactically cozy Russian–Chinese relations, the warming up in Indo–Russian relations may continue to gather momentum. Russia may be unhappy with the growing strategic proximity between India and the United States but it knows well that this is not aimed at hurting the Russian interests. Russia owes it to itself to provide space for India to retain and reinforce its strategic autonomy in a fast changing world. Russia's efforts to bring India into a triangular relationship with itself and China were rationalised in the name of evolving a multipolar world, but no less was it a reflection of Russia's own need for a stable balance in Asia and the undercurrent of the sense of unease toward a rising, and demographically expanding (into Russian territory) China.

Contributors

ISHTIAQ AHMED is a Visiting Research Professor at the Institute of South Asian Studies. He currently holds the position of Professor in the 'Politics of Development' Group at Stockholm University in Sweden.

SANJAYA BARU is a Visiting Professor at the Institute of South Asian Studies and the Lee Kuan Yew School of Public Policy at the National University of Singapore. Prior to arriving in Singapore, he was the designated Media Advisor to the Prime Minister of India and was also the Prime Minister's spokesperson and principle speechwriter.

ROMAR CORREA is a Professor of Economics at the University of Mumbai. He was a Visiting Senior Research Fellow at the Institute of South Asian Studies from October to November 2008.

DEEP K. DATTA-RAY is a D. Phil candidate at the University of Sussex. He is currently on attachment to the Ministry of External Affairs, New Delhi.

BIBEK DEBROY is a Visiting Senior Research Fellow at the Institute of South Asian Studies. He is also a Professor at the International Management Institute, New Delhi, and a Research Professor at the Centre for Policy Research, New Delhi.

SHREEKANT GUPTA is an Associate Professor at the Lee Kuan Yew School of Public Policy at the National University of Singapore. He was Visiting Senior Research Fellow at the Institute of South Asian Studies from August 2007 to July 2008.

M. SHAHIDUL ISLAM is a Research Associate at the Institute of South Asian Studies. He was a Research Associate at the Institute of Southeast Asian Studies (ISEAS) from September 2004 to August 2005 where he was the Assistant Editor of the *ASEAN Economic Bulletin*, the in-house ISEAS research journal.

RAJSHREE JETLY is a Research Fellow at the Institute of South Asian Studies. Prior to joining the Institute, she was a post-doctoral fellow at the South Asian Studies Programme at the National University of Singapore from 2001 to 2003 where, in addition to doing research, she co-taught two modules on South Asia.

IFTIKHAR A. LODHI is a Research Associate at the Institute of South Asian Studies. He completed his Master's in Public Policy from Lee Kuan Yew School of Public Policy, National University of Singapore, in 2006.

S.D. MUNI is a Visiting Senior Research Fellow at the Institute of South Asian Studies. He is also Visiting Senior Scholar at the Institute of Defence Studies and Analyses, New Delhi. He is India's former Ambassador to Laos.

S. NARAYAN is a Visiting Senior Research Fellow and Head of Research at the Institute of South Asian Studies. He is the former economic adviser to the Prime Minister of India.

ONG KENG YONG is Ambassador-at-Large in the Ministry of Foreign Affairs in Singapore and the Director of the Institute of Policy Studies. He was Secretary-General of the Association of South-East Asian Nations from 2003 to 2007. His diplomatic postings have taken him to Saudi Arabia, Malaysia, the United States of America, India and Nepal.

AMITENDU PALIT is a Visiting Research Fellow at the Institute of South Asian Studies. Prior to joining the Institute, he was a Deputy Economic Adviser in the Economic Division of the Department of Economic Affairs in the Ministry of Finance, Govt. of India.

NISHCHAL NATH PANDEY is currently the Executive Director of the Institute of Foreign Affairs in Nepal. He is also an Honorary Fellow and Consultant at the Institute of South Asian Studies.

GOPINATH PILLAI is the Chairman of the Management Board of the Institute of South Asian Studies. He is also Ambassador-at-Large with the Ministry of Foreign Affairs in Singapore.

K.V. RAMASWAMY is currently with the Indira Gandhi Institute of Development Research in Mumbai. He was a Visiting Senior Research Fellow at the Institute of South Asian Studies from July 2007 to July 2008.

MALMINDERJIT SINGH is an Assistant Director in the ASEAN Division of the Ministry of Trade and Industry, Singapore. He worked as a Research Associate at the Institute of South Asian Studies from July 2007 to December 2008.

E. SRIDHARAN has been the Academic Director of the University of Pennsylvania Institute for the Advanced Study of India in New Delhi since its inception in 1997. He was a Visiting Senior Research Fellow at the Institute of South Asian Studies from May to July 2008.

PARANJOY GUHA THAKURTA is a journalist and Founder of the 'School of Convergence' in India. He is also a Consultant at the Institute of South Asian Studies.